Modernizing
the Korean
Welfare State

Modernizing the Korean Welfare State

Towards the Productive Welfare Model

Ramesh Mishra, Stein Kuhnle,
Neil Gilbert, and Kyungbae Chung
editors

Transaction Publishers
New Brunswick (U.S.A.) and London (U.K.)

Library of Congress Catalog Number: 2003060384
ISBN: 0-7658-0221-X
Printed in the United States of America

Library of Congress Cataloging-in-Publication Data

International Symposium on Sharing Productive Welfare Experience (2001 : Seoul, Korea)
    Modernizing the Korean welfare state : towards the productive welfare model / Ramesh Mishra ... [et al.], editors.
        p. cm.
    Chiefly papers on the International Symposium on Sharing Productive Welfare Experience, held in Seoul, September 2001.
    Includes bibliographical references and index.
    ISBN 0-7658-0221-X (cloth : alk. paper)
    1. Korea (South)—Social policy—Congresses. 2. Korea (South)—Economic policy—1960—Congresses. 3. Welfare state—Congresses. I. Mishra, Ramesh, Dr. II. Title.

HN730.5.A8I62 2001
361.6'1'095195—dc22   2003060384

Contents

Preface and Acknowledgements

The chapters in this book (except chs. 6 and 9) are based on a set of papers presented at an international symposium held in Seoul in September 2001. The symposium brought together a group of leading scholars to consider the new departure in Korean social policy known as "Productive Welfare." The symposium was convened under the auspices of the Ministry of Health and Welfare of Korea and the World Bank, and organized by the Korean Institute for Health and Social Affairs (KIHASA). Subsequently KIHASA coordinated the collection of revised papers and provided secretarial and editorial assistance in the preparation of this volume. The final editing and preparation of the manuscript for publication was supervised by Stein Kuhnle at the Department of Comparative Politics, University of Bergen, Norway, with the secretarial assistance of Christine S. Nipen.

We would like to acknowledge the sponsorship, funding and support of the Ministry and the World Bank, and KIHASA for organizing the symposium as well as preparing this volume. We thank our contributors for their prompt response and cooperation in answering our queries and revising the papers.

The Editors

1

Introduction

Ramesh Mishra

The closing years of the last millennium saw a number of significant developments in South Korea (henceforth Korea). The country joined the OECD group of nations in 1996, was engulfed in a serious financial crisis in 1997, followed by a large bail-out loan from the IMF and for the first time elected a candidate from the opposition party—Kim Dae-Jung—as president who took office in 1998. These developments formed the context in which a symposium (International Symposium on Sharing Productive Welfare Experience) was held in Seoul, in September 2001. This volume brings together the papers presented at the symposium and two others especially prepared for this volume.

The focus of the International Symposium was "Productive Welfare"—a comprehensive approach to social welfare elaborated by the administration of President Kim Dae-Jung. The aim of this approach is to achieve a dynamic and progressive balance between efficiency and equity, between economic growth and social justice or, more broadly, between economic and social development. The articulation of this approach to welfare followed the financial crisis of 1997-98 whose aftermath revealed the limitations and weaknesses in Korea's existing social safety nets. However the Productive Welfare approach is more than a matter of strengthening the social safety nets in respect of unemployment insurance and social assistance. It aims at a thorough overhaul of the system of social protection informed by the principles of universality, comprehensiveness and social rights. The idea seems to be to fashion a system of social protection more in keeping with the needs of a country that is relatively advanced industrially, a member of the OECD nations, ready to embrace globalization and wishes to strengthen its fledgling democracy.

Although the financial crisis and the bailout loan provided by the IMF have been the trigger for the recent reforms, the conception of welfare underlying the new approach and the policies that have been implemented owe a great deal to President Kim Dae-Jung's social and political vision. Concern with social justice and equity is a notable feature of this vision. However Productive Welfare is also concerned with ensuring that the expanded system of welfare does not hamper work incentives, is sustainable and helps rather than hinders efficiency and economic growth. While the nature and significance of the new welfare paradigm and the reforms that are being carried out under its auspices remain a matter of some controversy (reflected in the symposium papers) there is little doubt that they represent an ambitious attempt to modernize, develop and consolidate the Korean welfare state. Moreover their significance may well extend far beyond Korea. For this new orientation—towards a comprehensive welfare state based on social rights—suggests a path breaking development in the East Asian context. The successful implementation and consolidation of the new social policies could conceivably have far reaching implications for the development of welfare in the rest of East and South Asia. Thus the theoretical and practical issues raised in this book have implications that go beyond the development of social policy in Korea.

The chapters in this volume are concerned with assessing the principles and policies of the new welfare paradigm. But they also address the problem of designing and implementing the new policies. The chapters divide logically into two main groups. A small group of chapters (Part I) is concerned with analyzing the concept and nature of the Productive Welfare paradigm and assessing its significance and that of recent reforms in Korea from a broader comparative and international perspective. A second and larger group of chapters (Part II) addresses specific issues and areas of policy.

In different ways the chapters in Part I seek to "situate" the Productive Welfare paradigm within an international and comparative perspective. For Gilbert (Chapter 2) the new departure in Korea is an example of the development of what he calls the "Enabling State," in which social welfare institutions serve largely as a handmaiden to the market economy. This is in line with the global trend of convergence, since the late 1980s, towards the enabling state. Welfare policies are being revamped to support individual responsibility, strengthen work incentives and enhance productivity. Thus Gilbert questions the commitment to welfare in the Productive Welfare paradigm. His analysis of the official statements and expressions on the subject suggests that the emphasis is more on production than welfare with the latter seen primarily as "an instrument for improved productivity" rather than as an institution for meeting human needs. In conclusion Gilbert argues that the "ultimate challenge" confronting Productive Welfare in Korea is to develop "more than as a handmaiden to the market economy" and to "devise a set of workable measures" that will enhance regard for welfare while maintaining the value of stimulating productive energy in the market economy.

In recent years globalization has emerged as a key issue in relation to the political economy of nation states. Mishra (Chapter 3) argues that Korea's Productive Welfare approach needs to be understood in this international context. He outlines the differing ways in which globalization is impacting on less developed countries, emerging market economies, former communist countries, and Western industrialized countries. Emerging market economies such as Mexico and Korea have been particularly vulnerable to the sudden destabilization of their economies as a consequence of financial openness resulting in a serious impact on employment, wages and living standards more generally. The problem is often compounded by fiscal austerity and other conditionalities set by international agencies such as IMF and World Bank in connection with bail out loans. Globalization also tends to undermine the national strategies of welfare or 'social protection by other means' (e.g. private sector full employment, company welfare) developed by East Asian and other countries necessitating a change in social policy. However as the contrasting cases of Mexico and Korea show how countries respond to these challenges depends on domestic economic and political configurations. For Mishra, the interaction between the global and the national provides the essential context for understanding the dynamics of welfare.

Kuhnle (Chapter 4) does not share Gilbert's reservations concerning the Productive Welfare paradigm. On the contrary he finds it to be emblematic of the development of a social citizenship state in Korea. He begins by outlining the development of the welfare state in the West, focusing on its European origins, and demonstrates that important differences continue to exist among Western countries with regard to values and institutions of welfare. Against this backdrop and with reference to East Asia he traces the development of statutory welfare in Korea and identifies the main elements in the vision and program of Productive Welfare. Kuhnle argues that in its bold attempt to expand and guarantee the fundamental democratic and social rights of all citizens, in its commitment of the state to a key role in the provision of welfare and in its indication of the lines of policy development the Productive Welfare paradigm promises to move Korean welfare towards the Scandinavian or "Social-democratic" type of welfare regime.

Chung's paper (Chapter 5) presents the rationale of the Productive Welfare approach, in its philosophical as well as practical aspects, and develops its implications in a systematic, if schematic, manner. The term "balanced" in the title refers essentially to a model of welfare that achieves a balance between the supply and demand for financial and other resources. But Chung's conception of a balanced order extends beyond the economic sphere. It embraces the notion of a harmonious and boundary-respecting relationship between different social spheres, e.g. the family, other groupings, and the nation-state, in their role in welfare. It also signifies a balanced and harmonious relationship between the human order and the environment. The term "generative" refers to economic development, creativity and improvements in quality of life. Thus Chung envisions the Productive Welfare paradigm to combine a balanced and a developmental approach in the broader sense. This is an ambitious interpretation and vision of the meaning of Productive Welfare. Chung's emphasis on the notion of balanced and generative approach in Korean welfare has, in part, to do with the view that many of the dysfunctionalities and weaknesses of the Western welfare states stem from lack of attention to balance and productive aspects.

In the last chapter (Chapter 6) in Part I Pinker focuses on the linkages between democratic, market and welfare values in the paradigm of Productive Welfare. The paradigm assumes a degree of institutional interdependence between the competitive market and agencies of social protection so that they can complement each other in the production and enhancement of welfare. Pinker finds this in line with the model of "welfare pluralism" which is based on a combination of individualist and collectivist values and an institutional "mix" of statutory and other forms of welfare provision. Pinker cautions that for this approach to succeed legal sanctions and statutory regulations need to be complemented by extensive measures of voluntary compliance and self-regulation on the part of individual citizens and institutions of civil society.

Part II is concerned with a range of specific issues and policy areas in relation to Productive Welfare. While some papers are strongly comparative (e.g. Takayama) others focus on Korean policies alone (e.g. Lee et al.) and others again take a more general approach to their subject matter (e.g. Bryant).

Kakwani and Son (Chapter 7) begin with the premise that the issue of "pro-poor growth" is relevant to the ideology and objectives of Productive Welfare in that the latter seeks to combine economic growth with a fair distribution of income and life chances. They go on to elaborate the concept of "pro-poor growth" and ways of measuring it ("pro-poor growth index"). Using such measures they find that Korea's pattern of growth between 1990 and 1997 was strongly pro-poor. Thus the poverty population dropped from 39.6 percent in 1990 to 8.6 percent in 1997. Although the economic crisis of 1997 interrupted this trend growth has once again turned markedly pro-poor and the estimated poverty rate of 8.38 percent in 2000 is lower than the pre-crisis low reached in 1997. In a comparison with Thailand they show that although pre-crisis growth in both countries was pro-poor, it was far more so in Korea.

The chapter by Lee et al. (Chapter 8) examines two vital components of Korea's social insurance system, viz. employment and work injury, in some detail. Although these programs had been expanding since their inception (1995 and 1964 respectively) the economic crisis of 1997 exposed the inadequacies of these programs. Far-reaching changes have followed with significant expansion of both programs. For example, unemployment insurance coverage has been expanded to include employees in smaller firms, minimum worker contributions have been lowered and duration of benefits extended. Workers' injury insurance has been expanded to include virtually all types of firms and new benefits such as nursing care have been added. However there are many gaps in coverage and other weaknesses. Thus non-standard workers, e.g. temporary and daily workers, continue to be excluded. Only about half the wage earners are covered by unemployment insurance and a smaller proportion by work injury. The authors make a number of suggestions for improving these two programs.

Park (Chapter 9) reviews the progress of policies developed under the aegis of Productive welfare with special reference to social insurance and public assistance. To a large extent his paper is about the gap between policies and their implementation. Faced with the crisis of 1997 Korea developed the Productive Welfare paradigm, which initiated a great leap forward in welfare. But the administrative infrastructure and database necessary for "achieving the welfare policies" of an "advanced society" are not yet in place. The expansion of coverage under social insurance and public assistance has underlined a range of problems that await solution. Thus in the case of public assistance conducting reliable means test of beneficiaries and their liable relatives is hampered by weaknesses in administration and lack of necessary information. In particular assessing the income of the self-employed - notorious for under-reporting of income - remains virtually an intractable problem. It also bedevils pensions and health insurance schemes. Yet income surveys of the self-employed have made only limited progress so far. It appears that businesses also can not be relied upon to provide accurate information. There remain large gaps in coverage, especially under employment and industrial injury schemes. While some of this relates to policy, administrative deficiencies are also contributing to the problem. The same is true of the provision of appropriate and timely benefits to those entitled to them. Park outlines a number of key measures which could help close the gap between policy objectives and practice.

Primus (Chapter 10) reviews in considerable detail the American system of income support especially as it concerns low-income families. He assesses the strengths and weaknesses of the US system and points to the lessons Korean policymakers can draw from the experience of the US as they seek to extend and strengthen their social safety net. The paper identifies three elements essential to a social safety net, viz. social insurance, work support and public assistance and concentrates on the last two. It highlights the variety of problems and issues that confront policymakers and planners in building and operating an effective safety net (e.g. the heterogeneity of the clients and the variety of barriers they face to employment, the difficult balancing act of promoting self-reliance and ensuring that clients' needs are met). The chapter emphasizes the important role of work support programs, notably Earned Income Tax Credit and Food Stamps in the US, in supplementing low wages and in helping families to maintain attachment to the labor market. Public assistance or "welfare" acts as a measure of last resort for those not in the labor force. Primus discusses recent welfare reforms in the US, which have sought to restrict access to public assistance by imposing time limits and instituting a variety of sanctions and inducements for families to be self-supporting. While reforms have played a part in reducing welfare caseloads substantially Primus believes that "poverty reduction needs to be given a higher priority."

In all industrialized societies aging populations and escalating costs have pushed the issue of financial stability and cost containment in health care center stage. Schulenburg (Chapter 11) addresses the issue in the wider context of different models and forms of care, notably private provision, tax-financed national health scheme, statutory health insurance, non-profit mutual health funds, and managed care. These are in the nature of ideal types, the actual pattern of medical care in a country is likely to be a mix of several types or comprise elements of different types. Schulenburg discusses these models and other variations in the organization and delivery of health care in terms of characteristics such as equity, cost containment, efficiency, choice, responsiveness to consumers, and quality. There are trade-offs between these. For example the tax-financed national health service is strong on cost containment (sometimes to the point of underfunding) and equity but weak on consumer choice and responsiveness, quality, and innovation. More specifically Schulenburg compares the Korean and German health care systems—both statutory health insurance schemes but with some significant differences. He concludes his chapter with a discussion of specific measures for financial stability and cost containment, such as out -of- pocket payments by patients, budgetary control in hospitals, positive and negative lists, and waiting list.

Pensions are a key element in any strategy to secure minimum living standards for all and to maintain human dignity. The Korean National Pension Scheme, which began in 1988, is a defined benefits scheme which aspires to universal coverage, redistribution, and solidarity. These principles are consistent with the philosophy of Productive Welfare. In a comprehensive overview of the public pensions system in Korea, Walker (Chapter 12) considers the implications of recent reforms as well as policy recommendations of various bodies that have examined the pensions system. While coverage has been extended replacement rates have been reduced and the redistributive element weakened. Long-term sustainability has emerged as a key concern. Walker considers the pros and cons of defined-benefits and defined-contribution schemes in light of World Bank's recommendations on pensions. He argues that although further reforms are needed much can be accomplished, including sustainability, without a radical overhaul of the present system. Thus retirement allowances should be phased out as public provision and the distinction between the National Pensions Scheme and the occupational pensions scheme ended. The management and operation of the Scheme needs improvement to allow for greater transparency, accountability and democratic representation.

Takayama's chapter (Chapter 13) considers the challenges confronting the Korean public pensions system in light of Japanese experience. There are many similarities in the way programs have evolved in the two countries as well as in their current structures and policies. For example, both have defined benefit schemes with a similar replacement rate. But there are also differences. The Korean system appears ' much more advanced' in several respects (e.g. private sector workers and the self-employed are covered by a unified program, both enjoying earnings-related benefits). In Japan, by contrast, the self-employed do not have an earnings-related component. Korea, unlike Japan, has decided not to allow contracting-out from the earnings-related component, a wise decision according to Takayama. Contracted out plans in Japan are currently suffering from huge unfunded pension liabilities.

However, as Takayama points out, Japan has had a much longer experience in handling public pensions. Thus portability among various schemes is not a problem. A great deal of progress has also been made in integrating and rationalizing the fragmented pension schemes including those of the public sector employees. Takayama looks at the Korean pensions system from the short-term as well as medium and long-term perspectives and presents a menu of strategies and reforms. He clearly does not share the optimism of Walker on the long-term sustainability of Korean public pensions and believes that changes in financing and/or the structure of benefits may be necessary.

A notable feature of the Productive Welfare paradigm is its holistic approach to welfare or rather quality of life. Hence the importance it accords to a safe, healthy and pleasant environment as well as a rich and flourishing culture. The chapters by Bryant (Chapter 14) and Van der Staay (Chapter 15) address the issues of environment and culture respectively. Environmental justice, Bryant argues, not only requires protecting the environment in general but also paying particular attention to those groups (e.g. the poor and people of color) that are disproportionately exposed to pollutants and environmental degradation. Tackling environmental issues successfully requires radical rethinking of the way we produce and consume. Governments need to rethink their tax structure. "Green taxes"—on emissions, effluents, solid waste disposal, products linked to environmental deterioration—will have to be a part of the interim though not long-term solution which requires a fundamental shift in the way we live. Moreover distributive justice must be attended to.

Turning to developments in Korea, Bryant finds the Green Vision 21 and the Eco-2 project commendable initiatives. The development of new environmental technologies, clean fuel, and new factories that produce low or zero-pollution vehicles, are steps in the right direction. Green Vision's support of environmental impact statements, call to governments to share information with local residents and to involve them in decision making and community organizations in the supervision of environmental policies are to be applauded. Projects for international cooperation under these initiatives are also on the right track. However for a more thorough-going people-centered approach Bryant suggests a phased strategy. The three phases concerned are a teach-in involving education on environmental injustice, community-based research, and an environmental justice revolution which involves a "regenerative" rather than "depletive" knowledge and technology of both production and consumption. Better management of a fundamentally flawed system will not do. There is a need to be "creative and visionary."

Van der Staay (Chapter 15) argues that development has entered a new phase with an emerging positive emphasis on culture. Historically viewed as a factor of resistance to development, culture—in terms of traditions and values—is now recognized as a vital element. More particularly with the growth of empowerment movements, the importance of people and their values has been incorporated into the definition of development. Thus culture should be viewed as an aim of development rather than as a means. Drawing on examples and observations from around the world, including Korea, the paper outlines a range of "strategies" for a cultural policy. These include maintaining a balance between "centers of power"—the cultural marketplace, the public sphere, and voluntary associations—as a way of strengthening quality and innovation; conducting scientific analyses of culture (e.g. time studies on leisure and opinion polls on values) with the aim of modernizing culture and strengthening the democratic process. The author emphasizes the importance of cultural development—the notion that cultural identity is flexible and should be open to learning and change. "Cultural scouting" is another valuable strategy for learning about global best practices in cultural policy. Although cultural policy is not generally given the same consideration and financial resources as given to economic development, social security, and the like, culture, suggests van der Staay, may be the 'entrance' to solving problems in these other fields and enhancing overall quality of life.

In the final chapter Mishra attempts an overall assessment of the nature of the Productive Welfare paradigm and, focusing on social security, highlights some of the key issues arising out of the development of social policy under its auspices. He finds that, on balance, Productive Welfare and the policies associated with it represent a substantial development of and commitment to social protection under state auspices. This is of particular significance, especially coming after a financial crisis and an IMF bailout, phenomena usually associated with fiscal austerity and retrenchment of social expenditure. Nonetheless echoing several of the papers in this volume Mishra also underlines the problem of ensuring adequate and sustained funding of programs and the successful implementation of policies.

Part I

The "Productive Welfare" Paradigm: Comparative and International Perspectives

2

Productive Welfare and the Market Economy: Korea's Enabling State

Neil Gilbert

In examining the philosophy of Productive Welfare, this chapter will address three matters. First since this section of the book deals with comparative and international perspectives, the policy orientation of Productive Welfare is examined within a larger context, so that we might see where it stands in relation to both the conventional ideal of the progressive welfare state and to recent patterns of reform that are reshaping the conventional paradigm to varying degrees in almost all of the industrial democracies. Here a number of large-scale trends are summarized, which have been more thoroughly documented elsewhere (Gilbert 2002). Next, several assumptions in the philosophy of Productive Welfare are explored with an eye to clarifying issues raised concerning the value of work and unpaid labor. Finally, the chapter ends on a philosophical note that concerns the broader consequences of Productive Welfare for the relation between the state and market economy, and their normative implications for the character of modern social life.

I. International Context: Social Reform at the Dawn of the 21st Century

Where is "Productive Welfare" positioned on the broad canvass of modern welfare state reforms? At the dawn of the 21st century, state sponsored care and social protection in all of the advanced industrialized countries have entered a new era, marked by substantive policy reforms that have deep and lasting implications. Social welfare scholars have variously characterized these developments as a movement from: the "Keynesian Welfare State to the Schumpeterian Workfare State" (Jessop 1994), "social rights to social obligations" (Mead 1986), "passive to active social policy" (OECD 1989), "from public to private activity, from entitlement to contract" (Richard 1994), and for those who favor more evocative metaphors—from "safety nets to trampolines" (Torfing 1997). In the U.K. this shift is referred to as the "third way."[1]

The gravity of these policy reforms, which emphasize work incentives, individual responsibility, and private initiatives is subject to varying interpretations. Some see them as a marginal adjustment in the borders of the welfare state—a retreat to the core—or a "fine tuning" of existing policies.[2] According to this view political forces have maintained the meat of existing principles of the welfare state, while trimming the fat of excessive provisions.[3] Others perceive these changes as major revisions in the guiding principles and philosophy of social protection, which are transforming the essential character of modern welfare states. Of course, to transform is not to dismantle or obliterate institutional arrangements for social protection. Social insurance, unemployment, disability, and public assistance programs and the like will continue to operate. What is being altered involves the basic policy framework for these programs on which the most progressive welfare states were modeled.[4]

The changes underway are spurred, in part, by the demographic challenge of aging societies. Indeed, the dramatic rise in aging has just begun and will take off at end of this decade, so that between 2001 and 2030 the ratio of the number of people over 65 to the number of people employed will on average virtually double in the OECD countries, climbing from 1 retired person for every three workers (a ratio of .33) to one retired person for every 1.6 workers (a ratio of .63) (OECD 1998). Although many of the OECD countries are raising the standard age of retirement in an effort to mitigate the crushing costs of aging, since 1970 the labor force participation rates for men over 65 have declined and declined substantially for men aged 60-64. However, there is much variation among countries, for example, in 1998, 70 percent or more of those aged 55-64 did not participate in the labour force in Hungary, Belgium, Luxemburg, Italy and Austria.

Aging is not the only demographic factor that is increasing demand—the growth in single parent families also necessitates various sorts of public aid. And although demographic shifts create powerful pressures for change, they are not the only forces at work. As shown in Table 2-1, social and economic forces have created at least four major lines of influence that are reshaping the institutional framework of social protection. While demand for social spending continues to push upward with the aging of populations, the constraints on additional spending are tightening in response to the pressures of the global economy, which have magnified interdependencies, heightened competitive markets, and shrunk time and space. There are differences of opinion about what exactly the process of globalization represents and it implications for the future of state sponsored social protection. However, many analysts agree that globalization has intensified pressures to scale back labor rights and welfare benefits (Standing 1999: 62-63).

In addition to what might be considered large-scale structural factors such as aging and the globalization of the economy, there are also socio/political pressures for change emanating from a shift in normative views about the consequences of social policies and the proper relationship between the state and the market. The weight of accumulated experience gained over the decades of welfare state growth has told us much about the unanticipated consequences of social benefits, particularly their disincentive effects. The idea that generous welfare benefits might inhibit one's inclination to work was once viewed as heresy by welfare state advocates—they charged it was a case of "blaming the victim." Yet the same idea, that welfare benefits produce "poverty traps" or "enforced dependency"—prudently worded not to blame victims—has become the received wisdom of the late 1990s.

Table 2-1
Social and Economic Pressures for Change: Four Lines of Influence

Four Lines of Influence	Social and Economic Pressures for Change
Demographic Transition	Aging Divorce rates Extra-marital births
Globalization of the Economy	Mobility of capital to where production costs are low Mobility of labor to where benefits are high
Knowledge of Unanticipated Effects	Disincentives to work Dependency traps
Capitalism	Rising faith in market economy Privatization

Finally, the collapse of the command-economy of the USSR has raised to record levels the stock of capitalism's public approval in the marketplace of ideas, which has been accompanied by a rising faith in the virtues and abilities of the private sector. These four lines of influence, representing complex and multiple forces lend impetus to the transformation of the welfare state. And what gives these pressures particular weight is that in different ways they all push away from the progressive welfare state model. What are the directions of change?

First and foremost, it has become almost universally accepted that social policies heretofore providing "passive" income supports to unemployed people should be replaced by measures designed to promote employment. Over the last decade, almost all of the industrial welfare states have initiated work-oriented reforms of public assistance, disability, and unemployment programs. The emphasis on work-oriented reforms is one of four critical dimensions in the transformation of the welfare state illustrated in Table 2-1. Social welfare policies of progressive welfare states were once framed by a *universal* approach to *publicly delivered* benefits designed to *protect labor* against the vicissitudes of the market and firmly held as *social rights*. Today these policies are increasingly being reformed to take a *selective* approach to *private delivery* of provisions designed *to promote labor force participation* and *individual responsibility*. The emerging emphasis on individual responsibility (to work and be self-sufficient) and the tightening of eligibility criteria for social benefits have eroded the social rights of citizenship—rights that T.H. Marshall saw as a defining element of citizenship that fostered a common sense of belonging and social cohesion (Marshall 1964). As Marshallian solidarity—the cohesion of shared rights—is on the wane, what we might call Durkheimian solidarity, the cohesion of membership in civic associations, which reinforce shared values and civic duties—is waxing with new energy (Durkheim 1933).

Overall, the transformation has been described by various terms, among which I prefer the designation from Welfare State to Enabling State (Evandrou et al. 1990; Gilbert and Gilbert 1989; Gilbert 1995; Marshall and Schram 1993; Wattenberg 1993: p. A12). The Enabling State draws upon what Richard Titmuss once called the "industrial achievement-performance" model of social policy, under which social welfare institutions serve as handmaidens to the market economy, rather than as a counter force supporting alternative values and objectives. This model of social policy, Titmuss explains, "holds that social needs should be met on the basis of merit, work performance and productivity. It is derived from various economic and psychological theories concerned with incentives, effort, and reward" (Titmuss 1974). The core philosophy of the Enabling State may be summed up in the principle of public support for private responsibility, where "private" responsibility includes individuals, the market, and voluntary organizations. Building on this principle, social welfare arrangements are increasingly designed to enable people to work and to enable the market and the voluntary sector to assume an expanded role in providing social protection. In contrast, the progressive welfare states of the 20th century emphasized public responsibility for care and protection of the vulnerable, and policies that decommodified labor. That is by providing a source of income outside of market exchanges, what are now described as "passive" welfare benefits gave unemployed workers a degree of independence, allowing them to withhold their labor making it less like a commodity bought and sold purely in response to market forces.

Table 2-2
Shift in Central Tendencies from Welfare to Enabling State

Welfare State	Enabling State

Public Provision
  - Delivery by public agencies
  - Transfers in the form of service
  - Focus on direct expenditures
	Privatization
	- Delivery by private agencies
	- Transfers in cash or vouchers
	- Increasing indirect expenditures

Protecting Labor
  - Social Support
  - Decommodification of labor
  - Unconditional benefits
	Promoting Work
	- Social inclusion
	- Recommodification of labor
	- Use of incentives and sanctions

Universal Entitlement - Avoiding stigma	Selective Targeting - Restoring social Equity

Solidarity of Citizenship
  - Cohesion of shared rights
	Solidarity of Membership
	- Cohesion of shared values and
	    civic duties

Source: Neil Gilbert, *Transformation of the Welfare State: The Silent Surrender of Public Responsibility* (New York: Oxford University Press, 2002)

Social protection and income maintenance were among the central functions of the progressive welfare state. Today, however, one finds the strong emphasis on designing social policies to enhance the productive forces of society expressed almost in one voice by political leaders and welfare scholars in industrial countries around the world. Thus, for example, one of the most popular textbooks on social welfare in the United States now teaches that "to reestablish and legitimate the welfare state it is necessary to demonstrate how social programs can contribute positively to the nation's productivity" (Karger and Stoesz 1994). In the Netherlands the Dutch Minister of Social Affairs and Employment calls for "re-shaping the welfare state into an economic performer" (Melkert 1997). Similar observations appear in Sweden, where Marklund sees welfare reforms as animated by the need "to increase the productivity and competitiveness of the economy" (Marklund 1992: 10). And in Britain, Anthony Giddens counsels movement toward the "social investment state," which features public investments in human capital over the provision of customary social welfare benefits (Giddens 1998). Indeed, since the late 1980s recommendations for the redesign of social policy to support productivity have been expressed in publications of the Organization for Economic Cooperation and Development (OECD 1988) and the International Social Security Association (1989).

A convergence toward the Enabling State paradigm described here should not be taken to mean that national systems of social protection will all follow the same heading and come to operate exactly the same way. While social welfare policies are increasingly being framed by new principles that emphasize work, privatization, individual responsibility, and targeted benefits, there certainly will be differences—rhetorical as well as substantive—in the way that countries interpret and apply these principles. Some will justify targeting on the basis of equity; others will accentuate efficiency. Different methods of targeting will be employed with varying grades of transparency.[5] The range of activities that qualify as "work" will differ as will the extent to which employment policies invest in human capital, job-creation, and wage subsidies, and the degree to which part-time paid employment is normalized. There will be alternative approaches to privatization from top-down contracting for services to bottom-up vouchers and ear-marked tax credits; contracting for services will be organized through varied arrangements that involve non-profit organizations in the voluntary sector, which are committed to delivering services in the context of broader social goals and community involvement as well as profit-making organizations dedicated mainly to the immediate business of providing services.[6]

All of which is to say that there will be assorted renditions of the Enabling State. Freud's axiom concerning the "narcissism of minor differences" suggests that the closer nations come to resemble each other the more they magnify minute dissimilarities, as a means to reinforce social cohesion.[7] If this proposition is correct, policy makers in the advanced industrialized countries are likely to go to great lengths to differentiate their social welfare initiatives from each other. The Nordic countries will have their version of the Enabling State, as will France, Germany, and others, including, perhaps, the Eastern European countries. But when one peels back the outer layers of rhetoric and sorts through the different measures to advance privatization, targeting, employment, and individual responsibility, we arrive at a common core of market-oriented social policies that emphasize the importance of work and private responsibility.

In this context, the principles of Productive Welfare as representing a Korean version of the Enabling State can be summarized as follows. A centerpiece of the philosophical foundation as laid out in *DJ Welfarism*, rests on the principle of "welfare through work," an approach that "replaces the traditional passive model of welfare with a dynamic model through which the right to work will be guaranteed" (Presidential Committee for Quality-of-Life

2000). And with this right comes the individual's responsibility to work and be self-supporting. Thus, "for example, low-wage earners with the ability to work who receive benefits *must* also participate in job-training programs or other programs that contribute to the public good, such as public works" (ibid.: 33). Under the tenets of Productive Welfare, welfare policies are "viewed as an investment for improved productivity, rather than as a simple transfer of income through administrative procedures"(ibid.:10). Plans in support of Productive Welfare link the citizens' rights and obligations to work with vocational training programs, equitable compensation, improved working conditions, and the security of minimum living standards.

The principles of Productive Welfare not only cultivate policies designed to encourage the private responsibility to work and be self-supporting, but also promotes an approach to the implementation of these policies that relies heavily on the private sector in local communities.[8] As explained in *DJ Welfarism* "rather than depending solely on central-government funding, a more efficient and flexible local welfare system can be constructed to solve local problems by forming a partnership between governing organizations, businesses, and civic groups in the local community and by utilizing volunteer services. A welfare network at the local community level will enable passive welfare recipients, who only receive benefits, to become active citizens, who participate in meaningful work" (ibid.: 15).

Finally, Korean scholars are not of one mind about how to characterize the emerging system of Productive Welfare. Some see this system as marked by neo-liberal tendencies, which are more closely related to the Enabling State than, for example, to the Social Democratic welfare state model. Among this group, Young-Hwa Kim suggests that although one finds neo-liberal tendencies in the emerging system of Productive Welfare, an accurate assessment of the Korean model ultimately must take into account unique cultural characteristics such as the traditional Confucian values of "familism," which to some extent may conflict with the role of the state in the provision of social welfare (Kim 2000). Others contend that while Productive Welfare policies may have some neo-liberal elements, on the whole they lean more toward a model that emphasizes the responsibility of the state over the market and the individual (Kim 2001).

II. Productive Welfare and the Apotheosis of Work

The positive and upbeat philosophy of Productive Welfare rests on several assumptions about the nature of work, at least two of which I think deserve closer examination. The first assumption involves what I would call the apotheosis of work. Throughout the discussion of Productive Welfare one finds references to the many virtues of work as an "essential means of attaining satisfaction and value"—an activity that confers independence and dignity (ibid.: 9). As clearly stated by the Presidential Committee for the Quality of Life, "the foundation of productive welfare will be laid by providing opportunities to experience the satisfaction and joy of work" (ibid.: 73). There is much truth in this statement that work is a source of satisfaction and joy for many people, but it is not entirely correct. Work encompasses a vast array of activities from those that are low-status, boring, physically demanding, poorly rewarded, and dangerous, to positions that are high status, exciting, physically easy, well rewarded, and safe. One might expect those laboring on the more favorable end of this continuum, for example, artists, writers, professors, lawyers, politicians, media personalities, and policy makers, to be happy in their work. Certainly professors, researchers, and policy analysts who fly around the world to conferences in splendid cities, such as Seoul, and receive magnificent treatment as guests from generous hosts at these events, must experience great joy and satisfaction in their work.

On the other side of the continuum—including for instance, coal miners, factory workers, taxi drivers, sales people, clerks, guards, service workers, graveyard cleaners, and mail carriers—where activities are dirty, dangerous and repetitive, the view of work as a thoroughfare to self-realization, satisfaction and joy, somewhat overstates the case. On closer examination the glorification of work runs up against a hard wall of an empirical reality. As previously noted, throughout the industrialized countries most people currently retire earlier than the standard age. From the early 1900s to 1970 the labor force participation rates for men over the age of 65 decreased markedly, from about 50 percent to 20 percent, while the participation rates for those aged 60-64 remained relatively stable and high. Since 1970, however, not only has the labor force participation rate of men over the age of 65 continued to decrease, but the rates for those aged 60-64 have declined substantially. By 1995, for example, the labor force participation rate for men aged 60-64 was less than 20 percent in France and about 30 percent in Italy; at the same time, the rates for men aged 55-59 were 60 percent in Italy and about 65 percent in France (Sorensen 1998). Some of this drop in the labor force participation of older workers can be attributed to labor-shedding adjustments in declining industries. However, one is hard pressed to find much worker resistance to early retirement. This suggest that although work may be a source of satisfaction that lends meaning to life, opportunity for congenial association, and a sense of personal achievement for many thinkers, policy analysts, academicians, and legislators who promote the virtues of work, it represents a daily activity that coal miners, bus drivers, sales people, postal workers, plumbers, and employees in a host of other occupations apparently seek to discontinue as soon as possible.

Of course work is important. But there are other things in life. The Presidential Committee for the Quality of Life notes that Korea has one of the longest work weeks in the world and that reducing the working hours might increase the individual's creativity and enthusiasm for work. Still they note that there is a strong argument that conditions in Korea do not yet warrant the introduction of shorter working hours. One response to the problem of unemployment in the European countries has been the increase in part-time work. This trend may be seen as a problem of substandard employment that should not be promoted by social policies or as a positive choice for many workers representing a functional adaptation to the family life cycle and educational needs, which subordinates work to other life interests. Whatever one's view, the rise of part-time work accounted for most of the additional jobs created during the 1980s in the northern states of the European Community where these positions were held disproportionately by women.[9] In the Netherlands, part-time employment has climbed from five percent to 37 percentage of total employment over the last twenty-five years—becoming in the process, a "normal form of gainful activity" (Walwei and Werner 2001). The decline in unemployment from a high of 14 percent in the summer of 1983 to under three percent in the winter of 2000 is often referred to as the "Dutch miracle." However once it is recognized as largely a redistribution from full-time to part-time work, the record appears still impressive, perhaps, but certainly less miraculous (Becker 2000).

A second assumption implicit in the model of productive welfare concerns the value of unpaid labor, particularly in the realm of social care. One might infer from the discussion of work and the plans for free child care for all children under five, that a parent who remains home to care for several young children, an elderly relative, and a disabled cousin is not engaged in "productive work." Though if the same person offered their child care services to strangers for a price, they would be seen as a productive member of society—engaged in an activity that confers dignity, satisfaction and the like. To what extent are people today expected to care for their dependent kin—young or old or disabled? In a cultural context marked by Confucian values of "familism," this normative question gains saliency, as state monies are increasingly being made available to subsidize labor for the private provision of social care, particularly for children and the elderly. Under these arrangements, time and effort hitherto invested in unpaid informal care both as a demonstration of mutual aid and an expression of the traditional norms of kinship obligation are now converted into a contractual exchange of service for payment on an hourly rate. The marketplace absorbs a large realm of social care that was previously in the domain of unpaid labor animated by compassion, obligation, and mutual aid. These activities were performed without pay mainly by women.

Although many women, no doubt welcome the opportunity to enter the paid labor force, evidence from surveys in Europe and the U.S. suggest that a large percentage of women with young children would prefer not to work outside the home or to engage in paid employment on only a part-time basis.

Data from a 1997 survey of families in the U.S. shows 49 percentage of women agreeing with the statement "When children are young, mothers should not work outside the home."[10] In many countries unpaid activities such as caring for children and disabled kin are being included among the criteria for entitlement to social benefits.

Of course, there is nothing sacred about the continuation of unpaid social care by women, which in the past was facilitated by "passive" welfare benefits. However, the commodification of this realm of care diminishes the opportunity and practice of voluntarily tending to the needs of others for reasons that transcend the immediate incentives of market exchanges. Different meanings can be attributed to this development. Some might interpret the trend as promoting equal opportunity and rewards, with women receiving greater financial compensation for their labors. Still others might associate the contraction of services that people perform for each other outside the market with a hardening of human relations—as intimate expressive relationships based on personal commitments are increasingly displaced by instrumental relationships based on commercial considerations. These views, of course, are not mutually exclusive.

III. Social Implications: The Challenge Ahead

This brings us to a broader philosophical question: What are the social implications of productive welfare? This model is largely, though not entirely, concerned with economic considerations—employment, productivity, and self-support. Although *DJ Welfarism* discusses the need for policies devoted to care of those unable to work, clearly the repeated thrust of this approach is to make people self supporting. Indeed, in the words of the Presidential Committee for the Quality of Life, "the objective is to include everyone in the workforce, regardless of ability, disability, deprivation, or privilege" (Presidential Committee for Quality-of-Life 2000: 11).

The expectations and values that frame the design of policies for Productive Welfare tend to celebrate economic productivity and private responsibility over passive social protection and expansive public aid. Certainly, there is much to commend the advent of "Productive Welfare" under the Enabling State as a beneficial corrective to the progressive Welfare State model of the advanced industrialized countries, which over time came to pay too little attention to the implications of social policy for productivity, merit, and responsibility.

However, the changing role of the state and the primacy of market-oriented policies in shaping the future course of social welfare raise an issue about how this development will effect the essential character of society. With the Enabling State serving as a handmaiden to the market and the expanding commercialization of family roles, the character of life in modern society is increasingly shaped by the market ethos of competition, individual choice, weighing measurable costs and benefits, and maximizing gain. Why is this a matter of concern? The market is a marvelous mechanism. Who in full possession of their senses would choose to live in the pork-barrel aesthetics of public housing over privately designed architecture tailored to individual tastes or to dine at the buffet of a state run restaurant over a table at almost any bistro in Paris? Whose children would rather be taken to the state run fair over a day in Disneyland? There is much to appreciate about the free market regarding material consumption within the domain of commercial life.

However, the domain of commercial life is just one arena of human interaction—an arena in which people engage in exchange and the satisfaction of material wants. But is it a virtuous domain? The relation between morality and the free market is a fascinating topic of long-standing debate (Schumpeter 1950; Hirschman 1977). On the right are those who argue that markets have positive moral implications and effects because they require the practice of honesty "to ensure fair dealing, and the virtues of thrift, diligence, and curiosity as guarantors of the self-reliant enterprise."[11] Rather than a breeding ground for probity and diligence, from the left competitive markets are seen as—red in tooth and claw—places where "dishonest and inhumane practices will drive out the honest and humane ones" (Schwartz 1999: 37). Centrists claim that the market is morally neutral.

Is the capitalistic marketplace an academy for hedonistic practices to which honesty and probity are denied entry or a school of virtuous activity? On this question the evidence suggests that we remain agnostic. The free market is a place where vigorous virtues vie with the villainous vices, morality and immorality are practiced without prejudice. Some people will disagree with this assessment. But whether one prefers the argument that virtue trumps vice in the market or vice versa, no one suggests that the free market is an incubator of the gentle virtues—charity, sympathy, kindness, public service, sacrifice, tolerance, mutual aid and the like. What Margaret Thatcher called the "vigorous virtues"—initiative, diligence, enthusiasm, productivity—are immensely functional within the domain of the market, but that is not the only plane of human activity and interaction (Letwin 1992). The value system of competition, choice, and profit yields vast material benefits, but little in the way of communal security.

When the habits and attributes of commercial life permeate the other spheres of human activity, the economic order engulfs society. As we enter the 21st century, a vague sense of apprehension about this development emanates from religious, academic, and political quarters. Addressing the moral implications of market activity, Christian social thinkers are at work forging a theory of what is termed *economic personalism,* inspired by the writings of Pope John Paul II.[12] Seeking a synthesis of theology and economics, "the idea is to promote a humane economic order that benefits from market activity but does not reduce the human person to just another element in economic phenomena" (Gronbacher 1998: 29). This humane order requires restraints on the market that are exercised not so much by political structures as by individual behavior influenced by moral instruction and socialization primarily through family and church and by a moral code promoted through voluntary associations. In academic circles the goals of communitarian economics go beyond increasing the productivity of the economy to incorporate social and political ends that serve the common interests and shared values of all citizens. Government is seen as having a distinct role in furthering these objectives, which include a safety net to protect the neediest members of society from the ruin of poverty and disease.[13] In the political arena, George W. Bush's 2000 presidential campaign ran on a platform of "compassionate conservatism," which relayed an evocative, though ill-defined, expression of the need to somehow incorporate the gentle virtue of compassion into his party's free market ideology.

In this context, the cause for concern about the emergence of Productive Welfare as a central activity of Korea's Enabling State is not so much that it promotes work-oriented policies and heightens public support for private responsibility as that in so doing may soon bow too deeply as a handmaiden to the market. As it has evolved among the industrialized countries since the early 1990s, the Enabling State generates no counter force to the capitalist ethos, no larger sense of public purpose that might be served beyond increasing productivity, no clear ideal of public service and dwindling support for the goals of social protection and security. In many respects the course of the Enabling State endorses anti-statist attitudes, which lends weight to the movement toward a market-dominated society.

What can be done to create a healthier balance between State and market forces, one which incorporates the self-serving vitality of private enterprise and the humanitarianism of shared public purpose? "The greatest asset of public action," Albert Hirschman points out, "is its ability to satisfy vaguely felt needs for higher purpose and meaning in the lives of men and women, specially of course in an age in which religious fervor is at a low ebb in many countries" (Hirschman 1992: 126). One need not return to expansive entitlements of the progressive welfare state model to revive the legitimacy of public purpose, the ideals of public service and appreciation for the state's special ability to insure social protection against the vicissitudes of the market and to organize communal security in the face of illness, disability, and the inevitabilities of old age.

The words used to frame social policy choices are important in clarifying the public purposes to be served. If policy choices are posed, for example, between "active" and "passive" social benefits—there is little doubt that all would prefer an "active" benefit. The word "active" speaks of life's energy, whereas "passive" suggests a state of mild depression. But if the choice is between "activation," which presses disabled people and women with young children into the labor force, and "social protection" against the risks of modern capitalism, the tendency to embrace "activation" would be less compelling. Policies devoted entirely to cultivating "independence" and "private responsibility" leave little ground for a life of honorable dependence for those who may be unable to work. And while work-oriented policies designed to increase "productivity" are insulated with amorphous claims of 'satisfaction," "empowerment" and "social inclusion," they are rarely confirmed as measures that ensure people more freedom to live fuller lives.

The ultimate challenge that confronts Productive Welfare in Korea is to develop as more than a handmaiden to the market economy. Earlier it was noted that "welfare through work" represents a basic principle of Productive Welfare. There are clear indications that the architects of Productive Welfare recognize the need for the State to do more than promote the principle of welfare through work. Although much of the discussion of Productive Welfare concentrates on the development and training of the labor force, a philosophical premise of Productive Welfare is that "all people have the right to enjoy life, health, and culture"—rights guaranteed by the State (Presidential Committee for Quality-of-Life 2000). Beyond what appears as the immediate objectives of cultivating work and generating greater material production, the architects of Productive Welfare endorse the broader principle of improving the quality of life through measures that involve access to lifelong education, better health care, enhanced cultural and leisure time activities, and safeguarding the environment. The devil resides in the details of the State's role in implementing these broader principles of Productive Welfare within a philosophical context that emphasizes work and market-oriented concerns. The purpose of this paper is not to draw a blueprint for the State's commitment to advance a broad vision of social well-being—but to illuminate the challenge ahead. This challenge is to devise a set of workable measures that might elevate regard for the "welfare" in Productive Welfare while maintaining a sober appreciation for the value of stimulating productive energy in the market economy.

Notes

1. Blair (1998). The British "third way" is reminiscent of the "middle way," Childs' popular account of Sweden's efforts to wend the path between individualism and collectivism in the 1930s. See Childs (1936).
2. Pierson (1996; 48); Sven Olsson Hort (2001) characterizes recent policy changes in the Swedish welfare state, including the unprecedented move toward the privatization of old age pensions, as "fine tuning."
3. Esping-Andersen's (1996: 265-266) curious claim that only "fat" was being cut, is followed on the very next page with a description of successful welfare state cutback policies including "the succession of increasingly severe cutbacks in the

Swedish welfare state, including the most cherished programmes such as pen sions, sickness absence and parental leave."

4. See for example Ferge (1996). For an analysis of the change in universalist prin- ciples and the institutional welfare model in Sweden, see Sunesson et al. (1998). Also see Glennerster (1999) for a view of the distinctive arrangements for social protection taking shape in the U.K.

5. Within the European Union Maurizio Ferrera (1996: 13) sees a "process of gradual institutional transformation" that could lead to a "qualitative convergence among the various systems." However, he suggests that, in relation to targeting for in- stance, such convergence would still be characterized by different countries em- ploying different methods.

6. Evers (2001) distinguishes between the neo-liberal approach to privatization, which emphasizes the business of services delivery and an approach that lends primacy to social goals, community involvement and the strengthening of civil society by voluntary non-profit providers.

7. Freud (1961) linked the narcissism of minor differences as a way to express hostility to outsiders and thereby satisfy the human inclination to aggression, while binding together the insiders.

8. For a detailed discussion of the various efforts and incentives to promote private sector participation in policymaking and implementation, see Presidential Commit- tee for Quality-of-Life 2000: 112-118.

9. For a breakdown of how definitions of part-time work vary within and between countries, see Hakim (1997).

10. These findings are reported in Wertheimer (2001). A similar reluctance to full-time employment when children are young is expressed by Danish mothers, despite the fact that in Denmark public day care is provided from the age of six months on and 90 percentage of mothers of young children are employed an average of 34 hours per week. When asked to describe the ideal arrangement for a nuclear family with children of nursery school age, only three percentage of the mothers preferred to have both parents working full-time, 15 percent chose to have the mother home full-time as a housewife, 42 percent favored part-time employment for the mother, and 40 percent preferred to have both parents working part-time, see Ministry of Social Affairs (1992).

11. Marsland (2001: 34-35). He shares James Q Wilson's (1993) view that trust and honesty facilitate commercial practices of buying, selling, lending and borrowing, which in turn inculcate habits of fair dealing.

12. For a review of the historical, philosophical, and practical aspects of economic personalism, see Gronbacher (1998).

13. For a statement of the goals of communitarian economics and how this perspective differs from the traditional ways of thinking about economic issues see Garfinkle (1996).

References

Becker, U. (2000) "Welfare State Development and Employment in the Netherlands in Comparative Perspective." *Journal of European Social Policy,* 10 (3).

Bell, D. (1976) *The Cultural Contradictions of Capitalism.* New York: Basic Books.

Blair, Tony (1998) "Forward and Introduction," *Green Paper on Welfare State Reform.*

Childs, M. (1936) *Sweden: The Middle Way.* New Haven: Yale University Press.

Durkheim, E. (1933) *The Division of Labor in Society.* Trans. George Simpson, New York: Free Press.

Esping-Andersen, G. (ed.) (1996) *Welfare States in Transition: National Adaptations in Global Economies*. London: Sage Publications.

Evandrou, M., Falkingham, J, and Glennerster, H. (1990) "The Personal Social Services: Everyone's Poor Relation but Nobody's Baby," in J. Mills (ed.) *The State of Welfare: The Welfare State in Britain Since 1974*. Oxford: Clarendon Press.

Evers, A. (2001) "Welfare Dynamics, The Third Sector, and Social Quality," in W. Beck, L. van der Maesen, F. Thomese, and A. Walker (eds), *Social Quality: A Vision for Europe*. The Hague: Kluwer Law International.

Ferge, Z. (1996) "The Change of the Welfare Paradigm—The Individualisation of the Social," paper presented at the Annual Conference of the British Social Policy Association, Sheffield.

Ferrera, M. (1996) *A New Social Contract? Four Social Europes: Between Universalism and Selectivity*. Badia Fiesolana, Italy: European University Institute.

Freud, S. (1961) *Civilization and Its Discontents*. Trans. and ed. by J. Strachey, New York: W.W. Norton.

Garfinkle, N. (1996) "Communitarian Economics," paper delivered at the 1996 Communitarian Summit, Genvea, Switzerland.

Giddens, A. (1998) "Ideology: Beyond Left and Right." *The Economist* (p.52).

Gilbert, N. (1995) *Welfare Justice: Restoring Social Equity*. New Haven: Yale University Press.

Gilbert, N. (ed.) (2001) *Targeting Social Benefits: International Perspectives on Issues and Trends*. New Brunswick, N. J.: Transaction Publishers.

Gilbert, N. (2002) *Transformation of the Welfare State: The Silent Surrender of Public Responsibility*. New York: Oxford University Press.

Gilbert, N. and Gilbert, B. (1989) *The Enabling State: Modern Welfare Capitalism in America*. New York: Oxford University Press.

Glennerster, H. (1999) "Which Welfare States are Most Likely to Survive?" *International Journal of Social Welfare*, 8 (1).

Gronbacher, G. (1998) "The Need for Economic Personalism." *The Journal of Markets and Morality* 1 (1).

Hakim, C. (1997) "A Sociological Perspective on Part-Time Work," in H. –P. Blossfeld and C. Hakim (eds) *Between Equalization and Marginalization: Women Working Part-Time in Europe and the United States of America*. Oxford: Oxford University Press.

Hirschman, A. (1977) *The Passions and the Interests*. Princeton: Princeton University Press.

_____ (1992) *Shifting Involvements: Private Interests and Public Action*. Princeton: Princeton University Press.

Hort, S. E. O. (2001) "From a Generous to a Stingy Welfare State? Sweden's Approach to Targeting," in N. Gilbert (ed.).

International Social Security Association (1989) "Developments and Trends in Social Security: 1978-1989," *International Social Security Review,* 42 (3).

Jessop, B. (1994) "From Keynesian Welfare to the Schumpeterian Workfare State," in R. Burrows and B. Loader (eds) *Towards a Post-Fordist Welfare State*. London: Routledge.

Karger, H. and Stoesz, D. (1994) *American Social Welfare Policy: A Pluralist Approach*. New York: Longman.

Kim, Y.–M. (2001) "Welfare State of Social Safety Nets: Development of the Social Welfare Policy of the Kim Dae-jung Administration." *Korea Journal* 41 (2).

Kim, Y.-H. (2000) "Productive Welfare: Korea's Third Way." *International Journal of Social Welfare* 12 (1).

Letwin, S. (1992) *The Anatomy of Thatcherism*. London: Fontana.

Marklund, S. (1992) "The Decomposition of Social Policy in Sweden." *Scandinavian Journal of Social Welfare*, 1 (1).

Marshall, T.H. (1964) *Class, Citizenship and Social Development*. New York: Anchor Books.

Marshall, W. and Schramm, M. (eds) (1993) *Mandate for Change*. New York: Berkeley Books.

Marsland, D. (2001) "Markets and the Social Structure of Morality." *Society* 38 (2).

Mead, L. (1986) *Beyond Entitlement: The Social Obligations of Citizenship*. New York: Free Press.

Melkert, A. P. W. (1997) "Conclusion" in *Family Market, and Community: Equity and Efficiency in Social Policy*. Paris: OECD.

Ministry of Social Affairs (1992) *Danish Strategies: Families and Children at Work and at Home*, Copenhagen.

OECD (1989) "Editorial: The Path to Full Employment: Structural Adjustment for an Active Society." *Employment Outlook*.

_____ (1998) *Maintaining Prosperity in an Ageing Society*. Paris: OECD.

_____ (1988) *The Future of Social Protection*. Paris: OECD.

Pierson, P. (1996) "The New Politics of the Welfare State." *World Politics*, 48 (2).

Presidential Committee for Quality-of-Life, Office of the President, Republic of Korea (2000) *DJ Welfarism: A New Paradigm for Productive Welfare in Korea*. Seoul: Tae Sul Dang, Korea.

Richard, W. (1994) "From Entitlement to Contract: Reshaping the Welfare State in Australia." *Journal of Sociology and Social Welfare*, 13 (3).

Schumpeter, J. (1950) *Capitalism, Socialism, and Democracy*. New York: Harper and Row Publishers.

Schwartz, B. (1999) "Capitalism, The Market, 'The Underclass', and the Future." *Society*, 37 (1).

Sorensen, O. (1998) "Variability of Retirement Age Practices: An Appropriate Response to Labour Market Developments?" *Harmonizing Economic Developments and Social Needs: ISSA Technical Conferences 1997, 1998*. Geneva: International Social Security Association.

Standing, G. (1999) *Global Labour Flexibility: Seeking Distributive Justice*. London: Macmillan Press, Ltd.

Sunesson, S. et al. "The Flight from Universalism." *European Journal of Social Work*, 1 (1).

Titmuss, R. (1974) *Social Policy*. London: George Allen & Unwin.

Torfing, J. (1997) "From the Keynesian Welfare State to a Schumpeterian Workfare Regime—the Offensive Neo-Statist Case of Denmark," paper presented at the 9th International Conference on Socio-Economics, Montreal, Canada.

Walwei, U. and Werner, H. (2001) "Employment Problems and Active Labout Market Policies in Industrialized Countries," in D. Hoskins, D. Dobernack, and C. Kuptsch (eds), *Social Security at the Dawn of the 21st Century: Topical Issues and New Approaches*. New Brunswick, N.J.: Transaction Publishers.

Wattenberg, B. (1993) "Let Clinton be Clinton." *Wall Street Journal*, January 20 (p. A12).

Wertheimer, R., Long, M. and Vandivere, S. (2001) *Welfare Recipient's Attitudes Toward Welfare, Nonmarital Childbearing, and Work: Implications for Reform?* Series B, No, B-37. The Urban Institute: Washington DC.

Wilson, J. Q. (1993) *The Moral Sense*. New York: Free Press.

3

Globalization, Social Protection and Productive Welfare: An International Perspective

Ramesh Mishra

I. Introduction

The debate on the implications of globalization for institutions of social welfare has focused mainly on western industrial societies. In doing so it has glossed over some crucial aspects of this relationship, namely: (a) the destabilizing effect of financial openness on national economies and its implications for social protection (b) the influence of international financial institutions (IFIs), notably IMF and World Bank, on the social policy of nations and (c) the erosion of "social protection by other means" and its implications for welfare. The chapter substantiates this argument by looking at the globalization and welfare nexus in four groups of countries: the less developed, newly industrializing, ex-communist, and western industrial. In conclusion it emphasizes the need for an international perspective, besides national and cross-national ones, for an adequate understanding of the relationship between globalization and welfare. Given the broad scope of the topic the chapter aims at providing an overview. Thus data are used to illustrate points rather than to provide a detailed examination of the issues concerned.

But how does the chapter relate to the Productive Welfare initiative of South Korea (henceforth Korea)? Essentially the chapter helps to locate this important initiative in the context of global developments. Thus each of the three points made above are relevant to Korean welfare. First, financial liberalization and the rapid movement of portfolio capital has had a major destabilizing effect on Korean economy resulting in a sharp rise in unemployment and social distress. It has underlined the need to develop and strengthen appropriate forms of social protection, at any rate as one of the policy options. Second, through the IMF loan conditionalities Korea has had first hand experience of supranational influence on economic and social policies affecting national autonomy in policy-making. Third, financial liberalization followed by the currency crisis of 1997 has seriously disrupted Korea's form of "social protection by other means," namely private sector full employment and steady economic growth within a relatively insulated economy. The new departure signaled by the Productive Welfare initiative seems to be about the need to develop adequate social protection, in the context of a globalizing economy, responsive to both economic and social needs of the nation. In short, Productive Welfare is a call for new forms of system (efficiency) and social (solidarity/justice) integration in the changed context of an open, market economy and a democratic polity in Korea. By extension the model should also be relevant to other countries—in East Asia and elsewhere—faced with a similar situation. However Productive Welfare is about many other things besides economic globalization, e.g. democracy, not dealt with in this chapter. Conversely this chapter is concerned with other issues, e.g. the need for an international perspective in the study of social protection, whose relevance to Productive Welfare is only indirect.

II. Enter Globalization

Until recently, the welfare state has been studied almost entirely within a national framework. This is not surprising given that it has developed as, and still remains, very much a national enterprise.

The basic assumption underlying the welfare state has been that of substantial policy autonomy on the part of the nation state in respect of macroeconomic management and the determination of monetary, fiscal and social policies. True, national economies and polities, especially the former have never been closed systems. They have been implicated in international and supranational systems and processes. Nonetheless it has been possible to study the welfare state with virtually little or no reference to the supranational dimension. At any rate this seems to have been the case with the welfare states in advanced industrial societies.[1]

It is not difficult to see why the focus has been on the national level. In its heyday, spanning roughly 1950-75, the welfare state functioned in the context of an international framework of trade and financial arrangements (Bretton Woods institutions, fixed exchange rates, capital controls) which provided the nation state with a good deal of economic stability as well as autonomy. The international framework was supportive of the welfare state and could therefore be taken for granted. It could thus, in a sense, be left out of account in the studies of the determinants and influences on social policy which were seen primarily, if not entirely, as national and endogenous. Moreover the process of the dissolution of the Bretton Woods framework since the early 1970s has been piecemeal and gradual. For example it was not until the 1990s that the abolition of capital controls was completed in the developed economies (Kelly 1995).

More recently, however, the relative insulation or the "national embeddedness" of welfare states has been increasingly challenged by a set of developments typically subsumed under the term "globalization."[2] Globalization is not so much a theoretical concept as a convenient label—a keyword—which has been employed widely to refer to a major societal trend which has gathered momentum over the last couple of decades. In broad terms it refers to a process through which the nation-state is becoming more open to influences that are supranational. These may be economic, cultural, technological or political in nature. As far as the welfare state is concerned, interest has centered on economic globalization which is seen as curtailing the policy—making autonomy of nations and putting a downward pressure on social protection and social standards in advanced industrial countries (Teeple 1995; Rhodes 1996; Mishra 1999). In this chapter, the focus will be on economic aspects of globalization understood as: i) economic liberalization, i.e. freer trade and especially financial flows across countries, and ii) the influence of global intergovernmental organizations (IGOs), notably the International Monetary Fund (IMF) and World Bank (WB), on economic liberalization and the social policy of nations.

The study of globalization from the perspective of the welfare state remains underdeveloped. Apart from the tradition of nation-centeredness, a part of the difficulty is that the global dimension requires an understanding and articulation of the nature of international political economy whereas students of the welfare state have been concerned primarily with the national-political economy (Rhodes 1996; Deacon 1997). In any case, since the mid-1990s there has been a growing perception that the international context of the welfare state has changed in significant ways and a literature concerned directly with the implications of global economic developments for the welfare state has been accumulating (Piven 1995; Teeple 1995; Rhodes 1996; Pierson 1998; Mishra 1999).

It is generally recognized that the international context or the "environment" in which the national welfare states operate today is different from the time when the Bretton Woods framework, with fixed exchange rates and capital controls, was firmly in place. But what exactly the new environment means for the welfare state remains contentious. Again how recent is the global influence on social policy of nations and what forms it takes remain underexplored issues. One problem here is that until recently the debate has been concerned mainly with the welfare state in advanced industrial societies and

thus remained confined within somewhat narrow limits.[3] Much of the literature has focused on the impact of global markets and financial openness on
the welfare state primarily in terms of curtailment of social programs or cutbacks in social benefits and expenditures. Framing the issue in this way it has
been possible to argue that the consequences of globalization per se have not
been particularly significant and that current trends and developments can be
explained adequately in terms of the influence of endogenous variables.
Others have argued the case for the continuing salience of social democracy
for welfare state policies despite the globalization hype (Garrett 1998). It is
not intended to join that debate here (Mishra 1999). Suffice to say that it has
been argued elsewhere that globalization needs to be taken seriously and that
its implications are somewhat contradictory as far as state welfare is concerned (Mishra 1998, 1999). Be that as it may, this chapter is concerned with
one of the major limitations of this debate, namely the lack of an international perspective, and its implications.[4]

Thus, one of the principal arguments of this chapter is that in order to
understand adequately the nature of globalization and its consequences for
social protection of nations it is necessary to look beyond industrial societies. In short one needs, so to speak, to globalize the globalization and welfare
debate. At present it remains compartmentalized with little or no connection
between the study of globalization and social protection in different group of
countries. The rest of this chapter will seek to highlight the relationship
between the global sphere and social welfare in the four "worlds" comprising
the less developed countries (LDCs), the newly industrializing countries
(NICs), the former communist countries, and Western industrial countries
(WICs). It will then consider the implications of this analysis for the globalization and welfare relationship.

III. Globalization and Social Protection in the LDCs

The comprehensive system of social protection which we know as the
welfare state in industrialized countries does not exist in most developing
countries or exists only in a rudimentary form. Full employment policies,
universal health care, insurance or assistance-based programs of income security are often non-existent or only partially developed. However, modes of
protection have to be seen in relation to the level of economic development
and the institutional setting of nations. Thus, it is more appropriate to focus
on the functions of social protection rather than on specific structures or
institutional arrangements through which they are met (Castles 1989).

While most developing countries share features of social protection with
developed countries, e.g. the provision of education, health care and housing, there are other distinctive programs such as consumer price subsidies,
price controls, food rations and the like which play a vital role in sustaining

incomes and/or living standards in LDCs. These measures, which constitute "social protection by other means" (ibid.), i.e. by means other than the formally recognized policies and institutions of welfare, have been the target of drastic cutbacks and restructuring at the behest of the IMF and the World Bank. The stabilization and structural adjustment programs, initiated by these IFIs as a condition for granting or rescheduling loans to LDCs, have been the means for implementing these policies.

As is well known, general debt management by the IMF involves two different measures: stabilization, and structural adjustment. The former aims at correcting the balance of payments deficit and involves such action as currency devaluation and a drastic curb on imports. The latter involves a more comprehensive program of restructuring the economy of the debtor country. It includes measures such as a sharp reduction in public spending, reduction or elimination of consumer subsidies on food and other necessities, retrenchment of social programs, privatization of state enterprises and reduction in wages in order to attract foreign companies and make exports more competitive.

Between 1978-92, more than 70 LDCs were involved in upwards of 500 programs under the auspices of the World Bank and IMF (McMichael 1996). How far the conditionalities were strictly observed and what were their precise economic and social consequences has been, not unexpectedly, a matter of contention and debate. It must be remembered too that in many countries there was a great deal of opposition to these conditionalities and adjustment programs. The draconian measures required by the IMF and their impact on living standards led to riots and disturbances in not a few countries (ibid.). Domestic political responses naturally varied. Moreover, circumstances differed from one country to another. Nonetheless, in broad terms conditionalities and adjustment programs meant the following. First, national autonomy in policy-making was substantially curtailed. Second, the economic medicine prescribed by the IMF led to substantial unemployment and reduction in wages. Measures of social protection, notably consumer subsidies, and social development were sharply curtailed. The result was a drop—sometimes severe—in living standards and a rise in poverty and deprivation. Third, the country's economy was opened up to foreign investors and more closely integrated into the global economy, with its attendant risks and benefits. For example, the strategy of export-led growth prescribed to these countries resulted in a glut of supply and a sharp fall in export prices (McMichael 1996). In any case during the 1980s there was a major reorientation in development policies. National development goals were replaced by those of participation in the world market. The reach of the global economy was extended.

The overall debt burden of LDCs rose by 61 percent during the1980s. And from the mid-80s the annual outflow of funds for debt servicing from the developing to the developed world exceeded the inflow. By 1997 the total debt burden of developing countries had reached almost $2.2 trillion (UNDP 1999). The hardest hit have been the forty or so heavily indebted poor countries, mostly in Africa. Since 1980 their debt burden has more than tripled, two-thirds of it the result of earlier loans and arrears unpaid. As the UNDP (ibid.) report sums up, this debt burden "drains public budgets, absorbs resources needed for human development and inhibits economic growth."

IV. The NICs or the Emerging Markets of Asia and Latin America

The term emerging market economies generally refers to the NICs of Asia and Latin America which offer opportunities for profitable investment. These countries share with the LDCs the experience of loan conditionalities and austerity policies imposed by IFIs, notably the IMF, with broadly similar implications for the living standards of the population. However, perhaps what is distinctive about the experience of emerging economies *is the way financial openness can destabilize the national economy* precipitating serious economic crisis and delivering the country into the arms of the IMF which then proceeds to arrange a bail out with various conditionalities. This is a different situation from that of the LDCs in that here it is essentially the financial openness of national economies and problems of private sector debt, rather than balance of payment difficulties or problems of public debt, that precipitates the crisis (Singh 1999). Here the impact of globalization is direct. Moreover as recent financial crises in Mexico (1994) and Korea (1997) show, these two NICs—both recently admitted to membership of the OECD with the latter boasting a sophisticated industrial economy—have been vulnerable to economic destabilization and the collapse of currency and stock markets (Grabel 1999) with serious consequences for the well-being of the population.

With the opening up of many NICs to foreign investment, in particular portfolio investment, a new chapter seems to have begun in the saga of globalization. As a part of the neo-liberal economic policies promoted by the "Washington consensus" more and more countries have been under pressure—directly or indirectly—to open up their economies to foreign investment. Down to the 1980s the NICs of East Asia, e.g. Korea, Taiwan and Indonesia, have had a variety of controls and restrictions in place on foreign investment. From about the mid-1980s many of these countries were persuaded to ease or remove these restrictions and to welcome foreign investment (Singh 1999). The result was a huge inflow of funds, mainly in the form of portfolio investment, in search of substantial returns. Moreover many companies and businesses in these countries borrowed heavily from foreign lenders in order to finance speculative and other economic activity. Although the principal causes of the financial crisis of South East Asia in 1997 remain a matter of contention, given the nature of the financial institutions and limited foreign exchange reserve of many NICs, financial liberalization must be considered an important precipitating cause of the crisis. For unlike many of the LDCs discussed above the Asian NICs, for example, did not have a balance of payment problem, their public sector was relatively small, budgets were not in deficit, and they had been hailed as model developing economies by IFIs such as the IMF (Felix 1998; Singh 1999). What then went wrong? In 1997 the perceived weakness of one of the currencies—the Thai "baht"—and the possibility of its devaluation caused a run on the currency and the "contagion effect" spread to neighboring countries. The result was a mass exodus of short-term foreign investment out of these countries. The collapse of the currency and the stock markets led to economic contraction, massive lay offs and a sharp drop in living standards (ILR 1999; OECD 1999a; UNDP 1999). At the same time foreign banks called in their short-term loans (denominated in dollar) which the private borrowers were unable to pay. The resulting shock to the global markets and the possibility of the contagion spreading further afield led the US and other G-7 nations to arrange a rescue package. In December 1997 Korea received a bail out of $57 bn. (the biggest so far, topping the $50 bn. Mexican bail out in 1995). Indonesia received a package of $43 bn (Grabel 1999). The Korean rescue package, overseen by the IMF, required the restructuring of the banking system, opening of the economy immediately to foreign imports, raising the limit on foreign ownership of stock, reducing government spending and raising taxes (ibid.). In the event, the severity of the economic downturn and other factors, including widespread criticism of IMF's policy of "one size fits all" and strong opposition from within Korea led the Fund to set aside its austerity policy.[5] However, overall the initial rescue package had a strong deflationary bias (Palley 1999; Singh 1999).

As a result of the economic crisis, production, consumption, employment and incomes—all suffered a sharp decline in, e.g. Korea, Indonesia and Thailand. The poverty population jumped another 12-20 percent, suicide and reported domestic violence increased sharply in, for example, Korea. In these and other Asian NICs, which virtually enjoyed conditions of full employment until then, unemployment rose sharply (ILR 1999; UNDP 1999). In Korea, for example, registered unemployment rose from just over two percent in mid- 1997 to over eight percent in early 1999 (OECD 1999a). Whereas before the crisis unemployment was concentrated among younger age groups, post-crisis unemployment hit the older (30-50) age groups who accounted for half of the unemployed workers. It was the relatively insulated nature of the Asian economies (their "strategic integration" in world economy as one economist puts it), which was in no small measure responsible for their spectacular economic success and which allowed them to maintain full employment through private sector jobs. Moreover along with relative job security went some work related benefits. That is one reason why unemployment insurance and other forms of income support programs for the unemployed were virtually non-existent or in a rudimentary stage of development in these countries. Sudden and unexpected onset of unemployment therefore had "disastrous consequences for the unemployed and their families" who "simultaneously lost their incomes and income-related benefits, such as health insurance" (ILR 1999). Indeed overall these countries have been slow to develop social programs, especially income security programs for the working age population relying instead on private sector full employment, corporate welfare and traditional family support (Goodman and Peng 1996).

One of the consequences of openness is that the system of social protection by other means has been weakened, if not undermined. Elsewhere I have made the point (with reference to Japan) that in so far as these forms of social protection are eroded the population will be far more vulnerable to economic insecurity and one of the options must be the expansion of state welfare (Mishra 1999). How different countries and governments respond to this problem of course depends on a host of domestic factors. Thus Korea seems to have accepted economic liberalization and greater market orientation of the economy while at the same time deciding to strengthen the social safety net especially in respect of unemployment insurance and social assistance (OECD 2000: Korea). Korea's response to unemployment, poverty and social inequities caused by the financial crisis has to do, in part, with the strength of trade unions and other social movements as well as recent political developments which have strengthened democracy (Cumings 1998; Gills and Gills 2000; Kim and Moon 2000). Although IMF loan conditionality has paid some attention to the need for social safety nets—a necessary corollary to the prescription for opening up these economies further—these concerns remain somewhat marginal and symbolic for the Fund. It has to be remembered too that in so far as loans demand fiscal austerity, reduction in public spending and the like it may be more difficult for these nations to develop or extend social protection measures.

In a sense the East Asian crisis was nothing new. In 1994-1995, Mexico had been hit by a not dissimilar crisis and illustrates very well the perils of financial openness for emerging market economies. By 1994, Mexico had not only joined the NAFTA but also the OECD thus symbolizing its coming of age as a relatively stable and maturing economy. These developments led to a large inflow of foreign portfolio investment in the early 1990s. Rising stock market prices and high interest rates on short-term bonds made the country very attractive for higher returns. However the bubble was to burst soon. During 1994 the stock market fell by about a third in value. In December the peso was devalued by 30 percent but in fact fell further. Confidence in the functioning of the "borderless" global economy as well as in the NAFTA were at stake. A bailout package of some $50 bn. (the biggest ever) was arranged hastily by the G-7 nations under US leadership to stabilize the peso and to restore investor confidence. Once again the task of setting the conditionalities and supervising the loan fell on the IMF (Grabel 1999).

The result of the economic crisis, high interest rates and the austerity policies demanded by the IMF was a massive inflation, sharp contraction in consumer demand, rising unemployment and falling wages. True, within a couple of years the economy improved, growth picked up and investor confidence had been restored. But it was a different story for the large majority of the people. During 1993-8, for example, average wages fell at a rate of 1.6 percent per annum while prices rose by an annual rate of 19.7 percent (OECD 1999b: "Basic Statistics, International Comparisons"). In the late 1990s, four-fifths of the country's population was still worse off than in 1982 (Pieper and Taylor 1998).[6] Moreover membership of NAFTA and the conditionalities attached to the loan means that the economy is now more open than before to global investors and thus at a higher risk for the repetition of the 1994-5 crisis through the sudden exit of portfolio capital.

In sum, financial liberalization has introduced a serious risk of the destabilization of the economies of the NICs through sudden outflow of portfolio capital and other forms of "hot money." Financial bailouts are aimed primarily at protecting the investors' and creditors' interest and the associated conditionalities often add to the diswelfare of the general population resulting from the crises. Moreover, the resolution of the problem within the framework of financial openness increases the risk of recurrent crises and diswelfare for the population likely to be followed by further bailouts. Thus a vicious cycle is set in motion. The consequences for systems of social protection are contradictory. On the one hand the commodification of the economy increases insecurity, undermines existing forms of social protection and thus underlines the need for adequate social safety net in an open globalized economy. On the other hand, the disruption of the economy, resource constraints and fiscal austerity, and the ideology of privatization militate against building programs of social welfare. How to manage this contradiction is an important problem of public policy in these societies.

V. Global Economy and the Former Communist Countries

As far as transnational influence on welfare is concerned, the ex-communist countries share a number of features with the LDCs and emerging economies—economic vulnerability due to financial openness, the influence of IFIs on social policy, the erosion of "social protection by other means"—but within a context that differs in important respects from that of the other two groups of countries. For one the former communist countries have been in a difficult process of transition from state socialism towards a market economy and open society. For another all this is taking place against the backdrop of a well-developed system of social protection. The impact of supranational forces needs to be seen in this context.

With the collapse of communism in the USSR and Eastern Europe in the late 1980s the former communist countries were faced with the task of reconstructing their economy and society. In broad terms this meant a transition from state socialism to some form of liberal economic and political order, a transition that had no historical precedents and thus no blueprints or models as a guide. At any rate it was also evident that these countries will need economic assistance to make the transition (a different model of economic transition is being followed by China and Vietnam), an assistance that could only come from the West. It came packaged with the dominant Western economic ideology of neo-liberalism. These countries were advised to go for an all out radical reform and to integrate their economies within the world economy. This meant moving away from a relatively closed economy and society to one completely open to global capitalism in terms of trade and financial flows. This approach to transition, which came to be known as "shock therapy"(ST) involved such things as trade and financial liberalization, currency convertibility and the unleashing of market forces in the domestic economy (Gowan 1995; Standing 1996).

The transition was expected to create some economic dislocation and problems of adjustment in the short run. In fact the policy of ST, combined with weaknesses inherited from state socialism, proved disastrous for many of these countries resulting in a huge drop in production, large scale unemployment, sharp decline in wages, large increases in poverty and deprivation and in economic inequality. This was accompanied with massive inflation, balance of payments problems and a serious lack of revenue for governments (ibid.).

The system of social protection these countries inherited was a part of the old order of state socialism with its ideological commitment to economic security and collective consumption. Its three major bases were: full employment for both men and women; a system of consumer price subsidies which held down the cost of living very substantially (these two comprised "social protection by other means"); a set of universal, if low quality, services such as health, education and child care, and a range of income transfer programs, e.g. pensions and child allowances, again at a low level of benefits. Employment related benefits were also important and in fact overlapped with state programs.

The decollectivization of the economy and its marketization under the ST approach meant the end of full employment and a drastic reduction, if not elimination, of subsidies. Each of these had considerable negative impact on living standards and the sense of economic security of the population. The third base of social protection—the social programs—has also been restructured resulting, in broad terms, in greater selectivity and residualism. Some income transfer programs, e.g. pensions, have seen a good deal of privatization. Given the policy of compulsory full employment (an aspect of state socialism), these countries did not have unemployment insurance or similar measures. These had to be put in place as a part of the transition (Standing 1996).

With balance of payments and other economic problems resulting from the transition these countries needed financial aid. This involved IFIs such as IMF and WB and, as in the case of the LDCs, the task of arranging and supervising loans provided these IFIs with the leverage for influencing economic and social policy. In general, fiscal austerity, the reduction of public expenditure and greater use of selectivity in social programs have been the guiding policy principles of the IMF for these countries. With the ST approach and associated adjustment policies the social costs of transition—varying in degree from one country to another—have been heavy in terms of impoverishment and destitution, inequality, falling life expectations and other quality of life indicators (Standing 1996; Truscott 1997; Ferge 2001).

Although the economies of some of the former communist countries, e.g. Poland and Hungary, have recovered well since the mid-90s the legacy of the transition and adjustment policies for social protection would appear to be more long lasting. Meanwhile the burden of foreign debt continues to weigh heavily on many of these countries (Strange 1998). In sum, supranational influences—working through global investors as well as IFIs—have been prominent in shaping economic and social policies with serious consequences for the living standards of the people. Moreover forms of social protection specific to state socialism—notably compulsory full employment and consumer subsidies—have been substantially dismantled making for a marked convergence towards the western welfare state model.

VI. Western Industrial Countries

At first sight the situation of the WICs seems to be very different from that of the other countries discussed above. First, as we have seen, in all three groups of countries the role of the IFIs—primarily IMF but also WB—in curtailing policy autonomy of nations and in restructuring social policy in a neo-liberal direction has been quite prominent. In the WICs, by contrast, IFIs have played no such role and these countries have not had their policy-making autonomy impaired in this way. Second, in emerging market economies financial liberalization has brought a large measure of volatility through the ebb and flow of short-term foreign investment resulting in the destabilization of the economy, fall in output, rise in unemployment, drop in living standards and rise in poverty. The loans and conditionalities that have usually followed under the auspices of the IMF contain a bias towards a deflationary policy and fiscal austerity. The "social protection by other means" that has characterized the emerging Asian economies, in conditions where state welfare remains less developed, has been weakened as a result. In the WICs, by contrast, financial liberalization and the free flow of investment across borders has not meant the destabilization of economies or serious currency crises—problems that a country's own economic and financial resources (including borrowing on the market) cannot cope with. In short, the kind of impact of globalization on economic and social welfare of nations seen in East Asia and elsewhere recently has no counterpart as far as WICs are concerned. These differences are not unimportant. Does it mean, then, that the WICs are immune to the destabilization of their economies and free from the influence of IGOs?

Let us begin with the influence of IGOs. The WB has little to do with WICs while the IMF has not been involved in bailing out any WICs for over two decades. Thus it has not had a direct say in the fiscal and social policy of these countries. On the other hand the indirect influence of the IMF on WICs—by way of the surveillance of monetary and fiscal management, offer of expert advice, regular meetings and consultations with finance ministers and other government officials of member countries—is not to be underestimated (O'Brien et al. 2000; IMF 1999; Gerster 1994). And by and large, this influence has been strongly monetarist and liberal in orientation. The OECD, which acts more as a think-tank for the WICs, also seeks to influence the economic and social policy of member countries. Although more eclectic and less orthodox in its approach than the IMF, the OECD also appears to favor financial liberalization, greater market-orientation of the economy and a smaller role for the social state (Deacon 1997; Mishra 1999).[7]

In sum, although IGOs such as the IMF and OECD do not exercise direct control over social policy of the WICs indirectly they influence policy options and choices of these countries. True, the pro-market liberal policies generally favored by these institutions is not an easy sell within member states. WICs are democracies and therefore government policies are subject to challenge by interest groups and opposition parties. In short democracy acts as a counterweight to global neo-liberalism. Here again the WICs may be in a somewhat different position than the LDCs, the NICs and ex-communist countries where democracy and civil society are not so well developed and institutionalized. Moreover, the European Union appears to be playing a progressive role by way of developing minimum social standards, albeit mainly concerned with the workplace, for member countries.

Although the WICs have not so far experienced any destabilization of the economy it would be wrong to conclude that they are immune to such a development. Thus, the Asian crisis of 1997 which was followed by financial crises in Brazil and Russia in 1998 did pose a threat to the stability of the global economy as a whole. The bailouts organized by the G-7 governments (led by the US) during the 1990s were, in part, meant to contain and defuse the crises and stop the contagion from spreading more widely. An example of a direct threat to Western financial institutions is provided by Long Term Capital Management, a leading American hedge fund which was highly leveraged and which faced almost certain collapse in the fall of 1998. The domino effect on stock markets and other financial institutions and through them on the US economy could apparently have been serious. A rescue package for the fund was put together hastily by Western banks at the initiative of the Chairman of the Federal Reserve and the President of the Federal Reserve Bank of New York (Warde 1998). Clearly the increased integration of the global economy itself together with financial openness means that the WICs are also potentially at risk.

Compared to the stable financial regime under the Bretton Woods dispensation the current regime of financial openness and flexible exchange rates increases the risk of large-scale economic destabilization, hardly a sound basis for sustaining national welfare states. Indeed as the experience of Sweden in 1992 shows, the currencies of WICs have at times come under severe pressure leading to significant shifts in social policy (Crotty et al. 1998).

Despite these commonalities between the WICs and other countries the impact of globalization on WICs takes a somewhat different form. It is more indirect and diffuse in nature although broadly in the same neo-liberal direction. We shall look briefly at three broad areas of social concern: full employment, social security, and taxation and inequality. Keeping in mind that conditions vary from one country to another and that global pressures are mediated through the political economy of the nation-state the following generalizations seek to capture the broad trend. First, financial openness and mobility of capital together with flexible exchange rates means that Keynesian macroeconomic management in order to create full employment and stable economic growth is not feasible—or at least not effective—in an open economy. Second, heightened international competition and associated changes in market conditions demand greater labor market flexibility and the acceptance of low wage employment. Governments are under pressure to cut back unemployment benefits and social assistance to the able-bodied. Third, conditions of openness and capital mobility are exerting a downward pressure on taxation and social spending as nations are placed in a competitive situation in order to attract or retain private investment and create a business-friendly environment. Bond markets are influencing the fiscal policy of nations through the credit rating of governments. Progressive taxation is becoming a thing of the past as top income tax rates plummet and there is a marked shift from income and corporate taxation to the more regressive consumption taxes. Both pre-tax and post-tax inequality of incomes has increased markedly. In sum, global capitalism, with the support of IGOs such as the IMF and others, has been exerting a good deal of pressure, directly or indirectly, to scale down the comprehensive systems of social protection developed within the context of a more stable international framework of finance and relatively closed national economies (Mishra 1999).

However, counter-pressures in the form of democratic opposition, long-standing national commitment to social partnership and social market approach, e.g. in Continental Europe, are moderating the neo-liberal thrust of global capitalism. Moreover, the idea that social programs could make a positive contribution to productive efficiency and social cohesion seems to be finding greater acceptance. Hence, overall, we find that WICs have not as yet traveled far down the road of shrinking the social state and reducing social protection.

VII. Summary and Conclusions

Evidence from the world outside of the WICs suggests that an exclusive focus on the latter in terms of the effect of globalization is limiting in a number of ways. For one it ignores almost entirely the role of IGOs in curtailing the policy-making autonomy of nations, one of the key issues in the relationship between globalization and social protection. This role has been direct and pronounced in the case of a large number of countries around the world and needs to be brought into focus. This is important for a number of reasons. First, it draws attention to the fact that globalization involves more than just pressure from markets and private enterprises; IGOs are also involved. Second, it highlights the fact that IGOs are also influencing the social policy of WICs and that the nature of this influence has yet to be examined systematically. And although these IGOs, especially the World Bank, are now far more aware of the social consequences of their economic policies as well as the fact that directly or indirectly they are involved in making social policy this social dimension needs to be made more explicit. Third, a focus on the IGOs, notably the IMF, OECD but also the World Trade Organization, underlines the fact that globalization is a process—rather than a finished state. This is important in that a good deal of complacency in the literature about the durability of the welfare state stems from treating globalization as though it was a finished state. A related point is that these IGOs are closely involved in the process of extending the reach of globalization. The Multilateral Agreement on Investment (MAI), a measure which was piloted through the OECD in near secrecy for about three years before being shelved, is a case in point (Clarke and Barlow 1997; Braunstein and Epstein 1999). Fourth, a focus on the role of these IGOs raises the issue of legitimate governance in the area of global policy-making. For IFIs such as IMF and WB are not democratic bodies but reflect the economic power of donor nations. Yet their decisions have direct implications for welfare policies of nations. Other IGOs, e.g. OECD, also suffer from lack of transparency and accountability (witness, for example, the secrecy surrounding the MAI).

We turn next to the implications of financial openness and cross-border flow of capital for nations. Here again an exclusive focus on WICs tends to miss out almost entirely on the role of financial openness in destabilizing economies. In Mexico (1994-1995), in Korea and other Asian countries (1997-1998), and in Brazil and Russia (1998) the sudden exodus of foreign capital has had a major impact on the economy resulting in loss of output, bankruptcies, unemployment, fall in living standards and poverty. Moreover these crises required bailout loans which generally involve further belt-tightening and public expenditure cuts. In the case of East Asian countries economic destabilization has disrupted, if not substantially weakened, the bases of their economic success and "social protection by other means," i.e. rapid economic growth and private sector full employment. One response to this, notably in Korea, has been to expand the scope of state welfare and strengthen social protection (Kwon 2001). Systems of social protection have also been undergoing a transformation in former communist countries bringing them closer to the Western welfare state model. Thus globalization appears to be resulting in a convergence in systems of social protection across different types of societies, a development that is missed out if the focus is exclusively on WICs. Moreover, the transition from the old forms of social protection to the new ones needs to be examined systematically as a problem of social policy development in its own right, a problem to which Korea under the presidency of Kim Dae-Jung seems to be devoting a good deal of attention.[8]

No doubt, financial openness and the flow of foreign investment has also brought economic benefits for countries outside the WICs. However the question must be asked at what cost? And what kind of benefits and for whom? For as the case of Mexico, for example, shows economic growth can resume within a short time following the crisis, stock markets surge and foreign investors return. But it is a different story as far as the majority of people are concerned. They may have to pay for the cost of adjustment in terms of fall in living standards and retarded social development for a long time. Whereas the bailouts protect the interests of foreign and domestic investors there may not be any kind of bailout for the people of the country concerned. Hence the importance of national responses to globalization and social protection. These responses will vary depending on a host of economic and political factors and determine whether and how the need for adequate social protection and labor market policies to help people to adjust to new conditions is met. The contrast between Mexican and Korean responses to financial crisis of the 1990s shows this quite clearly.

In any case, the drastic effect of financial openness raises the question of the need to regulate financial flows in order to prevent economic destabilization. Recent studies by UNCTAD show that the rising frequency of financial crises is associated with the growth of international capital flows in the 1990s (UNDP 1999). A look at countries outside the WICs underlines the serious consequences that can result from financial openness. Thus far the WICs have been spared the kind of dramatic destabilization we have seen elsewhere. But this does not mean that Western economies are immune to the virus of instability—they too seem to be potentially at risk in a global economy.

In sum, there is a case for bringing an international and global perspective to bear on the study of the relationship between globalization and social welfare. At present it tends to be compartmentalized in terms of different groups of countries due to academic specialization and the important differences that exist among countries. This chapter has argued that such a specialized approach needs to be complemented by a wider and more unifying international perspective. In such a perspective the consequences of (i) economic liberalization and (ii) the policies of economic IGOs, for social protection (including "social protection by other means") and social standards would have to be center stage. That could provide the common ground for the study of globalization and welfare relationship across major types of society, namely developed, developing, and transitional (ex-communist), and offer a more adequate database for understanding this relationship. Within such a framework the Productive Welfare paradigm can be examined as a significant response to problems of national welfare precipitated by globalization.

Notes

1. This is not to say that exogenous variables have not received some attention. Thus Cameron (1978) found a positive correlation between social expenditure and trade dependence of economies. Katzenstein (1985) advanced the thesis that international vulnerability of small trade-dependent countries leads to cooperation among social partners, in short corporatism, and results in a more developed system of social protection. Castles (1989) argued that high tariffs and restriction on immigration enabled Australia and New Zealand to develop a "wage-earners' welfare state" as part of a system of "social protection by other means."

2. The literature on globalization is immense. Held et al. (1999) provide an encyclopedic overview.

3. There is now a growing body of literature which explores the implications of globalization for economies outside the WICs. This is beginning to extend the parameters of the debate and to offer new insights into change and development in social protection. For example on Korea, see Lee (1999); Shin (2000); Kwon (2001).

4. Deacon et al. (1997) address this issue but focus on the social policies—manifest or latent—of supranational agencies such as IMF, WB, OECD, European Union and the differences among them. This paper, on the other hand, is concerned with an international perspective which includes IGOs and other global influences and which might help us understand their implications for social protection across a range of societies.

5. In fact given Korea's strong fundamentals it has been possible to apply a considerable fiscal stimulus to the economy. Thus government spending rose by about 17 percent in 1998 and the budget, which was in surplus earlier, went into deficit as a

result (OECD 1999a). See Lane et al. (1999) for IMF's concern with social issues in the East Asian crisis.

6. The Mexican case shows what can happen to industrializing nations as a result of financial liberalization. Clearly much depends on endogenous variables, e.g. the state of the economy, the nature of financial institutions and their management, the nature of the polity and the government. Thus, Korea's rapid rebound after the crisis of 1997, fall in unemployment rate to below 4 percent by 2000, low rate of inflation and the extension of social protection and labor market policies provides a useful contrast to Mexico. It has to be remembered, however, that Korea is world's eleventh largest economy with a per capita income double that of Mexico and now with very substantial foreign exchange reserves. On Korean rebound and social policies see OECD (1999a; 2000).

7. The OECD's attitude to social expenditure and social protection seems to vary between the "European" and the "American" approaches. Since the mid-1990s the European approach seems to have gained ground somewhat.

8. See Presidential Committee for Quality-of-Life, Office of the President, Republic of Korea (2000: 9) An example of recent initiatives in this respect is the International Symposium on the development of Productive Welfare organized in Seoul in September 2001. It would be of considerable interest to see how Japan handles the problem of transition from its highly institutionalized system of social protection by other means, i.e. private sector full employment and enterprise welfare, to a form of social protection commensurate with an open globalized economy. In light of the combined weight of endogenous and exogenous factors it seems likely that Japan will expand state programs of welfare substantially.

References

Braunstein, E. and Epstein, G. (1999) "Creating International Credit Rules and the Multilateral Agreement on Investment" in J.Michie and J.Grieve Smith (eds) *Global Instability*. London: Routledge.

Cameron, D.R. (1978) "The Expansion of the Public Economy: A Comparative Analysis." *American Political Science Review*, 72 (4).

Castles, F. (1989) "Social Protection by Other Means" in F.G. Castles (ed.) *The Comparative History of Public Policy*. New York: Oxford University Press.

Clarke, T. and Barlow, M. (1997) *MAI: Multilateral Agreement on Investment and the Threat to Canadian Sovereignty*. Toronto: Stoddart.

Crotty, J. et al. (1998) "Multinational Corporations in the Neo-Liberal Regime" in D. Baker et al. (eds) *Globalization and Progressive Economic Policy*. Cambridge: Cambridge University Press.

Cumings, B. (1998) "The Korean Crisis and the End of "Late" Development." *New Left Review*, 231.

Deacon, B.et al. (1997) *Global Social Policy*. London: Sage.

Felix, D. (1998) "Asia and the Crisis of Financial Globalization" in D. Baker et al. (eds) *Globalization and Progressive Economic Policy*. Cambridge: Cambridge University Press.

Ferge, Z. (2001) "Welfare and "Ill-Fare" Systems in Central-Eastern Europe" in R. Sykes et al. (eds) *Globalization and the European Welfare State*. Houndmills: Palgrave.

Garrett, G. (1998) *Partisan Politics in the Global Economy*. Cambridge, Cambridge University Press.

Gerster, R. (1994) "A New Framework of Accountability for the IMF" in J. Cavanagh et al. (eds) *Beyond Bretton Woods*. London: Pluto.

Gills, B.K. and Gills, D.S. (2000) "Globalization and Strategic Choice in South Korea: Economic Reform and Labor" in S.S. Kim (ed.) *Korea's Globalization.* Cambridge: Cambridge University Press.

Goodman, R. and Peng, I. (1996) "The East Asian Welfare States" in G. Esping-Andersen (ed.) *Welfare States in Transition.* London: Sage.

Gowan, P. (1995) "Neo-Liberal Theory and Practice for Eastern Europe." *New Left Review,* 213.

Grabel, I. (1999) "Rejecting Exceptionalism: Reinterpreting the Asian Financial Crises" in J. Michie and J. Grieve Smith (eds) *Global Instability.* London: Routledge.

Held, D. et al. (1999) *Global Transformations.* Stanford: Stanford University Press.

Hirst, P. and Thompson, G. (1999) *Globalization in Question.* Cambridge: Polity Press.

International Labour Review (1999) "Social Aspects of the Follow-Up to the Asian Financial Crisis." *International Labour Review,* V. 138 (2).

International Monetary Fund (1999) *Annual Report 1999.* Washington DC.

Katzenstein, P. (1985) *Small States in World Markets.* Ithaca: Cornell University Press.

Kelly, R. (1995) "Derivatives: A Growing Threat to the International Financial System" in J. Michie and J.G. Smith (eds) *Managing the Global Economy.* Oxford: Oxford University Press.

Kim, Y.C. and Moon, C. (2000) "Globalization and Workers in South Korea" in S.S. Kim (ed.) *Korea's Globalization.* Cambridge: Cambridge University Press.

Kwon, H. (2001) "Globalization, Unemployment and Policy Responses in Korea." *Global Social Policy,* 1 (2).

Lane, T. et al. (1999) *IMF-Supported Programs in Indonesia, Korea and Thailand.* Washington DC: IMF.

Lee, H.K. (1999) "Globalization and the Emerging Welfare State: The Experience of South Korea." *International Journal of Social Welfare,* 8 (1).

McMichael, P. (1996) *Development and Social Change.* Thousand Oaks: Pine Forge Press.

Mishra, R. (1998) "Globalization and the Welfare State: The Contradictory Imperatives" in M.P. Singh and R. Saxena (eds) *Ideologies and Institutions in Indian Politics.* New Delhi: Deep and Deep Publications.

_____ (1999) *Globalization and the Welfare State.* Cheltenham: Edward Elgar.

O'Brien, R.O. et al. (2000) *Contesting Global Governance.* Cambridge: Cambridge University Press.

OECD (1999a) *Economic Surveys 1998-1999: Korea.* Paris.

_____ (1999b) *Economic Surveys 1998-1999: Mexico.* Paris.

_____ (2000) *Economic Surveys 1999-2000: Korea.* Paris.

Palley, T.J. (1999) "International finance and global deflation" in J. Michie and J. Grieve Smith (eds.) *Global Instability.* London: Routledge.

Pieper, U. and Taylor, L. (1998) "The Revival of the Liberal Creed: The IMF, the World Bank, and Inequality in a Globalized Economy" in D. Baker et al. (eds) *Globalization and Progressive Economic Policy.* Cambridge: Cambridge University Press.

Pierson, P. (1998) "Irreversible Forces, Immovable Objects: Post-Industrial Welfare States Confront Permanent Austerity." *Journal of European Public Policy,* V. 5(4).

Piven, F.F. (1995) "Is It Global Economics or Neo-laissez Faire?" *New Left Review,* 213.

Presidential Committee for Quality-of-Life, Office of the President, Republic of Korea (2000) *DJ Welfarism: A New Paradigm for Productive Welfare in Korea.* Seoul: Tae Sul Dang, Korea.

Rhodes, M. (1996) "Globalisation and West European Welfare States: A Critical Review of Recent Debates." *Journal of European Social Policy,* 6 (4).

Shin, D. (2000) "Financial Crisis and Social Security: The Paradox of Korea." *International Social Security Review.*

Singh, A. (1999) "Asian Capitalism" and the Financial Crisis" in J. Michie and J. Grieve Smith (eds) *Global Instability*. London: Routledge.

Standing, G. (1996) "Social Protection in Central and Eastern Europe" in G. Esping-Andersen (ed.) *Welfare States in Transition*. London: Sage.

Strange, S. (1998) "The New World of Debt." *New Left Review*, 230.

Teeple, G. (1995) *Globalization and the Decline of Social Reform*. Toronto: Garamond Press.

Truscott, P. (1997) *Russia First: Breaking with the West*. London: I.B. Tauris.

UNDP (1999) *Human Development Report 1999*. Oxford: Oxford University Press.

Warde, I. (1998) "LTCM, a Hedge Fund above Suspicion." *Le Monde Diplomatique*, English Internet edition.

4

Productive Welfare in Korea: Moving Towards a European Welfare State Type?

Stein Kuhnle

The chapter looks at President Kim Dae-Jung's vision of "Productive Welfare"—a conception of a Korean welfare state. "Productive Welfare" is put in a historical and comparative perspective, starting with a brief resumé of the origins of the modern welfare state and its differentiation into institutionally different types of welfare state regimes in Western Europe. The main elements of the vision are presented. The problems and concerns forming the basis for Productive Welfare, as well as its goals, are briefly introduced. Productive Welfare is described as an interesting attempt to expand and guarantee the fundamental democratic and social rights of all citizens. The government is given a more central, responsible and responsive, role in welfare provision. It is assumed that the policies already implemented after the economic crisis of 1997, and those spelled out for future decisions, in some sense will move the Korean welfare system closer to the so-called "social-democratic" or Scandinavian or "Nordic" type of welfare regime.

I. European Origins of Welfare States: When, How, and Why

The welfare state is a European invention (Flora 1986) developed, expanded, adjusted, refined and modified over a period of more than 100 years since a comprehensive compulsory social insurance program was initiated by the government of Chancellor Bismarck in Germany in the 1880s. The early German legislation on social insurance spurred European-wide legislative initiatives on 'the social question' or *Arbeiterfrage*. Germany was not the world's or Europe's most democratic country at the time, nor the most industrialized. The beginning of social insurance is widely interpreted as an example of the politics of legitimation, as "a pre-emptive strike" to subvert the growing socialist threat to the conservative-authoritarian regime (Flora and Heidenheimer 1981; Kuhnle 1983; Kwon 1999). By granting workers social rights, social insurance and—benefits, Bismarck hoped to maintain the regime and quell political demands for radical and socialist political organization, participation and mobilization. Later, and in other countries, social insurance legislation and welfare policies, were introduced and developed as a response to democratic political mobilization, articulation of demands for social security and equality and as a result of political conflict, competition and compromises between political parties.

In the 20th century, social insurance and welfare state development in Europe is basically a correlate to democracy and economic prosperity. Again, one should warn against any conception of a one-to-one relationship between democratic development, economic modernization and commitment of the state to provide welfare and guarantee social rights for its citizens. Among developed democratic capitalist states we observe great variations as to taxation levels and composition of taxes, and to the share of national budgets and national products spent on welfare purposes of various kinds. We observe variations as to population coverage, scope and generosity of social and welfare policies, and different ways of organizing and financing cash transfers and service provision. Over time, different types of welfare states in Europe have developed, based on different pre-industrial socio-structural prerequisites and interests, and different social and political philosophies, values and visions. The role of the state varies, as does the concept of the state.

In all societies, a number of distinct providers offer welfare: the family, civil society, the market and the state. Typologies of welfare provision (Titmuss 1958) and welfare states (Wilensky and Lebeaux 1958) can be traced to the late 1950s, mainly based upon the kind and scope of responsibility for welfare assumed by the state. Wilensky and Lebeaux' major distinction was between a residual and an institutional welfare state, the first being one where the state seeks to limit its commitments to marginal and deserving social groups or individuals, the second being universalistic with state commitments encompassing the entire population. Titmuss (1974) uses these concepts and introduces also an intermediary type that is labeled "the industrial achievement-performance model," in which welfare needs might be met on the basis of merit, work performance and productivity. The most quoted elaboration of these concepts must be Esping-Andersen's notion of "welfare state regimes" in his work on *The Three Worlds of Welfare Capitalism* (1990). Esping-Andersen's conceptualization, or labeling, is slightly more politicized. He distinguishes between "liberal" welfare states, which are more market based and in which means-tested assistance and only modest universal transfers are supposed to predominate; "conservative-corporatist" welfare states, in which the state furthers the preservation of class and status differentials achieved through employment and market participation; and lastly the "social democratic" welfare state, in which the principles of universalism and "de-commodification" of social rights are strongly promoted. Countries can more or less clearly be placed in one or the other category,[1] but most welfare states will tend to contain elements of organization and principles of entitlements and obligations from all three types of welfare states distinguished between.

I shall not elaborate much on the concept of welfare state regimes or on the many and contested dimensions of any typology, but would like to, as a background for the later exposé of the Korean case, present two tables as illustrations of variations among European welfare states on some selected and important indicators. Table 4-1 offers a comparison of government employment as a percentage of total employment, while Table 4-2 gives a picture of social expenditure as a percentage of gross domestic product in different types of European welfare states. The groups of countries roughly fall within the theoretical-political conceptual categories mentioned, with Scandinavia representing the institutional or so-called social democratic type,[2] Continental European countries representing the industrial achievement or conservative-corporatist type, and the United Kingdom representing the residual or liberal type. The Southern European countries supposedly represent a mix of all the other types, but with particular additional traits such as a stronger role for the family and elements of clientilism, especially in Italy and Greece (Ferrera 2000).

Most of government employment is for welfare purposes broadly defined, and Table 4-1 indicates significant variations of state involvement and commitment across different types of European welfare states or welfare regimes. The variations are to a large extent a reflection of much greater state and local government responsibility for personal social services and care in Scandinavian countries than elsewhere in Europe. Variations in relative total social expenditure, however, have become less conspicuous over the last decade, as seen from Table 4-2.

Whatever the shape of the welfare state, economic growth has, even if sometimes only modestly, persisted over recent decades. Given the widespread "conventional wisdom" that a big public sector and comprehensive welfare state is bad for economic performance, it is of interest to note that the Scandinavian countries had higher labor productivity, defined as GDP per person employed, in the 1990s, than the average of European Union countries and the USA (Elmeskov and Scarpetta 2000).[3] Labor productivity growth was higher in the 1990s than in the previous decade. For some time being ignored as victims of a kind of "welfare state sclerosis" by many economists and commentators, Scandinavian or Nordic countries have made a remarkable comeback at the center-stage of the theory and practice of social and economic development (Scharpf 2000; Ferrera and Rhodes 2000; Kuhnle 2000).

Table 4-1
**Public Sector Employment as Percent of Total Employment 1974-1995 in
Different Types of European Welfare States: Unweighted Averages**

Countries	1974	1985	1995
Continental Europe	14.7	18.7	18.8
Scandinavia	20.0	26.9	29.4
Southern Europe	10.5	14.2	15.5
United Kingdom	19.6	21.5	14.4

Source: Kuhnle and Alestalo, 2000

Note: Continental Europe includes Austria, Belgium, France, Germany, The Netherlands, Scandinavia, Denmark, Finland, Norway, Sweden, Southern Europe: Greece, Portugal, Spain and Italy.

Table 4-2
**Social Expenditure as Percent of Gross Domestic Product in Different Types of
European Welfare States, 1980-1995: Unweighted Averages**

Countries	1980	1990	1995
Continental Europe	28.1	29.6	30.1
Scandinavia	25.6	28.1	32.1
Southern Europe	15.0	18.0	22.2
United Kingdom	21.5	24.3	27.7

Source: Kuhnle and Alestalo, 2000

In one of several recent surveys of the global business environment, the world-wide ranking of nations according to indicators of competitiveness made by the World Economic Forum,[4] Finland, most severely hit by the recession in the Nordic area (Kuhnle 2000), was ranked number one, replacing the US which was on top of the ranking the previous two years (*Financial Times*, 9 August 2000). Moreover, the other three main countries of the far North of Europe belonged to the 'top 20': Denmark, no. six (up from seven in 1999 and eight in 1998), Sweden no. seven (nos. four and seven in previous years), and Norway no. 20 (previously 18 and 14).

Alternative visions of a 'good public economy' or a 'good society' have always been theoretically possible. A comprehensive welfare state is not a necessary prerequisite for a 'good society', but neither is it necessarily incompatible with such a concept. Economic growth is possible with or without an advanced welfare state and a strong role of government for welfare responsibility. Developments during the last 20 years bear out the empirical possibility of alternative visions of a good democratic society, based on different value assumptions and political choices. It is perhaps timely that this fact is generally taken into account—not least when considering lessons to be drawn for other regions of the world, with political histories, traditions, and cultures different from both the American and European countries which spearheaded the industrial modernization of society and development of social security institutions.

Table 4-3 indicates that people in different economically developed countries do not share identical expectations as to what the state should do in terms of welfare provision and commitments to social rights. At the end of the 20th century, European voters expect much more from the state than American voters. The possible historical reasons for these differences shall not be spelled out here, but the impact of different historical legacies for current politics of welfare should not be underestimated. Apparently a significant political cultural difference between the United States of America and Europe (as a whole) exists, which gives the state different roles in social and welfare matters on the two continents, and which also implies that political debates and the politics of welfare are framed differently. This contrast takes on a global political significance in a world where more and more countries—especially democratizing countries in East and Southeast Asia—develop a modern and affluent economy. Global political, economic and organizational integration is expanding and ideas and lessons are spread more rapidly across territorial boundaries than ever before. Some countries and regions of the world command substantially more economic, political-ideological and cultural power and leverage than others, and some welfare philosophies are thus more easily spread and transmitted than others.

The politics of welfare policy development and welfare state construction is about equalization of life chances, social justice, social security, social cohesion and stability, and about how to create the optimal conditions for sustainable economic growth and productive development, which again provides the foundations for the other goals of the welfare state. But also political preferences, ideologies, interests and values, more or less independently of level of economic development and prosperity, make up foundations of welfare policy development. Thus, what kinds of welfare state policies are possible is at all times a question of what is considered desirable by governments and voters. And what is considered desirable—what the state *ought to* do and *can* do (Rothstein 1994)—is a question of political and cultural context (norms, expectations, value structures) as much as a question of level of economic development and theories and knowledge of pre-requisites for economic growth and efficiency.

Whether welfare states—with developed programs for retirement and disability pensions, sickness insurance, occupational injury insurance, maternity insurance and paid parental leave, child and family benefits, unemployment insurance and labor activity programs, health and personal social services, kindergartens, etc.—are a blessing or not for economic growth and efficiency is a topic for much research and dispute (Atkinson 1999; Sandmo 1995; Midgley 2000). At least seen at the macro-level and over longer time-spans, the welfare state and economic growth has gone hand in hand (Kuhnle 2000a). An educated, healthy and satisfied population, with guaranteed social rights and democratic rights of expression, organization and participation, is a likely pre-requisite for productive activity, sustainable economic growth and political stability. Economic growth is possible with a number of welfare state constructions, of different scope, organization and generosity. But economic growth and efficiency have, as indicated above, not been the only goals of national welfare politics in Europe, and are not likely to be the only goals in societies with democratic participation rights and democratic governmental accountability. It has been shown, for example, that governments in countries with great social inequalities spend relatively more on police and domestic security matters than governments in countries with more egalitarian distributions of resources (Alber 2000), and the type of welfare state construction and policies can thus affect the mode of "production" of social problems and need and scope for other (expensive) kinds of public policy.

Table 4-3
Support for the Welfare State, Selected Countries, 1992 and 1996

The State should be responsible for:	Reducing income Differences		Providing work for all	
	1992	1996	1992	1996
USA	38.3	48.0	47.1	39.4
United Kingdom	65.2	67.7	56.1	69.4
Germany (West)	65.5	62.5	66.3	74.6
Germany (East)	89.2	83.7	92.6	91.9
Italy	80.0	75.4	86.2	76.6
Hungary	74.6	78.6	85.0	86.9
Norway	60.0	73.3	78.3	80.8

Source: International Social Survey Programme 1992 (Social Inequality II) and ISSP 1996 (Role of Government II). Data are documented and made available by *Zentralarchiv für empirische Sozialforschung* and Norwegian Social Science Data Services.

Note: Percentage of population who strongly agree that the State (Government) should have the responsibility for reducing income differences and for providing work to everybody.

One important lesson to be learnt from the European experience is the simple one that the welfare state does and may serve many functions. Debates on what are proper lessons to be learnt and what are proper welfare policy solutions in other, non-European, contexts can thus be framed in many ways. Social protection and welfare are topics often discussed in terms of poverty relief and meeting minimum needs for income and services. Poverty reduction was historically one aim for many governments putting social legislation on the agenda. But the establishment of European welfare states is about much more, especially in their Nordic and Continental European variants, but also in America (where the concept of "welfare state" has a largely negative connotation in contrast to what is the case in Europe). Originally, considerations of social harmony and regime support (in non-democratic contexts) were important. Over time, many programs were developed thanks to democratic mobilization and decision-making to insure against events and risks, which cause income loss, to enable reallocation of income over the life-cycle and redistribution across social groups, and to provide a sense of security for all citizens (Atkinson 1999: 5-6). Although a controlled experiment is impossible, I dare claim that the welfare state in the democratic European context appears to have been a societal "stabilizer," which has prevented serious social rebellion, strong revolutionary movements (except for right-wing extremism in the pre-WWII period when the welfare state as well as parliamentary democracy were still weak and "underdeveloped" institutions in many parts of Europe), and extensive poverty. The combination of structures of democratic governance, regulated capitalist market economies, and relatively comprehensive welfare institutions have rather successfully accommodated changing social needs. Social and political challenges have continuously filled government agendas, but dramatic "crisis-theories" since the mid-1970s have fared rather poorly empirically in the European context (Van Kersbergen, 2000).

One common element or principle of welfare (state) policies across countries and cultures is "the principle of less eligibility" (Kuhnle, Hatland, Hort 2000). Already the British Poor Law report from 1834 coined a basic principle for economic transfers that is still crucial to social security, although with different names. The 'principle of less eligibility' stated that the income of those people in receipt of benefits should always be lower than the lowest paid members of the labor force. It is still a general principle that it never shall pay for individual citizens or households to prefer social security benefits to work or gainful employment. This principle is defended partly with economic arguments (incentives), partly with arguments of justice or fairness. But there are important exceptions from this principle. The first and most important one is basic pension (and other basic benefits). The main goal for basic benefits is to prevent and relieve poverty. But if income from paid work is on a lower or similar level, these benefits may create a disincentive to work.

The second exception from the principle that benefits should be lower than wages is sickness benefits. It happens quite often in Europe, especially in Scandinavia, that employees in collective agreements, and sometimes in legislated schemes, receive full pay, or close to full pay or income compensation, during periods of sickness. How different compensation levels of health related benefits affect labor participation and duration of absence, is a major theme in political debates in many European countries.

European nation-states have developed welfare state institutions and programs of varying characteristics, but whatever the brand of the welfare state, it must in its post-World War II shapes be seen as a significant institution conducive to the consolidation of democratic development. It may be claimed that present European welfare states face challenges of an entirely new character in history: "rapid transition to post-industrialism, increasing globalization, sweeping changes in demography and social relations, trends towards supranational integration and a new, "post-cold war politics" (Ferrera and Rhodes 2000: 1). But European welfare states facing problems of greatly varying severity have more or less successfully coped with what seemed crucial new challenges in the 1990s (Kuhnle 2000; Ferrera and Rhodes 2000). Recent European experiences give support for the hypothesis that developed democratic welfare states are quite good at making adjustments of public policies in such a way that the legitimacy of the system can be preserved at the same time as new vitality and transformations in the economy can be brought about. Here may be a lesson for other regions of the world, for rapidly modernizing economies and newly democratizing countries.

II. The South Korean Welfare System Development and Productive Welfare

In Western social science and politics, welfare state schemes establishing the social rights of citizenship are usually perceived as a fourth stage in the process of state and nation building (Marshall 1950; Rokkan 1970; Titmuss 1974; Flora 1986). In the mid-1990s, during the years before the currency and stock market crisis in 1997, the low-spending "welfare states" of East and Southeast Asia not only attracted increasing attention among Western scholars and politicians, but were actually pointed out as potential welfare models for the West. Governments of capitalist East and Southeast Asia presented themselves as supportive of a small public sector, the market and family-based social provisions, and, at least in the rhetoric (e.g. Malaysia, Singapore), distanced themselves from the welfare institutions and value orientations of Western countries. In contrast to European countries, which spent an average of 25 percentage of the gross domestic product for social purposes in the mid-1990s, Japan's social spending accounted for a little more than 15 percent, while Korea and Taiwan reached 10 percent and other countries in the region recorded even markedly lower figures (Hort and Kuhnle 2000).

Several authors have postulated that East and Southeast Asian countries in many cases are following, or seem likely to follow, the "route to modernity" taken by their developed predecessors in Europe (Therborn 1993; Hort and Kuhnle 2000). Or, as it is formulated in a similar assessment: "as they grew richer, the more advanced Asian economies began exhibiting a public attention to social welfare that is more in keeping with some European conditions than with liberal market developments" (Godement 2000). When the 'miracle' took off in East and Southeast Asia two or three decades ago, all of these countries were low-tax and low-wage entities with an absence of democratic structures and practices and labor rights and entitlements. Now, with the partial exception of Indonesia and the Philippines, different types of social security schemes have been developed, though not always implemented, particularly from the mid-1980s onwards. During the first years after World War II growth policies in some countries in the region deliberately included a social dumping component, as no welfare or social insurance laws other than mere paper laws were enacted. Nevertheless, there was at least some legislative activity in most countries. The picture is rather different for most countries during the miracle period. Existing schemes were extended rather than entrenched, and there has been no competitive "race to the bottom."

The introduction of social welfare programs in Korea from the early 1960s has been interpreted as part of a political strategy aimed at enhancing the legitimacy of the political regime (Kwon 1999), partly, at least, because of a perceived potential threat from the student movement by Park Chung Hee who seized power through a military coup in 1961. A Civil Servants Pension Act had been enacted in January 1960, and was reformed in 1962 (extended coverage, and sickness benefits introduced). The first (limited, but compulsory) Industrial Accident Insurance was introduced in 1963, the same year as a (limited, voluntary) National Health Insurance Act was adopted. A National Welfare Pension Act was passed in 1973, but implementation postponed, and a general National Pension Program was not adopted until 1988 (Kwon 1999). The early development of social policy in Korea coincided with economic development, but economic growth was not a sufficient condition for reform activity (Kwon 1999), neither was the increased industrialization (Tang 2000; Park 1990). As in Europe historically and now, political factors played and play an important role in accounting for social policy development.

Korea offers an example of rapid and strong reform activity during the miracle decade from the mid-1980s, although the problems related to the old mutual aid networks and the poverty issue did in no sense completely disappear as growth took off (Kwon 1998; Ramesh 1995; Son 1999; Park and Kim 1998). In the late 1980s, Korea became a front-runner among the "tiger economies" in terms of social security reform. Big and active steps were taken in connection with a transition to democracy. The National Pension Program in 1988 and the extension of the National Health Insurance Program during the same year came under the banner of "social justice" after the democratic breakthrough in 1987. During the course of rapid economic expansion substantial changes in benefit levels, duration and qualifying conditions also occurred (Son 1998). Wage dumping more or less disappeared as total labor costs rose to European levels in the early 1990s. Before the crisis of 1997, job security existed in the big conglomorates (*chaebols*) and unemployment was virtually non-existent. Since the outbreak of the crisis, lay-offs have become more common and the unemployment rate trebled. An Employment Insurance Scheme was introduced in 1993 (implemented 1995), and the government has gradually extended the scheme to cover workers in smaller and smaller firms. This program has been important in assisting unemployed people to weather the Asian economic crisis (Tang 2000). Combined with the election of Kim Dae-Jung as president, the 1997-crisis induced a number of reforms, "coupled with moves towards a more Western welfare system: not only a stronger safety net and more generous unemployment benefits, but a restructured National Health System, more liberal pension entitlements and an expanded Labor Standard Law" (Gough, 2000). Korea is gradually building the foundations of a modern welfare state, and the (temporal?) collapse of the miracle does not seem to have buried these ambitions. "Korea differs from the other three Asian tigers in espousing the goal of a welfare state" (Tang 2000: 17). But according to one leading scholar in Korean welfare development, Kwong-leung Tang, "Korea is not a welfare state. [Although] It does have a full array of social welfare services. Education, health, and housing have developed extensively along with social security. The idea of social solidarity is fostered; but social entitlement as of right is not deeply rooted" (Tang 2000: 109). On the other hand, welfare ambitions on the part of the present government are vivid. In fact, the President's notion of "Productive Welfare," elaborated in his Liberation Day speech in August 1999, presents a rather unique political document of governmental welfare philosophy and vision.[5]

President Kim Dae-Jung's vision of a system of productive welfare is made against a background of a serious financial crisis that started at the end of 1997 and brought the impressive economic growth record to a sudden and unexpected halt. The crisis forced the government to agree to a rescue package with the IMF. Unemployment grew rapidly and peaked at more than eight percent in early 1999, and more than one million Koreans were thrown into poverty (OECD Observer, October 2000). The economic crisis hit vulnerable groups harder, increased the proportion of temporary workers, and reversed the trend of steady improvement of income distribution, according to one recent analysis of the impact of the crisis (Kwon 2001). As a social policy response, the government has introduced reforms in the areas of labor market policies and social safety nets which helped the economy to renewed growth, and the unemployment rate to fall.

Does the President's welfare vision point towards a development of a welfare state, and how does it relate to philosophies of existing welfare states or regimes? How do the goals of "Productive Welfare" relate to democratic ideals, and how to judge the effectiveness of specific policies and incentives prescribed? Let me briefly look at these questions.

Following Esping-Andersen (1990) and Gough (2000) the concept of welfare regimes refers to the pattern of state social policies and programs; to the division of responsibilities between state, the market, civil society and voluntary organizations and the household; to the welfare outcomes of these institutions—i.e. to what extent a person's standard of living is dependent upon the labor market and family membership; and to the stratification outcomes of these institutions, i.e. to what extent and in what way the welfare system affects inequalities, interests and power in society. Combining characteristics on these dimensions, the literature distinguishes, as mentioned earlier, four welfare regimes in the Western OECD world: the liberal Anglo-Saxon, the conservative Continental European, the social democratic-Scandinavian, and the more family-based Southern European regime. Ian Gough (2000) questions whether this welfare regime approach can be applied to East Asia, and concludes that it can, if reformulated. By that he argues that the welfare regime approach is basically concerned with the broader "welfare mix": the interactions of public sector, private sector and households in producing livelihoods and distributing welfare, and that it is also "a political economy" approach which embeds welfare institutions in the "deep structures" of social reproduction (Gough 2000: 3-4). I cannot here discuss and spell out all implications of this conceptual mapping of welfare regimes. In a very summary way, one might say that the East Asian type of welfare regime, including Korea, has until now been both more market-based and family-based, than European welfare regimes in general, which are more state-based. Education has been the exception to this pattern in East Asia, with the state being the dominant provider of services and playing a crucial role. Does the notion of "Productive Welfare" imply any significant change in the Korean welfare regime orientation? Is Korea moving towards a liberal, conservative, social democratic type of regime—or towards a new type of "East Asian regime"? Is the balance between welfare providing institutions set to change? What are the main features of the program for "Productive Welfare"?

The vision of Productive Welfare spells out why and how a balanced and harmonious interaction of democratic, market, social and cultural forces can provide a model for a desired future Korean welfare society. It is argued that only the interplay of institutions and forces can overcome the economic crisis and provide a sustainable future welfare society. A number of problems and concerns form the background for the program, which is presented both as an ideology and a policy.

Problems and concerns:

- deteriorating social integration
- poverty in the outskirts of urban areas
- inequality in the distribution of income and wealth
- regional imbalance in the distribution of resources
- weak rights and interests of the socially underprivileged
- old age pension coverage for people who have not paid contributions
- high rate of unemployment
- instability of employment
- protection of needs of people (young, old, disabled) outside the labor market
- present system hinders self-support as a means to escape poverty
- monopolistic tendencies in business-government collusion
- globalization and high labor costs

Among the *goals* of Productive Welfare can be listed:

- develop a welfare system that nurtures both growth and equitable income distribution
- reach consensus between the government, the market and civic society
- revive (lost) community spirit through civic organizations
- develop a local-community based system of welfare
- fair, equitable distribution of wealth
- active policy of welfare through work; generate social capital, i.e. "labor power"
- increased socio-economic participation
- more comprehensive social security system that covers the entire population
- increase the percentage of total government spending on social welfare
- improve organization of the welfare system
- raise taxes for high-income earners
- constitutional recognition of social welfare as a basic human right; of the right to life; the right to minimum living standards; the right to minimum education; the right to healthcare; the right to housing; the right to work
- develop social participation programs
- increase opportunities for (labor force) participation of women
- strengthen the protection of children's living standards
- strengthen active labor market policy
- strengthen the role of the private sector and of civic groups/voluntary associations
- develop and maintain new health care services
- enhance cultural participation of alienated regions and people
- reduce socio-economic disparities among nations in the East Asia region
- advance global harmony

Both the problem definitions and concerns, and the list of goals to be pursued as well as many of the institutional means proposed in the vision of Productive Welfare all imply a more active role for the government or state than earlier in the Korean welfare system. The vision also implies a more active interplay with both business and civic organizations, and greater participation from below in the formulation of problems and provision of welfare. But the program is not concrete as to how to develop this active interplay. As to state responsibility, reforms introduced already may offer some indication of the direction of change. State responsibility has been enhanced considerably after the financial crisis of 1997, and plans for further improvement in coverage and benefits of social insurance schemes are formulated. A Planning Board is established to integrate the four major insurance schemes. The Minimum Living Standards Security Act was furthermore legislated in 1999 guaranteeing all households, whose incomes do not meet the minimum cost of living, welfare benefits from the government to equal the difference, and a Lifelong Education Act introduced in 1999. Employment Security Centers are set up, and active labor market programs introduced. The government will develop and maintain new healthcare services and long-term care. In general more institutional co-operation between the private and public sector is to be developed, and the welfare system shall include democratic decision-making procedures in order to build public confidence and consensus. Productive Welfare is considered a means to enhance the development of democracy, by actively facilitating socio-economic democratization and meeting people's demand for welfare. Productive Welfare promotes more local self-government, and aims to promote harmonious development through sustained economic growth and broad-based democracy. Welfare policies are considered an investment for improved productivity, rather than as a simple transfer of income through administrative procedures.

In an analysis of Korean welfare state development up until the mid-1990s, it was concluded that the Korean welfare system does not fit any of the types of welfare regimes known from the typology of Western, particularly European, welfare states (Kwon 1999). But the conservative, Continental European type was considered to come closest, partly because emphasis is on maintaining rather than transforming the prevailing order, and because the initiative come from those in power rather than from those who were not.

Since the economic crisis of 1997-98, Korea has witnessed a rapid expansion of the welfare state following a series of reforms (Kwon 2001). The crisis produced new problems of poverty, unemployment, and insecurity conducive to the rise of more solidaristic attitudes and popular support for a stronger role of the state in welfare matters. Both of these attitudinal changes contributed to the historic victory of the opposition party in the 1997 Presidential election (Kwon 2001). The reforms implemented, and reforms implied in the Productive Welfare vision, are bound to increase relative scope of state expenditure for welfare from the present relatively low level among OECD countries.

The mixture of problem interpretations, policy ideas, initiatives and proposals presented in the Productive Welfare document may—everything taken into account—well represent a new model or type of welfare regime in its own right, building on historical characteristics of Korean culture and social institutions, and tailored to the current economic, political and social circumstances in Korea. On the other hand, ideas, institutions and programs developed historically and in recent years in other parts of the world, perhaps in Western Europe in particular, are also reflected in Productive Welfare. If anything, a reading of the vision on Productive Welfare gives rise to the impression that the type of welfare system conceived for Korea is one which holds the potential of pushing Korea more in the direction of a so-called social democratic, Scandinavian type of welfare regime, and in its modern, topical disguise. Productive Welfare emphasizes a stronger state commitment to welfare, social inclusion, that all citizens should be covered by government welfare schemes; social rights; equalization of life chances; a more equal and fair distribution of income and wealth; and social integration, democratic participation, self-government and democratic accountability. Emphasis on public investment in education, health and institutions to promote labor market participation combined with income and social safety nets for low income families and comprehensive social insurance schemes is conducive to less welfare dependency on family membership. Emphasis on developing active labor market programs and strong incentives for finding gainful employment could be interpreted as a step towards "re-commodification" rather than "de-commodification" in the conceptual world of Esping-Andersen (1990), but this is also in accordance with current trends of thinking and practice of Scandinavian social democratic parties and governments (as well as the thinking and practice of other parties which may have influenced the social democratic thinking). The combination of trends towards "de-familialization" (Esping-Andersen 1999) and "re-commodification" in welfare policy development can thus be said to be in accordance with the Nordic "social democratic" type of welfare regime, and more so with this type than with any of the other types of welfare states. Likewise, the policies and institutions proposed in favor of income equalization, consensus-building and power-sharing underpin the picture of an emerging active welfare state akin to the type developed in Northern Europe. That this type of welfare state can be effective, both in terms of social security, low levels of poverty, standards of quality of life, and economic growth and productivity has been proven in the North European context.

Understandably, not all goals are operationalized, but many concrete proposals for expanding the welfare system are put on the agenda, and there is little doubt about the intended overall direction of change. But the program or vision as it now stands does not address the problems of timing and sequence of introduction of new reforms. The timing and sequence may be important in itself, but any reforms enacted may also affect the character of subsequent reform activity.

The evolving Korean welfare system is not likely to closely fit any of the theoretical-empirical types of welfare regimes in the research literature. Although it is likely to include characteristics rooted in norms and values in Korean and East Asian philosophy and history of social and family institutions, the cursory overview of elements in the Productive Welfare model links it—in my view—much closer to the so-called social democratic type of welfare regime than any of the other types. Three formulations succinctly give the direction: "Neither simple redistribution nor laissez-faire policies can support sustainable economic development in the 21st century," "Social equality cannot be achieved by the competitive market alone," and "Equitable redistribution will contribute to strengthening social integration."

III. Conclusion

South Korea has been characterized as a developmental-universalist productivist welfare state where social policy is subordinated to economic policy, social rights are limited, and where the state is understood to underpin market and families with some universal programs (Holliday 2000). But the vision and partly implemented program of Productive Welfare can also be said to represent a new, bold ideological and policy formulated attempt to consolidate and foster the further development of a democratic welfare state within the framework of a recently democratized country and rapidly developing economy. The vision of Productive Welfare shares many characteristics of the various kinds of welfare regimes in the Western OECD area. It is premature to state which type Korea will resemble the most in its future development, but tentatively it looks as if the Korean welfare system may in due time have more in common with the "Nordic" or Scandinavian, "social-democratic" welfare regime than any of the other European and Western types. In Scandinavia, the government is given a core role in all matters related to the welfare of citizens, and in such a way that citizens through investment in education, active labor market programs and health can be productive and through taxes contribute to the generation of incomes and wealth which can be redistributed to equalize the life chances of all citizens in society. State expenditures for health, pensions, and welfare purposes are still relatively low in Korea, but set to increase gradually as entitlements and rights established in recent social reforms take effect. Ideas of universalism, equality, and employment seem strong at both the societal and political level, as in Scandinavia more than elsewhere in Europe. The ideology and policy for Productive Welfare appear to indicate a significant change in the thinking about welfare state development in Korea, and it may well form the basis of inspiration for government welfare policy development in the wider East and Southeast Asian region—and beyond.

Notes

1. See a state-of-the-art report on typologies of welfare states in the article by Arts and Gelissen (2002).
2. "Social-democratic" is the concept used by Esping-Andersen (1990) and many other authors. I say *so-called* social democratic type because the concept may lead readers to think that this is a type of welfare state that only social democratic parties and governments have promoted, and this is definitely not the case, neither in Scandinavia nor elsewhere. All major parties have favoured and contributed to a strengthening of this type of welfare state regime historically and in the present time in Scandinavia, both in and outside of government positions. A high degree of cross-party consensus exists on the desirability of comprehensive welfare states, although there will always be different opinions and priorities as to how, when and what to reform and adjust in the welfare state. The term "social-democratic" may be defended on the grounds that the social-democratic movement over time has been the strongest political force in the development of the modern state and welfare state, but preferably a politically and analytically more neutral label should be sought.
3. It is interesting to note that the IMF (*Financial Times*, 9-10 September 2000) does not credit the recent years' renewed Swedish economic upswing, creativity and entrepreneurship, to the persistent Swedish government emphasis on core welfare state policies such as a broad tax basis, high tax revenues, security in the labor market, the world's most generous paid parental leave schemes, increased child allowances, and extra resources for universal pre-schools and public care. Sweden, as other Scandinavian countries, illustrates that a combination of high tax revenues, labor market security, declining unemployment, generous universal welfare services, and economic growth is possible.
4. The list was compiled in co-operation with the Center for International Development at Harvard University, available at *http://www.cid.harvard.edu/cidglobal/compet.htm*.
5. The vision is published in an extended and elaborate form in a book published by the Office of the President (2000), which has also formed the basis for the presentation of the program or vision in this chapter.

References

Alber, J. (2000) "Hat sich der Wohlfahrtsstaat als soziale Ordnung bewährt?" Paper for the Congress of the German Sociological Association, Cologne, 27 September 2000.

Arts, W. and Gelissen, J. (2002) "Three Worlds of Welfare Capitalism or More? A State-of-the-Art Report." *Journal of European Social Policy*, 12 (2).

Atkinson, A.B. (1999) *The Economic Consequences of Rolling Back the Welfare State*. Cambridge, Mass./London: The MIT Press.

Elmeskov, J. and Scarpetta, S. (2000) "New Sources of Economic Growth in Europe?" Paper presented at 28th Economics Conference of Österreichische Nationalbank, Vienna 15-16 June 2000.

Esping-Andersen, G. (1990) *The Three Worlds of Welfare Capitalism*. Cambridge: Polity Press.

Esping-Andersen, G. (1999) *The Social Foundations of Post-Industrial Economies*. Oxford: Oxford University Press.

Ferrera, M. (2000) "Reconstructing the Welfare State in Southern Europe" in S. Kuhnle, (ed.) *Survival of the European Welfare State*. London/New York: Routledge.

Ferrera, M. and Rhodes, M. (eds) (2000) *Recasting European Welfare States*. London: Frank Cass Publishers.

Flora, P. and Heidenheimer, A. J. (1981) "The Historical Core and Changing Boundaries of the Welfare State" in P. Flora and A. J. Heidenheimer (eds) *The Development of Welfare States in Europe and America*. New Brunswick/London: Transaction Publishers.

Flora, P. (ed.) (1986) *Growth to Limits. The Western European Welfare States Since World War II*, Vol I. Berlin: Walter de Gruyter.

Godement, F. (2000) "Models and Politics for Asian Social Policies." Paper, ASEM Project, May 22, 2000.

Gough, I. (2000) "Welfare Regimes in East Asia and Europe." Paper presented ASEM Conference, Paris 27 June 2000.

Holliday, I. (2000) "Productivist Welfare Capitalism: Social Policy in East Asia." *Political Studies*, 48.

Hort, S.E.O. and Kuhnle, S. (2000) "The Coming of East and South-east Asian Welfare States." *Journal of European Social Policy*, 10 (2).

Kuhnle, S. (1983) *Velferdsstatens utvikling. Norge i komparativt perspektiv* (The development of the welfare state. Norway in a comparative perspective). Oslo/Bergen: Universitetsforlaget.

Kuhnle, S. (ed.) (2000) *Survival of the European Welfare State*. London/New York: Routledge.

Kuhnle, S. (2000a) "European lessons of the 1990s" in S. Kuhnle (ed.) *Survival of the European Welfare State*. London/New York: Routledge.

Kuhnle, S. and Alestalo, M. (2000) "Introduction: Growth, Adjustments and Survival of European Welfare States" in S. Kuhnle (ed.) *Survival of the European Welfare State*. London/New York: Routledge.

Kuhnle, S., Hatland, A. and Hort, S. (2000) "Work-Friendly Welfare State: Lessons from Europe." Paper presented at International Conference of ASEM/World Bank/KSSA on "Flexibility vs. Security? Social Policy and the Labour Market in Europe and East Asia." Seoul, November 30- December 1.

Kwon, Huck-ju (1999) *The Welfare State in Korea. The Politics of Legitimation*. Houndmills, Basingstoke/ London: Macmillan Press.

Kwon, Huck-ju (2001) "The Economic Crisis and the Politics of Welfare Reform in Korea." Paper presented at the International Workshop on Asian Welfare Policy Responses to the Crash of 1997, University of Bergen, 16- 18 August.

Kwon, S. (2001) "Economic Crisis and Social Policy Reform in Korea." *International Journal of Social Welfare,* 10 (2).

Marshall, T. H. (1950) *Citizenship and Social Class*. Cambridge: Cambridge University Press.

Midgley, J. (2000) "Social Security and the Economy: Challenges and Response to Economic Uncertainty." Proceedings, 2nd Regional Conference on Social Security, Hong Kong, 24-26 January.

OECD Observer (October 2000) "Labour Market Reform and Social Safety Net Policies in Korea," Policy Brief. Paris: OECD.

Office of the President (2000) *DJ Welfarism. A New Paradigm for Productive Welfare in Korea*. Seoul: Tae Sul Dang.

Park, Byung-Hyun (1990) "The Development of Social Welfare Institution in East Asia: Case Studies of Japan, Korea and the People's Republic of China." Ph.D. dissertation, University of Pennsylvania.

Park, Chanyong and Kim, Meesok. (1998) *Current Poverty Issues and Counterpolicies in Korea*. Seoul: Korea Institute for Health and Social Affairs and UNDP.

Ramesh, M. (1995) "Politics of Illiberal Capitalism: The State, Industrialization, and Social Security in South Korea" in J. Dixon and R. Scheurell (eds) *Social Security Programmes—a Cross-cultural Comparative Perspective*. Westport, CT: Greenwood.

Rokkan, S. (1970) *Citizens, Elections, Parties*. Oslo: Universitetsforlaget.

Rothstein, B. (1994) *Vad bör staten göra?* Stockholm: SNS-förlag.

Sandmo, A. (1995) "Social Security and Economic Growth" in *European Institute of Social Security Yearbook 1994*. Leuven: Acco.

Scharpf, F. W. (2000) "The Viability of Advanced Welfare States in the International Economy. Vulnerabilities and Options." *European Review*, 8 (3).

Son, A. (1998) "The Construction of the Medical Insurance System in the Republic of Korea, 1963-1989." *Scandinavian Journal of Social Welfare* , 7.

Son, A. (1999) "Health Insurance for Every Citizen—the Development of the National Health Insurance System of the Republic of Korea, 1963-1989, the Republic of Taiwan, 1950-1995." Ph.D.dissertation, Uppsala University.

Tang, Kwong-leung (2000) *Social Welfare Development in East Asia*. Houndmills, Basingstoke/New York: Palgrave.

Therborn, G. (1993) "Routes to and through Modernity" in R. Torstendahl (ed.) *State Theory and State History*. London: Sage.

Titmuss, R. M. (1958) *Essays on the Welfare State*. London: Allen and Unwin.

Titmuss, R. M. (1974) *Social Policy.* London: Allen and Unwin.

Van Kersbergen, K. (2000) "The Declining Resistance of Welfare States to Change?" in S. Kuhnle (ed.) *Survival of the European Welfare State*. London/New York: Routledge.

Wilensky, H. and Lebeaux, C. (1958) *Industrial Society and Social Welfare*. New York: Russell Sage.

5

Generative Balanced Model of Welfare

Kyungbae Chung

I. In Search of a New Welfare Model

In the existing welfare states, unemployment and income disparity are severe problems and excessive welfare expenditure has threatened government finance, driving it towards a budget deficit crisis. Their over-generous welfare benefits have been criticized for diminishing welfare recipients' work incentive. To cope with these problems comprehensively, efforts need to be made to find a new welfare model. In the establishment of a new welfare state model, several essential elements are to be considered: unemployment, income inequality, financial crisis, stagnation and deteriorating work incentives.

The social democratic welfare model allows active governmental intervention in order to improve equality, thereby increasing the size of government. As a result, the expanded governmental function creates a burdensome bureaucracy and hampers effectiveness. Serious financial imbalances, primarily caused by over-generous benefit schemes that do not take into account the balance between contributions and benefits, creates a climate inimical to sustainable development, and the subsequent decline of work incentive and the withering investment motivation appear as clear signals of an unsuccessful model. Meanwhile, the neo-liberalist model seeks minimized governmental intervention and places priority on efficiency based on the free-market system. However, there are serious social problems resulting from this scheme, including massive unemployment, an aggravated poverty ratio and the increasing social isolation. These two welfare models play major roles in today's economies with starkly contrasting policy goals. However, they fail in addressing effectively several concerns, including continuing unemployment and the poverty gap.

Welfare models of advanced western countries have evolved over long periods; however, many problems such as excessive welfare dependency and bloated non-productive welfare expenditure have resulted. States working to downsize welfare expenditure have met resistance from welfare recipients and political elements. Korea has achieved a very compressed economic growth in contrast to other advanced countries. As a result, rapid income increases and explosive welfare demands may create a more severe welfare expansion crisis than that of advanced western countries. Therefore, to prevent problems experienced in the western welfare system, design of a new welfare system should set its priority on human development and active labor market operation. Productive Welfare's fundamental purpose lies in enhancing national competitiveness and further extending welfare capacity into cultural and environmental sectors to achieve improved quality of life.

Productive Welfare can be defined as an active welfare policy aimed at social productivity improvement through economic value creation, based on the fundamental welfare drive towards equality. That is, Productive Welfare begins on the firm premise that every single citizen in the society should be guaranteed and secured basic livelihood as one of their basic rights. With this premise, Productive Welfare acknowledges and stresses human development and self-actualization by means of education and work opportunity. Combining these elements, it aims at balanced development of equality and efficiency.

Table 5-1
Comparison of Welfare States

	Social Democracy	Neo Liberalism	A New Model
Govt. Size	• Big govt.	• Small govt.	• Functionally efficient government
State Intervention	• Intervention increase	• Citizen autonomy	• Generative[1] motivation
Market Economy	• Mixed economy	• Free market	• Mixed Economy
Labor Market	• Active labor policy	• Laissez-faire	• Active labor policy
Policy Target	• Income redistribution	• Supply economy	• Generative and balancing
Social Security (Quality of Life)	• Social Security System (active)	• Social Safety Net (passive)	• Social Safety Net (linking, generative)
Unemployment	• unsolved	• unsolved	• Self actualization
Income Disparity	• unsolved	• deepened	• Poverty escape
Financial Crisis	• deepened	• n.a.	• balancing resources [2]

1. Generative ➡ generation of income and quality of life
2. Balancing ➡ Resources Supply = Resources Demand

While the existing social welfare system has been selective and temporary with a comparatively stronger function as a relief system, Productive Welfare aims at universal welfare based on civil rights and both productive and contribution-oriented policies that provide self-support through human development and job creation. Furthermore, considering welfare expenditure as a productive investment, Productive Welfare supports continued human development through job mediation and continuing education, and promotes job creation through systematic self-support in conjunction with training and workfare programs.

In this study, Productive Welfare policy is going to be discussed from the point of view of its generative and balanced measures and will focus on the development of policies to achieve these aims. To this end, each chapter will cover important aspects of Productive Welfare policy. Section II will look at balanced resource distribution; Section III will address value generation; Section IV will review generative balanced policy; and Section V covers Productive Welfare programs and evaluation of the scheme.

II. A Balance-Oriented Welfare Economy

Welfare economy balance occurs when there is equilibrium between resource supply and resource demand. Resources can be divided into two categories: material and non-material. The latter is composed of several components comprising the quality of life, knowledge, information, culture, patents, intellectual property rights, technologies and sports talent, to name a few.

Balance : | resource supply = resource demand |

Balanced order accepts mankind's given resources as finite. Within this constraint, balanced order assesses resource demand and promotes optimal and efficient distribution of available resources. Resource supply is identified as the total amount of aggregated goods and services, which is equal to the sum of aggregated national income and national wealth.

Balanced Distribution of Resources

Under balanced distribution (RS=RD), the economic structure should create balanced growth, and the economy can be stabilized without any inflationary gap or deflationary gap. Hence, efficient resource distribution can be executed and overall economic and societal quality can be improved.

For balanced distribution, the annual social welfare expenditure should be within annually utilizable resources (budget). The four major social insurance schemes including pension, medical insurance, employment insurance and work injury insurance should maintain financial balance. Excessive borrowings from the next generation to satisfy the needs of the current generation may disrupt resource distribution between generations, resulting in economic stagnation and social decline.

Unbalanced allocation causes supply-demand imbalance followed by an inflationary gap or deflationary gap. Economic disruption caused by imbalances between Resources Supply and Resources Demand distorts resource distribution and alters real price value. The major economic players face myriad external influences in their decision-making. If ineffective distribution becomes prevalent in the society as a whole, and altered terms of trade result, social disorder may occur.

Wage and interest rate policies are examples of balancing mechanisms related to Resources Supply. The former purports to balance labor supply and demand, and the latter to balance capital supply and demand. Low interest rates increase capital demand and investment opportunity, which stimulates production activity. In contrast, high interest rates reduce capital demand and depress investment, which results in declines in production activity. In relation to resource demand, consumption can change in accordance with price, consumption level, and interest rates. Government expenditure is determined by external factors and is composed of ordinary expenditure, treasury loan and investment, and social welfare expenditure.

Under the stagnation period, a consumption stimulation policy can be adopted to boost aggregate demand, or a policy to lower interest rates can be applied to raise investment and consumption, or a financial policy can be adopted to increase government expenditure. All these policies can contribute to increased resources demand and stimulating production activity. Conversely, in an overheated phase, a resources demand restraint policy can be adopted, through which aggregate demand can be carefully regulated by monetary and fiscal policies.

One of the most difficult problems for advanced welfare states is that an overloaded financial burden due to social welfare allowances may put national finances in risky straits. Since The New Model aims at balancing resource supply and demand, finding balance of all segments is desirable only within the range of utilizable resources.

Value System for Balanced Order

The balanced order determines an optimal distribution arrangement where resource demand falls within resource availability. It assumes that excessive consumption beyond the limitations of available resources and exhaustive utilization of resources reserved for the next generation is a destructive practice. Rational order does not operate on the basis of resource utilization without constraint, deviating from optimal levels. Therefore, adhering to the concept of "balanced order" requiring supply and demand balance is a crucial requirement for rational order.

The value system of balanced order relies on respect for boundaries where individual interests exist within family and community interests. Likewise family interest should not override group interest and there can be no group interest beyond national interest. When any group brings a negative impact on national interest, sanctions should be imposed based on national law. Interests of a single state can be attained by respecting the interests of other nations; hence, violation of other nations' interests is likely to cause conflict. Therefore, there will be a global acknowledgement that abiding by international convention for coexistence brings mutual benefits.[1]

Even with the coexistence of the global community, endless human need will continuously demand inordinate exploitation of natural resources and thus adversely affect ecosystems, for it is part of human nature to pursue what is beyond our need. Possessed by the never satiable desire, we eat and drink to death, and take to excess. But what gives one the time and capability to work are the lives of others in nature. Implicit here is the notion that playing havoc with nature is tantamount to destroying the source of our being. Also, one's neighbor is as much a part of nature as oneself is, for all humanity is interconnected: my root is my neighbor's and vice versa. It is one and the same roots from which all humanity emerged, and we all live in a community of common-rooted individuals. This is what our ancestors, who held the Taoist Weltanschauung, a cosmology of common-rootedness, called "the oneness of heaven-earth-man."[2] Balanced order can be achieved only when the needs of humanity and nature are in harmony. In other words, mankind's continued viability relies on individual or group interests being restrained by community interest and national interest is sought after within the coexisting boundary with other nations. Eventually coexisting with nature in harmony and respecting balanced order will rescue mankind.

Balanced States and Unbalanced States

A *Balanced State* is defined as a state equipped with an institutional arrangement for maintaining balanced order. When the balanced order is disrupted, or is non-existent, it is called an Unbalanced State. Many of today's problems can be traceable to unbalanced order. The ethical order of mankind -and justification of the state—are provided for within a balanced order, and an unbalanced state that threatens such elements cannot be supported. Breach of environmental convention, exclusion of other nations' interests, violent protests made by extremist groups, and other challenges to balanced order made by injuring the foundation of peace do not have ethical justification. Consequently, isolation will follow, ultimately leading to further difficulties by the groups or countries engaged in these activities.

The institutional arrangements of balanced order include several components: (i) a budget system to maintain financial balance, (ii) social security system for efficient resource distribution, (iii) adherence to international conventions for peace and prosperity, (iv) adherence to environmental conventions for protection of ecosystems and natural resources, (v) property legislation for balance of intergenerational resource distribution.

Meanwhile, under unbalanced state conditions, several negative results can be observed such as a widening gap in income between the rich and the poor, increased unemployment, economic depression, and price instability. Also the incomplete social security arrangement for income redistribution will make people socially vulnerable, increase national debt, and cause resource depletion and ecosystem destruction.

Table 5-2
Comparison between Balanced and Unbalanced States

Institutional Arrangement	Balanced State	Unbalanced State
1. Resource distribution (resource conservation law)	• Efficient Equality	• Deepening inequality (gap between the rich and the poor, unemployment)
2. Financial balance (budget law)	• Financial Stability	• Financial risk (economic depression, inflation)
3. Distributional equity (property law)	• Prevention of social risk	• Neglecting social risk
4. Intergenerational balance (property law)	• Intergenerational balanced distribution	• Debt increase in next generation
5. Interstate balance (international convention)	• Coexistence and co-prosperity among states	• International conflict
6. Ecosystematic balance (environmental treaty)	• Ecosystem protection	• Ecosystem Destruction/ Resource Depletion

*Balance: resource supply = resource demand

III. Generating Quality of Life

The term "generative" applies to economic development and quality of life improvement. Economic development contains both economic growth and qualitative improvement of the economy. Quality of life, the element providing satisfaction at the level of consciousness, covers security, self-respect, self-actualization (Giddens 1994), environmental elements and administrative service, etc. The latter is related to subjective consciousness, whereas the former is a material element. Considering this, material elements cannot replace human security, self-respect, and self-actualization; thus any-one lacking quality-of-life elements cannot find well-rounded well-being.

Our value is related to providing satisfaction through material goods, or satisfaction through quality of life. Total supply of value means total supply of both material value, including goods and services, and quality of life provided by self-satisfaction. Meanwhile, material value can bring satisfaction only when it contributes to mankind's spiritual satisfaction. Hence, the former is a necessary element for achieving the latter. In this sense, proper provision for quality of life may become as significant as economic and material supply.

In the welfare state, achievement of equality is set as its supreme goal (Titmuss 1958; Giddens 1998). However, equality as a result of a social wel-fare system makes mankind a passive recipient, which in turn hampers satis-faction from self-actualization using given capabilities and potentialities. Therefore, welfare recipients cannot effectively escape poverty, and their overall work incentive deteriorates. Setting equality as one of the goals of the social system is important, as is reducing inequality in the area of self-choice; however both are inferior compared to the satisfaction gained from self-actu-alization. Since value generation is aimed at material income creation and spiritual quality of life creation concurrently, new assessment in the welfare state will be required.

Generative Process

Under the social welfare system, recipients are provided with welfare ben-efits from the state, and these often serve to decrease people's work incentive, creating passivity. Many advanced welfare states in the West have been strug-gling with low productivity, stagnation, a widening poverty gap and severe unemployment issues that are attributable to recipients' "passive psychol-ogy."[3] Mankind has survived because of the presence of competition and subsequent honing of ability. Secured income may deprive people of com-petitiveness and vitality, and the potential risk for the depression of the entire social structure, as has occurred in many socialist countries, may result.

A new paradigm for the welfare system requires a "generative motives system." The "generative" force is defined as generative innovation which aims at bringing new productivity increases and quality of life improvements by means of new technology, new markets, new resources, new information and new services, etc. Generative innovation[4] can be classified into two ar-eas: the material and the quality of life innovations. Quality of life innova-tion comes through better information and knowledge, education and physical exercise, sightseeing and entertainment, and system innovation through new management skills and structural efficiency. New welfare states need to intro-duce a "generative motivation system" to escape from growth depression.

A "generative motivation system" should streamline the associated legal system for investment motivation, technology innovation, capacity building, social service, and quality of life improvement. Along with this work, it should focus on developing a comprehensive institutional arrangement to systematically link financial policy, monetary policy and administrative service. Stimulated profit-making motivation increases investment and input. Consequently, this will increase employment and capital goods consumption, which will eventually increase gross national production.

Table 5-3
Generative Motivation Policies

Policies	Targets	Instruments
• Investment Inducement Policy	• Income Generating	• Interest Rate Policy
• Technology Innovation Policy	• Productivity Improvement	• Secure Profit
• Human Development Policy	• Capacity Improvement	• Training and Education
• Work Incentive	• Self-actualization	• Low Income Saving
• Voluntary Work	• Social Solidarity	• Service-time Saving
• QOL (Culture, Sports, Leisure, Education)	• Welfare improvement	• Cultural Improvement

Generative Policy for Degenerative Society

The community establishes national legal order based on the social contract and creates common interests by yielding part of its private interests to others. However, social development will be deterred, and a degenerative process will be accelerated, in cases where exclusive group interest is stressed and legal order is violated by emphasizing individual interest and specific group interest over public interest and national interest.

The deterioration of states and organizations occurs when specialized group interest precedes community interest. When the fundamental regulation of community is unstable, due to conflict of group interests, regional conflict, political feuds, corruption, legal order violation, public order disturbance, it becomes very difficult to address structural inefficiencies that add to social costs. Deterioration results in the loss of national competitiveness and causes economic stagnation that brings on economic crises. Economic recession and the social degenerative process are cyclical processes.

To block the social degenerative process,[5] an institutional arrangement to effectively address different group interests is required. Under the three-tier coordination scheme,[6] an interest adjustment committee, such as a "Tripartite Coordination Committee," executes the first step of coordination. Pending issues are brought to the "pubic interest protection committee" within the constitutional court and go through the second coordination process. The most serious conflicts, which cannot be resolved at the second tier, become a subject of the third coordination scheme that requires a referendum to make a final decision and creates legislation to solve the conflict.

Lack of committed effort made to secure social order affects the overall structure of the society. Especially in Korean society, there has been a plague of social disorder, and people have a deep-rooted negative perception towards societal/governmental/labor processes because consultation, negotiation and coordination are not expected, and group interest suppresses national interest and public interest. Such a negative perception originated in our long history of suffering from numerous foreign invasions and financial crises causing massive layoffs. Therefore, only balanced social order can remedy the prevalent social pathology and bring stability into society in order that we may recover rationality.

Several preconditions should be satisfied to convert degenerative society into generative society: clear policy targets, active and productive welfare economic policies, efficient and improved social systems.

IV. Generative Balancing Policies

Generative Balanced Policies Program

Generative Balanced Policies aim at attaining distributional equality and productive efficiency through productive interaction between balanced resource distribution and development motives.

Balanced distribution occurs when resources supply and demand balance, resulting in optimal resource distribution. The term "balance" can be seen in two ways: quantitative balance and power balance. Generative elements include investment, technology, human resource development, etc., and resulting income creation and employment levels are dependent on the size and effectiveness of such generative elements.

For the discussion of generative balancing policies, specific policy goals including poverty escape, human resource development, employment policy, financial stabilization, investment facilitation are to be explained as comprising two elements: balancing and generative. The *Generative Social Safety Net* is designed to assist people to escape poverty through policies aimed at providing basic security and helping welfare recipients achieve self-support through work and training programs. As a result, wage levels decrease allowing increased investment and subsequently, the development process is actively spurred. The *Human Resource Development Network* is designed to improve labor efficiency and productivity through education and training. Human resource development can help people escape poverty and results in

Generative Balanced Policies = Balancing Element + Generative Element

Table 5-4
Generative Balanced Policies

Degenerative Society ⇒	Generative Balanced Policies
I. Policy Targets: Confused ⇒	I. Policy Targets: Clear
Social Instability (Social conflict, QOL deterioration)	Social Stability (QOL improvement with social welfare)
Economic Growth/Economic Depression	Balanced Growth (Balanced economic growth and stability)
Deepened poverty gap, increased unemployment	Coexistence of the rich and the poor; Resource conservation; Ecosystem Protection
II. Passive Welfare Economic Policy ⇒	II. Active Welfare Economic Policy
Incomplete Basic Security lack of SSN	Basic Security Policy (SSN) Income
-Income Security(State Dependent)	-Security (stimulate self-help effort)
-Medical Security(Increasing self-burden)	-Medical Security (Completed)
Poverty Trap, Poor Living condition	Active Program for poverty escaping
-Depending on the Passive welfare allowance	-Self-supported improvement (Social Sector Job Creation Network)
-Insufficient Education and Training	-Lifelong Improvement Network
Insufficient Innovative Investment	Innovative Investment
-Lack of technology innovative and investment opportunities	-Investment for Technology innovation, Management Innovation
-Low social investment	-Social Investment, QOL Improvement
Financial Crisis from finance exhaustion	Finance Balancing Policy
-Benefit-defined Social Insurance	-Contribution-defined social insurance
-Harming work incentive by basic income security system	-Generative Basic Income Security
Economic Depression Economic Instability	Attaining Economic Balance
-RD ≫ RS	-RD = RS
-Increased Unemployment	-Unemployment, Price, Stable distribution
III. Adverse Function of Social System ⇒	III. Social System Improvement
Incomplete social order	Securing Basic Order
-Confusion of Basic Social Order	-Rearrangement of basic order
-Lack of Rule of Law	-Rule of Law
Intense Group Interest	Coordination of group interest
-Insufficient Public interest seeking	-Interest coordination among groups
-Prioritization on group interest	-Priority in Public Interest
Bureaucracy	Efficient Government
-Inefficient Bureaucrat	-Efficient Government, Service oriented
-Bureaucratic Corruption	- Administrative transparency
Inefficient Society	Efficient social system and QOL improvement
-Inefficient social system	-Effective linkage to social system
-High cost structure by inefficiency	-Cost retrenchment by efficiency

Table 5-5
Generative Balancing Policies

Policies	Generative Features	Balancing Features	Policy Instruments
1. Poverty Escape Policy	•Activating /Empowering	•Independence	•Social Safety net - Income Maintenance Prog. - Low Income Business - Low Income Skill Training
2. Human Resources Dev. Policy	•Factor of production	•Increase in Distribution	•Retraining Programs •Continuing Education
3. Full Employment Policy	•Income Generation	•Increase in Wage Income	•Labor Net Working •Unemployed, Elderly, Women, Handicapped
4. Financial Balancing Social Insurance	•Funding for investment	•Income Transfer	•Social Insurances (HI, PL, UI, WI) •Defined Contribution
5. Social Investment Policy	•Employment Increase	•Income Increase	•Training/Education •SOC, Parks, Libraries, Social SVC.

productivity improvement, which is an essential element for national competitiveness. Basic livelihood security for trainees and special education for adjustment to the labor market are required for successful policy implementation. Active employment policy provides substantial assistance for the unemployed and subsidies provide minimum livelihood compensation when they are employed. It is a generative policy aimed at promoting active job placement. *Social Insurance Finance Stabilizer* entails a fixed contribution system that makes payment contingent upon the insurance fee collected from workers. The Reserve Fund will provide a long-term income guarantee through market investment.

Generative Social Safety Net (GSSN)

Social Safety Nets have three areas of operation: The first area of safety net operation includes the social insurance system; the second area addresses social assistance; and the third area of safety net activity covers public work, social-sector job creation and emergency aid. Although social safety nets provide basic security, those unemployed with working capacity, or the elderly in good physical condition with work experience, may actively seek - and desire—more active working opportunities. This will add to their self-actualization and enhance quality of life. Social safety nets have created a passive attitude in many welfare recipients. Because of this phenomenon, the motivation to work of welfare recipients is diminishing, and also, concern is growing that income creation may pull those welfare recipients just out of the reach of social assistance programs.

Surmounting these difficulties require, inter alia, Generative Social Safety Net, a social safety net enriched with two additional elements: Productive WorkNet and Generative Motivation System.

A national network keyed toward increasing employment by providing job information and job training opportunities for the capable unemployed and the socially marginalized alike, Productive WorkNet combines several categories including employment network, social sector job network, aged labor force network and social volunteer network. This is an organic information system in which an individual can easily access to job market depending on his/her job-skill development and cumulative work experience over time.

In western welfare states, the concept of "equality" can create a passive attitude that may directly link to economic depression. Therefore, stimulating the major motivation for economic development is required to effectively coordinate "development and balance" for the enhancement of national competitiveness. Generative Motivation System can satisfy self-actualization needs by providing self-support works for low-income workers. Specifically, the system should concentrate on extending its capacity to support wage assistance, education assistance, skill-set advancement, paid social volunteer work, self-support community activity, and seek to build linkages between them. Adding Generative Motivation System to the social safety net results in the Generative Social Safety Net aiming at converting passive recipients of basic security into active participants. Through such a process, the Generative Balanced Model can be completed for balanced development of society as a whole and improved quality of life.

The ultimate goal of working lies in maximizing satisfaction by attaining self-satisfaction, self-respect, and self-actualization, as well as income creation. Providing an unemployed, skilled labor force with comparatively lower-skill jobs may increase self-satisfaction through working though their wages are insufficient. Currently, a number of retirees have been participating in social volunteer work aimed at generating self-satisfaction, not creating income.

When a nation provides basic livelihood security to its people, numerous jobs including low-skill work, social sector jobs or social volunteer work can be included as part of the total national economic unit. Considering this, any incentive that induces free exchange among sub-units can contribute to increased total labor (L) of a nation and results in increased income creation and self-satisfaction.[7]

Table 5-6
Generative Social Safety Net

Goal	Elements
Generative Social Safety Net	Social Safety Net + Productive WorkNet + Generative Motives
1. Social Safety Net	Basic Security, Social Insurance, Emergency Aid
2. Productive Work Net	Employment Network, Social Sector Job Network, Aged Labor Force Network, Social Volunteer Network
3. Generative Motivation	Investment Motivation, Technology Innovation, Human Resource Development, Work Incentive, QOL Improvement

Note: SSN → Productive WorkNet → Increased Labor Supply → Decreased Wage level → Stimulate Investment Motivation → Innovation, Development

Income Generation Process of Generative Social Safety Net

Having the minimal national living standard provided by the social safety net, the low-skilled unemployed can work for low wages (workfare), and the income generated can then be reserved under the self-support preparation savings system. This, in turn, not only protects the income deduction system, but also brings an increase in the real income by raising total labor, lowering wages (Torfing 1999) and resulting in price reduction. Increased income is reflected in increased consumption, stimulating production. A fall in wages and prices expands the window of profit opportunity, bringing increased investment along with increased employment, this then leads to the increased demand for high-skilled laborers and boosts income.

SSN support results in an increase of low-skilled workers. Income increase leads to increased demand for mid-level managers and young adults in the labor force. Increased labor supply decreases wages and increases investment, employment and high-skilled labor. The previously illustrated cycle is

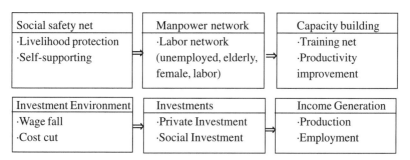

based on the generative process. Problems associated with the aging society and long-term unemployment can be also solved with the same policy.

Experience of OECD Countries

The aim of activation strategies is to encourage the unemployed to be more active in job search and keep more in touch with the labor market. Such strategies range from attempts to provide more effective job-search assistance to the unemployed and monitoring their search activity at one end of the spectrum to making it obligatory on the unemployed to satisfy work tests or participate in active programs or in education and training if they are to continue to draw benefits. Such activation strategies are becoming quite common for young people in OECD countries (e.g. Australia, Denmark, Ireland, United Kingdom), and they are even being extended to other groups of the unemployed in some countries. The recent U.S. welfare reform, with its emphasis on work requirements, time limits for benefits and sanctions for non-compliance, can be viewed as an extreme example of this approach (Martin 2000).

The role of active labor market policies changes subtly in the context of activation strategy. They can be viewed as a vehicle for enforcing a work test on the unemployed, especially in cases where the supply of jobs is low. In such cases, continued receipt of unemployment benefits becomes conditional on program participation, as in the case of Denmark or Switzerland, and/or by offering a sufficiently wide range of programs so that a maximum number of the unemployed will choose to enter them voluntarily. In a related manner, there is a growing interest in many countries to implement effective activation strategies to promote job-search activities and curb benefit abuse by claimants of unemployment benefits. As noted in the previous section, the evaluation literature suggests that these strategies, if used intelligently and supported by effective sanctions, can help stimulate job search and serve to keep benefit claimants in touch with the labor market (Martin and Grubb 2001).

The introduction of workfare policies in Denmark is inspired by the workfares strategies which re-emerged in the UK and the US in the late 1980s. However, the Danish government, inspired by the Swedish experience, managed to detach workfare from its neo-liberal "origin" and to reformulate its contents in accordance with the sociopolitical legacy in Denmark. As such, the Danish workfare strategy is an offensive rather than a defensive strategy. The offensive Danish workfare strategy puts emphasis on: (1) activation rather than benefit and wage reductions; (2) improving the skills and work experience of the unemployed rather than merely increasing their mobility and job-searching efficiency; (3) training and education rather than work-for-the-benefit; (4) empowerment rather than control and punishment;

(5) more inclusive workfare programs rather than programs which only target the unemployed.

Generative Balanced State (GBS)

A new model of welfare seeks income creation, improved quality of life and balanced resource allocation in order to reach the ultimate goal of producing a welfare economy with a combination of efficiency and equality. A new model must be a Generative Balanced Model for Welfare Economy as an alternative of welfare state (GBS).

Firstly, a new model calls for dynamic balance between welfare benefits and current societal and economic conditions. In other words, the model constantly alters the size and pattern of resource allocation in welfare sectors in response to ever-changing conditions such as technology innovation, aging population growth, family disbanding, etc. Also, a new model may be applicable to all conditions since it transcends a specific society or time period.

Secondly, a new model is a system in which all people can coexist in peace and harmony. Human society needs a balanced order of competition and coexistence similar to a natural ecosystem. Mere competition emphasizing effectiveness, or distribution that stresses only equality, cannot sustain human society. The balanced combination of "equality" as a social value and "efficiency" as an economic value can play a crucial role in sustaining human society.

Thirdly, a new model requires an institutional arrangement to reach social agreement for the balance of interests. Determining "the optimal balance point" for coexistence under incessant social change should involve all aspects of society. Therefore, a proper institutional arrangement involving the opinions and concerns of corporations, labor, professionals, civil servants, government, civil groups, unions, NGOs, etc. is necessary for the successful implementation of the balanced welfare model.

Fourthly, a new model needs to support the self-actualization motivation of mankind. Through positive self-actualization motivation of welfare recipients, it aims at promoting an active and voluntary welfare policy. Further, it emphasizes the incubator role of the welfare system, with a final goal towards returning the unemployed to active economic and social activities.

Table 5-7 describes the new model of generative balanced state as compared to the other three state categories, namely, degenerative unbalanced (DGUB), degenerative balanced (DGB), and generative unbalanced (GUB) states. A degenerative unbalanced state is a country where its resource demand outstrips its resource supply, thereby leading into socioeconomic problems involving stagnation, inflation, and income disparity. Countries of this type usually have passive and reactive, rather than active and proactive, social safety nets. Russia, North Korea, and some South American countries are examples in point.

In degenerative balanced states, resource supply is less than or equal to resource demand. Typical socioeconomic problems these countries - Cuba, Iran and Iraq for example—face are stagflation and deficit growth, and, like their degenerative unbalanced counterparts, their social safety nets are usually passive.

Meanwhile, the category of generative unbalanced states includes European countries, the United States and Japan whose resource supply is either larger or smaller than resource demand. It is characteristic of these countries that they face problems of inflation and social conflicts ensuing from their unbalanced growth and inefficient social safety nets.

Table 5-7
Generative Balanced State

Allocation[2] / Value added[3]	Unbalanced	Balanced [1]
Generative [4]	• RS $\gtreqless$ RD • Unbalanced growth, inflation, social conflict • Generative SSN • GUB (Europe, US, Japan)	• RS = RD • Balanced growth (Growth, Quality of Life) • Generative SSN • GBS (Singapore)
Degenerative	• RS « RD • Stagnation, inflation, income disparity • Passive SSN • DGUB (Argentina, North Korea)	• RS ≤ RD • Stagflation, Deficit growing • Passive SSN • DGB (Cuba, Iran, Iraq)

1. Aggregate Supply/Aggregate Demand = Material + Quality of Life
2. Resources Allocation: balanced $\Rightarrow$ AS = AD, unbalanced $\Rightarrow$ AS $\gtreqless$ AD
3. Value Added: generative $\Rightarrow$ Income Creation + QOL Improvement
   $\therefore$ generative = Income {Productivity [Investment Labor Skill] Security}
   degenerative $\Rightarrow$ Decrease in Income & QOL
4. Generative process: Active Income Creation & QOL improvement
Development motivation $\uparrow \Rightarrow$ Factor Input $\uparrow$ Investment Increase(L, K) $\Rightarrow$ Productivity increase $\uparrow \Rightarrow$ Income Creation $\uparrow$ QOL $\uparrow$

A Generative balanced state, on the other hand, is an economy whose resource demand is more or less equal to its resource supply. The best example of this category is Singapore. With its social safety net highly generative in character, the country has been making significant headway toward creating balanced growth and continuous improvement in quality of life.

Productivity improvement by balanced resource distribution, human resource development, and self-actualization can eventually contribute to making our society better and stronger. And also, further emphasis should be given to achieving common peace and prosperity by establishing strong commitments towards coexistence with nature as well as among nations.

Generative Balanced State(GBS) aims to pursue the above-mentioned goals; they are:

- A Basic Security System including all people in the society in a balanced manner
- A Basic Security pursuing co-prosperity and coexistence;
- Resource-saving balanced development satisfying resource demand within the limits of resource supply;
- Generative Motives encouraging work and further development;
- Human Resource Development, developing human capability and boosting productivity;
- International Convention securing equal coexistence among states;
- Environmental Convention aimed at protecting ecosystems.

V. Assessment of Productive Welfare Program

Productive Welfare is largely composed of four components: establishment of basic social safety nets; establishment of a self-support system for socially vulnerable classes; job creation, social investment, human development; and welfare system streamlining and modernization. All four components are essential to Productive Welfare and cannot be pursued independently, but should be closely associated, maintaining a mutually complementary relationship. In other words, effective self-support assistance can be provided only on the basis of a solid basic social safety net system. Human development and job creation will also be facilitated when society is well equipped with a basic social safety net system. Furthermore, self-support, human development, job creation and institutional streamlining can eventually reduce social burden and function as building blocks for a stronger industrial foundation. Additionally, these elements can foster improvement of the basic livelihood security system of all people in the society. As mentioned previously, all four Productive Welfare pillars when combined create a synergistic effect, contributing to quality of life and national productivity improvement. Therefore, when all four programs are fulfilling their roles effectively, Productive Welfare supports social development and balances resource demand and supply.

Establishment of a basic social safety net is the most fundamental prerequisite of Productive Welfare for promoting social solidarity. Centerpieces of the basic social safety net are basic livelihood security, basic welfare service provision, and human resource development.

The National Minimum Living Standards Security Act aims at protecting people's basic livelihood. In order to achieve this, a range of efforts is under-way with a view to efficiently providing basic income, healthcare, and educa-tional opportunities. The Korean government executed a comprehensive and general revision of the Livelihood Protection Act and introduced the Na-tional Minimum Living Standards Security Act in October 2000. Under this Act, the Government will ensure that basic needs are met for all people living below minimum living standards regardless of their work capabil-ity. As a result, the number of beneficiaries of Basic Livelihood Security reached 1.55 million, three percent of total population and three times the number of people covered before the Act. The Act seeks to secure a "home-like" society by implementing various programs to strengthen family func-tion and to ensure that people have at-home welfare services they need. To achieve this goal, a multi-layered and organic social support system should be established to strengthen family self-care system; at the same time, in the spirit of social solidarity society should implement non-gov-ernmental caring mechanisms for those needing social protection. To this end, family-support service delivery systems should be extended to comple-ment diversified family arrangements. Introduction of a tax benefit system and incentives for protection providers should be actively reviewed for en-hanced family protection.

The social safety net has a three-tier structure. The first tier consists of four social insurance schemes including medical insurance, national pension, employment insurance and industrial-injury insurance. The Korean govern-ment has introduced these social insurance schemes and through rapid expansion has established universal coverage of the social insurance scheme. The second tier represents social assistance for people under the poverty line. In Korea's case, introduction of the National Minimum Liv-ing Standards Security Act has allowed all people living under the pov-erty line to receive social assistance benefits. The third tier is emergency aid to provide prompt assistance at the time of an emergency situation including natural disaster, war, economic crisis and massive unemployment. Emergency food aid and medical service are good examples of third tier of social safety net programs.

Self-support policy can be divided into counter-poverty measures on one hand, and supporting instruments for the socially vulnerable such as the elderly, women and the disabled on the other. Although counter-poverty efforts are underway to create community-based volunteer jobs, social jobs and self-support small businesses, more active and progressive mea-sures are required to help the poor to climb out of the poverty trap.

Productive welfare policies for the elderly aim at utilizing their expertise and skills. Related efforts include a number of programs that provide support for elderly business startups, elderly job searchers, and paid volunteers. To make the policy more efficient, a full-scale elderly workforce network is required. Productive Welfare policies for women should be directed toward full utilization of women's labor through development of women-oriented programs. Currently, a far-reaching network for human resource development is required along with childcare assistance programs aimed at activating women's participation in the economic sector. The new policies aim also to promote rehabilitation of all persons with disabilities by implementing a range of pro-disabled programs. Vocational rehabilitation education and business incubator programs are available to the disabled.

Job creation measures and social investment seek to counter unemployment, create social-sector jobs, increase the incentive for people to work, and create impetus for greater labor flexibility. Some of the existing measures include an employment network, productive welfare networks, and wage-assistance employment. Also, a number of programs are in place to create social jobs that serve public interest, including the home-helper project, community-based volunteer works, community cleaning, environmental protection works, public projects, and public enterprise development. However, a greater investment is required to improve the performance of these programs.

The social investment policy on preventive health care seeks to achieve increased productivity by promoting health and preventing diseases through health education centers, health expositions, and health zones. Health/welfare industry policy aims to transform this industry into a knowledge-based and high value-added industry. A comprehensive set of strategies is under preparation with a view to fostering new innovations in drugs, medical instruments, food, cosmetics, information technology and biotechnology. Health and biotechnology industries require further concentrated investment.

The existing welfare system will achieve greater efficiency with current efforts to stabilize social insurance finances, formulate a social insurance information infrastructure, build linkages among social insurance schemes, establish improved delivery mechanisms, and invigorate performance-based management. Currently, a comprehensive set of financial measures is under preparation to ensure long-term stability of social insurance funds.

To ensure wider public accessibility to social insurance information, an array of new programs are under development, among them an individual health/welfare card, and establishing a national healthcare/welfare information infrastructure. The efficiency of the social insurance system will be further improved with additional measures to be taken to establish linkages among the four social insurance schemes.

To achieve increased efficiency in the service delivery system and heath/welfare management, further efforts are required to initiate health/welfare service evaluation and implement performance-based management systems for social insurance agencies.

Table 5-8
Productive Welfare Policy: Programs and Assessment

Policies	Goals	Programs	Assessment
I. Basic Social Safety Net			
• Basic Livelihood Security	•Livelihood security	•Basic income/health/housing/education •Simultaneous and sufficient benefit provision required	•System framework is completed (1.55 million beneficiaries)
• Basic Service Provision	•Homelike society	•At-home welfare service, strengthening function •Caregiver allowance	•Service delivery system is in need of improvement
• Overhauling of Social Safety Net	•Social integration	•Primary safety net (social insurance)- secondary safety net (social assistance)- tertiary safety net (emergency aid)	•System framework is completed
• Human Resources Development	•Functional capacity improvement	•Vocational training, social education/lifelong education •Caseworker retraining	•In need of further improvements in education/ training system in connection with job provision
II. Self-support Policies			
• Anti-poverty Measures	•Poverty eradication	•Community-based voluntary works/self-support project/creation of social jobs · Anti-poverty support	•Progressive anti-poverty measures required
• Productive Welfare Policy for the Elderly	•Utilization of elderly expertise and skills	•Job information service and small business incubator programs •Support for paid community volunteer workers	•Elderly manpower network is required
• Productive Welfare Policy for Women	•Utilization of female laborpower	•Female labor power development, public educare programs, women laborpower network	•Female laborpower network is required
• Self-support Policy for the Disabled	•Increasing self-support ability of the disabled	•Education programs, vocational training, and small business incubator program, disabled workforce network	•Rehabilitation projects are in need of further substantiation
III. Job Creation and Social Investment(Healthcare/Education/Housing/Culture)			
• Employment Network	•Employment enhancement •Increase work incentives	•Employment network, productive welfare network • Wage-assisted employment	•Unemployment network is completed
• Creation of Social Jobs	•Creation of social jobs that serve public interest	•Home helpers and community-based volunteer workers, community cleaning works, environment protection project, public project, public enterprises (cooperatives)	•In need of increasing social investment
• Investment in Preventive Healthcare	•Heath promotion/disease prevention	•Health education center/Health Expo/ health zone	•Health investment plan is under establishment

• Health and Welfare Industries	•Knowledge-based, high value-added industry	•New medical instruments and drug development, food and cosmetics, and biotechnology & information technology	•In need of concentrated investment in health and biotechnology industries
IV. Improvement of System Efficiency			
• Financial Stabilization for Social Insurance	•Financial balance	•Financial stabilization of the National Pension •Financial stabilization of the National Health Insurance	•In need of long-term measures for financial stabilization
• Informatization of Social Insurance Sector	•Information accessibility	•Health/welfare cards •Health/welfare information infrastructure	•Informatization project is underway
• Linking Various Social Insurance Schemes	•Efficiency of management and operation	?Institutional link among the four major social insurance schemes	•Efforts are underway to link social insurance schemes
• Performance-based Management	•Increased efficiency and responsibility in management	•Health/welfare service evaluation system •Performance-based management of social insurance organizations	•In need of further institutional measures

VI. Conclusion

Although the development of science and technology has considerably enhanced industrial productivity and brought affluence to people around the globe, welfare state models including neo-liberalism and social democracy have failed to establish welfare systems which fulfill the fundamental goal of peaceful coexistence between human beings. A considerable number of the unemployed has been excluded from regular social activities, and the problem of income disparity has not been adequately addressed. The socially underprivileged and poor populations have been dependent on welfare allowances provided by the state, and have struggled against the vicious cycle of poverty. Income disparity between nations has been widened, leaving some nations fighting against famine and struggling to protect natural resources and ecosystems.

The recent trend toward globalization has driven nations around the world into an arena of unrestrained competition. While many nations have been making great leaps in technological innovation and efficiency increases for improved national competitiveness, they have also provided active assistance for excluded populations by means of social safety net systems that ultimately help them re-enter the job market. In the wake of the 1997 financial crisis, Korea has improved its social safety net to aid crisis recovery, and has stressed the leading role of the state in financial recovery and protecting the unemployed by putting them back in the job market.

The social safety net is an institutional arrangement aimed at protecting all people in the society from social risks including unemployment, aging, disease, natural disaster, and death. Social Safety Nets can provide resource redistribution for the poor - including the socially vulnerable - and help achieve social equality and maintain balanced resource distribution. Balanced resource distribution can be defined as a process of finding balance between supply and demand of resources. Within the scope of total resource use and allocation, Social Safety Nets seek to ensure the coexistence of rich and poor and improve equality and efficiency through effective resource distribution.

Human beings have throughout time adapted to the natural environment and produced survival techniques from food gathering in the wild to making and improving technology. Noteworthy technological developments brought mass production and wealth. However, to survive international competition amid globalization, nations should combine continuous growth and social development, and any nation excluded from this competition may fall onto a degenerative path. To continue productive and generative growth, generative incentive policy for social development is necessary. Generative policies can provide investment incentive through productivity enhancements such as human development, technology development, capital productivity improvement aimed at economic development. These steps should result in quality of life improvement.

A Generative Balanced Model of welfare based on the combination of growth factors for balance and improved productivity resulting in coexistence is required. Problems seen in Western welfare states such as unemployment, economic downturn, income disparity and budget deficit can be linked to social safety nets and development motives that maximize productivity. Minimum living standards are guaranteed by the social safety net, and people with the ability to work are helped to become self-supportive and independent. The balance of supply and demand for the unemployed, elderly, females and disabled human resources is maintained with the help of the establishment of an employment network. Skill training is provided to unskilled people for capacity building. This in turn brings an increase in the labor supply, a wage hike and the reduction of costs. As a result, the investment climate is improved encouraging more investment. Production and employment are increased creating income, and ultimately, sustained growth and development of a society can take place.

A Generative Balanced Model which combines balanced elements and productive elements can make it possible to perform comparative analysis between welfare economic status and social development levels, and further can be utilized in the evaluation of Korea's Productive Welfare system. Productive Welfare is equipped with systems such as a basic social safety net and training programs to enhance human resources and to help people to be self-supporting and independent. Job opportunities are expanded due to increased investment, and the supply of human resources is regulated through the employment network. Moreover, balanced combination of efficiency and advanced information sharing of social security system can improve effectiveness and reduce cost. Productive Welfare has made the minimum living standard security comprehensive, thereby improving the self-support and training programs. However, given the fact that Productive Welfare aims at the harmony of equality and effectiveness, much time is required in order to achieve the financial stability of the social insurance system through systematic reform in stages.

Notes

1. Individual Interests < Family Interests < Group Interests < National Interests < Global Coexistence < Coexistence with Nature. Individual interests should not precede group interests.
2. Taoism has been forming building blocks for a large part of value systems, ethos, and cultures in many parts of East Asia for well over two millennia. Here, the great influence of philosophical Taoism on people's understanding of interpersonal and environmental perceptions is worth a brief discussion. Many scholars define the term Tao as the "way" or, more aptly, as the way of nature. One of Taoism's quintessential tenets is that *nature is an inseparable whole*, an interconnected organic unity, with all its manifestations operating according to a set of inexorable natural laws. This is to say that nothing stands unconnected from anything else, and nowhere is this idea of the interconnectedness of all life and manifestations is grasped more succinctly than in the notion of yin-yang, according to which seemingly opposing elements in nature are not in conflict but in a state of *interdependent and complementary harmony*, continually balancing one another. This runs antithetical to the traditional Western view that humans, separate from one another and from nature, can exercise manipulation and control over all situations and that with our intelligence we are able to have our environment in hand. Taoist views that the self-regulated mechanism of nature works toward harmony and balance, and any part of nature that develops inordinate qualities creates an imbalance that in turn triggers a corresponding reaction. There are abundant evidences in natural phenomena and human affairs that attest this. Imbalances in nature are counterbalanced by spontaneous reactions, and the more excessive the initial imbalance, the more powerful will be the reactionary force. The actions of individuals and collectives are subject to similar principles of nature. Any individual or group that develops extreme qualities or that disturbs the natural harmony of the world will beget corresponding consequences, and the ultimate human goal is to realize consonance with one another and with nature.
3. Difficulties with the welfare state (distributional equality / passivity):
   - Welfare recipients $\Rightarrow$ passivity $\Rightarrow$ work evasion $\Rightarrow$ poverty trap;
   - Equality does not always ensure satisfaction. Other elements such as security, self-respect, and self-actualization can also influence the satisfaction of mankind.

   The maximum point of self-satisfaction does not lie in equality but in opportunities for choice. One who achieves goals through their own choosing is superior to one loaded with external burden under an equitable state.

4.	Generative Innovation	• Material Innovation → new technology, new market, new resources • Quality of Life Innovation → Better Service, Information/Knowledge Service, Cultural Education/Physical Exercise, Sightseeing, Entertainment • System Improvement → New Management Skill, Structural Efficiency

5.	Degenerative Process • Interest Group → Public Interest Destruction → Social Disorder → Insecurity → Inefficiency → Loss of Competitiveness → Disinvestment → Income Reduction → Degenerative Stagnation

6. Three-Tier Coordination Scheme: TCS
   = (I. Tripartite Coordination Committee) + (II. Public Interest Protection Committee in the Constitutional Court) + (III. Referendum)
7. Total Labor Supply (L) = Ls (Specialized Labor Force) + Lu (Low Skill) + Ld (Simple Work) + Lv (Social Sector Volunteer)

References

Department of Social Security (1999) *Opportunity for all: Tackling Poverty and Social Exclusion*. United Kingdom: The Stationery Office.

Giddens, A. (1994) *Beyond Left and Right. The Future of Radical Politics*. Cambridge: Polity Press.

_____ (1998) *The Third Way. The Renewal of Social Democracy*. Cambridge: Polity Press.

Gilbert, N. and Van Voorhis, R. A. (2001) *Activating the Unemployed: A Comparative Appraisal of Work-Oriented Policies*. New Brunswick & London: Transaction Publishers.

Grover, C. and Stewart, J. (1999) "Market Workfare: Social Security, Social Regulation and Competitiveness in the1990s," *Journal of Social Policy,* 28 (1).

Judge, K. (2000) "Evaluating Welfare to Work in the UK," in N. Gilbert & R. Van Voorhis (eds) *Activating the Unemployed: A Comparative Appraisal of Work-Oriented Policies*. New Brunswick & London: Transaction Publishers.

Keizer, P. (2000) "From Welfare to Workfare: Dutch Policies in the Nineties," in N. Gilbert & R. Van Voorhis (eds) *Activating the Unemployed: A Comparative Appraisal of Work-Oriented Policies*. New Brunswick & London: Transaction Publishers.

Mackey, R. (2000) "Welfare-to-Work: New Direction in New Zealand," in N. Gilbert & R. Van Voorhis (eds) *Activating the Unemployed: A Comparative Appraisal of Work-Oriented Policies*. New Brunswick & London: Transaction Publishers.

Martin, J. P. (2000) "What Works Among Active Labour Market Policies: Evidence from OECD Countries' Experiences," OECD, *Economic Studies* 30. Paris: OECD.

Martin, J. P. and Grubb, D. (2001) "What Works and for Whom: A Review of OECD Countries' Experiences with Active Labour Market Policies," mimeo. Paris: OECD.

Mishra, R. (1984) *The Welfare State in Crisis: Social Thought and Social Change*. Great Britain: Wheatsheaf Books Ltd.

OECD (2000) *Pushing Ahead with Reform in Korea: Labour Market and Social Safety-Net Policies*. Paris: OECD.

Titmuss, R.M. (1958) *Essays on the Welfare State*. London: Allen & Unwin.

Torfing, J. (1999) "Workfare with Welfare: Recent Reforms of the Danish Welfare State," *Journal of European Social Policy,* 9 (1).

6

Implementing Productive Welfare: From Philosophical Theory to Everyday Practice

Robert Pinker

I. Introduction

When they were preparing the agenda for their *International Symposium for Sharing Productive Welfare Experience*, the organizers wisely designated one of the five plenary sessions for a review of its philosophical principles and policy objectives. Three papers were presented in this session. Stein Kuhnle (Chapter 4) explored the democratic credentials of productive welfare philosophy. Neil Gilbert (Chapter 2) and Ramesh Mishra (Chapter 3) examined its economic connotations, respectively with regard to the institutions of the competitive market and the process of globalization. Welfare institutions make up the third major component of what is generally described today as the modern pluralist nation-state. All three contributors discussed the normative linkages between democratic, economic and welfare values.

All of these components are embodied in the Republic of Korea's model of Productive Welfare. The title of this model is distinctive, insofar as it implies a degree of institutional interdependence between the ends and means of the competitive market and the agencies of social protection. The key assumption that underpins this model is the belief that both sets of institutions can be made to complement each other in the production and enhancement of welfare. In this respect, welfare is conceptualized as having both a material and a moral dimension.

In this retrospective chapter, I will give further attention to the philosophical principles or values that seem likely to shape the ends and means of

Korea's productive welfare policies in the years ahead. I will, however, give particular attention to the ways in which these principles conflict with or complement each other in a pluralist political context, how these conflicts can best be reconciled or accommodated, and—most importantly—how they can be put into practical effect.

The academic literature of social policy is replete with normative models of welfare systems in which their authors set out the core principles or values that they believe ought to direct and shape the ends of social policy. These models cover a wide range of ideological perspectives. Some give priority to individualist values and the role of the non-governmental sector in raising living standards and enhancing social welfare. Others commend collectivist values and argue that government agencies ought to be the main funders and providers of social services.

In the middle ground between these ideological extremes, welfare pluralists advocate models based on a combination of individualist and collectivist values and an institutional 'mix' of statutory and non-statutory forms of welfare provision. The Korean model of productive welfare fits clearly within the compass of this pluralist middle ground.

Formulating normative models of welfare is a necessary but relatively straightforward task in the making of social policy. It is far more difficult to translate these abstract principles into practice. In democracies, governments will only succeed in doing so if they are able and willing to raise and spend the necessary revenues on an equitable basis in ways which command the respect and support of their citizens. Conversely, citizens as tax-payers and social service users, must accept their responsibilities in ways which command the confidence and trust of their governments.

Kyungbae Chung (Chapter 5) draws attention to the reasons why many Korean citizens lack confidence in the integrity and competence of their government. He argues that the past mismanagement of economic crises, the pursuit of sectional interests at the expense of the public interest, corruption and lack of transparency and accountability in the conduct of political affairs have all contributed to Korea's crisis in public confidence.

Sang-Kyun Kim focuses on the urgent need to restore the government's confidence in the personal integrity of those citizens who cheat on their tax-returns and their benefit claims. He describes these practices as a "black market" of corruption, which currently accounts for revenues in excess of twenty percent of Korea's gross domestic product. He argues that the "curtailment" of this black market is "one of the most serious barriers" to the successful development of Korea's productive welfare policies (Kim, S.-K. 2001). In default of an effective remedy, this "black market" will become a "black hole" in Korea's welfare universe that drains away its public revenues and public confidence in equal measure.

II. Setting the Issues in Context

Many other nations throughout the world face similar threats to the solvency of their welfare budgets. Some have had notable successes in reducing the incidence of tax evasion and benefit fraud as well as in raising the standards of conduct in public life. There are, however, no ready-made and universally relevant strategies to hand that one nation can take over and adopt from other nations for its own purposes without modification. Nevertheless, nations can learn from the experiences of others, provided that they are careful to adapt these strategies in ways that build on the strengths of their own distinctive political cultures. Such transfers of knowledge and experience are most likely to succeed when they occur between nations that have reached roughly similar stages of political and economic development, are moving in similar political and economic directions, and confront similar kinds of political and economic challenges.

Stein Kuhnle (Chapter 4) draws attention to the many different kinds of function that welfare systems perform. In addition to the provision of social services, they also act as agents of political and social stability. They can be understood as both a response to democratic pressures for social reform and social justice and as one of the institutional means by which democracies can create those conditions of political stability without which the continuous production of wealth would not be possible. Kuhnle goes on to describe the ways in which the dual processes of industrial growth and democratization have begun to complement each other in the Republic of Korea since the mid-1990s—despite the impact of recurrent economic crises. Indeed, President Kim Dae-Jung's productive welfare policy proposals can best be understood as a bold attempt at turning an economic crisis into an opportunity for creative change and national renewal. Other industrial nations throughout the world are facing similar challenges to their political and economic stability under the impact of global change.

Kuhnle also speculates about the likely future outcomes of the President's productive welfare initiative. He suggests that, if these policies are successfully implemented, Korea will eventually move "more in the direction of a so-called social democratic Scandinavian type of welfare regime, and in its modern topical disguise." At the same time, he predicts that many of the cultural characteristics of this new regime will remain distinctively Korean.

Gilbert (Chapter 2) suggests that Korea has already begun moving in a different normative direction. He describes the model of productive welfare as "the Korean version of the Enabling State," a type of welfare state regime which has much in common with Titmuss's "industrial-achievement" model. Both of these models are characterized by "a common core of market-orientated social policies that emphasize the importance of work and private responsibility." They describe the kind of welfare state regime which relies on selectivist rather than universalist forms of service provision. Professor Gilbert points out that in such a pluralist welfare system there is always a danger that the values of the competitive market will come to dominate those of the statutory social services. He argues the case for what he describes as "a healthier balance between state and market forces."

At this point it is worth noting that, in the 1970s, when Titmuss was setting out his three contrasting models of social policy, the concept of welfare pluralism was rarely, if ever, used by social policy analysts. In his three-fold typology, Titmuss defines his "Residual Welfare Model of Social Policy" as one in which statutory social services are only provided to people in need as a last resort when family and charitable aid have failed. He defines his "Industrial Achievement-Performance Model" as one in which social needs are met "on the basis of merit, work performance and productivity." His third and ultimate "Institutional Redistributive Model" is defined as one in which social welfare operates "as a major integrated institution in society, providing universalist services outside the market on the principle of need: it is basically a model incorporating systems of redistribution in command-over-resources through time" (Titmuss 1974: 30-32).

In my view, the Korean model of productive welfare incorporates elements of both the industrial achievement and the institutional redistribution models, as Titmuss defines them. Productive welfare philosophy, as its title clearly indicates, attaches as much importance to the economic values of self-help and competitive efficiency as it does to the social values of solidarity, welfare rights and redistributive justice.

The Korean model of productive welfare is also based on a network of partnerships between both the state and market institutions and the statutory and non-statutory sector social services. It is these kinds of partnership that place the model unequivocally within the pluralist tradition of social policy. Titmuss was opposed to any type of welfare system that would be described as pluralist in our current terminology. He was sceptical of all claims that it might be possible to achieve "a healthier balance" between the claims of statutory welfare and market forces without prejudice to the redistributive ends of social policy.

The hard experience of he 1980s and 1990s has taught most governments and social policy analysts that the kind of welfare state regime that Titmuss preferred and defined as an "institutionally redistributive" model was fundamentally flawed simply because it polarized the values of the economic market and statutory welfare and elevated the one to the detriment of the other. Private markets, he argued, fostered egoism and alienation—statutory social services fostered altruism and social integration. There is no doubt, as Gilbert (Chapter 2) observes, that "the free market is a place where vigorous virtues vie with villainous vices" but so, for that matter, are the statutory social services which can be prone to the vices of inefficiency, undue secrecy, insensitivity to consumer choice and even corruption (Pinker 1993: 58-60).

Titmuss thought that the redistributive ends of statutory social services were self-evidently morally superior to those of the competitive market. He also assumed that the ends and means of competitive markets could be subordinated to those of social welfare without detriment to economic productivity. Competitive markets, however, are neither amoral nor morally inferior institutions. They are not driven exclusively by self-interest. Indeed, they can only operate effectively on the basis of trust. The challenge Korea faces today in the context of productive welfare, as Gilbert suggests, is to find ways of extending and strengthening the social responsibilities of competitive business enterprises and establishing a more equal relationship between the values of the competitive market and those of the statutory social services (Gilbert, Chapter 2).

At the start of this essay, I suggested that the concept of welfare possesses both a material and a moral dimension. This moral dimension can best be defined as a commitment to upholding and raising personal and collective standards of social responsibility in both of the related fields of wealth creation and social protection. These standards of responsibility should be seen as being equally binding on governments, employers and citizens alike. Only from such a commitment will it be possible to develop networks of social solidarity and interdependence that are strong enough to provide Korea's productive welfare policies with a shared sense of moral purpose and philosophical credibility. Korea must achieve this goal if it is to succeed in a highly volatile global economy.

The successful development of productive welfare policies also requires a commitment to setting all policy objectives within the constraints of something like the 'golden rule' that the British and some other Western governments are currently trying to follow. Jenny Scott defines this rule in terms of a requirement that, "over the economic cycle, the government will borrow only to invest. In other words, it can issue bonds and add to its debt if it is going to spend the proceeds on building more schools and hospitals. But spending on things like unemployment benefits must come out of tax revenues. In this way it can run a total budget deficit over the cycle, but not a current one (Scott 2001). In addition, government debt must be held down at a prudent level, relative to GDP over the whole economic cycle.

Globalization undoubtedly increases the risk of conflicts between the ends and means of competitive markets and social welfare institutions. It also makes it more likely that the consequences of such conflicts will have seriously adverse effects on living standards and job security. Nevertheless, it has always been the case that business cycles can have damaging as well as beneficial effects on personal and collective well-being. What has changed in recent years is the sheer momentum with which global markets have grown more powerful and all-pervasive.

Mishra (Chapter 3) addresses these and other related issues with reference to a range of nation-states, including Korea. He does, however, focus our attention on the contradictory consequences that frequently affect systems of social protection in a global economy.

"On the one hand," he argues, "the commodification of the economy increases insecurity, undermines existing forms of social protection and thus underlines the need for an adequate social safety net in an open globalized economy. On the other hand, the disruption of the economy, resource constraints and fiscal austerity and the ideology of privatization militate against building programs of social welfare" (Chapter 3).

Mishra makes these points with regard to the newly industrializing countries. He goes on to suggest that the impact of globalization on Western industrialized countries takes a more "indirect and diffuse form." These countries have long standing traditions of democracy and social partnership which have so far allowed them to resist any drastic residualization of their statutory social services. In conclusion, he sets out a case for developing a common framework for the study of globalization and its impact on the welfare systems of all the main types of society. Globalization, he argues, is a dynamic process which seems to be producing a degree of convergence in systems of social protection across a great diversity of societies. At the same, even the wealthiest industrial nations remain potentially at risk of instability and destabilization. For this reason alone, they should also have vested interests in developing more effective international regulatory institutions.

III. Towards a Philosophy of Productive Welfare

Under the impact of globalization, some degree of value convergence is already taking place across the broad spectrum of different kinds of welfare state, or welfare society, regimes in the world today. The general trend is towards the middle ground of welfare pluralism. In democratic societies, however, it seems likely that significant differences will persist with regard to such issues as the balance that is struck regarding the division of formal welfare responsibilities between statutory and non-statutory agencies and, similarly, the division that is struck between formal social services and the informal networks of social care based on families and neighborhoods.

These differences will persist in democracies because elected governments must take account of the customary values and beliefs of their citizens, notably with regard to their views on the status of citizenship, the scope and limits of entitlements and responsibilities and the terms on which and the extent to which social services should act as agents of redistribution. Kuhnle (Chapter 4) for example, suggests that the idea of social entitlement as a right of citizenship is not deeply rooted in the political culture of Korea. This may well be the case at the present time but the concept of familial duty or obligation has always been a powerful factor in Korean society. It is also worth noting that, in recent years, western conceptualizations of the status of citizenship have begun to attach as much importance to its duties as to its rights.

At the informal levels of everyday life, familial and civic notions of obligation and entitlement change over time in response to the impact of external political, economic and social developments. Familial notions of obligation and entitlement can frequently conflict with the rights and duties of citizenship and the pursuit of more general national interests. When ordinary people lack confidence in the integrity of their governments, they are more likely to resort to forms of tax evasion and benefit fraud in defense of what they see as the best interests of their families.

At the same time, it is in the context of family life that we learn to accept restraints on our more selfish dispositions and show consideration for other people. We become moral beings as family members and through example and the lessons of experience. Familial altruism may be a limited form of altruism but it is the mainspring from which all our other moral concerns for other peoples' welfare flow. As we mature and become active citizens of a wider community, our notions of obligation and entitlement also grow more extensive and take on the character of social rights and duties.

This gradual extension in our range of social awareness is driven by a combination of egoistic and altruistic considerations. We learn from personal experience that familial altruism alone cannot guarantee our welfare in an uncertain world. We learn that collective forms of social provision—statutory and non-statutory—are sensible ways of pooling risks and helping each other in times of need. The compassion we feel for those less fortunate than ourselves is also an important factor but, as I once wrote, the welfare institutions of a society can best be understood in terms of "an unstable compromise between compassion and indifference, between altruism and self-interest" (Pinker 1971: 211).

Nevertheless, this growth in moral development from a familial to a civil awareness of our obligations and entitlements is most likely to occur in societies where some elements of the trust we repose in our closest relatives and friends extends outwards to the institutions of civil society and government. Trust grows only in social contexts where promises are kept, obligations are discharged and entitlements are met.

IV. Citizenship and Productive Welfare

The concept of citizenship, expressed in legal terms and sustained by popular sentiment and practice, will play a vitally important role in giving practical reality to the abstract principles of productive welfare philosophy.

The legal components of citizenship are already clearly set out in the constitution of the Republic of Korea, notably in the stipulations of Article 10. The welfare components of these constitutional rights, however, have not yet "been translated into real rights, because economic growth and development has consistently been prioritized over welfare" (Presidential Committee for Quality-of-Life 2000).

As Hyung Shik Kim points out, the concept of citizenship "as a mechanism for integrating the principles of market economy and welfare objectives" has long been a subject of debate among Korean policy makers and social policy scholars (Kim, H.- S. 2000). Apart from these economic and social considerations, the concept of citizenship is certain to have important implications for the future re-unification of North and South Korea.

The writings of T. H. Marshall stand out as having a significant relevance to the political, economic and social objectives of President Kim Dae-Jung's productive welfare program. Marshall developed a theory of welfare and citizenship that was explicitly pluralist in character and positive with regard to the roles of both competitive markets and statutory social services in the generation of welfare. In many respects, his approach to these issues has affinities with the values and aims of Korea's productive welfare policy plans. Marshall defined citizenship as "a status bestowed on those who are full members of a community. All who possess the status are equal with respect to the rights and duties with which the status is endowed" (Marshall and Bottomore 1992). Citizenship in this sense becomes a basis for social solidarity in Marshall's welfare theory.

Marshall identified three key elements in the status of citizenship. The first of these elements includes our civil rights and obligations with regard to "personal liberty, freedom of speech, thought and faith, the right to own property and to conclude valid contracts and the right to justice" (ibid.). Economic rights and obligations are, of course, intrinsic to this definition. The second of these elements is "the right to participate in the exercise of power" either as a voter or as a representative. The third element encompasses our social rights and obligations "to a modicum of economic welfare and security and to live the life of a civilized being according to the standards prevailing in the society" (ibid.).

Marshall's essay on Value Problems in Capitalism explored the problem of reconciling the claims of democracy, socialism and welfare in a free society (Marshall 1981). In contrast to Titmuss' unitary model of society, Marshall sets out a pluralist model of "democratic welfare capitalism" in which "the rights of citizenship inhibit the inegalitarian tendencies of the free economic market, but the market and some degree of economic inequality remain functionally necessary for the production of wealth and the preservation of political rights" (Pinker 1995: 119).

Marshall was in no doubt at all that the task of abolishing poverty must be "undertaken jointly by welfare and capitalism; there is no other way" (Marshall 1981). In Marshall's mixed economy of welfare the aims of collectivist social policies and the operation of competitive markets will, at times, conflict but in his view these "apparent inconsistencies are, in fact, a source of stability, achieved through a compromise that is not dictated by logic" (ibid.).

Marshall believed that economic, political and social rights all expressed different dimensions of welfare, and that it was not possible to go on extending any of these rights at the expense of the others without crossing the critical threshold at which the relationship between freedom and security becomes one of diminishing marginal utility (Pinker 1995).

Since Marshall's death in 1981, major policy changes have transformed the institutional map of British social welfare with the introduction of internal markets and purchaser/provider contracts within the statutory sector, the privatization of large sectors of the public services and the growth of occupational welfare schemes. Overall levels of public expenditure on the statutory social services, however, have remained high despite sustained efforts to contain and cut them. There has been a fundamental paradigm shift towards the pluralist middle ground between the extremes of collectivism and individualism.

There is no doubt that under the present Labour Government the state will continue to play a major role in the funding and the provision of social services. Nevertheless, it is equally certain that new kinds of public/private sector partnership will be encouraged and that the role of the private sector in the fields of pension provision, health care, housing and education will be expanded.

In the past, policy analysts like Titmuss supported the idea of the state as the main provider of social services because they were convinced that only the state could guarantee the social rights of citizenship. They believed that these rights could be guaranteed if they were embodied in statute law and delivered by governments that were accountable to their citizens in parliament and through the processes of democratic elections.

To a considerable degree these expectations have not been fulfilled. In Britain today, millions of elderly citizens have paid a lifetime of pension contributions only to find that, in their retirement, their incomes must be supplemented by selective means tested benefits. If they become so infirm that they require long-term community or residential care and cannot pay for it they must, again, submit to means tests of their incomes and capital assets before help can be provided.

Nevertheless, the expectations that are currently being invested in the occupational and private sector services may also remain unfulfilled with the passage of time. Occupational and private sector schemes are subject to the pressure of market forces. The value of investments and annuities can fall as well as rise. When they fall, members of such schemes receive lower retirement incomes than they originally expected.

V. Citizenship and Welfare Pluralism

As more of the social rights of citizenship become dependent on the integrity and efficiency of the non-governmental sector, governments will have to play a more assertive role as regulators and indirect guarantors of civil rights in market contexts. Citizens may enjoy more choice as purchasers of non-governmental social services but they will need easier access to impartial advice if they are to make wise and well-informed choices. In the 1980s and early 1990s, many British citizens received bad advice and were sold the wrong kinds of pensions. In recent years, the private pension sector has been subjected to much more stringent statutory regulation. The private sector pension industry has also had to strengthen its own self-regulatory mechanisms.

As welfare systems become more pluralist, they also become more dependent on non-governmental agencies as direct providers of social services. In the statutory welfare sector, the linkages between the status of citizenship and social rights are legally defined. Similar kinds of protection will have to be developed in the more volatile contexts of non-statutory market relationships if the rights of citizens as welfare consumers are to be adequately safeguarded. In such contexts, the principle of consumer sovereignty will be tested to its limits with regard to the rights of the poorest citizens who will always be the weakest bidders in competitive market contexts. And it is extremely questionable whether the private welfare sector will be able or willing to meet their needs at premiums that they can afford.

Korea's new model of productive welfare will be based on a pluralist network of public and private sector partnerships, its government will also have to assume a more pro-active regulatory role with regard to the non-statutory social services if the rights of citizens as consumers are to be adequately protected. It will also have to retain a substantial responsibility for meeting the welfare needs of its poorest citizens.

Writing in the 1960s and 1970s, Titmuss opposed the growth of the occupational and private welfare sectors on the grounds that non-statutory welfare agencies were an impediment to the kinds of income redistribution that he favored. He also criticized their lack of accountability to their policy holding customers and questioned the extent to which occupational based welfare schemes provided "both freedom of choice in welfare benefits (pensions, medical care and so forth) and a sense of participation in the organization and administration of the system" (Titmuss 1974: 141). These questions still have relevance to current debates about the ends and means of welfare pluralism, the status of citizenship and the degree to which the non-statutory welfare sector should be made accountable to government for the conduct of its business. Titmuss, however, was writing on these matters in the 1960s and early 1970s and he tended to assume that the integrity and accountability of government itself was both self-evident and beyond question. No such assumptions are made in today's political climate of general scepticism and disenchantment.

Insofar as Korea's model of productive welfare is based on a model of political as well as welfare pluralism, these issues of public confidence extend beyond the immediate concerns of social policy. Citizens need to be convinced that people who hold high office in government and the other institutions of civil society are held as accountable for their personal conduct as they themselves expect to be. Indeed, it can be argued that those people with the greatest access to power and influence are more likely to use their positions of authority for personal profit than anyone else. Consequently, their conduct should be subject to more rather than less public scrutiny.

Throughout the late 1980s and early 1990s, there was a marked increase in the level of public concern about the apparent decline in the standards of conduct in British public life. This crisis of confidence followed a series of high-profile cases in which Government office-holders and Members of Parliament were accused of exploiting their positions for personal financial gain (HMSO 1995: 106-107).

In 1994, the Government of the day responded to these concerns by setting up a Committee on Standards in Public Life. The Committee's terms of reference required it:

> To examine current concerns about standards of conduct of all holders of public office, including arrangements relating to financial and commercial activities, and make recommendations as to any changes in present arrangements which might be required to ensure the highest standards of propriety in public life.

For these purposes, public life should include: Ministers, civil servants and advisers; Members of Parliament and UK Members of the European Parliament; members and senior officers of all non-departmental public bodies and of national health service bodies; non-ministerial office holders; members and other senior offices of other bodies discharging publicly funded functions; and elected members and senior officers of local authorities" (HMSO 2001: 1).

In the following year, the Government appointed a Parliamentary Commissioner for Standards who was made responsible for monitoring the effectiveness of the Register of Members' Interests outside the House of Commons, advising the Parliamentary Select Committee on Standards and Privileges on all proprietorial matters relating to the disclosure of interests by Members of Parliament and investigating complaints about their conduct in cases where she believed such investigations were necessary.

In its First Report of 1995, the Committee on Standards in Public Life set out seven principles to be applied in determining where the boundaries of acceptable conduct should lie in public life. It also recommended that urgent remedial action should be taken to maintain and enforce these standards. The seven principles laid down were those of selflessness, integrity, objectivity, accountability, openness, honesty and leadership.

The Committee, however, went further than prescription and exhortation. It recommended that all public bodies throughout the United Kingdom should be required to prepare their own Codes of Conduct that incorporated the seven principles. They were also required to set up internal monitoring procedures and independent forms of scrutiny, designed to maintain and enforce these principles.

Since its establishment in 1994, the Committee has published seven reports covering its extensive enquiries across a wide range of British public institutions. Detailed comment on its findings and numerous recommendations is not possible in a short essay of this kind. Nevertheless, the clear and consistent message that comes through all of these reports is the Committee's insistence that the seven principles must be operationalized and incorporated into the daily practice of Government and other public institutions at all levels—and that there should be "appropriate penalties for failing to observe Codes of Conduct" (HMSO 2001: 10).

In addition to the formal institutions of central and local government, much of the day-to-day conduct of British public affairs is delegated to a variety of single purpose non-governmental and extra-governmental agencies which are wholly or largely publicly financed. They include quangos (quasi-autonomous non-governmental organizations) and other kinds of quasi-governmental agencies which play a major role in the day-to-day management and delivery of social and other public services.

As Butcher observes, this whole field of service provision "is surrounded by definitional uncertainty" and their steady growth has been widely criticized because they are insufficiently subject to "democratic accountability and control" (Butcher 1995). There are currently 5,750 such extra-governmental organizations in Britain today and they are responsible for spending over £50 billion of public money. The ultimate responsibility for the appointment of most of their non-elected members rests with Ministers.

The Committee on Standards has reviewed these arrangements and recommended that these appointments should be subject to closer independent scrutiny by a Commissioner for Public Appointments. A Commissioner was appointed in 1995. Vacant posts are now advertised and appointments are made on merit with conditions of greater 'transparency' and 'openness', Quangos fulfill many useful functions in the conduct of British public life but they are still widely criticized for their lack of accountability in an increasingly 'consumer-orientated' society (Dearlove and Saunders 2000). At the same time, it should be noted that most of these agencies recruit a proportion of their committee members from the general public. They offer considerable scope for the involvement of so-called ordinary citizens who want to become active in the conduct of public life.

Many other statutory and non-statutory bodies are involved in the regulation of British public life. The Audit Commission for Local Authorities and the National Health Service in England and Wales regulates stewardship and efficiency of these authorities. The Charity Commission undertakes similar duties with regard to the 187,000 registered charities in the United Kingdom. The Financial Services Authority regulates the activities of the occupational and private pensions, life insurance and investment industries. It also works closely with the various self-regulatory bodies of these industries. Disputes between policy holders and insurance companies that cannot be resolved at these levels of mediation may be referred to the offices of the Insurance Ombudsman.

In the more general field of civil rights, aggrieved citizens can appeal for remedy to statutory bodies like the Equal Opportunities Commission, the Commission for Racial Equality, the Health and Safety Commission and a diversity of other Tribunals that mediate disputes between citizens and service providers, employers and so forth.

Conversely, successive Conservative and Labour Governments have required the statutory social security agencies to enforce stricter checks on the incidence of benefit fraud. Labour's New Deal social welfare program includes a Benefits Integrity project designed to discover and sanction fraudulent claimants and to encourage genuinely needful citizens to claim benefits to which they are entitled. In 1997, benefit fraud was costing the Government and tax-payers in the region of £1.7 billion a year. The value of benefits not claimed by eligible citizens was in the region of £1.14 billion. The Inland Revenue now enforces stricter deadlines for the assessment and payment of income and other taxes and imposes financial penalties on individuals and companies that fail to meet these requirements.

The law and statutory forms of control and regulation have a vitally important role to play in the maintenance of social order and the conduct of public life. There are, however, some cogent reasons why these regulatory tasks ought not to be left exclusively to the agencies of government. First, governmental agencies do not possess the skills and competencies that are required to regulate all of the institutions of civil society. Secondly, whenever they attempt to do so, they soon acquire too much power and become oppressive, inefficient and unaccountable in the conduct of affairs. Thirdly, and most importantly, nations only become genuine democracies when their citizens become actively and continuously involved in running and regulating their own lives with a minimal degree of government intervention. Fourthly, democratic freedoms are most likely to flourish when as much regulation as possible is based on voluntary consent rather than the threat of legal sanctions.

This is not to deny that government will always have a vitally important role to play in the regulation of civil affairs. Indeed, throughout the nineteenth and twentieth centuries, there has been a steady growth in the powers and activities of the state affecting the institutions of civil society and the day-to-day lives of ordinary people. The growth has continued regardless of the political complexion of governments.

One of the few counterweights to this long-term trend towards centralization has been the parallel growth of self-regulatory bodies in British civil society. Self-regulation has developed most successfully in major industries like advertising, the press, aviation, insurance, gas, electricity and water, as well as in all the major professions. They regulate their activities and deal with complaints from members of the general public in accordance with the requirements of their own codes of ethical conduct. Many of them also appoint members of the general public to serve on their regulatory councils.

The history of nineteenth century political and social thought shows that all the great advocates of liberty warned against the rising tide of statutory encroachments on the institutions of civil society. They vested their hopes in the growth of intermediate self-regulatory and voluntary associations which would mediate between the state and the individual citizen and would prevent the undue concentration of power and influence in the hands of politicians and government bureaucrats.

The principles and practices of self-regulation have always occupied a central and distinctive place in the context of British civil society. The case for self-regulation rests on the premise that in complex democratic societies self-imposed rules are likely to carry a greater moral authority and, consequently, to work with greater effectiveness than externally imposed legal rules.

Self-regulation works well because it is accessible to everyone, rich and poor alike. It is generally fast and flexible in its conduct of business and it operates at no cost whatever to the government or tax payers. Nevertheless, since self-regulation depends on voluntary compliance it can only work effectively if its codes of ethical conduct are based on the civic traditions and customary values of the industries and occupations which it oversees and the general public which it serves and protects. Self-regulatory codes of conduct must be informed by the realities of everyday professional practice and the expectations of ordinary people. These practices and expectations are, in turn, underpinned by their attachment to more general principles of ethical conduct and formal doctrines of natural rights and obligations.

These formal doctrines may claim to have universal validity but the business of self-regulation is a highly practical activity. Regulators have to apply general principles—which often conflict with one another—to specific cases as they arise in specific societies, each of which are characterized by their own distinctive political and civil cultures. For these reasons, any society that decides to encourage the growth of self-regulatory institutions can learn much of benefit in general terms from the experience of other societies. It must, however, develop its codes of practice from the ethical components of its own distinctive culture.

We also need to remind ourselves that in democratic pluralist societies the opportunities for active civic participation in public life extend far beyond the boundaries of formal governmental and non-governmental institutions. In the contexts of social welfare, family members provide countless unpaid acts of care and support to each other, their friends and neighbors, without need or benefit of expert advice. Schools, churches, neighborhood associations and informal volunteer groups all have significant contributions to make in the renewal and enrichment of community life. At the same time, it is important to remember that pluralist societies are characterized by a high degree of cultural diversity. In seeking to nurture the growth of responsible citizenship and the bonds of social solidarity, it is vitally important—in the interests of personal freedom—to respect and tolerate these cultural differences. Too little social control leads to anarchy but too much control—notably at the informal levels of everyday life—produces new kinds of authoritarianism. As in the formal conduct of political and public life, we have to find middle way between extremes.

Finally, we must take account of current trends in the international economy. Over the past twenty years, as we have noted, the globalization of industrial production and trade has given rise to much speculation and uncertainty about the future development of national welfare states. This process of globalization is already beginning to undermine the economic sovereignty of independent nation states, the welfare expectations of their citizens and the institutional frameworks of interdependency and reciprocity through which these expectations are met.

The real challenge that faces governments throughout the global world of today is that they cannot guarantee the right to work for their citizens. Consequently, governments can only place on citizens an obligation to seek work and citizens, for their part, are obligated to demonstrate a genuine willingness to seek work and to accept the offer of a job if they are unemployed. This trend towards placing more emphasis on the obligations of citizenship than on its concomitant rights and entitlements has been given added momentum by the processes of economic globalization.

When sovereign nation states lose control over their own economic and political policies, their citizens are effectively disenfranchised. When international authorities are unable to regulate the free play of global market forces, we reach the point at which the gradual evolution of civil, political and social rights comes to a halt and then goes into reverse. Citizens, thereafter, will live as hostages to economic forces which neither they, nor their governments, control.

In the years ahead, it will not be possible to reconcile the imperatives of competitive market capitalism and social protection unless we are willing to sacrifice some elements of our national sovereignty and become more outward looking and inclusive in our thinking about the ends and means of social welfare policies. All the past challenges that we faced and the compromises that we reached in the creation of our national welfare states must be confronted and resolved again in the context of a global economy.

We have to find a new kind of global middle way between the extremes of competition and co-operation because: "we cannot pursue the philosopher's tone of market individualism without unravelling the delicate strands of interdependency that hold civil societies together. No can we give unqualified support to the collectivist ideologies of equality, fraternity and co-operation. If we neglect the imperatives of wealth creation, we will end with equal shares in poverty. Ideologies, like material goods and services, are subject to a law of diminishing returns. As with material goods and services, so with the doctrines of individualism and collectivism—and for the same reason—no single political ideology can encompass or reconcile the diversity of human principles and desires that find expression in the institutions of a free society" (Pinker 1995a: 113).

If we fail to resolve these issues at an international level, we will end by destroying the institutional frameworks of democratic citizenship and social protection that have taken us so long to build at the national levels of economic and social policy. If we succeed, we will begin making the global future into our future. We will stop treating the global economy as if it were a phenomenon driven by impersonal and unaccountable market forces. Given the necessary political will, these forces can be better regulated and made more accountable. But the exercise of prudent budgeting and responsible self-regulation must always begin at home in the context of independent nation states.

Finally, it needs to be emphasized that welfare expenditures and other social costs are not impedimenta to wealth creation. These forms of social protection were key elements in the structures of political order and solidarity which have made possible the continuous creation of wealth in competitive markets since the end of the nineteenth century. This positive association between competitive markets and social protection has been developed and sustained throughout the greater part of the twentieth century in the contexts of many sovereign nation states. The challenge facing us in the coming century is to make this mixed economy of work and welfare function more effectively in the context of a global economy, without detriment to the status of citizenship and the legitimate claims to social welfare associated with that status.

VI. Conclusion

In this essay, I have tried to describe what I consider to be the essential philosophical and institutional preconditions for the successful development of productive welfare policies or—for that matter—all other kinds of pluralist welfare policies, so I have given particular attention to the institutional and cultural foundations that must be firmly established before citizens will begin to trust in the integrity of their governments and, conversely, governments will begin to trust in the integrity of their citizens. I have also argued that democratic societies work best and democratic freedoms are most secure when legal sanctions and statutory regulations are complemented by an extensive measure of voluntary compliance and self-regulation on the part of individual citizens and the institutions of civil society.

I have made extensive reference to examples drawn from British experience in regulating the conduct of public life. In doing so I am mindful that, despite the impact of recent reforms, financial scandals and abuses of power and influence still occur from time to time across all the dimensions and levels of public life. And they will continue to do so because no regulatory system will ever be perfect. Nevertheless, I remain convinced that significant progress has been made in recent years and that the current state of affairs is much better than it would have been had these reforms not been implemented.

A welfare society—as distinct from a welfare state—is a society in which people assume a substantial degree of responsibility for their own welfare and the well-being of their families. These informal networks of concern and social care provide the moral and cultural foundation on which the formal structures of statutory and voluntary social services develop. Taken together, these interactive networks and structures make up the institutional elements of welfare pluralism and productive welfare. Although conflicts of interest and value frequently arise between these institutional elements they are, in the last analysis, dependent upon each other. The welfare of many individuals and families would be jeopardized if statutory social services were to disappear. Conversely, the statutory social services could not compensate for or provide adequate substitutes if the structures of familial altruism ceased functioning.

It is an encouraging portent for the future development of Korea's productive welfare model that it makes provision for building closer partnerships between its statutory and non-statutory social services.

References

Butcher, T. (1996) *Delivering Welfare: The Governance of the Social Services in the 1990s*. Buckingham: Open University Press.

Dearlove, J. and Saunders, P. (2000) *Introduction to British Politics*. Cambridge: Polity Press.

HMSO (1995) Volume I. Report, Committee on Standards in Public Life. London, Cm 2850-1.

_____ (2001) *The First Seven Reports: A Review of Progress*. London, available only on http://www.public_standards.gove.uk/stocktakerep/stock01a.htm.

Kim, H.- S. (2000) "Competing Strategies for Integrating Communist and Capitalist Social Welfare Systems of North and South Korea," Korea National College of Rehabilitation and Welfare, Kyunggi-Do, Korea, mimeo.

Kim, S. K. (2001) "A Precondition for Productive Welfare." Paper presented at the International Symposium for Sharing Productive Welfare Experience, Seoul, Korea.

Marshall, T. H.(1950) *Citizenship and Social Class and Other Essays*. Cambridge: Cambridge University Press.

_____ (1981) *The Right to Welfare*. London: Heinemann Educational Books.

Marshall, T. H,. and Bottomore, T. (1992) *Citizenship and Social Class*. London: Pluto Press.

Pinker, R. (1971) *Social Theory and Social Policy*. London: Heinemann Educational Books.

_____ (1993) "Social policy in the Post-Titmuss era" in R. Page and J. Baldock (eds). *Social Policy Review 5*, Social Policy Association, University of Kent, Canterbury.

_____ (1995) "T. H. Marshall" in V. George and R. Page (eds) *Modern Thinkers on Welfare*. London: Prentice Hall / Harvester Wheatsheaf.

_____ (1995a) "Golden Ages and Welfare Alchemists." *Social Policy and Administration*, 29 (2).

Presidential Committee for Quality-of-Life (2000) *D. J. Welfarism*. Republic of Korea Office of the President, Seoul, Korea.

Scott, J. (2001) *Living Economy*. London: Reuters / Pearson Education.

Titmuss, R. M. (1974) *Social Policy: An Introduction*. London: George Allen and Unwin.

Part II

Aspects of Public Policy and the New Welfare Paradigm

7

Korea's Pro-Poor Economic Growth

Nanak Kakwani and Hyun Hwa Son

President Kim Dae-Jung has articulated productive welfare as "an ideology, as well as a policy, that seeks to secure minimum standard of living for all people." The theme of this paper is pro-poor growth, which is somewhat consistent with the idea of productive welfare in the sense that the people, who do not enjoy the socially accepted minimum standard of living, should be able to share the benefits of economic growth proportionally more or at least no less than the rest of the society. This chapter attempts to answer the questions: Is economic growth in Korea pro-poor? And if so, what is its degree? How does Korea compare with Thailand in terms of its degree of pro-poorness? The chapter also develops a regression model that can be used to forecast the incidence of poverty on the basis of information on growth rate per capita GDP and unemployment rate.

I. Introduction

Until the financial crisis in 1997, the Korean economy had been perceived as one of the fastest growing economies in South East Asia. Its growth of per capita real GDP surpassed an annual rate of more than five percent during the period of 1990-97. Along with high economic growth, Korea is also known as the economy with relatively equal distribution of income and with full employment. Before 1997, inequality had declined gradually, while the rate of unemployment had been only two to three percent. This seemingly sound economic outlook was shattered by the financial crisis in 1997.

The adverse effect of the crisis had been widespread throughout the economy. The unprecedented rate of economic growth for the past three decades turned into negative: per capita real GDP declined at the rate of 7.6 percent in 1998. Unemployment surged to 6.8 percent in the same year. As the economy slowed down substantially, the unemployment rate increased and many people were pushed into poverty. The incidence of poverty jumped dramatically from 8.6 percent in 1997 to 19 percent in 1998. Coupled with poverty, the crisis also precipitated worsening inequality in the society.

In some sense the economic crisis has been a blessing in disguise. Prior to the crisis, the government of Korea gave a high priority to economic growth that was deemed to enhance welfare of the people. In order to accomplish this objective, the government emphasized the importance of macro policy management such as stable low inflation and promoting domestic and foreign investment. This emphasis seems to be shifting towards achieving a more equitable economic growth that would benefit all Koreans.

President Kim Dae-Jung has proposed a policy called productive "welfarism." He defines productive welfare as "an ideology, as well as a policy, that seeks to secure minimum living standards for all people, while expanding opportunities for self-support in socio-economic activities for the purpose of maintaining human dignity" (Presidential Committee for Quality-of-Life 2000, Chapter 3).

A major focus of productive welfare lies on enhancing the people's standard of living through aspiring both equity and efficiency objectives. An equity objective or an equitable distribution of wealth establishes a basic framework that ensures that every individual in the society is able to enjoy his or her minimum level of standard of living. Equally important, this minimum standard of living can be sustained or uplifted by means of stable economic growth that generates employment opportunities and constant income sources. In this respect, productive welfare puts an equal importance to both growth and equity. More importantly, productive welfare can make a significant contribution to mitigating the adverse effect of the crisis and thus to strengthening social integration. Further, the idea of productive welfare is somewhat consistent with the theme of our paper, pro-poor growth, in the sense that the ultimate goal of productive welfare is to achieve a society, of which the disadvantaged group of people can share the benefits of economic growth proportionally more than or at least no less than their counterpart.

The prime objective of this study is to know whether the Korean economic growth has (or has not) been pro-poor for the last decade. A view held widely in development economics is that the benefits of rapid economic growth rates diffuse automatically across all segments of society. This trickle-down theory implies that the rich become richer and after a while the poor also will benefit from the increased wealth in society. In this view, the poor tend to benefit indirectly from economic growth. The benefits of economic growth accruing to the poor are likely to be proportionally less than the benefits accruing to the rich. However, by the early 1970s this trickle-down myth had proven to be insufficient for presenting ways to reduce poverty. Today pro-poor growth, advocating proportionally more benefits to the poor than to the rich, is becoming a major factor in poverty reduction strategies of the international development organizations (ADB 1999).

This chapter attempts to answer the questions: Is economic growth in Korea pro-poor? And if so, what is its degree? How does Korea compare with Thailand in terms of its degree of pro-poorness? The chapter also develops a regression model that can be used to forecast the incidence of poverty on the basis of information on growth rate per capita GDP and unemployment rate.

The chapter is organized in the following manner. Section II looks into the relationship between economic growth, measured in per capita real GDP and standard of living. Sections III and IV describe trends in inequality and poverty respectively in the 1990s. The next section, Section V, defines pro-poor growth and develops an index that would measure the degree of pro-poor growth. Section VI presents an empirical analysis of the nature of economic growth in Korea and Section VII presents a regression model that explains the incidence of poverty in terms of macroeconomic indicators. This model is then used to forecast the incidence of poverty in the second quarter of 2000 to the first quarter of 2001. Finally, Section VIII gives some concluding remarks.

II. GDP Growth and Average Standard of Living

The growth rate of per capita Gross Domestic Product (GDP) is commonly used to evaluate a country's economic performance. It is true that GDP per capita is an important determinant of welfare on the grounds that the levels of consumption or our demands for goods and services are closely related to the economy's output capacity. It does not necessarily imply, nevertheless, that a high growth in per capita GDP means higher welfare. A conventional measure of GDP excludes many factors that contribute to economic welfare while incorporating other factors that have adverse effects on welfare. More importantly, aggregate output measures are completely insensitive to the distribution of welfare among individuals in the society. As such, GDP per capita should be used as an indirect measure of people's standard of living.

Economic welfare can be directly measured by utilizing household surveys that in general provide information on households' incomes and consumption expenditures. There are two approaches to the measurement of individual welfare. One approach is based on income, deemed the major resource for each individual to consume goods and services in the market economy. The other approach is related to the standard of living, measured by current consumption expenditure. If economic welfare is viewed as an indicator of the standard of living, consumption enjoyed by the people in the current period will be a better measure of individual welfare. Moreover, as advocated by the permanent income hypothesis, consumption tends to exhibit a stable trend over time through savings and borrowings.

In measuring economic welfare, it is important to take into account different needs of each individual belonging to a household. Since households vary according to their size and composition, their needs are expected to be different. Hence, the measurement of individual welfare should reflect different needs of individuals.

Suppose that x_i is the per capita income (or consumption expenditure) of the ith household and z_i is the household specific poverty line, which was obtained from the minimum cost of living study conducted in 1994 by the Korean Institute of Health and Social Affairs as given in Bark (1994). Kakwani and Prescott (1999) have updated the poverty line estimates on the basis of appropriate consumer price indices for different years. Then, it is possible to define the welfare of the ith household as $y_i = 100$, which takes any value greater than zero. This measure of welfare can be interpreted as the percentage of excess income (or expenditure) the ith household has over its poverty line. If y_i is less than 100, then the ith household is identified as poor and zero otherwise.

Table 7-1 presents three alternative measures of average standard of living covering the period from 1990 to 2000. The per capita real GDP was estimated using the Korean National Accounts data in conjunction with the population projections. The second measure is the per capita household real expenditure, which was estimated from the Korea's Family Income and Expenditure Surveys (FIES), which are conducted quarterly every year. The yearly figures of per capita household real expenditures were calculated as the average of four quarters in every year. The real expenditure from each quarterly survey was estimated by adding the real expenditure on ten items of consumption which included food; housing; clothing and footwear; furniture and utensils; utilities including fuel, light and water charges; education; culture and recreation; health; transport and communication; and other consumption expenditure including tobacco and personal care. The third measure of average standard of living is the average per person welfare, which was obtained by weighted average of per person welfare with weight proportion to the population. Recall that individual welfare, which was estimated by dividing the per capita household expenditure by the household's poverty line, takes into account different household needs and therefore is a better measure of average welfare than the per capita real expenditure.

All these three measures tell us that people's standard of living had been improving rapidly during the period between 1990 and 1996. It is interesting to note that there was a sign of slowdown in 1996-97 before the economic crisis actually started. While both real consumption and welfare per capita have virtually become steady during 1996-97, real GDP per capita increased relatively by a larger magnitude. In the crisis period, 1997-98, all the three measures show a substantial fall in the average standard of living although the fall in per capita real GDP is much less than in the other two measures of standard of living. During the post-crisis period, all measures indicate that people's standard of living started to improve but at different degree. In 1999, GDP per capita recovered and even exceeded its pre-crisis period, whereas real consumption and welfare per capita were still far below compared to their pre-crisis levels. Based on indicators—including high unemployment and worsened inequality and poverty, it seems that people's living standards have not been fully restored at the pre-crisis level.

Table 7-1
Average Standard of Living in Korea

Year	Per capita Real GDP	Per capita Real exp	Per capita Welfare Percent
1990	1394	229	134
1991	1534	253	146
1992	1596	279	160
1993	1675	296	168
1994	1801	316	180
1995	1955	339	191
1996	2072	369	208
1997	2109	371	209
1998	1955	304	173
1999	2157	340	193
2000	2345	388*	218*

*Estimated from the regression model.

Figure 7-1
Per Capita Real GDP

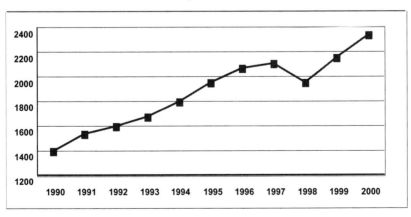

III. Inequality in Korea

Concerning income inequality in Korea, there have been numerous studies that have produced widely conflicting conclusions. The major problem underlying this inconsistency is due mainly to the non-availability of data on incomes for non-wage and non-salary earners. Many researchers have attempted to estimate the income of employer and self-employed household heads but these attempts have lead to conflicting results because of the different assumptions made by them. In our study, per capita consumption expenditure is utilized to compute inequality in the 1990s.

Figure 7-2
Per Capita Real Consumption

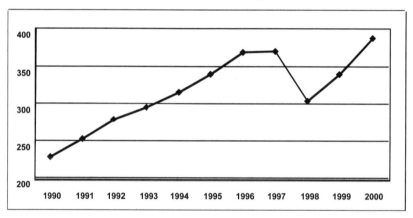

Figure 7-3
Per Capita Welfare

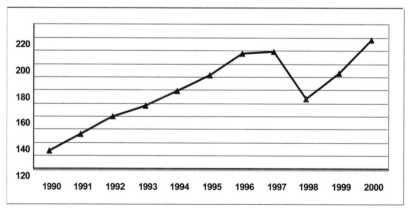

Table 7-2
Growth Rates of Per Capita Standard of Living: Korea

Year	Per capita Real GDP	Per capita Real Exp	Per capita Welfare Percent
1991	9.6	9.8	8.9
1992	4.0	9.8	8.7
1993	4.8	5.8	5.0
1994	7.3	6.7	6.7
1995	8.2	7.1	6.4
1996	5.8	8.4	8.3
1997	1.8	0.5	0.5
1998	- 7.6	- 19.8	- 18.7
1999	9.8	11.0	10.8
2000	8.4	13.4*	12.2*

* Estimated from the regression model.

Figure 7-4
Growth Rates of Average Standard of Living

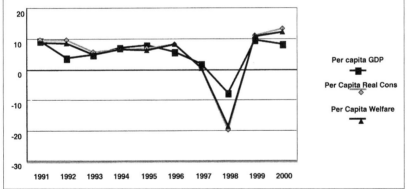

Table 7-3
Gini Index and Quintile Shares

Year	Gini	Quintile1	Quintile2	Quintile3	Quintile4	Quintile5
1990	29.0	9.4	13.4	16.8	21.6	38.8
1991	28.7	9.4	13.5	17.0	21.7	38.4
1992	29.0	9.2	13.5	17.0	21.6	38.7
1993	28.3	9.4	13.6	17.1	21.8	38.1
1994	28.3	9.4	13.6	17.2	21.7	38.1
1995	28.0	9.5	13.6	17.2	21.9	37.8
1996	28.7	9.4	13.5	17.0	21.7	38.5
1997	27.9	9.5	13.7	17.2	21.7	37.8
1998	28.5	9.2	13.6	17.2	22.0	38.0
1999	29.1	9.1	13.4	17.1	21.9	38.5

In our study, we use the Gini index to estimate inequality. The Gini index is the most commonly used method of measuring inequality. As shown in Table 7-3 and Figure 7-5, inequality in Korea had been gradually declining until 1997. Since 1997, inequality has continued to increase sharply, with the Gini index reaching a highest level at 29.1 percent in 1999. In 1999, as indicated in Figure 7-6, the share of the bottom 20 percentage of population has been declining until 1997 and since then has been increasing. It means that the economic crisis hurt the poor proportionally more than the rich.

IV. Incidence of Poverty in Korea

The present study utilized the Minimum Cost of Living (MCL) basket developed in 1994 by the Korean Institute for Health and Social Affairs (KIHASA) as the poverty line. Kakwani and Prescott (2000) modified this poverty line in order to take account of different costs of living between Seoul and other cities. The poverty line was updated for other years using the separate consumer price indices for Seoul and other cities.

It must be emphasized that we have used Korean specific poverty line, which measures the minimum acceptable standard of living in Korea. Therefore, the incidence of poverty computed here cannot be compared with the incidence of poverty in other countries. Our main objective here is to analyze changes in poverty and how it has been affected by the economic growth in Korea.

We estimate poverty based on consumption. We compute the three most widely used poverty measures, namely, head count ratio, poverty gap ratio, and Foster-Greer-Thorbecke (1984) index. While the head count ratio simply computes the percentage of poor living below the poverty line, the other two measures calculate the depth and the severity of poverty after taking into account the distribution of consumption among the poor.

Figure 7-5
Gini Index: Urban Households

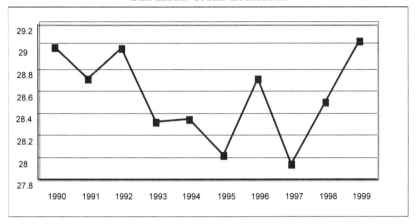

Figure 7-6
Consumption Share of the Bottom 20 Percent Population

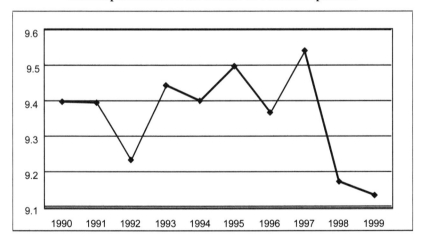

As presented in Table 7-4, poverty declined sharply between 1990 and 1997. For instance, the percentage of poor dropped dramatically from 39.6 percent in 1990 to 8.6 percent in 1997. The crisis, however, pushed a number of people down to poverty and led to 19 and 13.4 percentage of poor in 1998 and 1999, respectively. Although the head count ratio improved substantially in 1999, it was far higher than its pre-crisis level.

Table 7-4
Poverty Incidence: Korea

	Actual Incidence			Annual Growth Rate		
Year	Percentage of poor	Poverty gap ratio	Severity of pov index	Percentage of poor	Poverty gap ratio	Severity of pov index
1990	39.6	9.6	3.4	-	-	-
1991	31.3	7.1	2.4	-23.4	-30.5	-33.9
1992	24.5	5.4	1.8	-24.7	-27.9	-31.2
1993	20.5	4.2	1.3	-17.7	-25.0	-29.0
1994	16.5	3.2	1.0	-21.5	-25.5	-29.7
1995	12.7	2.4	0.7	-26.7	-29.8	-31.3
1996	9.6	1.8	0.5	-27.5	-30.0	-30.0
1997	8.6	1.6	0.5	-10.7	-11.2	-14.1
1998	19.0	4.2	1.5	78.8	97.2	115.3
1999	13.4	2.7	0.9	-34.7	-42.5	-50.1
2000	8.38*	1.48*	0.44*	-47.2	-62.0	-70.9

* Estimated from the regression model.

Since we did not have the survey data for the year 2000, we estimated the poverty incidence for 2000 using the regression model, presented in Section VII. Given the quarterly growth and unemployment rates, we estimated the percentage of poor in the year 2000 as 8.38 percent, which is lower than its pre-crisis level. Similarly, the poverty gap ratio and severity of poverty index were estimated to be 1.48 and 0.44, respectively. Thus, we can say that the incidence of poverty in Korea is now lower than its pre-crisis level.

It is noteworthy that the rate of reduction in poverty slowed down considerably during the 1996-97 period, when the percentage of poor decreased by only 10.7 percent compared to a reduction of 27.5 percent in the previous year. The same story emerges from the other two poverty measures. These results suggest that there did exist signs of a forthcoming crisis one year earlier, which was not picked up in time.

V. What is Pro-Poor Growth?

The relationship between economic growth and poverty has been studied extensively. A large amount of cross-country evidence suggests that growth and poverty reduction are strongly positively correlated. The countries that have experienced high growth over a sustained period have made a greater reduction in poverty. This result is consistent with the "trickle down" theory that some benefits of growth will always trickle down to the poor. Thus, the incidence of poverty can diminish with growth even if the poor receive only a small fraction of the total benefits.

Figure 7-7
Percentage of Poor in Korea

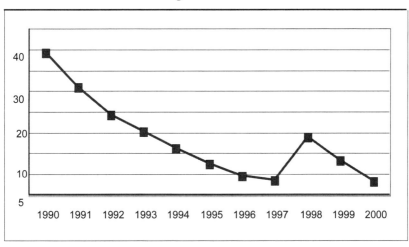

Pro-poor growth requires a strategy that is deliberately biased in favor of the poor so that the poor benefit proportionally more than the rich. Such an outcome would rapidly reduce the incidence of poverty. The trickle-down development also reduces poverty but the rate of poverty reduction may be much slower. It is the slowness of poverty reduction that has generated interest in the concept of " pro-poor growth."

The degree of poverty depends on two factors: average income and income inequality. The increase in average income reduces poverty and the increase in inequality increases it. Economic growth increases average income (or consumption), but at the same time an increasing or decreasing inequality may accompany it. An increase (decrease) in inequality implies that the proportional benefits received by the poor are less (more) than those by the non-poor. Thus, growth is pro-poor when it is accompanied by a reduction in inequality.

To make the concept of pro-poor growth operational, we need to choose a measure of inequality. The Gini index is a widely used measure of inequality. Unfortunately, there exists no monotonic relationship between changes in the Gini index and poverty reduction. With mean income remaining the same, an increase or a decrease in the Gini index can still leave poverty unchanged. Similarly, poverty can increase or decrease without any change in either mean income or the Gini index. Thus, changes in the Gini index cannot always tell whether or not growth has been pro-poor. As a matter of fact, none of single measures of inequality proposed in the literature can be used to measure the degree of pro-poor growth.

The Lorenz curve is widely used to analyze inequality in the size distribution of income. It can be easily established that there is a monotonic relationship between changes in the Lorenz curve and poverty reduction. If the entire Lorenz curve shifts towards the egalitarian line, then poverty will always reduce even if the mean income does not change. Thus, the Lorenz curve provides a criterion for measuring the degree of pro-poor growth. Growth is pro-poor if the entire Lorenz curve shifts towards the egalitarian line. The major difficulty with the Lorenz curve is that it may not provide an unambiguous measure of pro-poorness of growth. In practice, we may have a situation, when we cannot say whether growth has been pro-poor.

Kakwani and Pernia (2000) have developed an index of pro-poor growth, which is tailored to any specific poverty measure. It is based on a decomposition of total change in poverty into (i) the impact of growth when the distribution of income does not change, and (ii) the impact of income redistribution when total income does not change.

Suppose η is the poverty elasticity with respect to growth, which is defined as the proportional change in poverty when there is a positive growth rate of 1 percent. η can be decomposed into two components, η_g and η_I such that

$$\eta = \eta_g + \eta_I \qquad (1)$$

where η_g is the pure growth effect and η_I is the inequality effect. η_g is the proportional change in poverty when the distribution of income does not change, whereas η_I is the proportional change in poverty when inequality changes in the absence of growth. η_g will always be negative, when growth rate is positive because positive growth always reduces poverty, with distribution remaining constant. η_I can be either negative or positive depending on whether change in inequality accompanying growth reduces or increases poverty. Growth will obviously be pro-poor if η_I is negative. Thus the degree of pro-poor growth can be measured by an index

$$\phi = \eta/\eta_g \qquad (2)$$

ϕ will be greater than 1 when $\eta_1 < 0$. Thus, growth will be pro-poor when $\phi > 1$, meaning that the poor benefit proportionally more than the non-poor, i.e., growth results in a redistribution in favor of the poor. This would be the first-best outcome. When $0 < \phi < 1$, growth is not strictly pro-poor (i.e. growth results in a redistribution against the poor) even though it still reduces poverty incidence. This situation may be generally characterized as "trickle-down" growth. If $\phi < 0$, economic growth actually leads to an increase in poverty. This situation may be characterized as "immiserizing" growth (Bhagwati 1988).

During a recession, the observed growth rate is negative, resulting in an increase in the incidence of poverty, which means that η is positive and so is η_g. If there were no income redistribution due to recession, the incidence of poverty would increase by η_g percent (due to an one percentage decline in the growth rate), whereas the actual increase in poverty is η percent. Thus, the recession will be pro-poor if $\eta < \eta_g$ and pro-rich if $\eta > \eta_g$. This implies that the recession will be pro-poor if $\phi < 1$ and pro-rich if $\phi > 1$.

Index ϕ measures how the benefits of growth are distributed across the population. Suppose g is the growth rate and θ is a poverty measure, the proportional change in poverty may be written as

$$\frac{\Delta\theta}{\theta} = f(g,\phi) \qquad (3)$$

which implies that there are two factors that determine a country's performance in poverty reduction. First is the growth rate g, which affects the mean income of society and second factor relates to the distribution of benefits of economic growth, which is measured by the pro-poor index ϕ. Obviously, the growth rate alone is not sufficient to achieve a maximum reduction in poverty. It may, of course, be necessary.

To determine $f(g, \phi)$, we introduce the idea of poverty equivalent growth rate $g*$ which is defined as the growth rate that will result in the same level of proportional poverty reduction as the present growth rate with no change in income inequality, i.e. when everyone receives the same proportional benefits of growth. It is obvious that $g*$ will be given by

$$f(g*, 1) = f(g, \phi) \qquad (4)$$

noting that $\phi = 1$, when everyone receives the same proportional benefits. From (1), we write

$$\frac{\Delta\theta}{\theta} = f(g,\phi) = g\,\eta$$

and

$$f(g*, 1) = \eta_g g*$$

which in view of (4) immediately gives

$$g^* = g \ \phi \qquad (5)$$

It is the poverty equivalent growth rate that controls for how equitable growth rate is. This suggests that the performance of a country should be judged on the basis of poverty equivalent growth rate and not by growth rate alone. Maximizing g^* will be equivalent to maximizing the total proportional reduction in poverty.

For instance, if a country's growth rate is nine percent and pro-poor index is two-thirds, then its effective growth rate in terms of poverty reduction is only six percent. If the same country achieves its growth rate of nine percent but the proportional benefits going to the poor are more than the non-poor, in which case, suppose ϕ is 1.2, then the effective growth rate will be 10.8.

Therefore, a rapid poverty reduction can be achieved by maximizing g^* (or $g\phi$) but not g alone.

VI. Is Korean Economic Growth Pro-Poor?

The results in Table 7-5 illustrate that economic growth in Korea has generally been highly pro-poor, as indicated by the pro-poor index with most of the values close to or greater than one. It is noteworthy that in 1996-97 the index shot up to 5.1 for the headcount ratio. This is the period when economic growth began to slow down sharply but the incidence of poverty continued to fall markedly. This is because the distribution of consumption became more equal, contributing to a reduction of 4.8 percent in the percentage of poor. During the crisis in 1997-98, the pro-poor growth index for the headcount ratio was 1.2, suggesting that the poor were proportionally more adversely affected than the non-poor. What is more, the values of the pro-poor growth index for the poverty gap and severity of poverty were 1.3 and 1.4, respectively, implying that the ultra poor suffered proportionally even more during the crisis period.

Table 7-6 presents actual as well as poverty equivalent growth rates for Korea. Before the crisis, poverty equivalent growth rates were higher than actual growth rates for most of time period. In particular, the poverty equivalent growth rate of nine percent in 1996-97 was far higher than the actual growth rate of 1.8 percent in that same period (Figure 7-8) suggesting that the poor benefited proportionally much more than the rich, which resulted in a larger percentage reduction in poverty than what is indicated by the actual growth rate.

Table 7-5
Pro-Poor Growth Index for Korea

	Elasticity	Growth	Inequality	Index
		Poverty Explained by Pro-Poor		
		Percentage of poor		
90-91	-2.4	-2.2	-0.3	1.1
91-92	-6.2	-6.0	-0.2	1.0
92-93	-3.7	-3.0	-0.6	1.2
93-94	-3.0	-3.0	0.0	1.0
94-95	-3.3	-2.7	-0.5	1.2
95-96	-4.7	-5.4	0.6	0.9
96-97	-6.0	-1.2	-4.8	5.1
97-98	-10.4	-8.7	-1.7	1.2
98-99	-3.5	-3.6	0.1	0.98
		Poverty gap ratio		
90-91	-3.2	-2.9	-0.3	1.1
91-92	-7.0	-7.6	0.5	0.9
92-93	-5.2	-3.8	-1.4	1.4
93-94	-3.5	-3.5	0.0	1.0
94-95	-3.7	-3.1	-0.5	1.2
95-96	-5.2	-6.0	0.9	0.9
96-97	-6.3	-1.3	-5.0	4.7
97-98	-12.8	-9.7	-3.1	1.3
98-99	-4.3	-4.0	-0.3	1.07
		Severity of poverty		
90-91	-3.5	-3.4	-0.2	1.0
91-92	-7.9	-8.6	0.7	0.9
92-93	-6.0	-4.2	-1.8	1.4
93-94	-4.1	-3.9	-0.1	1.0
94-95	-3.8	-3.5	-0.3	1.1
95-96	-5.2	-6.6	1.4	0.8
96-97	-8.0	-1.5	-6.5	5.4
97-98	-15.2	-10.6	-4.7	1.4
98-99	-5.1	-4.4	-0.7	1.17

After the crisis, actual growth rates have become higher than poverty equivalent growth rates. This implies that the poor have been more adversely affected by the crisis, and that even if there was a positive growth in 1998-99, its benefits did not go to the poor proportionally more than to the non-poor. If we measure poverty by the poverty gap ratio and severity of poverty index, we find that the poverty equivalent growth rate in 1998-99 is higher than the actual growth rate, which suggests that the ultra-poor benefited more than the poor. This could have happened because in response to the economic crisis, the Korean government introduced many welfare programs including public works program, which might have helped the ultra poor more than the poor or the non-poor.

Table 7-6
Actual and Equivalent Growth Rates: Korea

| Period | Actual Growth Rate | Equivalent Growth Rate | | |
		Percentage of Poor	Poverty Gap Ratio	Severity of Poverty Ratio
90-91	9.6	10.7	10.4	10.0
91-92	4.0	4.1	3.7	3.6
92-93	4.8	5.8	6.6	6.8
93-94	7.3	7.2	7.3	7.5
94-95	8.2	9.7	9.5	8.9
95-96	5.8	5.1	5.0	4.6
96-97	1.8	9.0	8.3	9.6
97-98	-7.6	-9.0	-10.0	-10.9
98-99	9.8	9.6	10.5	11.5

Figure 7-8
Actual and Equivalent Growth Rates: Korea

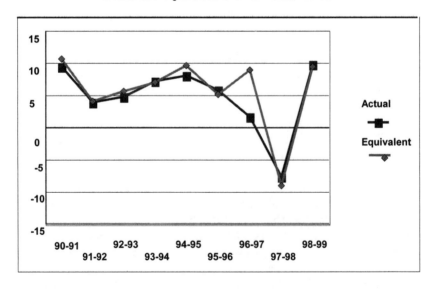

In comparison with Korea, we look at the case of Thailand. Thailand achieved remarkable economic growth over the two decades prior to the Asian financial crisis. The consequence was a rapid decline in the incidence of poverty. However, the pace of poverty reduction would have been much faster if income distribution had improved or at least not worsened (Table 7-7). For instance, had inequality stayed constant between 1988 and 1990, a 1 percent growth in the economy would have reduced the incidence of poverty by 3.25 percent or better, but the actual reduction in poverty was only around one percent. The corresponding value of the pro-poor growth index was about 0.3. Nevertheless, it is commendable that the pro-poor growth index increased markedly to 0.64 for the headcount ratio in 1994-96, the period before the crisis.

Table 7-7
Growth and Inequality Components and Pro-Poor Index: Thailand

| Period | Elasticity | Poverty Explained by | | Pro-Poor Index |
		Growth	Inequality	
		Percent of Poor		
88-90	-0.99	-3.25	2.26	0.31
90-92	-1.08	-3.77	2.69	0.29
92-94	-2.29	-3.96	1.68	0.58
94-96	-3.12	-4.88	1.75	0.64
96-98	-6.50	-4.74	-1.76	1.37
		Poverty Gap Ratio		
88-90	-1.46	-4.50	3.04	0.33
90-92	-1.10	-4.85	3.75	0.23
92-94	-2.97	-5.20	2.23	0.57
94-96	-3.61	-5.77	2.16	0.63
96-98	-7.59	-5.96	-1.63	1.27
		Severity of Poverty		
88-90	-1.77	-5.27	3.50	0.34
90-92	-1.12	-5.56	4.44	0.20
92-94	-3.38	-5.87	2.49	0.58
94-96	-4.04	-6.42	2.38	0.63
96-98	-8.38	-6.61	-1.77	1.27

In the aftermath of the financial crisis that erupted in mid-1997, the high positive growth rates achieved by the Thai economy prior to 1996 reversed sharply into negative growth in 1998 (Table 7-8). Consequently, the monotonic improvement in the poverty incidence achieved until 1996 halted abruptly, and the number of poor increased from 11.4 percentage of the total population in 1996 to about 13 percent in 1998. Did the economic crisis hurt the poor more than the non-poor? The results in Table 7-8 show that if the crisis were inequality-neutral, one percentage reduction in per capita income would have increased the percentage of poor by 4.74 percent, but the actual increase was 6.5 percent, which resulted in a pro-poor growth index of 1.37. Thus, the economic crisis adversely affected the poor proportionally more than the non-poor.

Table 7-8
Actual and Equivalent Growth Rates: Thailand

| | Actual | Equivalent Growth Rate | | |
Period	Growth Rate	Percent of Poor	Poverty Gap Ratio	Severity of Poverty Ratio
88-90	9.1	2.8	2.9	3.0
90-92	7.5	2.1	1.7	1.5
92-94	7.7	4.4	4.4	4.4
94-96	5.7	3.7	3.6	3.6
96-98	-1.0	-1.4	-1.3	-1.3

Unlike Korea, economic growth in Thailand has not been pro-poor. This can be clearly seen in Table 7-8 and Figure 7-9. The poverty equivalent growth rates have always been lower than actual growth rates, implying that although Thailand achieved high economic growth in the 1990s, the benefits going to the poor were proportionally much less than to the non-poor. However, the difference between the two growth rates has become increasingly narrower over time indicating that the economic growth has become increasingly more pro-poor particularly in the period after 1996.

Figure 7-9
Actual and Equivalent Growth Rates: Thailand

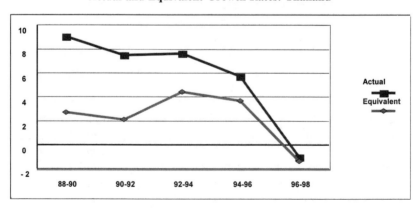

On the whole, both Korea and Thailand had high economic growth in the 1990s before the crisis. Nevertheless, the Korean economic growth generated proportionally more benefits to the poor than to the non-poor, whereas the Thai economic growth benefited the non-poor proportionately more the poor.

VII. What Determines Poverty?

Due to the economic crisis, the growth rate of per capita GDP in 1998 became –7.6 and at the same time unemployment rate increased almost three fold from 2.7 percent in 1997 to 6.8 percent in 1998 (Table 7-9). If the labor force participation had not declined during the crisis period, the unemployment rate would have been much worse. These adverse macroeconomic indicators reflected an immediate increase in the percentage of poor from 8.6 percent in 1997 to 19 percent in 1998. This section explores the question: To what degree can the growth in per capita GDP and unemployment rate explain the incidence of poverty?

We propose a simple regression model in which the dependent variable is the logarithm of poverty incidence (log PI) and the explanatory variables include the log of per capita real GDP ($log(PCGDP)$), the log of the rate of unemployment ($log(u)$), and a quarterly dummy variable (D_i) that captures seasonal effects. The proposed model is

$$\log(PI) = \alpha_0 + \alpha_1 \log(PCGDP) + \alpha_2 \log(u) + \beta \sum_{i=1}^{4} D_i + \varepsilon$$

Table 7-9
Unemployment and Labor Force Participation Rates

Year	Unemployment Rate	Labor Force Parti Rate
1990	2.4	60.0
1991	2.3	60.6
1992	2.4	60.9
1993	2.8	61.1
1994	2.4	61.7
1995	2.2	61.9
1996	2.0	62.0
1997	2.7	62.0
1998	6.8	60.7
1999	6.4	60.6
2000	4.1	N/A

Figure 7-10
Unemployment Rate: Korea

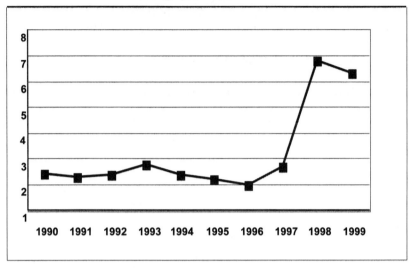

Figure 7-11
Labor Force Participation Rate

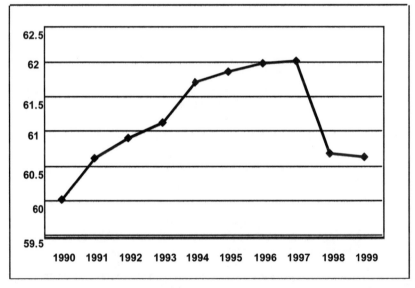

Note that α_1 and α_2 measure elasticities of poverty with respect to per capita real GDP and unemployment rate, respectively. This model was estimated using 41 quarterly observations covering the period from the first quarter 1990 to first quarter 2000. Since this is a fairly large sample, therefore, we can expect to get fairly accurate estimates of the model.

Table 7-10
Regression Model to Explain Poverty in Korea

Explanatory Variables	Coefficient	t_Value
Log head count ratio		
Constant	28.27	29.8
Log per capita GDP	-3.41	-27.0
Log unemployment rate	0.42	8.6
1st quarter	-0.80	-13.2
2nd quarter	-0.34	-6.1
3rd quarter	-0.22	-4.2
R square	0.96	
Log poverty gap ratio		
Constant	31.37	27.6
Log per capita GDP	-4.05	-26.7
Log unemployment rate	0.54	9.2
1st quarter	-0.90	-12.4
2nd quarter	-0.37	-5.5
3rd quarter	-0.20	-3.2
R square	0.96	
Log severity of poverty		
Constant	32.98	24.8
Log per capita GDP	-4.44	-25.0
Log unemployment rate	0.67	9.9
1st quarter	-0.94	-11.1
2nd quarter	-0.36	-4.6
3rd quarter	-0.18	-2.4
R square	0.95	

The results are presented in Table 7-10. As would be expected, poverty declines with a positive economic growth but it increases with a higher rate of unemployment. The growth elasticity of the headcount ratio is estimated to be −3.41 with the t value of 27 implying that economic growth has a highly significant impact on the incidence of poverty. The percentage of poor will on average decline by 3.41 percent in response to one percentage increase in per capita GDP. On the other hand, the unemployment elasticity is estimated to be 0.42 with the t value of 8.6, which suggests that an increase in unemployment rate also has highly significant impact on poverty. If unemployment rate increases by one percent, the percentage of poor will on average increase by 0.42 percent.

The coefficients of quarterly dummy variables are statistically significant as is indicated by their t- values. It means that the incidence of poverty in Korea is significantly affected by the seasons. The incidence of poverty is expected to be lowest in the first quarter of the year and highest in the fourth quarter. From the policy point of view, this is an important result. This suggests that the government's poverty alleviation policies should be geared to those quarters, when the incidence of poverty is expected to be highest.

The coefficient of determination of the estimated regression equations is .95 or more, which means that the growth rate in per capita GDP, unemployment rate and seasonal dummy variables explain more than 95 percent of variation in the incidence of poverty. Given the sample size of 41, the value of R^2 of more than .95 can be regarded as giving a reasonable goodness of the model (see Figure 7-12). Thus, we may use the estimated regression models in Table 7-11 to forecast the incidence of poverty using the macroeconomic variable, namely, growth rate of per capita GDP and unemployment rate and seasonal information.

The regression equations were estimated using the quarterly data beginning from the first quarter 1990 to the first quarter 2000. We utilized these equations to forecast the poverty incidence for the next four quarters from the second quarter 2000 to the first quarter 2001. These forecasts are presented in Table 7-11. The percentage of poor in the first quarter of 2001 is expected to be 6.67 percent. This result suggests that Korea has recovered remarkable well from the economic crisis, which had an enormous adverse impact on poverty.

Figure 7-12
Goodness of Fit of the Regression Model

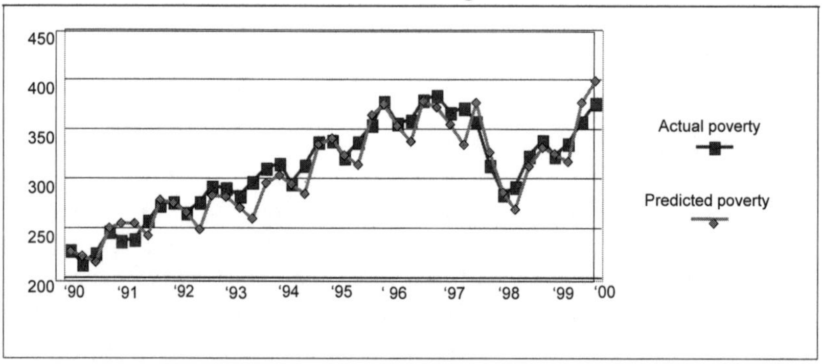

Table 7-11
Forecasting Poverty Incidence

Period	Percentage of Poor	Poverty Gap Ratio	Severity of Poverty
2nd quarter 2000	8.85	1.59	0.48
3rd quarter 2000	9.77	1.73	0.50
4th quarter 2000	7.15	1.19	0.33
1st quarter 2001	6.67	1.17	0.35

VIII. Concluding Remarks

Until the onset of economic crisis, Korea had been a roaring tiger in terms of its economic achievements. It maintained sustained high economic growth with relatively equal distribution of income and with a generally low level of unemployment rate. The impressive economic growth achieved in the past contributed to a sharp reduction in the incidence of poverty. The recent economic crisis changed this situation. The past gains made in reduction of poverty and income inequality came under threat from the crisis. Fortunately, prior to the crisis, Korea had some welfare programs in place. When the crisis hit the economy, the government responded quickly by expanding the existing programs and thus could provide timely help to the people most affected by the crisis. Consequently, the social sector in Korea recovered rapidly. The incidence of poverty is now estimated to be lower than its pre-crisis level. In some sense, the economic crisis has been a blessing in disguise. It has shifted the government's exclusive policy focus on rapid economic growth towards a mixture of growth enhancing and direct poverty alleviation policies. This has now become evident from President Kim Dae-Jung's vision of productive welfare, which endeavors to improve the quality of life for all citizens by promoting social development and a fair distribution of wealth.

The theme of this chapter is pro-poor growth, which is somewhat consistent with the idea of productive welfare in the sense that the people, who do not enjoy the socially accepted minimum standard of living, should be able to share the benefits of economic growth proportionally more or at least no less than the rest of the society. The empirical analysis presented in the paper suggested that economic growth has generally been pro-poor in Korea at least until 1997, when the financial crisis struck the Korea economy. The analysis also suggested that the impact of the economic crisis has not been pro-poor; the poor suffered proportionally more than the non-poor during the crisis. It was also found that the rapid economic recovery benefited the ultra-poor more than the poor or the non-poor. This may have happened because in response to the economic crisis, the Korean government introduced many welfare programs including public works program, which helped the ultra-poor more than the poor or the non-poor.

The major component of productive welfare will be to alleviate poverty. The rapid and sustained economic growth can play an important role in achieving a rapid reduction in poverty. The chapter suggests that economic growth is not sufficient to achieve this objective. The chapter developed the idea of poverty equivalent growth rate, which is the product of the growth rate in per capita GDP and the pro-poor index, which measures how the benefits of economic growth are distributed. The proportional reduction in poverty is monotonically related to the poverty equivalent growth rate. Thus to achieve a rapid reduction in poverty we should maximize the poverty equivalent growth rate rather than the growth rate alone. This means that the government should follow a mixture of growth enhancing and direct poverty alleviation policies.

A clear message that emerges from the economic crisis is that there is need for comprehensive social security systems that provide adequate safety nets to the people in desperate need on a permanent basis. In most developing countries, family and friends provide informal safety nets. These safety nets can be quite effective during normal times. But when there is widespread economic crisis, the informal safety net system breaks down. Moreover, with increasing prosperity brought by rapid economic growth, traditional family values are fast disappearing, reducing the effectiveness of informal safety nets. Thus, the government needs to play an active role in providing safety nets to the people on a permanent basis.

References

ADB (1999) *Fighting Poverty in Asia and the Pacific: The Poverty Reduction Strategy.* Manila: Asian Development Bank.

Bark, S. I. (1994) "The Estimation of Minimum Cost of Living." *Korean Institute of Health and Social Affairs* (in Korean).

Bhagwati, J.N (1988) "Poverty and Public Policy." *World Development Report* 16(5):539-654.

Foster, J., Greer, J., and Thorbecke, E. (1984) "A Class of Decomposable Poverty Measures," *Econometrica*, 52 (3): 761-66.

Kakwani, N. (2000) "On Measuring Growth and Inequality Components of Poverty with Application to Thailand." *Journal of Quantitative Economics*, 16 (1): 67-80.

Kakwani, N. and Pernia, E. (2000) "What is Pro-poor Growth?" *Asian Development Review*, 18 (1).

Kakwani, N. and Prescott, N. (2000) "Impact of Economic Crisis on Poverty and Inequality in Korea," unpublished mimeo. The World Bank, Washington D.C.

Presidential Committee for Quality-of-Life, Office of the President, Republic of Korea (2000) *DJ Welfarism: A New Paradigm for Productive Welfare in Korea.* Seoul: Tae Sul Dang, Korea.

8

Korean Employment Insurance and Work Injury Insurance as Social Safety Nets: An Assessment

Won-Duck Lee, Jai-Joon Hur, and Hokyung Kim

I. Introduction

On July 1, 1995, before the financial crisis, Korea put into place the ambitious Employment Insurance System (EIS) as the fourth pillar of the social insurance system. The Korean EIS consists of three components: unemployment benefits, job training, and employment maintenance/promotion subsidies (for more details on the structure of the Korean EIS, see Yoo 2000). Prior to the introduction of the EIS, Work Injury Insurance (WII) was established in 1964 as the nation's first type of social insurance. WII includes seven benefit programs to compensate for injury, disability and death caused by work-related accidents. Both the Korean EIS and WII are types of compulsory social insurance.

In November 1997, the Korean economy was hit by a devastating financial crisis. The following year, declining macroeconomic conditions brought about major disruptions in the labor market. Soaring unemployment caused disproportionate suffering among non-regular and low-educated workers. Remaining jobs became unstable and the hard-core disadvantaged group in the Korean labor market experienced recurrent unemployment. Wage differentials between low-end workers and others widened while income distribution was aggravated.

The existing welfare system, including the WII and EIS, turned out to be insufficient to cover all types of workers. In light of such shortcomings, the Korean welfare system, including the social insurance system, went through major revisions. Scope of eligibility was extended so that all employees are appropriately protected from unemployment or potential hazards of work-related injuries throughout their lifetimes. Beyond the extension of application, EIS took other meaningful measures during the crisis to protect against the risk of income loss due to unemployment such as introducing the extended benefit and lengthening the duration of benefits.

The objective of this chapter is to assess the role of the Korean EIS and WII as social safety net components of Korea's productive welfare policy and to set forth a list of complementary tasks to be carried out for these two social insurance schemes. Section II evaluates the roles implemented by the Korean EIS to cope with the labor market turmoil. Section III explains the role of Korean WII as a social safety net and presents some policy alternatives for further development of the system. Section IV presents a summary as well as a commentary on remaining policy initiatives.

II. Role of the Employment Insurance System as a Social Safety Net

The Korean labor market fell into unprecedented turmoil after being hit by adverse shocks. In the face of high and continued increasing unemployment, the Korean EIS implemented diverse and intense measures to alleviate the adverse impacts of the crisis on the labor market. Services of the EIS can be classified into four categories: (1) unemployment benefits as a means of income support, (2) job training for reemployment, (3) employment subsidies for job maintenance and employment promotion for disadvantaged workers, and (4) public employment service (PES) and labor market information (LMI) system.

Labor Market Context

Before assessing the role of the EIS, it is worthwhile to take a brief look at the evolution of the Korean labor market after the financial crisis.

The unemployment rate in Korea was as low as two to three percent before the financial crisis. However, the unemployment rate made a dramatic jump to 5.6 percent in the first quarter of 1998 and began to rise continuously until it reached 8.4 percent in the first quarter of 1999 (Figure 8-1). The unemployment rate has since decreased to 3.5 percent in the second quarter of 2001, the lowest level subsequent to the onset of the financial crisis in 1997.

The proportion of regular employees stood at 54.1 percent in 1997 and continued to decrease, reaching 47.6 percent in 2000. During the same span, the proportion of temporary and daily employees rose correspondingly (Figure 8-2). This increasing tendency of non-regular employment was observed even before the crisis, although the crisis seems to have accentuated the trend.

Figure 8-1
Trends in the Unemployment Rate (percent)

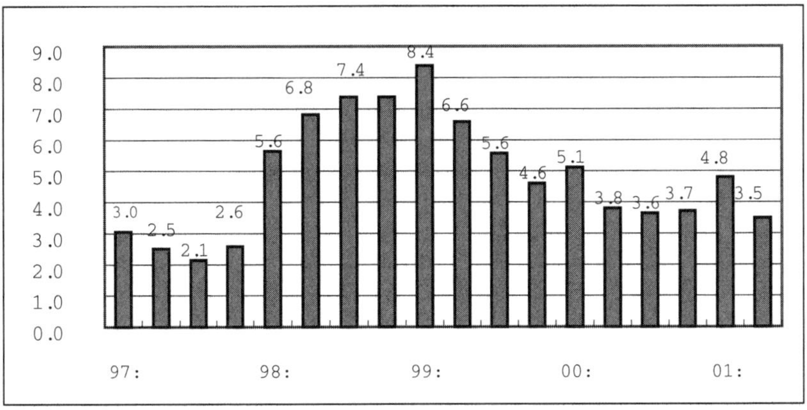

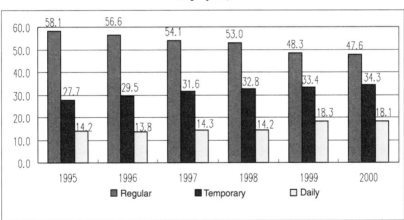

Source: National Statistical Office, *Monthly Report on the Economically Active Population Survey*, various issues.

Figure 8-2
Trends in the Proportion of Employees by Employment Type (percent of total employees)

Source: National Statistical Office, *Annual Report on the Economically Active Population Survey*, various issues.

After the financial crisis, the Gini coefficient drastically increased to 0.316 in 1998 and has not fallen below that mark since (Figure 8-3). A recent study by Jeong and Choi (2001) confirms that the aggravation of income distribution results from the reduction of low-income earners' wages rather than from a fall in medium-income earners' wages.

Figure 8-3
Trends in the Gini Coefficient

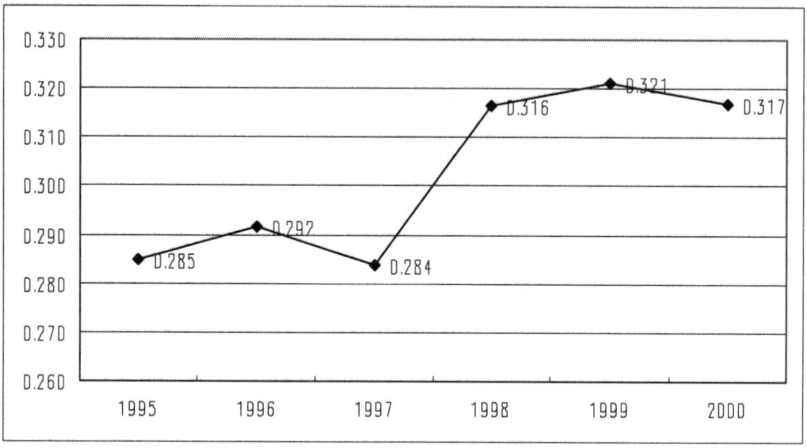

Source: National Statistical Office, *Family Income and Expenditure Survey* database.

During the crisis, non-regular workers and less-educated workers suffered disproportionately. Jobs were precarious and the hard-core disadvantaged group in the Korean labor market experienced recurrent unemployment, even if they did not fall into the long-term unemployment trap. Wage differentials between low-end workers and others widened and income distribution became highly skewed. Given the labor market situation, non-regular workers were most in need of a social safety net, but most of them were not covered by the EIS. This situation, however, provoked a need for more refined social safety net and contributed to the extension of the Korean social safety net.

Unemployment Benefits

With severe economic recession and massive unemployment, poverty among the jobless and low-income families emerged as a critical social issue that needed to be addressed immediately. Income support programs were implemented in two directions. First, in order for the EIS to care for as many unemployed as possible, its scope of application was extended, qualification requirements were relaxed, and UB beneficiaries were given up to 60 additional benefit days. Second, the low-income jobless were given income or credit support such as loans for living expenses (including family medical and educational expenses) and other public aid benefits.

When the EIS was first introduced, scope of UB application was limited to workers employed at firms with 30 or more employees. In the face of rising unemployment and growing unemployment vulnerability of low-wage earn-ers at small size firms, extending the scope of UB application was deemed critical to expand the social protection of the unemployed. In response, the Korean government extended scope of UB application to firms with ten or more employees in January 1998, to firms with five or more employees in March 1998, and finally, to all firms with at least one employee in October 1998 (Table 8-1). After these three consecutive amendments of the Employ-ment Insurance Law in 1998, only those part-time employees working less than 80 hours a month and daily workers employed for less than a month remained 'legally' excluded from EIS application.

The extension of EIS application had a very limited effect on protecting the unemployed in that simply being insured did not suffice for UB eligibil-ity. Under the old rules, one must be involuntarily laid off after having con-tributed insurance premiums for more than 12 out of the last 18 months to be qualified for UB. With these requirements, however, temporary workers and other unstably employed workers at small firms found it difficult to be eli-gible for UB. To better protect those marginal workers and newly covered employees, the government relaxed eligibility conditions, including easing the minimum contribution requirement from 12 out of the last 18 months to 180 days out of the last 12 months.

Table 8-1
Scope of EIS Application

Date	Unemployment Benefit Component	Employment Maintenance/ Promotion Subsidies & Job Training Component
July 1, 1995	≥ 30 employees	≥ 70 employees
January 1, 1998	≥ 10 employees	≥ 50 employees
March 1, 1998	≥ 5 employees	≥ 50 employees
July 1, 1998	≥ 5 employees	≥ 5 employees
October 1, 1998	≥ 1 employee	≥ 1 employee

Source: Ministry of Labor (2001a), *White Paper on Employment Insurance*, Seoul

The duration period of UB varies depending on the insured's employment period and the claimant's age. The range was from a minimum of 60 days to a maximum of 210 days. However, since Korea's EIS was implemented only on July 1, 1995, the insured period of employees could not exceed five years and thus the actual duration of UB could not exceed 150 days until June 30, 2000.

Given the limited benefit duration and the unprecedented unfavorable labor market situation, the extended benefit rule was put into operation from July 1998 so that the qualified unemployed could receive up to 60 days more than the period designated by the benefit duration matrix. Further, the UB duration matrix from 60 to 210 days was modified to 90 to 240 days, with the new matrix going into effect in January 2000 (Table 8-2). In essence, the average duration of UB increased to 126 days in 1999 from 85 days in 1997 and 91 days in 1998.

Table 8-2
Benefit Duration Matrix (no. of days)

		Insured Employment Period				
		Less than 1	1-3 years	3-5 years	5-10 years	Over 10 years
Age of	Below 30	90	90	120	150	180
Claimant	30-50	90	120	150	180	210
	Over 50 and Handicapped	90	150	180	210	240

Source: Ministry of Labor

Despite all these efforts implemented by the government such as extension of scope of application, relaxation of eligibility criteria and lengthening of benefit period, the beneficiaries represented a too limited portion of the unemployed for UB to be considered as a primary safety net against unemployment. In 1999, the beneficiary ratio was 10.7 percent, which is significantly lower than that of any other OECD country (Table 8-3).

Table 8-3
Ratio of UB Beneficiaries Relative to Total Unemployment (Unit: thousands, percent)

Country	Unemployment (A)	Beneficiaries (B)	B/A×100
Germany (1990)	1,971	858	43.5
Japan (1992)	1,420	395	27.8
Korea (1999)	1,353	145	10.7
U.S.A. (1990)	6,874	2,475	36.0
U.K. (1993)	2,900	870	30.0

Source: National Statistical Office, *Annual Report on the Economically Active Population Survey*, 2000.
Central Employment Information Office, *Monthly Statistics of Employment Insurance*, various issues.Phang, 1999

Five reasons can be attributed to the low beneficiary ratio. First, wage workers explain only 62.4 percent of total employment while UB, by nature, does not cover non-wage workers (the difference between A and B in Table 8-4).

Second, the compliance rate is low. This shortcoming comes from two different origins. Daily workers who work less than a month in a firm are legally excluded from EIS application (a considerable part of the difference between B and C in Table 8-4). Also, all legally insurable employees are not actually insured because of the disincentive for frequent turnover of non-regular employees, regular worker-oriented burdens such as the declaration process and filling of administrative forms, limited administrative capacity, and informal characteristics of economic agents in the labor market (Hur 2001a; Hur and Yoo 2001). As of December 2000, the compliance rate was only 73.4 percent, which means that there is a large gap between the scope of application *de jure* and the scope application *de facto* (the difference between C and D in Table 8-4). Many temporary and daily employees are still excluded from UB application and remain exempt from protection.

Third, actual benefit duration is limited because the benefit duration matrix depends on the insured employment period whereas the EIS has only been in existence for six years. Fourth, the eligibility criteria for Unemployment benefits are strict, in particular, the criteria judging whether or not a claimant is involuntarily unemployed. Workers who quit their jobs without justifiable reasons are generally regarded as voluntary unemployed and are not eligible for benefits even though they remain unemployed. This requirement is much stricter than in most countries except for a few such as the U.S., Czech Republic, and Spain (OECD 2000). Fifth, there is a considerable number of white-collar unemployed who feel shameful about presenting themselves at the Employment Security Center to receive unemployment benefits.

Table 8-4
Compliance Rate of EIS (December 2000) (Unit: thousand persons, percent)

Employment	Employees	Legally Insured Employees	Actually Insured Employees	(D/A)x 100	(D/B)x 100	(D/C)x 100
(A) 20,857	(B) 13,265	(C) 9,190	(D) 6,747	32.3	50.9	73.4

Source: Authors' calculations based on the *Economically Active Population Survey* database and *Employment Insurance* database.

Job Training for Reemployment

Programs in the job training component of the EIS accommodated the unemployed to enhance their job skills and thus increase their employability through providing retraining opportunities for the unemployed.

Since the outbreak of the economic crisis, the EIS expanded training programs for the unemployed. In 1998, about 163 thousand unemployed participated in and benefited from EIS job training programs, approximately eight times as many as those in the preceding year. The expenditure amounted to 191 billion won. In 1999, the EIS provided training opportunities for 171 thousand jobless workers with a budget of 307 billion won. In 2000, 132 thousand unemployed workers participated in training programs and the expenditure was 216 billion won. On average, 48.6 percentage of job trainees for reemployment benefited from job training component of the EIS (Table 8-5).

Those unemployed workers who had worked at firms covered by the EIS were eligible to apply for the reemployment training programs and received training allowances that lasted from one month to one year, up to a total of three times, until they found a new job. Training allowances were cut in half if participants continued to partake in the second training course and were reduced to zero for the third training course.

Training allowances ranged from 200,000 to 300,000 won (equivalent to 60-90 percentage of the minimum wage). Trainees who were learning skills for non-favored jobs, which had been facing a labor shortage amidst the deep recession, received additional bonuses. Similar training opportunities, financed by the general government budget, were given to those unemployed who had not been insured by the EIS. Therefore, substantial opportunity for vocational training was provided to all of the unemployed.

Table 8-5
Job Training for Reemployment (Unit: billion won, thousand persons)

	1998		1999		2000	
	Expenditure	Beneficiaries	Expenditure	Beneficiaries	Expenditure	Beneficiaries
Training for Reemployment by the EIS	191.0	163	306.7	171	215.5	132
Training for Reemployment, Total	656.8	363	514.4	371	440.3	222

Source: Central Employment Information Office, *Employment Insurance* database. Ministry of Labor, *White Paper on Policy against Unemployment*, 2001b.

Job training programs for the unemployed offered opportunities to those out of work to retrain themselves in order to enhance their own future employability, while training allowances helped alleviate their immediate economic difficulties. That is, apart from the formal purpose of job training, such programs served as a type of social safety net—those unemployed who could not receive cash benefits participated in job training programs and received training allowances.

However, diverse training programs that were loosely regulated and lacked appropriate monitoring and inspection led to the moral hazard of some training institutions and trainees. Some unqualified training institutions took advantage of the training programs and provided time-killing courses in order to receive reimbursement from the government, thus limiting the effectiveness of the training programs. Also, some trainees were solely interested in receiving the training allowances instead of acquiring actual skills.

Furthermore, an underdeveloped labor market information system and lack of experts to manage the training programs tended to limit the effectiveness of the training programs. Training institutions and programs were authorized depending purely on preexisting conditions such as available equipment, facilities, etc. Little consideration was given either to changing demand in the labor market or to the needs of the potential participants. Training institutions tended to routinely provide the same training programs as were conducted in the past. As a result, some training programs did not significantly aid in the reemployment of the trainees. As of October 2000, the reemployment rate of training program participants stood at 32.5 percent, which is lower than in other countries.

Lee and Kang (1999) identify factors that underlie the low reemployment rate. First, the number of trainees increased rapidly while labor demand was still low during the economic crisis. Second, the quality of training programs did not catch up with the pace of quantity expansion. Third, the contents of training programs were not suitable for the changing demand in the labor market. And fourth, the PES (Public Employment Service) had little capacity to reintegrate the participants into the labor market.

Employment Subsidies

Subsidy programs were implemented via the employment maintenance/ promotion component of the EIS. Employment maintenance subsidies intended to minimize employment adjustment through dismissals by providing wage subsidies to firms that made efforts to avoid laying-off redundant workers.

Table 8-6
EIS Employment Subsidies (Unit: million won, persons)

	1998		1999		2000	
	Expenditure	Beneficiaries	Expenditure	Beneficiaries	Expenditure	Beneficiaries
Employment Maintenance Subsidies	74,223	654,375	79,197	369,591	29,297	148,246
Hiring Subsidies	5,878	169	75,888	101,550	42,204	63,407
Employment Promotion Subsidies	16,186	120,721	29,149	198,783	42,148	233,426
Total	96,287	775,265	184,234	669,924	113,649	445,079

Source: Central Employment Information Office, *Monthly Statistics of Employment Insurance,* various issues.

To receive subsidies, firms needed to be in a situation in which employment reduction was inevitable for managerial reasons and had to adopt subsidizable practices such as: (1) temporary shut-down, (2) reduction of working hours, (3) provision of training to redundant workers, (4) provision of paid/unpaid leave, and (5) dispatch or reassignment of workers. Subsidies equivalent to one-half to two-thirds (depending on the size of the firm) of the wages or allowances paid to their workers were refunded for a maximum of 6 months.

The requirements of employment maintenance subsidies were relaxed during the crisis and the assistance level was increased to provide more incentives and to cover more firms and workers. In 1998, a total of 74.2 billion won was paid for the employment maintenance of about 0.7 million workers while, in 1999, 79.2 billion won was spent for a total of 0.4 million workers. With the improving labor market situation in 2000, the employment maintenance expenditure decreased to 29.3 billion won covering 0.15 million beneficiaries (Table 8-6).

Subsidy programs were first criticized by some economists on the grounds that they might hamper or delay structural adjustment of the economy by subsidizing marginal firms that had lost competitiveness in the market. However, subsidized firms were not necessarily bad firms destined to end up in bankruptcy. Good firms could face temporary cash flow difficulties in the midst of financial crisis as financial institutions did not function properly. In addition, since firms were free to decide whether to make use of subsidy programs or lay off redundant workers, there were no *a priori* reasons to believe that the subsidy programs prevented firms from restructuring. Thus, subsidy programs were advocated and maintained as an important element of labor market policy. In fact, according to Hwang (1999), firms with good human resources tended to utilize the employment maintenance subsidies.

However, the contribution of employment subsidies in reducing unemployment should not be exaggerated. The number of workers that benefited from the program was, on average, around 25,000 per month in 1998-99. Kim et al. (1999) analyzed the employment maintenance effects of employment subsidy programs using employer surveys as well as case studies. The estimated effect was 22.3 percent on average, which implied that deadweight loss was in the 70 percent range. According to the assessment of PES staff and monitoring reports, deadweight loss and substitution effects of the 'grants to promote employment of displaced workers' have been serious (Hwang 1999; Kim et al. 1999).

The other two subsidy programs in the employment maintenance/promotion component of the EIS are hiring subsidies and employment promotion subsidies, which are intended to assist disadvantaged workers of the labor market such as those involuntarily laid off, elderly workers, female workers, female household heads, and the long-term unemployed.

Table 8-7
Composition of Employment Service Agencies and Staff
(Unit: agencies, persons)

	1997	2000
Local Labor Office	46	-
Employment Security Center	3	126
Manpower Bank	3	7
Employment Service Center for Daily Workers	-	16
Total PES Agencies	52	149
No. of Staff	141	2,436

Note: 1. PES agencies and staff of the central government only. 2. Manpower Bank is a PES agency co-invested and co-managed by the Ministry of Labor and local government. It specializes in job matching and job counseling, but does not deal with UB payment service.
Source: Ministry of Labor

Public Employment Services and Labor Market Information System

With the surge in unemployment benefit claimants, the number of public employment service staff was insufficient to administer even Unemployment benefit payment service. Immediate expansion of PES capacity to meet the demand for both benefit payment and administration of other active labor market programs was deemed urgent.

In 1998, to improve the quality of employment services and to promote a user-friendly environment, the government combined the employment insurance division and the job information service division of local labor offices into PES centers called "Employment Security Centers" (Table 8-7). These centers were based on the concept of "one-stop service" to provide job seekers with job vacancy and vocational training information as well as Unemployment benefit payment service all at the same place. The government also eased regulations on job brokerage by private agencies and strengthened its support of free job placement services to trade unions and employers' organizations.

Although one may marvel at the progress that the Korean PES has made during the three consecutive years after the economic crisis, the capacity of the Korean PES still remains insufficient to play an active role in meeting labor market needs. Rather, it has made the government realize future policy tasks required to effectively meet the demands of job searchers via the PES. For example, strengthening "counseling" services in a proper sense based on improvement of counselors' expertise, development of a new occupational classification system that will serve more effectively in job matching, collaboration with private sector employment service agencies, etc. are some of the remaining areas to be addressed.

One way to evaluate PES capacity is to look at the ratio of workers in the labor force to PES staff. For example, Germany's PES has a ratio of 450 workers per PES staff, while that of Sweden and the United Kingdom has 403 and 882, respectively. Each of these countries' PES has a relatively high capacity level. In contrast, an average Korean PES staff has to deliver service to 9,011 workers (Table 8-8).

As for the labor market information system, the government launched an electronic system in May 1999, called "Work-Net," benchmarking Canada's "WorkInfoNet." Work-Net, accessible on the Internet, provides various types of information on job vacancies, vocational training programs, career guidance, employment policies, employment insurance services, labor market statistics, and labor laws. Almost all job vacancies registered at public employment agencies can be found on Work-Net unless employers refuse to allow the information to be uploaded. In order to make the system more effective and easier to use, the government plans to introduce a number of improvements including faster access speed and more user-friendly interface; development of job vacancy information based on new occupational classification; provision of detailed information on labor market trends, employment outlook and wages.

Table 8-8
Number of Public Employment Service Agencies and Staff
(Unit: agencies, persons)

Country	No. of Agencies	No. of PES Staff	No. of Labor Force per PES Staff	No. of Employees per PES Staff
Germany	841	87,570	450	364
Japan	666	15,290	4,388	3,445
Korea	149	2,436	9,011	5,395
Sweden	570	11,000	403	339
United Kingdom	1,159	33,000	882	711
USA	2,538	71,378	1,953	1,717

Source: Authors' calculations based on internal document of the Ministry of Labor and KLI Foreign Labor Statistics

Evaluation and Policy Directions

As of December 2000, there were 13.2 million wage workers in the Korean labor market. Of these, only 6.7 million employees (50.9 percentage of wage workers) were insured. Thus, one of the major problems with Korea's unemployment insurance is that even if the scope of EIS application has been extended to all firms, the compliance rate is still quite low. The main obstacle to providing EIS to temporary and daily workers is the lack of any mechanism certifying employment career for them. EIS should refine its employment record-keeping system and cover daily workers in order to overcome this shortcoming.

Enhancing the efficacy of the training system is another important issue to be addressed. Training allowances helped alleviate economic difficulties for trainees who are unable to receive other cash benefits or participate in public works programs. But job-training programs should place more emphasis on enhancing the employability of the unemployed rather than just providing income support.

The capacity of the PES has been expanded quantitatively during the economic crisis. But the counseling services and the labor market information system still leave much room for improvement. Counselors do not spend much time in in-depth counseling. Rather, they are preoccupied with such activities as registration of workers' records, recording job vacancies, and processing unemployment benefit claims of workers and subsidy claims of firms. Now that the labor market has been stabilized, counseling should play a greater role through improvement in the quality of counseling services. Besides, improvements should also be made in the labor market information systems through developing the occupational classification system appropriate to the labor market.

III. Role of Work Injury Insurance as a Social Safety Net

Key Features of Work Injury Insurance

Like other social insurance programs, WII was designed to provide protection against economic insecurity and catastrophic losses. WII benefits include medical treatment benefits for work-related injuries or illnesses and wage-replacement benefits for the lost earnings during the period of injury or illness. It also provides disabled workers with a substantial proportion of income loss.

In Korea, WII differs from other social insurance programs in the following ways: first, employers contribute to WII through payment of premiums to government insurance funds. There is no direct employee contribution, although much of the cost may be shifted to employees in the form of lower wages. A large part (about 85 percent) of the premium is experience-rated, and thus varies among firms based on the benefit. The other part (about 15 percentage) of the premium is set at a fixed-rate and is evenly spread among all the firms in the industry.

Second, WII is a "no-fault" system. Employers are liable regardless of fault, and employees qualify as recipients only if the injury or disease is work-related. Employers' liability is limited to the benefits in the program. And employees can receive benefits regardless of the employers' ability to pay.

WII coverage is mainly financed by the premiums paid by employers and the returns from asset management, while a part of the operation costs is financed by the government budget. The Ministry of Labor is in charge of estimating, with the help of the Korea Labor Institute, the approximate amount of payments for the following year, and thus, the rough estimate of total premiums to be collected from the owners of firms. The Ministry of Labor also determines the premium rate for each type of business based on the experience rate of the past three years. Once the premium rates for the different types of businesses are determined, each firm has to submit its own premium, which is adjusted by the variation rate depending upon the individual firm's experience rate.

Classifications and Contents of WII Payments

There are seven classifications of WII benefits according to the different conditions of work-related injury or illness: medical treatment benefit, income indemnity benefit, disability benefit, nursing benefit, survivors' benefit, funeral expense benefit, and long-term indemnity pension benefit. Most of these are cash benefits with the exception of medical treatment. Medical treatment is provided when the injury requires more than three days of treatment.

If the injury requires up to three days of treatment, employers are supposed to pay the medical expenses in accordance with the Labor Standards Act. Income indemnity benefits cover 70 percent of income loss when a worker is not able to resume his/her job within three days due to the injury or illness. Disability benefits are paid either in the form of a lump sum or pension: a lump sum payment is provided for those who fall in the class of degree eight to 14 of impediment, and pension payment for degree one to three of impediment. Those who fall in the class of degree four to seven of impediment can choose between a lump sum or pension payment.

Survivors' benefits are also paid either in the form of a lump sum or pension: in the case of lump sum, the average income for 1,300 days is paid; while in case of pension, 47 percentage of the average annual income plus five percent for each additional recipient is paid. The maximum annual pension payment should not exceed 67 percent of the average annual income.

Trends in Work-Related Injury

An amount of 120 days of average income is paid for funeral expenses. Long-term indemnity pension benefits are the payments to those injured

Figure 8-4
Benefits of WII

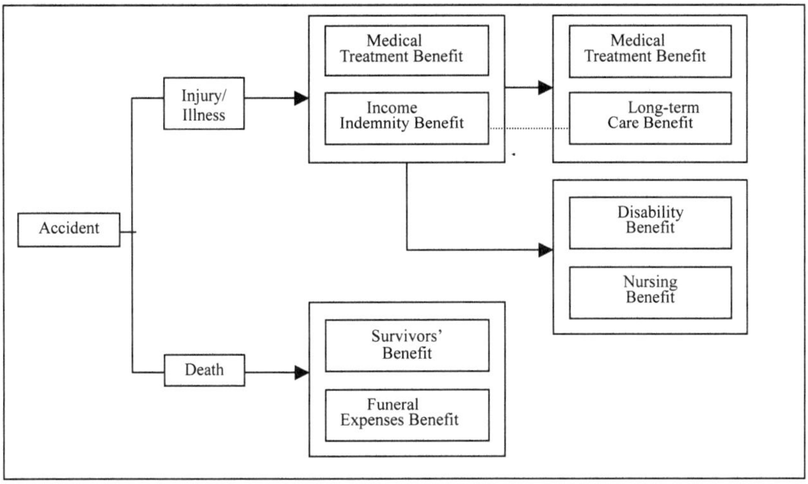

Source: Kim, Hokyung, et al. 2000, p. 9

Figure 8-5
Number of Injured Workers

Source: Ministry of Labor; Korea Labor Welfare Corporation database

workers who do not recover after two years of medical treatment and fall in the incurable disease classification of degree one to three.

For the recipients of long-term indemnity pension, income indemnity benefits are not applied. Long-term indemnity pension benefits are paid in the form of a pension, the amount of which differs according to the severity of the disease: As for Degree 1, the average income for 329 days will be paid; for Degree 2, 291 days; and for Degree 3, 257 days. The amounts of these payments are the same as those for disability benefits.

As represented in Figure 8-5, the number of injured workers had been decreasing for the last decade. In 1998, there was a sharper decrease in the number because of the recent economic recession. In 1999 and 2000, however, the number of injured workers began to increase as the economy recovered and thus hired more employees as the operation ratio of manufacturing industry rose. In general, manufacturing firms are faced with a higher risk of work-related injuries.

The number of deaths, which had been on a rising trend, decreased in 1998 and 1999 due to the economic recession. In 2000, the number of deaths rose once again as the economy recovered, especially in those industries characterized by high risk of work-related injury such as construction, manufacturing, etc. (Figure 8-6).

Figure 8-6
Number of Funeral Expense Recipients

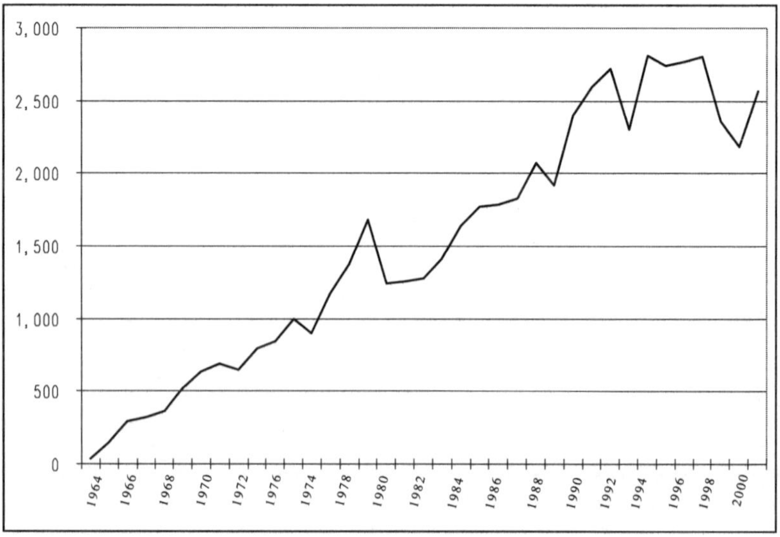

Source: Ministry of Labor, Korea Labor Welfare Corporation database

Figure 8-7
Trends in the Portion of Benefit Payments

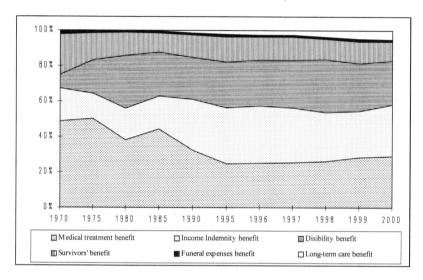

Source: Ministry of Labor, Korea Labor Welfare Corporation database

This kind of phenomena can be seen also from Figure 8-7, which represents the progress of the portion of each type of benefit payments of WII. This chart indicates that the portion of long-term indemnity pension benefits grew in the last couple of years while income indemnity benefit payments decreased over the last half-decade. Medical treatment benefits have increased for the last half-decade due to the rise in medical fees.

Scope of the WII Application

In 1964, WII was initiated for a total of 64 firms and 80,000 employees in the mining and manufacturing industries. In order to apply for WII, a firm had to employ at least 500 workers. Thereafter, as represented in Table 8-9, the target industries for WII have been expanded, and the minimum number of employees required per firm has been alleviated up to now. From 1998, WII was extended to student apprentices and students in vocational schools, and from 1 July of the year, finance and insurance firms with more than four employees were included in the WII system. From July 1, 2000, the minimum number of employees required was reduced to one and thus virtually any firm is now a target of WII. Moreover, employers with no more than 50 employees are able to join WII under the notion that most of them actually participate themselves as workers.

Table 8-9
Minimum Number of Employees Required for WII

Year	Required Number of Employees in a Firm	Industry
1964	≥ 500	Mining, manufacturing only
1965	≥ 200	Addition of electrical, gas, transportation, and warehouse industries
1966	≥ 150	All existing industries
1967	≥ 100	All existing industries except brassware, which requires at least 25,000 employees annually.
1969	≥ 50	Addition of construction, service, water service, sanitary equipment, telecommunication
1974	≥ 16	All existing industries
1976	≥ 16 (5)	All existing industries except mining, chemical, petroleum, coal, rubber goods, and plastic, which require at least 5 employees.
1982	≥ 10	Addition of logging industry
1983	≥ 10	Addition of agricultural goods brokerage business
1986	≥ 5	14 industries only including veneer plywood
1987	≥ (5)	20 industries including timber, which require at least 5 employees
1988	≥ 5	16 industries including electronics appliance manufacturing
1991	≥ 10	Addition of mining, forestry, fishery, hunting, retail/wholesale business, real estate brokerage
1992	≥ 5	Mining, forestry, fishery, hunting, retail/whole sale business, real estate brokerage industries
1996	-	Addition of education, health, and social work services
1998	-	Addition of financial, insurance, and overseas dispatch industries
2000	≥ 1	All existing industries, including owners of firms with at most 50 employees

Source: Kim, Hokyung et al. 2000, p. 13, Ministry of Labor

Even with this extensive application of WII, some contingent low-income workers and atypical workers are still not included in this social safety net, which poses a potentially significant hazard. Among those are insurance solicitors, home visiting test-kit providers for children, golf caddies, etc. Since their main source of income is commissions rather than salaries, the owners of the businesses that they work for often do not acknowledge them as employees. This is an issue that is still under heated debate. It is argued that since these workers maintain some kind of continuous employment relationship with specific companies, they must be treated as employees in the event of work-related injury. However, the counter arguments point out that, in many cases, it is hard to prove that they work for specific companies, and moreover, it is hard to determine whether the injuries are indeed work-related.

As mentioned above, WII has recently extended its application to virtually all firms (except self-employees) by alleviating the minimum required number of employees to one. However, some types of businesses are still excluded because of the difficulties in administration and confirmation of employment relationships. Among them are construction businesses with less than 20,000,000 won of total expenses; private construction businesses with total project areas of less than 330m²; farming, fishing, hunting, and home care service businesses with less than five employees; other types of businesses or industries where the work injuries are covered under different laws; and firms whose regular number of employees is less than one due to the irregular use of part time workers.

Coverage of WII

When WII was first introduced in 1964, medical treatment was provided only for those injuries or illnesses that required more than nine days of treatment. (Table 8-10) However, the required number of days was reduced in 1971 to more than seven, and in 1982 to more than three days.

Table 8-10
Expansion of WII Coverage

Date of Implementation	Medical Treatment Benefit	Income Indemnity Benefit/ Long-term Care Benefit	Disability Benefit	Survivors' Benefit	Funeral Expense Benefit
1964.7.1	Lapse period: more than 10 days	60percent of average of income Lapse period: more than 10 days	Lump sum: Maximum (Grade 1: 1000 days) Minimum (Grade 10: 50 days) Lump sum amount: 1000 days of average income in case of incomplete recovery after 1 year of progress	Lump sum: 1000 days of average income	90 days of average income
1971.1.1	Lapse period: more than 7 days	Lapse period: more than 7 days	Subdivision of grade: Maximum (Grade 1: 1340 days) Minimum (Grade 14: 50 days) Pension benefit introduced Target: Grade 1-3 Annual benefit: Grade 1 (240 days of average income) Grade 2 (213 days) Grade 3 (188 days) Lump sum amount: 1340 days of average income in case of incomplete recovery after 2 years of progress	Introduced pension benefit Amount of benefit according to the number of survivors: 1 survivor: 30 percent of annual income 2 survivors: 35 percent of annual income 3 survivors: 40 percent of annual income 4 survivors: 45 percent of annual income	

1977.12.19			Increased annual pension benefit: Grade 1 (279 days of average income) Grade 2 (248 days of average income) Grade 3 (219 days of average income)	Increased annual pension benefit: 1 survivor: 45 percent of annual income 2 survivors: 50 percent 3 survivors: 55 percent 4 survivors: 60 percent	
1982.1.1	Lapse period: more than 3 days	Lapse period: more than 3 days	Increased annual pension benefit: Grade 1 (313 days of average income) Grade 2 (277 days) Grade 3 (245 days) Grade 4 (213 days) Grade 5 (184 days) Grade 6 (156 days) Grade 7 (131 days)	Increased annual pension benefit: 1 survivor: 52 percent of annual income 2 survivors: 57 percent 3 survivors: 62 percent 4 survivors: 67 percent	
1983.7.1		Long-term care benefit Amount of payment established Grade 1 (313 days of average income) Grade 2 (277 days of average income) Grade 3 (245 days of average income)	Discontinuance of lump-sum benefit payment		
1989.4.1		Level of income indemnity increased 70percent of average income Level of long-term benefit increased: Grade 1: 329days of average income Grade 2: 291days of average income Grade 3: 257days of average income	Mandatory pension payment introduced Amount of lump sum benefit increased: Grade 1: 1474 days Grade 2: 1309 days Grade 3: 1155 days Grade 4: 1012 days Grade 5: 869 days Grade 6: 737 days Grade 7: 616 days Grade 8: 495 days Grade 9: 385 days Grade 10: 297 days Grade 11: 220 days Grade 12: 154 days Grade 13: 99 days Grade 14: 55 days The amount of pension benefit Increased. : Grade 1: 329 days Grade 2: 291 days Grade 3: 257 days Grade 4: 224 days Grade 5: 193 days Grade 6: 164 days Grade 7: 138 days The amount of lump sum benefit increased: 1300 days of average income Amount of benefit increased: 120 days of average income		
2000.7.1	Treatment for after-effects introduced		Pension payment of the 50percent of the lump sum amount for grade 4-7 became mandatory Nursing benefit newly established: Full-time: 24,775 won/day Part-time: 16,516 won/day	Pension payment became mandatory: either 100percent in pension, or 50percent in pension and 50percent in lump sum	Maximum / minimum level of payment established

Source: Kim, Hokyung, et al. 2000, pp. 17-18

Income indemnity benefits, which paid only 60 percentage of average income in 1964 was increased to 70 percent in 1989. Disability benefits paid according to ten different degrees of disability in 1964 were subdivided into 14 degrees in 1971, and the payment level was increased as well for each of the different degrees. In 1989, those who fell into the category of Degree 1-3 were obligated to receive benefits in the form of pension, while those between Degree 4-7 were given the choice of lump sum or pension. However, from 2000, they are also obligated to receive 50 percentages of benefits in the form of pension.

Survivors' benefits, which were provided in the form of lump sum payments in 1964 and paid in the amount of 1,000 days of average income, were increased to 1,300 days of average income. In 1970, pension type payment was introduced and the amount of payment increased in the years 1971, 1977, and 1982. Payment in the form of pension was basically obligatory, however in 1999, recipients were given the option of receiving half the benefit amount as a lump sum.

As for funeral expenses, the benefit was increased in 1989 from the original 90 days of average income to 120 days. However, in 1999, the maximum and minimum limits were fixed in order to reduce the difference between low and high benefit recipients. Long-term indemnity pension benefits had been paid in the form of lump sums since 1964, but a pension type form of payment was introduced in 1982.

A major revision was made to workers' compensation in July 2000, the content of which is as follows.

First, when it is difficult to calculate total income of the employee to determine the premium and coverage, 'standard income' is applied. Standard income is typically applied to those firms that are bankrupted, closed, or when employers file the total income gathering the reports of workers. The standard income in this case is the same as that of unemployment insurance – monthly payments are 723,000 won and hourly payments are 3,200 won.

Second, nursing benefits were newly introduced to cover the care service cost for the severely disabled workers. This benefit is restricted to those who fall into the disability classification of Degree 1-2. Full-time care benefits are 24,775 won/day and part-time benefits are 16,516 won/day.

Third, the indemnity payment for old-aged workers whose age exceeds 65 is decreased from the existing level of 70 percent to 65 percent.

Fourth, a maximum compensation standard, 28 times as much as the low benefit recipients, was set to alleviate the difference between low and high benefit recipients.

Fifth, in order to determine the total income for those who work in construction business and whose working days are typically far less than other workers, the "coefficient of usual working period" will be applied.

In addition, in order to enhance the services for the rehabilitation of disabled workers, WII will extend its service range for the after-effects of an injury/illness to include respiratory diseases. Moreover, WII plans to strengthen the financial support for the (economic) restoration of the disabled by extending the number of disabled workers who have access to the fund for opening small businesses at low interest rates from the present 80 to 500 in 2005. It will also run vocational adjustment programs for the disabled.

Evaluation and Policy Directions

In retrospect, the WII system has made great strides in Korea, yet there are several major tasks that still need to be accomplished.

First, although the application of WII has been continuously extended since its establishment in 1964 to include virtually all kinds of firms, the actual number of firms covered by WII is around 65.2 percent of the total industry as of Jun 30 2001. Many employers, typically those of small businesses, have been unwilling to join WII, even though they are required to pay 50 percent of the coverage and the premium for three years after a work-related injury has occurred and is reported. Thus, in order to extend the WII's scope of application to include as many workers as possible, specific measures are needed to help firms automatically join WII as they establish or continue their businesses.

Another issue that needs to be addressed is to find ways to reduce the rate of accidents (i.e., work injuries). The Korea Occupational Safety & Health Agency (KOSHA) implements risk management programs in the workplace such as the KOSHA 2000 program, which is designed to reduce work injuries and is operated on voluntary basis. However, since the application of the program is not compulsory, it has generally been applied to large firms that maintain relatively good safety conditions and can afford the program fee. Thus, in order to achieve the best effects in reducing work injuries, policy devices are needed not only to enhance the efficiency and credibility of the safety check itself, but also to implement a compulsory safety check program in work area. Moreover, in order to set forth a pro-incentive device for the owners of firms to reduce injuries at the work place, a rate discounting system that applies the degree of workplace safety when rating WII premiums may be called for.

On the other hand, in the face of increasing number of pension receivers and thus escalating benefit payments in the future, the WII program needs to be more carefully applied to maintain financial soundness. In order to accomplish this, an extensive information system including a well-maintained database as well as more rigorous studies on the financing methodology, the rate making system and the effectiveness of work-injury insurance policies and related programs are needed.

In summary, under the perception that every worker faces the risk of being injured, even if the probability is very small, the role of WII is very important for the economic stability of employees. In light of this, WII has extended its scope of application and increased its coverage since 1964 in order to strengthen its role as a social safety net and thus reduce the potential hazards of workers throughout their lifetime.

However, regardless of the extension of the application of WII, there still remain some contingent workers that are not covered by the existing safety net because of the irregularity in their employment relationship and the difficulty in proving that the injury is related to work. For some of these workers, whose incomes are substantially low and are thus unable to pay WII premiums, it may be necessary to consider a separate social aid program rather than try to include all types of workers into WII. In order to maintain a stable social insurance system and to reduce the problem of moral hazard and/or reverse selection in the system, different programs may have to be considered for different groups of workers according to their varying needs.

IV. Conclusion

The protection of workers from various risks such as illness, work injury, disability, unemployment, and retirement, without deterioration of work incentives, and thus ensuring improved welfare and productivity of workers is at the core of the philosophy of productive welfare. Hence, it seems evident that the extension of the coverage of EIS and WII will improve workplace safety and productivity of small firms as well as the welfare of workers

Every worker faces the risk of being injured or unemployed. In this sense, the WII and EIS are required to play an important role for the economic stability of employees. The WII and EIS have extended their scope of application since their introduction in order to strengthen their role as a social safety net and thus reduce the potential hazards of workers throughout their lifetime.

The WII and EIS have actually extended their application to include workers of small firms with less than five employees in 2000 and 1998, respectively. However, despite the extension of WII and EIS application, there remain a considerable number of contingent workers who find it difficult to be covered by the existing insurance programs.

The remaining issues that need to be addressed are the following. First, for those who are legally insured for WII and EIS coverage but are actually uninsured, some policy measures that help to raise the participation rate should be implemented. Second, for those who are currently legally uninsured, the WII and EIS should extend their scope of application in order to cover workers who work on daily basis or whose employment arrangements are not typical, particularly daily workers. For this, it is vital to keep good employment records. Another thing that needs to be addressed in the near future is whether we should protect those workers within the framework of the WII and EIS or whether we should design a new system appropriate for them.

References

In Korean:
Hur, J-J. and Yoo, K-S. (2001) *A Design of UI for Daily Worker.* Seoul: Korea Labor Institute.
Hwang, D. (1999) *Measures to Activate Employment Maintenance/Promotion Programs in Small Businesses.* Seoul: Ministry of Labor.
Jeong, J-H. and Choi, K-S. (2001) *Changes in Wage Structure and Income Distribution.* Seoul: Korea Labor Institute.
Kim, D.-H. et al. (1999) "Evaluation of Employment Maintenance Subsidies." Seoul: Korea Labor Institute.
Kim, H. (2000) "Forecasting the Medium and Long-term Benefit Payments of Work Injury Insurance." Seoul: Korea Labor Institute.
Lee, B-H. and Kang, S-H.. (1999) "Vocational Training," *Unemployment Policy in Korea.* Seoul: Korea Labor Institute.
Ministry of Labor (2001a) *White Paper on Employment Insurance.* Seoul.
Ministry of Labor (2001b) *White Paper on Policy against Unemployment.* Seoul.
Phang, H. (1999) "Evaluation of Four Year's EIS Experience." Seoul: Korea Labor Institute.

In English:
Hur, J-J. (2001a) "Expanding the Coverage of Korea's Unemployment Insurance," in Park, F. et al.(eds) *Labor Market Reforms in Korea: Policy Options for the Future.* Seoul: World Bank/Korea Labor Institute.
Hur, J.-J. (2001b) "Economic Crisis, Income Support, and Employment Generating Programs: Korea's Experience," Paper prepared for the UN ESCAP regional seminar on *Evaluation of Income/Employment Generating Programs to Alleviate Socio-Economic Impacts of the Economic Crisis,* Bangkok, May 23-25, 2001.
OECD (2000) *Review of Labour Market and Social Safety-net Policies in Korea.* Paris.
Phang, H. (1999) "Labor Market Issues and Employment Policies in Korea after the Economic Crisis." Paper presented at Manila Social Forum, Nov. 9-12.
Yoo, K.-S. (1999) *The Employment Insurance System in Korea.* Seoul: Korea Labor Institute.

9

Productive Welfare: Achievements and Limits

Chanyong Park

I. Background

The economic crisis in 1997 exposed the inability of Korea to deal with external shock and also exposed the weak domestic social infrastructure's inability to cushion against the impact of shock. As a result, based on the understanding that the already existing social policy system had a fundamental limit in dealing with economic crisis, Productive Welfare was established. It was established after reviewing the national policies on welfare, labor, environment, culture and education with scholars and experts in these fields. With such a background, Productive Welfare was born in 1999 as a new paradigm of Korean social policy.

Productive Welfare is an ideology that seeks to secure minimum living standards for all low income households, provide human resource development programs to support self-reliance of the poor and guarantee a basic living standard by expanding the coverage of social insurance to all people for the purpose of maintaining human dignity. As such, Productive Welfare endeavors to improve the quality of life for all citizens by promoting social development and a fair distribution of wealth.

Productive Welfare is one of the three major pillars of national policy, alongside Democracy and Market Economy. In fact, prior to adopting Democracy, Market Economy and Productive Welfare as the three pillars of national policy, President Kim Dae-Jung's Government had already experienced basic themes of Productive Welfare laying foundations for social policies. For instance, one of the policies driven under the Productive Welfare ideology was social insurance for which the coverage was expanded in 1998 and 1999.

Establishment of Productive Welfare's theoretical structure along with Democracy and Market Economy could provide a clearer vision of the Korean government's will to pursue balanced development of politics, economics and society. However, the reasons why Democracy, Market Economy and Productive Welfare should be emphasized as pivotal directions of national policies and the way each of the three pillars can be operated from a view of social integration, is a point to be discussed further.

In a democratic society, the administration of the state might be directly influenced by the majority.[1] Thus, national policies in general are formed and administered for the majority, which mainly consists of the middle class. Market Economy is often considered as a system which provides more benefits to those who have more capacity of winning fair competition in the market. These people tend to be in a comparatively good environment, for example, born to a wealthy, highly educated family or have outstanding intelligence, bright entrepreneurial skills or good health, which endows them with an advantage to win competition in the market. Therefore, under the circumstance where only Democracy and Market Economy are emphasized, the outcome would be biased benefiting mainly the middle class, who are the political majority and the high-income class. However, in our society, there are still considerable numbers of people who experience difficulties in accessing the labor market such as the old, disabled, orphans and also people with low ability to work and therefore face greater obstacles in being employed. Moreover, in reality, the vulnerable have not been sufficiently protected by the social security system in Korea. Thus, it could be argued that the government, through introducing Productive Welfare based on social solidarity as one of the pivotal directions of national policy, tries to resolve conflict among classes resulting from the economic crisis and seeks to achieve social integration among all classes. This helps us to have a better understanding of why Productive Welfare is one of the three pillars of national policy including Democracy and Market Economy.

II. Welfare Reform and Its Achievement

There are two difficulties in discussing what has been achieved by policies under the theme of Productive Welfare. First, Productive Welfare does not equate to a concrete policy program but is one of the pivotal directions of national policies including Democracy and Market Economy. Hence, it is not always easy to decide which programs should be classified into policies based on Productive Welfare.

Second, it is a little bit early to discuss what Productive Welfare has achieved at this point since it was only established in 1999 and most of the projected polices under Productive Welfare have not yet been settled. Nevertheless, this paper classifies these policy programs under the criteria of Productive Welfare and evaluates them even though they have not been settled yet.

Productive Welfare was born due to the extremely unstable societal atmosphere, which was caused by the 1997 economic crisis. Hence, whether policies based on Productive Welfare have stabilized society through protective programs for the poor and the unemployed is a key criterion for considering the achievement of Productive Welfare. In this dimension, Productive Welfare can be evaluated as a national management direction that enabled society to overcome the difficult situation. As argued above, introduction of the National Basic Livelihood Security Act (hereinafter NBLSA) and expanding the coverage of social insurance are characterized as the projected policies under Productive Welfare. In addition to these are the following: enhancing the accessibility of the vulnerable class to the labor market through human resource development which lays stress on labor welfare, taking measures to protect irregular employees and extending the application of the minimum wage system to all industries. Other projected policies based on Productive Welfare such as augmenting cultural and leisure lifestyles for the poor, building a healthy environment and providing education are too broad to be discussed in this chapter. Hence, discussion is narrowed down to policies that are relevant to social security and examine their achievements and limits.

Public Assistance

The NBLSA, which started in October 2000 as a replacement of the Livelihood Protection Act, guarantees minimum living standards to all low income families whose income is below the official poverty line, without considering their ability to work. So all low-income earners with the ability to work also become eligible for benefits unlike the previous system. The NBLSA puts emphasis on the nation's responsibility for the low-income class. Its introduction has tripled the number of livelihood payment beneficiaries from 540,000 in 1999 to 1.51 million in 2001 (Park et al. 2000).[2]

The official poverty line for the NBLSA beneficiaries or recipients is described in Table 9-1. Those who meet the criteria and do not have any family support will be considered as eligible. The criteria for those who support the eligible are quite complex but limited to immediate family members, spouses, and any siblings who are financially supporting them. The supporters are furthermore divided into three groups based on their asset and income: those able to support, those who have difficulty in supporting and those unable to support. Only in the latter two cases are poor families eligible for the benefit.[3]

Table 9-1
Official Poverty Line (2001)

No. of household member / Criteria	One	Two	Three	Four	Five	Six	Seven & More
Income (thousand Won)	330	550	760	960	1,090	1,230	Add 120 per person
Property (thousand Won)	31,000		34,000		38,000		

Source: Ministry of Health and Welfare, White Paper, 2001

Livelihood payment of the NBLSA is designed to provide supplementary payment to households whose income does not meet the official poverty line, and the amount of support is equal to the difference of household income and the official poverty line. Also, civil rights were enhanced through acknowledging the NBLSA as a social duty. The NBLSA fostered a condition in which the number of *Self-Reliance Aid Centers*[4] increased from 6 in 1997 to 161 in 2001 and the number of social workers increased from 3,000 in 1997 to 5,500 in 2001. Specifically, the increase in the number of *Self-Reliance Aid Centers* participating in self-supporting assistance programs within the community, and the inducement to bring social concerns to the program can be regarded as an achievement.

Nevertheless, the National Basic Livelihood Security (NBLS) system still has room for improvement. Firstly, the NBLSA was legislated in response to a plea stemming from the bad circumstances of the 1997 economic crisis without a full examination of its implications. For instance, the complement of officials who are charged with social welfare has not reached its goal, and the Ministry of Health and Welfare, in charge of the NBLSA, has had difficulties in inducing relevant Ministries to collaborate with the investigation into the financial assets of relatives who have a duty to support. This caused some mis-targeting towards the poor at the beginning of its implementation. However, it is expected that this problem will remain due to difficulties in surveying the income of the self-employed. Secondly the self-support system has not been fully enforced due to the lack of administrative networks at the Ministry of Labor. The self-supporting programs of the Ministry of Health and Welfare have been projected to work in collaboration with the Ministry of Labor, a necessary condition for the official poverty line of eligibility to be applied equally among all regions, i.e., metropolis, medium and small-sized cities, and rural areas (Park et al. 2000; Ministry of Labour 2001).

Social Insurance

The Social insurance system has undergone rapid change since 1998. The thrust of this change is to reduce drastically uncovered groups through applying the National Pension scheme to all[5]; integrate the management systems of *the Health Insurance Funds for Wage Earners* (hereinafter HIFW) with the *Health Insurance Funds for Non Wage Earners* (hereinafter HIFNW); and expand coverage of Employment Insurance and Industrial Injury Insurance to all workplaces.

As a result, anyone who has an income is now covered by the National Pension scheme, regardless of employment category thus opening an era of universal National Pension. Now, even if a pension premium is paid only once, pension is payable for the disabled and survivors.[6] In addition, the integration of management systems of Health Insurance could help to enhance social solidarity and actualize fair charges.[7] Also by abolishing time

Table 9-2

Process of Korea's Social Insurance Coverage Expansion: By Year and Group

National Pension	Health Insurance
1960: government employees	1977: wage earners at workplace with
1963: military personnel's	500 or more people
1975: private school teachers	1979: employees in government, private
1977: private school personnel's	school and wage earners at
1988: wage earners at workplace with	workplace with 300 or more people
10 or more people	1980: wage earners at workplace with
1992: wage earners at workplace with	300 or more people
five or more people	1982: wage earners at workplace with
1995: fishermen and farmers	16 or more people
1999: urban residents (national coverage)	1988: wage earners at workplace with
	five or more people and
	fishermen and farmers
	1989: urban residents (national coverage)
Employment Insurance	**Industrial Injury Insurance**
1995: workplace with 30 or more people	1964: workplace with 500 or more people
1998: workplace with 10 or more people	1965: workplace with 200 or more people
1998: workplace with five or more people	1967: workplace with 100 or more people
1998: workplace with one or more people	1969: workplace with 50 or more people
	1974: workplace with 16 or more people
	1982: workplace with 10 or more people
	(some with over five people)
	1992: workplace with five or more people
	2000: workplace with one or more people

Source: Ministry of Health and Welfare, White Paper, 1963-2001 and Ministry of Labor, White Paper, 1990-2001

limits on periods for Health Insurance services it has been made possible to provide medical service throughout the year (Kim, Y-M. 1997b).[8]

Following the 1997 economic crisis, economic recession and dramatic restructuring sharply accelerated the unemployment rate. As a result, Employment Insurance coverage was expanded earlier than previously planned. Beginning March 1998, unemployment benefits became available even to workers at the workplace with five or more persons. With the severe unemployment situation, coverage was expanded again in October 1998 to include workers at the workplace with four or less persons as well as temporary or part-time workers.[9] As for Industrial Injury Insurance,[10] membership has become mandatory even for a workplace hiring less than five persons beginning July 2000. Expanded coverage of social insurance by reducing the mandatory employment period was geared towards including temporary and daily workers.

Under the National Pension scheme, temporary, daily, and other part-time employees are classified as local participants.[11] As for Health Insurance, since July 2001, temporary and daily workers were transferred to the workplace participant group. Initially, Employment Insurance was not applicable to those who work for less than a three-month period and less than 30.8 hours a week. Since October 1998, the mandatory employment period was shortened to include those who work more than one month and more than 80 hours per month (or more than 18 hours a week). Recent changes in regulations regarding expanded coverage of employment insurance, by shortening the mandatory work period, are described in Table 9-3.

Table 9-3
Rules to Implement Social Insurance for Non-Full-Time Workers
(as of December 2000)

Classification	Pension Scheme	Health Insurance	Employment Insurance	Industrial Injury Insurance
Temporary daily workers	three months or more	two months or more	one month or more	Applied
Part-time workers	Classified as locally insured persons	classified as locally insured persons	More than 80 hours or more than one month (18 hours or more a week)	Applied

Source: Park, Chanyong, Yeon-Myung Kim and Taewan Kim, 2000
Note: Temporary and daily workers join as local participant group in national pension and as non wage earners in Health insurance.

However, there are still difficulties in improving the systems of National Pension and Health Insurance because of the low rate of income survey of the self-employed. The self-employed often report less than their actual income in an effort to pay a low insurance premium and it is not easy to assess the scale of the problem. In contrast, salary earners pay their full National Pension and Health Insurance premiums since it is deducted at source. This is unfair in that the self-employed and the salary earners receive the same medical service and the salary earners' discontent may result in a boycott of payment of social insurance premiums. The problem remains unresolved due to the fact that the Ministry of Health and Welfare, which is facing this problem, is not the Ministry that has the ability to handle it. On the other hand, the Ministry in charge of the income survey of the self-employed finds enforcing the income survey simply for the effective management of social insurance burdensome. Consequently, a low rate of income survey of the self-employed has continued and no resolution has been reached up to this point (Kwon 2000; Noh 1999; Noh and Lee 2000).

Moreover, the destabilization of Health Insurance finance, which was in fact predicted several years ago, has become a core issue these days. Although increasing Health Insurance premium is the most viable option, it is not being followed because of people's resistance. Instead the government announced a policy of increasing its subsidy for Health Insurance.

Limits of Welfare System

Thanks to the reduction in the employment period for eligibility and the expansion of qualifying workplaces, the number of marginal workers,[12] who are not covered by social insurance, has decreased for the past two to three years. Despite the concentrated efforts to extend coverage of social insurance, however, a substantial number of persons still do not have access to income maintenance benefits under social insurance.

Figure 9-1 shows the coverage of Korea's social insurance. Health insurance has a wider coverage than the national pension as it has liberalized age and other eligibility conditions. Employment Insurance and Industrial Injury Insurance basically targeted for employees, but those at workplaces with four or less employees in the agricultural and fishery industries have been excluded. Considering that agricultural or fishery companies with four or less employees are likely to deal with labor-intensive work which may expose workers to greater risk of injuries, such workplaces should be covered by the Industrial Injury Insurance. Furthermore, temporary and daily workers employed for one month or less and those who work less than 18 hours a week are not covered by Employment Insurance (Hwang 2000). But as seen above, measures to bring marginal workers under the social security system have been implemented; the reduction of the qualifying employment period, a

Figure 9-1
Coverage of Social Insurance

Age		15-18							18-60																						60-65
Section	Non Economically Active population	\<- Economically active population: Workers -\>							\<------------------------------ Economically active population ------------------------------\>																	Officials	Teachers & staffs at private school	Sailors	Special Post officials	The self-employed	Candidates for application	Non-candidates for application	Person in military services	Professional soldiers	Special applicants
Social Insurance — Pension	NP	NP	NP	NP	NP	NP	NP	NP	NP	NP	NP	NP	NP	NP	NP	NP	NP	NP	NP	NP	CP	PP	NP	CP	NP	NP		NP	NP	SP	
Health																															
Employment																															
Industrial injury																															

Within the Economically active population, Workers are classified by workplace ("Workplace with 5 or more persons" and "Workplace with less than 5 persons"), industry type ("Industry", "Agriculture & Fishery"), employment status ("Full-time", "Temporary daily" [3 months or more; Less than 3 months: 1 month or more / Less than 1 month], "Part-time" [18 hours or more per week; Less than 18 hours per week]) and "The Unemployed". The Non economically active population includes "Candidates for application", "Non-candidates for application" and "Soldiers".

Note 1: Shaded area represents subjects that have been covered and unshaded/blank area represents subjects that have not been covered.

Note 2: NP: National Pension, CP: Pension for Officials, PP: Private School's Pension, SP: Pension for Soldiers

NP[1] applicable if two-thirds of workers in the relevant workplace agreed

NP[2] applicable for those who want to register

decrease in weekly work hours, and expansion of coverage to workplaces with four or less employees have already been put into action. Nevertheless, the system is still faced with obstacles in providing coverage for all workers under the social insurance schemes.

The issue of shortfalls in Korea's social insurance scheme has only recently come to surface despite its importance. Korea's social insurance schemes had provided a protective umbrella for salary and wage earners, but excluded those at workplaces with four or less employees and the lowest paid temporary contract-based workers. Hence it is important to figure out the types of uncovered zones existing in the social insurance scheme and their impact on the system. It is also essential to realize that the government's efforts to expand the coverage of the social insurance schemes for the past two or three years have not been sufficient to overcome the problem of excluding some people from coverage. The problem should be dealt with on multiple fronts.

The people not insured for social security are of two types. The first consists of those to whom the social security scheme is not applied. The second consists of those qualifying for benefits but not awarded due payment. Salary and wage earners may not be covered because the contract term is too short. They do not receive benefits, although entitled, when they have intentionally avoided paying contribution[13] or because of the lack of administration infrastructure for screening and providing benefits in a timely manner. Measures to overcome those difficulties are addressed below.

III. Counter Policies for Improvement

Guiding principles to establish counter policies that are comprehensive, complete, and fair are discussed below. Earlier we discussed how government has tried to reduce groups uncovered by social security programs. However, the benefit level is also important. Provision of reasonable welfare benefits under the principle of sufficient income support is essential. For public assistance, appropriate amount of payments should be guaranteed based on minimum cost of living. As for social insurance, the basic rule should be that the insured pay their due contribution and receive corresponding benefits. Even if the uncovered groups are eliminated and benefit levels are reasonable, problems would remain if the principle of equity is not applied. More effort must be made to apply the rule of equity in selecting beneficiaries and providing benefits.

Affiliation of Information Systems with the Four Social Insurance Management Bodies

The management of workplaces and insured persons by one administrative body instead of four, can create synergy effects on insurance administration. In particular, by affiliating the channels of qualification management, charging and collection into one, it would be much easier to establish eligibility of marginal workers, workplaces with four or less employees, and the self-employed. Under such a system, insured persons under one social insurance can be immediately recognized as insured under other social insurance, making it less likely for them to be left uncovered. The possibility of applying insurance to marginal workers, who are affected by frequent workplace closure and bankruptcy as well as frequent job changes, depends on whether or not their employment status and wage level can be fully verified.

For these reasons, countries with a long history of social insurance often opt for consolidated charging and collection of social insurance contributions. For instance, in Germany, pension, employment insurance, and health insurance premiums are charged and collected by the health insurance administrative organization in the form of a comprehensive social insurance premium.

Collection of Insurance Premium by National Tax Authority

Another way to reduce uncovered groups in social insurance (by preventing intentional contribution avoidance) is to make social insurance contribution mandatory. In fact, in many countries taxes and social insurance contributions are linked or integrated. National tax agencies collect social insurance contributions by including them in taxes and transfer the amount to related social insurance organizations. One of the problems in applying social insurance to marginal workers is that both employers and insured persons tend to avoid paying contribution. No doubt the national tax authority is in a better position to resolve this problem as it has access to massive data regarding income and assets as well as much stronger authority to charge and collect. Since the National Tax Service of Korea manages all assets, income, and tax payment documents on an individual basis, it is also better poised to transform the social insurance scheme to an individual based management scheme. Also, if employers make false reports regarding wage or employment status, tax authorities can correct the wrong data based on other documents in their possession. The involvement of the taxation agency would be an excellent way to check for moral hazards in terms of contributions and benefits. (contribution payment avoidance, falsely scaled-down income reports, and redundant receipt of benefits). Beyond that, combining collection of taxes and social insurance payments will boost administrative efficiency and reduce collection costs, and thereby also benefit employers.

This method is adopted by the US (the national tax agency charges and collects social insurance contributions), the U.K. (its national tax agency has taken the responsibility of charging and collecting social insurance contributions beginning in 1999), Sweden, and Argentina. In particular, the consolidation of social insurance payment collection with tax collection in Argentina is regarded as a model case for improvement in managerial and operational efficiency (ILO 2000).

Strengthening the Ability to Survey Income of the Self-Employed

By strengthening income survey levels of the self-employed (National Committee for Self-Employed Income Assessment 1999), blind spots in the NBLS, and the National Pension and the Health Insurance could be scaled down. Undeclared income and the under-reporting of income of the self-employed is so prevalent that it has become one of the major problems in social security. The reason for concentrating major effort into the income survey of the self-employed is that public assistance, especially determining the financial assets of the family supporters in regard to NBLS and poverty related monitoring function, cannot operate properly in cases where the income of the self-employed is not surveyed adequately. The low rate of accurate income survey carried out for the self-employed is causing major concern for social insurance as well. However, in the case of Korea, in spite of the absence of complete income survey data, not only National Pension is being expanded to include the self-employed in the urban area, but also the integration of Health Insurance Funds and their financial integration is under-way. Basically a society which has difficulty in carrying out the income survey effectively is thus left to face the challenge of achieving the welfare policies of an advanced society. Moreover, the success of social insurance schemes based on integration and social solidarity is jeopardised. In order to raise the income survey level active participation and co-operation from the Ministry of Finance and Economy and the National Tax Service is necessary. Otherwise it would be unavoidable to convert the existing social insurance scheme into a different system that can operate even with the low income survey level.

In 1999, the *National Committee for Self-employed Income Assessment* recommended various measures designed to resolve the issue of mis-declaration of income. In the course of 1999 and 2000 taxation reform was carried out by the National Taxation Service including several measures to revamp the value added tax system, accelerate credit card use, and restructure ways to improve relevant income data of the self-employed. This overhaul can be said to set the tone for assessing the accurate income status of the self-employed. It is also expected to play an important role in understanding the employment and wage status of employees at small workplaces, as well as the documentation on charging contributions for social insurance schemes. A variety of measures to promote credit card use, in particular the credit card lottery scheme, have almost doubled its use for the first half of 2001 compared to the same period of 2000. The use of credit cards has been on a steady rise, becoming a significant factor in exposing the undeclared income of the self-employed. However, the implementation of these various taxation reforms will take too long to be a useful basis for collecting social insurance contributions. Therefore it would be desirable to carry out tax investigations on a random basis, as done in many other nations, and in case of violation, strict penalties should be imposed. This measure will boost public awareness that tax evasion is a serious crime. Only then will it be possible to get a better grip on the size of income of the self-employed, within a short period of time (National Tax Service 2000a; 2000b).

Optimizing the Level of Social Security Benefits

Adequate protection against risks cannot be provided if the social security benefit level is too low. The level of NBLS payment is based on the research on minimum cost of living conducted by the Korea Institute for Health and Social Affairs (KIHASA). The minimum cost of living measured by KIHASA goes through a thorough review of *the Central Minimum Living Standard Committee* which consists of government officials, scholars, labor unions and NGOs. Thus, the level of NBLS payment has been estimated to be appropriate for the current situation.

Under Industrial Injury Insurance, the cash benefits have met the international level set by the ILO, except for rehabilitation and medical services (Kim, Y.-M. 1997b). Job seeking benefits under Employment Insurance were pointed out to be less than they should be and therefore measures have been introduced to boost the benefits (beginning January 2000, benefit provision period was increased from 60-210 days to 90-240 days and minimum job seeking benefits have been raised from 70 percent to 90 percent). This means that as long as they are entitled for coverage, the marginal workers will find it more beneficial. In the case of Health Insurance, it has been estimated that it provides relatively low benefits and no cash benefits for disease or injury. As for National Pension, it is designed so that those with shorter contribution period receive smaller pensions. Therefore the marginal workforce whose insured period is relatively short may appear to face disadvantages. However, given the fact that the National Pension is designed for income redistribution, from which the low-income class is likely to benefit the most (Kwon 2000), the marginal workforce and employees belonging to small workplaces and earning low income are not so disadvantaged when it comes to National Pension.

Benefit levels under social insurance are generally proportional to contribution levels and contributory periods. The system has limited ability to adjust benefit levels and contributory periods given its insurance framework. In any case, the issue of increasing benefit levels and of entitlement periods should be discussed in line with the mounting burden of contribution payments and government support. In the case of the marginal workforce and employees at small workplaces, government assistance with paying contributions should be considered.

IV. Concluding Remarks

It was only as recently as three to four years ago that the general public began to regard the social welfare system as being substantial to their daily life. This is because the welfare system has been applied mainly to the poor population unable to work or to workers employed in big companies, excluding often the self-employed or the poor with working ability. However, the 1997 economic crisis made the Korean government speed up its response to the surging unemployment rate and poverty ratio. It was an event, which prompted the government to declare Productive Welfare as one of the fundamental governing principles in parallel with Democracy and Market Economy. The effort to strengthen the social security system allowed it to take another leap forward. However, inherent problems have appeared in the course of trying to develop a comprehensive social welfare system within a short time frame, something which had taken advanced nations several decades. As a result, blind spots in social security coverage and the lack of effective links among systems have become the downside of the process.

This paper presented a comprehensive review of the social security system including major public assistance programs and social insurance schemes. It also discussed counter measures to scale down blind spots in social security coverage. Korea's social security has developed based on the two pillars of social insurance and public assistance. Despite problems arising in the process of evolution, Korea's Health Insurance system is cited as one of the most successful social security systems of developing nations. Therefore, assuming that these issues could be resolved through revision and reform of the existing scheme, this study focused on exploring ways to create an environment, where the functioning of the existing social security scheme can be improved. Additionally, ways to resolve defects in the system were also reviewed.

To sum up: measures to scale down blind spots in social security coverage boil down to dealing with the marginal workers. Their exclusion from social insurance coverage is a major shortcoming of Korea's social insurance, along with the lack of accurate assessment of the income of the self-employed.[14] Problems also stem from the combination of several characteristics: the economic structure (size of black market), contribution rates of social insurance by employers and employees (contribution avoidance), income level of insured persons, level of taxation administration, managerial capability of social insurance administration, and others. Nonetheless, strengthening the managerial capability of social insurance organizations by transferring the function of determining of recipient eligibility and charging contribution to the National Tax Service will help to consolidate the social insurance funds and enhance the effectiveness of the social insurance expansion. Administrative organizations for social security systems will need to improve the targeting for benefits and service provision in order to boost social credibility. For all these matters, relevant government authorities and social insurance officials will need to have a creative approach.

Notes

1. However, the extent to which this is observed is much less in the exceptional circumstance where the structure of income distribution is extremely bipolar.
2. Legislated in September 7, 1999 and enacted in October 1, 2000, the NBLSA, which is one of the public assistance programs, has improved the nation's welfare system greatly.
3. If the combined income or asset of an applicant's household and his financial supporter's household is over 120 percentage of income criteria or property criteria of the official poverty line, the supporter under question is regarded as an official supporter. If the applicant is unable to work and have no income, but owns a house, then the combined income level is raised to over 150 percentage of the official poverty line.
4. The Self Reliance Aid Center was established in 1996 to support recipients of the Livelihood Protection System (LPS) as well as the low-income earners who are not covered by the LPS. The main activities of the center is to provide information on available jobs, to offer job counselling and job placement services to support the community-based business and self-employment, to mediate the self-reliance fund, and to teach skills and management techniques. Self-reliance Aid Centers are operated by the civil groups and designated by the Government, but both the central and local governments can partly or wholly provide the operating funds. (http://www.mohw.go.kr/english/intro8.html)
5. Major changes brought by the amendment of the National Pension Act in January 1999 are as follows. First, the self-employed in urban areas were included into the scheme beginning in April 1, 1999. The beneficiaries of the scheme are divided into two groups: wage earners employed by workplaces and local scheme members. Persons insured through the workplaces refer to employees aged between 18 and 60, who are either employees or employers at a workplace with five or more full time workers. Those 18 or younger are able to join the workplace pension plan with employer consent. Those 60 or older can have the extended contribution period to age 65 if their insured period is less than 20 years. However, excluded from the coverage of the National Pension Scheme for the workplace are those who have temporary work with contracts of three months or less, those who have seasonal work with periods of three months or less, and those who often move from workplace to workplace. Temporary and part-time workers are also excluded from coverage of the National Pension Scheme for the work place. But those who are excluded from coverage of the National Pension Scheme for the workplace are nevertheless insured through the Local scheme of National Pension (Park et al. 2000).
6. The new National Pension scheme strengthened pensioners' rights and sought for livelihood stability. The minimum contribution period was shortened from 15 years to ten years. Pension installment is provided for those who turn 60 after divorce or those who divorce after 60 in case marriage has lasted for five years or

more (But benefit provision is terminated when they are remarried). Deferred payment for pension contribution arrears is permitted for those obligated with child rearing and military service, as well as for students and those serving prison terms. Legislation is being formulated to provide loans to unemployed for livelihood stability (Park et al. 2000).

7.   Since the introduction of Health Insurance in 1977, it has gone through several phases before maturing into a universal Health Insurance scheme. However, the Health Insurance system had inherent problems. Specifically, Health Insurance Funds did not have the same premium calculation systems. As a result, the insured could have ended up paying different premiums if they belonged to different Health Insurance Funds, although their income and asset levels were the same. This caused equity problems and at the same time, widened the financial gap among Health Insurance Funds. The independent management of small-size Funds also brought up operational inefficiency. Previously, the Health Insurance system was divided into Health Insurance Corporations for Employees of Government, Private School, Military, HIFW, and HIFNW. To resolve the problems, the government consolidated the HIFNW and Health Insurance Corporations for Employees of Government and Private Schools. It was the first step towards the grand consolidation of Health Insurance taken on October 1998. As the second step, the plan integrated HIF-WE into the already consolidated comprehensive Health Insurance Funds, to be the National Health Insurance Corporation. The new universal Health Insurance Corporation has the integrated management system for the insured but classifies them into two groups: HIFW and HIFNW. Those, who are covered by HIFW, consist of employees and employers at the workplace with five or more people, employees of government and private schools, who earn monthly wages. Those, who are covered by HIFNW, consist of the self-employed and employees at the workplace with four or less people. The new system applies the same premium rates in line with income level, regardless of which Health Insurance Fund in charge of the coverage. The new Health Insurance system has shifted its focus from treatment-orientation to prevention, rehabilitation and health promotion (Park et al. 2000).

8.   The Health Insurance system abolished the regulation of limiting the period covered by Health Insurance to a certain level. Instead it promises unlimited Health Insurance coverage year-round beginning July 1, 2000. Previous Health Insurance laws covered only disease, injury, and death excluding pre-natal care from coverage. The new Health Insurance expanded the scope of coverage to include preventive care, diagnosis, rehabilitation, health promotion, not to mention treatment and death (Park et al. 2000).

9.   Since its introduction and implementation in 1995, Employment Insurance has become the primary social safety net for the unemployed during the economic crisis when the jobless rate surged. The number of recipients of Employment Insurance was estimated at 50,000 throughout 1997, but in 1998, the number surged to 438,000. Unemployment benefit provision also skyrocketed to 799.1 billion Won, ten times that of 1997 of 78.7 billion Won. Likewise, the sharp increase in the number of beneficiaries for 1998 is attributable to the expanded scope of coverage, a string of bankruptcies and closures of firms, lay-offs, early retirement, the reduction of minimum coverage period, and the implementation of special expanded payments. In the end, the contribution income of 1998 worth 576 billion won was exceeded by unemployment benefits expenditure worth 799.2 billion won. In other words, the ratio of contribution income to benefit payment recorded 139 percent. Unemployment benefit serves the primary social safety net

with extended coverage scope, eased eligibility criteria, extended coverage period and extended average coverage period. But despite the eased beneficiary standards, the ratio of unemployment benefit recipients to the total jobless is 10.5 percent, which is significantly lower in comparison to those of advanced nations such as Japan (27.8 percent, 1992), Germany (43.5 percent, 1990), the US (36.0 percent, 1990), and Britain (30.0 percent, 1998).

10. Industrial Injury Insurance was the first social insurance to be adopted in Korea. In the initial stage of introduction, its implementation scope was limited to mines or manufacturing factories with 500 or more people. In industrial injury insurance, employers are fully liable for the contributions, which is different from other social insurances. The premium per person is determined by multiplying the premium rate and the total amount of salaries. In 1999, a major legal amendment was made to the industrial injury insurance system. The amendment was made to enhance the fairness by setting maximum and minimum coverage limits with the aim to narrow the benefit gap. Thanks to the amendment, new insurance payments were introduced, and more small and medium size firms were included into the system, thereby strengthening its role as a social safety net.

11. National Pension classifies workers between 18 and 60, at workplaces with five or more employees, and daily or temporary workers who work for more than three months, into workplace pension groups. Those between 18 and 60 who are not workplace workers or insured under the special occupation pension schemes are classified as local pension participant groups. Full-time workers employed for three months or less, part-time workers at workplaces with five or less workers, all workers at workplaces with five or less employees, and the self-employed can join the National Pension but many of them are believed to be delinquent contributors to the insurance (Park et al. 2000).

12. Marginal workers in this paper refers to full time workers at the workplaces with four or less employees as well as 'part-time workers' including temporary daily workers. They share the common ground: their employment status is incomplete and they are excluded from national welfare or company welfare benefits.

13. In July 2000, among total participants (16,585,390 persons), there are 10,879,281 local participants (5,144,000 are free from contribution payment duties). Those, who delay their insurance contribution due to unemployment, bankruptcy, and livelihood difficulties and those who were unable to pay contributions due to military service, education, and prison sentence, numbered 4,813,000. Here the problem is the large number of insured persons unable to pay contributions. As of April 2000, 30 percentage of insured persons under the National Pension or 5,141,000 are unable to pay insurance contributions due to low income. 85 percentage out of them or 4,375,000 are either unemployed, have their businesses suspended, or unaccountable with unclear whereabouts. Among those who delay their pension insurance contributions are the unemployed, economically inactive persons, full-time housewives, and women with no spouses. Under the current system, they are allowed to defer insurance premium payments. However, there is a group of people who should not be allowed to delay their payment, but who are classified as permissible delayers. These are the high-income asset owners who are estimated to total about 200,000 to 300,000 (Park et al. 2000).

14. Accurate assessment of income of the self-employed will determine success of Korea's social insurance scheme as well as the ability to cover employed persons with social insurance schemes. It seemed impossible even two to three years ago, however, it is now possible not only to figure out the income size of self-employed persons but also to assess the income and employment status of employees at the workplaces run by self-employed persons, more accurately.

References

In Korean:

Hwang, D. S. (2000) *Changes in Unemployment Benefits and Management System of the Insured following the Extension of the Unemployment Insurance Coverage.* Korea Labor Institute.

Kim, Y.-M. (1997a) "Application Procedure of Korea Social Insurance and Inequality," *Korea Social Welfare and Inequality,* Study Center of Social Welfare.

_____ (1997b) "Standards of ILO's Social Security and Problems of Improving Korea Social Security," *Korea Journal of Social Welfare*, 31, Academic Society of Social Welfare.

Kwon, M.-I. (2000) "Profit Survey of National Pension: Is the National Pension Payment a fair profit for an Insurance Bill?," *Korea Journal of Social Welfare*, 41, Academic Society of Social Welfare.

Lee, G. (1999) "Problems of Korea Work Injury Insurance and Guide for its Improvement," *Journal of Social Welfare Policy,* 9, Academic Society of Korea Social Welfare Policy.

Ministry of Health and Welfare (1963-2001) *White Paper.*

Ministry of Labor (1990-2001) *White Paper.*

National Committee for Self-Employed Income Assessment(1999) *Policy Proposal for the Self-Employed Income Survey.*

National Tax Service (2000a) *Announcement of Modifying a Value Added Taxation System.*

_____ (2000b) *Six-month Operation of Credit Card Receipt Lottery System.*

Noh, I. (1999) "Self-employed Income Survey and Levy System of Insurance," *Journal of Social Welfare Policy*, 9, Academic Society of Korea Social Welfare Policy.

Noh, I. and Lee, Y. (2000) "Evaluation of A Year Extension of National Pension into City Areas and Guide for its Improvement," Materials for Seminar on Evaluation of A Year Extension of National Pension into City Areas and Guide for its Improvement, National Pension Corporation.

Park, C., Kim, Y.-M. and Kim, T. (2000) *Schemes for Reforming Korean Income Maintenance System to Expand the Social Safety Nets.* Korea Institute for Health and Social Affairs.

In English:

ILO (1989) *Introduction to Social Security.* 3rd ed, 2nd impression, ILO, Geneva.

_____ (2000) *World Labour Report: Income Security and Social Protection in a Changing World.* ILO, Geneva.

Presidential Committee for Quality-of-Life (1999) *DJ Welfarism.* Seoul: Office of the President of Korea.

10

United States' Experience with Welfare Reform: Lessons for Korean Policy

Wendell E. Primus

Individuals (and particularly children) can be or become poor for a number of reasons: because they live in families that have experienced death, disability (of both short and long duration), unemployment, low wages, or due to problems securing and retaining employment. Different programs are needed to address these different situations. In the United States, social insurance programs address the first three, work support programs such as the Earned Income Tax Credit (EITC), child care assistance, and food stamps address low wages, and the public assistance system provides income and services to enable individuals to overcome their employment barriers.

Both work support and public assistance programs underwent considerable changes in the 1990s. In the early 1990s, the primary public assistance program in the United States was Aid to Families with Dependent Children (AFDC). In 1996, it was replaced with Temporary Assistance for Needy Families (TANF), and new time limits and enforced work sanctions were introduced in the cash welfare assistance program. At the same time, the funding for work support programs—including the Earned Income Tax Credit, health insurance coverage for low-income children, and child-care subsidies—was increased substantially.

Let me begin by applauding the philosophy and vision of the Korean National Basic Minimum Living Standard. To implement this vision in Korea or in any country, policymakers need to understand the heterogeneity of the population that should be served by a safety net. This chapter begins with a discussion of this issue and then proceeds to a discussion of some guiding principles that should form the basis for a safety net. The chapter then briefly describes the three main elements of the safety net—social insurance, work support programs, and public assistance—and their appropriate roles in serving individuals and families. I then draw some lessons from a U.S. perspective which reflect both successful aspects of the current system and ways in which it could be improved. The chapter then turns to the overarching topic of parental responsibility and the government's role in supporting children, especially in cases where the parents are separated. Finally, the chapter addresses a number of specific administrative issues that can have a substantial impact on the success or failure of implementing safety net programs.

This chapter does not address health insurance coverage, retirement programs, education, or macro-economic changes that might increase job availability. The chapter also does not discuss the safety net for the elderly; the primary focus is on families with children. The goal of this chapter is to make a few suggestions regarding the design and implementation of a safety net in Korea.

I. Heterogeneity of the Population Served by the Safety Net

People who are poor are heterogeneous and have low-incomes for a variety of reasons. Some families and children are poor because of a death or disability of the primary breadwinner. Some are poor because adults lose jobs during an economic slowdown or recession. Others lose jobs because of the natural workings of a dynamic economy where firms go out of business because demand for products or services shifts or because technological change produces economic dislocation. Still others are poor because the particular skills or human capital that a person possesses does not result in a wage rate high enough so that the individual and his dependents can realize a minimal level of income to meet basic food, shelter, and other needs. Finally, some individuals have one or more barriers to employment that make it difficult or impossible for them to secure and retain employment.

Policymakers designing safety net programs often try to differentiate the "deserving" poor—that is, people who are unable to work, from the "undeserving poor"—those who are able to work but choose not to. Distinguishing between people who can work and those who cannot is more complicated than it may seem. A substantial portion of the population served by cash welfare assistance has a number of barriers to employment. At the same time, a national profile of people with incomes below the poverty line suggests that they have a stronger attachment to the labor force than many people assume. Dividing the population of people who need assistance from safety net programs into these different categories is further complicated by the fact that a given individual's employability can change over time, for example, with the onset of illness, disability, or recession.

Over the past few years, a number of studies have shown that the population served by cash welfare assistance in the United States has a high incidence of various barriers to employment (Zedlewski 1999; Danziger et al. 2000). While this research describes the employment barriers facing individuals in the United States, these barriers are probably a universal phenomenon and it is likely that they exist in South Korea as well, although the percentage of the population exhibiting these various barriers will vary. In the United States, roughly one-fourth to one-third of current welfare recipients have a serious mental health problem; it appears that upwards of one-fifth of current recipients have physical impairments that limit their ability to work; a substantial proportion have learning disabilities, and two studies that tested the IQs of current recipients found that one-fifth to one-quarter had low IQs (less than 80) (Sweeney 2000). Finally, substance abuse problems are also significant. An estimate of the extent of substance abuse problems is more difficult: the figures range from about 2 percent to 20 percent and depend partially on how the questions about substance abuse are asked (ibid.). Many individuals have multiple employment barriers. These same studies indicate that the probability of employment decreases significantly as the number of barriers faced by a given individual increases (Zedlewski 1999; Danziger et al. 2000).

In terms of work effort, a national profile of the 5.2 million poor families with children in the United States in which the parents were not ill, disabled, or retired counters the perception that most poor families include adults who could work but do not.[1] Of these families, 3.9 million—or 76 percent — had one or more working parents. Most of these families—3.4 million—showed a clear connection to the labor force, with parents working more than one calendar quarter. Nearly one-third of these families had workers employed full-time and year-round. In many instances, the primary issue is that wages are not high enough to provide a livable income (Bernstein et al. 2000).

Most families in the United States that receive public assistance have adults with recent work experience. As a result, these families' yearly incomes are a combination of public assistance and earnings. This group of families includes those who use public assistance as a temporary safety net when a job is lost due to a layoff, disruption in child care or transportation arrangements, illness, family crisis, or other factors; many such families remain on assistance for relatively short periods of time. This group of families also includes families that leave welfare when a parent finds work. Finally, this group includes families in which a parent is working but the family remains eligible for assistance as a result of low earnings. Some 72 percent of the families with children that received public assistance at some point in a year during the late 1990s had a parent who worked at least part of that year.[2]

II. Guiding Principles

Even though the reasons that an individual or family is poor at a given time may overlap and divisions between the groups are not clear-cut, different programs are appropriate for families in different circumstances. When an individual or a family needs income assistance, the first line of defense should not be public assistance programs. The first major component of a nation's safety net should be social insurance programs which provide a social insurance payment when an event such as recession, disability, or death occurs. Eligibility for these payments depends upon having a work record and the payment replaces a percentage of lost wages. These programs, in keeping with Korea's vision of productive welfare, are based upon work, and should help families avoid the need for public assistance programs.

The second major component of a safety net should provide working families that earn low wages with an earnings supplement and child care subsidies to ensure that their work effort is rewarded. Some of these working families may need additional assistance in meeting housing and food needs. They should have access to these work supports only if they are working and their earnings are low enough that they are in need of support.

Public assistance should be the third major component of a nation's safety net. The guiding philosophy behind the National Basic Minimum Living Standard is appropriate: "Productive welfare is an ideology, as well as a policy, that seeks to secure minimum living standards for all people, while expanding opportunities for self-support in socio-economic activities for the purpose of maintaining human dignity" (Kwan 2000). Public assistance programs should ensure that recipients are engaging in activities that will make them more productive and allow them to become financially independent. The nature of these activities will vary for families and individuals with different needs and barriers to employment and may include employment training, publicly-funded jobs, education, and substance abuse treatment.

In brief, the guiding principles of a strong safety net should be:

- a minimum living standard for all people so that poverty and deprivation are minimized;
- a strong emphasis on work among all non-elderly adults (with exceptions for some adults taking care of young or disabled children) which seeks to promote self-sufficiency and financial independence while minimizing dependency upon government assistance. Work should be rewarded by keeping marginal tax rates[3] as low as possible within budget constraints. For any family, work should increase their standard of living significantly. In certain programs and for certain adults, work should be required and enforced with appropriate sanctions, and publicly funded transitional jobs should be provided when employment in the private sector is not possible. These transitional jobs can provide valuable work experience, build a work ethic, and provide a bridge to jobs in the private sector;
- barriers to employment should be eliminated wherever possible through the appropriate provision of services that effectively and efficiently address these barriers;

- that the public view the safety net as just, and that the safety net reflect the culture and ethic of the vast majority of the populace. For example, requiring single mothers to work should be based upon Korea's culture and societal norms about the value of child-rearing versus requiring the mother to support herself by earning wages;
- that the minimum living standard is adjusted for inflation each year and reflects regional differences, if any, in the cost of living;
- that the provision of this minimum living standard seeks to minimize interference with the market economy;
- that clients of assistance are treated with dignity, but with the expectation that earnings are honestly reported and other program requirements are met; and
- that both parents and the government have a role in supporting children. When a child's family is poor, when the child is disabled, or when the child is a victim of abuse or neglect, the government's role is greater than it would be otherwise. Nevertheless, in most cases, the children's primary source of financial support should be their parents, regardless of whether they are living together. When parents are separated, this obligation should be enforced through a child support enforcement system.

III. The Role of Social Insurance

Consistent with Korea's vision, the first set of programs that families and individuals without jobs should be directed to are the work-based social insurance programs. Individuals who have become unemployed or who are unable to work due to a temporary or permanent disability, or who are dependent survivors should not be immediately referred to the social welfare system.

The social insurance system provides cash benefits to replace earnings lost as a result of unemployment, disability, or death. This protection is obtained by working in jobs that are covered by the social insurance programs. Social insurance programs in the United States are financed by taxes paid by employers, employees, and the self-employed, and pay benefits to individuals largely on the basis of work histories. Once workers are employed in covered jobs long enough to be insured, they are automatically eligible to receive benefits and are not subject to a means test nor required to accept any available job; instead, they are permitted to look for jobs similar to previously held jobs. In contrast, public assistance programs are financed by general taxes and pay benefits according to a family's need without taking into account work history or previous earnings.

Social insurance programs differ from traditional private-sector insurance programs in that the programs are national, and coverage is generally compulsory and nearly universal. They are designed to prevent poverty by providing additional protection for families with children, and by providing a larger degree of earnings replacement for low-paid versus high-paid workers. In the United States as of 1999, there are about 1.4 million children (2.0 percent of all children) who receive survivor benefits because one or more of their parents are deceased. Another 1.4 million (2.0 percent) children receive disability payments because their parent became disabled (Social Security Administration 2000). Because these benefits are fairly generous, very few of these children are poor.

The main components of the social insurance system in the United States include:

• *Old-Age, Survivors, and Disability Insurance (OASDI)* pays benefits to retired workers and their dependents, to disabled workers and their dependents, and to the survivors of workers who die. Nearly all American workers are covered. Benefits are based on a worker's average earnings, and are financed by a payroll tax shared by workers and employers. In 1999, of a total work force of approximately 158.5 million workers, about 151.7 million workers and an estimated 96 percentage of all jobs in the United States were covered under Social Security (US House of Representatives 2000).

• *Workers' Compensation* pays the cost of medical care and compensation for lost income for employees who are injured in a job-related accident or who contract a disease as a result of their job. Workers' compensation also provides payments to dependents of workers in case death occurs. Benefits vary by state and depend on the type and duration of the worker's disability and previous weekly earnings. Most states set minimum and maximum limits on benefits, and limit the duration of receipt of benefits.

• *Unemployment Insurance* has two main objectives: (1) to provide temporary and partial wage replacement to involuntarily unemployed workers who were recently employed; and (2) to help stabilize the economy during recessions.

Unemployment benefits vary. In order to qualify for benefits, an unemployed person usually must have recently worked for a covered employer for a specified period of time and earned a certain amount of wages. About 125 million individuals were covered by unemployment compensation programs in 2000, representing 97 percent of all wage and salary workers and 89 percent of the civilian labor force. Most states provide benefits for up to 26 weeks. The unemployment benefits are weekly cash payments that are generally equal to about half of the worker's full-time weekly pay rate, with minimum and maximum limits (US House of Representatives 2000).

These programs are conceptually similar to the four major social insurance programs in South Korea: the national pension system, health insurance, unemployment insurance, and industrial injury insurance. However, coverage and benefit levels under these programs are considerably less in South Korea in comparison to the United States. According to one assessment, "Despite advancements, the entire population has yet to be covered by the social insurance system and the level of benefits is still insufficient" (Kwan 2000). Current government efforts to enhance the employment insurance system will increase the number of eligible employment insurance recipients to 7.6 million, or 80 percentage of total workers, and to 20 percentage of the total number of unemployed by the end of 2002 (ibid.). Korea should continue to strive for more universal coverage in its social insurance programs.

Since these programs are conceptually similar to those in the United States, the discussion of issues surrounding these programs will not be extensive. However, there are several improvements that could be made to these programs in the United States, and may be applicable in Korea as well. The tax base for these various social insurance programs should be better coordinated. This would ease considerably employer reporting burdens (and probably increase compliance and lower administrative mistakes). Unemployment tax rates are to some extent employer specific. In other words, if an employer does not manage his work-flow properly and is constantly hiring and firing workers, his tax burden will be higher. As a result the employer has an economic incentive to be concerned about the impact of layoffs on his employees.

To receive unemployment benefits, an individual must have been laid off because of economic reasons and must be looking for work. These two requirements mean that only 35 to 50 percent of unemployed persons in the United States receive benefits. New entrants or reentrants to the labor force are not eligible for benefits. In addition, if a person had to quit employment because child-care arrangements fell apart, or because a worker followed a spouse to another part of the country and could not find work immediately, or because of the birth of a new child; the worker is probably ineligible for benefits. The safety net in the United States could be improved by allowing some of these workers to be eligible for benefits. Policymakers in Korea will have to decide whether some or all of these situations should be covered through unemployment benefits.

Another instance where the American safety net could be improved is our treatment of dislocated workers. These are workers who have been employed for a considerable period of time but because of technological change or other reasons, they become unemployed with little chance of returning to their industry or firm. These workers need income support as well as training, vocational counseling and job seeking assistance. They should not have to turn immediately to the public assistance component of the safety net.

IV. Supporting Low-Wage Working Families

In the United States, the wage and career opportunities available to less-skilled workers have substantially worsened in the last 20 years or so. Employment no longer provides these workers the economic security it once did

(Blank 1997). For 23 years, from 1973 through 1996, wages and benefits deteriorated for most workers. However, a turn-around began in 1997. While there are still many losses to be regained, the wage trend is finally moving in the right direction.

- Wages paid at the median of the pay scale declined between 1973 and 1996, but finally began rising in 1997-99. However, this median wage did not surpass the 1989 level until mid-1999 and it remains substantially below the level reached in 1973 when the downturn began.[4]
- There are a growing number of jobs paying poverty-level wages, defined as an hourly wage so low that a worker employed full time cannot pull a family of four above the poverty line. In 1998, 29 percent of all workers were in jobs paying poverty-level wages, a larger share than in the past.[5]

These declines in wages are due to both the increasing internationalization of the U.S. economy as firms move their production facilities (and jobs for low-skill workers) across international borders and technological changes in the U.S. economy that require a more skilled workforce (Blank 1997).

These trends are not unique to the United States, and have become apparent in Korea in more recent years. The impact of Korea's labor market crisis in the late 1990s has disproportionately affected low-skilled and low-wage workers: about one million jobs for technicians and unskilled workers were lost, with production workers and laborers losing jobs at higher rates than others (Fields 1999). Workers with the lowest levels of education and lower-incomes made up an increasing share of the total unemployed population (ibid.).

There are two basic options for improving low wages to achieve a minimal level of income. The first option is to regulate the market and impose a minimum wage that is high enough to meet the basic needs of working families. The second is to supplement low wages through government programs — an earnings subsidy like the EITC or a wage rate subsidy. A minimum wage is an important policy tool to prevent exploitation of and increase the earnings of low-income workers. As a policy matter, one should employ both options. Because of employment effects on low-wage workers and to ease the transition from school to work for first-time job seekers, the minimum wage should not be increased to such a level that wages from full-time employment at the minimum wage yields an adequate income. Instead, there should be a minimum wage and the earnings of low-income workers (particularly those with dependents) should be enhanced through wage supplements. Wage-rate subsidy programs were not adopted in the United States because of their considerable administrative burden. Wage rate subsidy programs provide an increase in the wage rate—the total value of the subsidy is the hours of work multiplied by the amount of the subsidy. It is more administratively complex because hours of work and the wage-rate must be ascertained, not just earnings.

Work support programs play a crucial role in helping low-income working families make ends meet. The two primary programs that provide assistance to working poor families are the Earned Income Tax Credit (EITC) and the food stamp program. A family of four with one person earning the federal minimum wage (currently $5.15 per hour) who is employed full-time and full-year has income close to the poverty line only if that family also receives both the EITC and the food stamp benefits to which it is entitled. The poverty line in the United States is one measure of the minimum amount of income required to meet basic needs in a household—food, shelter, and clothes. As Figure 10-1 illustrates, for that family, the minimum wage job (less withholding for the employee share of payroll taxes) brings in $9,512 of income, the EITC and child credit adds $4,038, and the cash value of food stamps adds $3,696. These three sources of income equal $17,246, or 95 percent of the poverty line for a family of four, which is estimated to be $18,094 in 2001. Without food stamps, the family's income would equal only 75 percent of the poverty line; without food stamps or the EITC, the family's income would equal only 52 percent of the poverty line.

The support programs that provided additional assistance to poor families were changed in the 1990s. These policies were expanded as part of an effort to "make work pay." As a single parent with no earnings begins to work, that parent's earnings increase, her TANF and food stamp benefits decline, and her work-related expenses such as child-care, transportation, and work-related clothing increase. To "make work pay," government benefits must be structured in a way that ensures that when families become employed and increase their earnings, they are economically better off after benefit reductions and increased expenses are taken into account.

- The *Earned Income Tax Credit (EITC)* is the most important safety net program for supporting low-income workers, and was substantially ex-

Figure 10-1
Helping Working Families Reach the Poverty Line, 2001

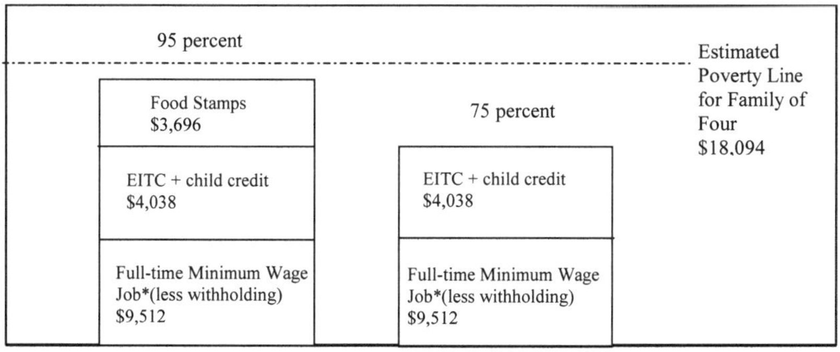

*Assumes 2,000 hours per year of work, and no work or child care expenses

panded in 1990 and again in 1993. The EITC provides a refundable tax credit to low-wage workers with children. The largest credit is available to taxpayers with more than one child—they may claim a credit in calendar year 2001 of 40 percent of earnings up to $10,020, resulting in a maximum credit of $4,008. The maximum credit is available for those with earnings between $10,020 and $13,090. At $13,090 of earnings the credit begins to phase down at a rate of 21.06 percent of earnings above $13,090. The credit is phased down to $0 at $32,121of earnings. Families with one child receive a somewhat smaller credit, and childless workers also are eligible for a much smaller EITC.

- The *food stamp program* provides in-kind nutrition assistance to low-income families. Historically, food stamp benefits were provided as paper coupons that could be spent for food at authorized grocery stores. Today, however, over forty states deliver some or all food stamp benefits through electronic benefit transfer (EBT) systems that work with cards very much like ATM cards. Food stamps generally are limited to families whose gross incomes are no more than 130 percent of the federal poverty line ($1,848 per month for a family of four) *and* whose net incomes are no more than 100 percent of the federal poverty line ($1,421 per month for a family of four). Food stamps is both a work support and an income support program. A household's food stamp benefit depends on the number of people in the household, the household's gross income, and deductions for expenses (such as housing costs that exceed half of the household's income) that can significantly affect a household's ability to purchase a nutritionally adequate diet. The maximum a family of four can receive is $434 per month, but the overwhelming majority of food stamp households receive less than the maximum and are expected to spend some of their own incomes to supplement their food stamp allotments. The average food stamp benefit

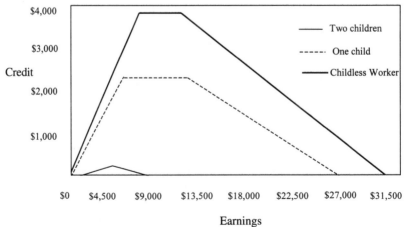

Figure 10-2
EITC Credit in 2000

during the first half of fiscal year 2001 is less than $75 per person per month, or 81 cents per person per meal (Super 2001).

• The U.S. Department of Housing and Urban Development (HUD) operates three major federally-funded programs that provide *housing assistance* to low-income families: public housing and Section 8 certificates or vouchers which provide recipients with subsidies to rent housing in the private market, and Section 8 project-based programs, which are rental units in buildings that are owned and operated by private owners who have received a subsidy from the federal government (Sard and Daskal 1998). Families receiving housing assistance typically pay 30 percent of their income in rent. The government typically covers the difference between the tenant contribution and the full rental cost. As a result, families required rent payments generally rise with an increase in income and fall with a decrease in income. There are many more families eligible for assistance than there are families provided assistance, and waiting lists for housing assistance are very long in many jurisdictions.

• Funding for *childcare* for low-income families was consolidated into a single childcare and Development Block Grant and increased available resources for childcare. The maximum income eligibility levels were raised, but states were not longer required to guarantee childcare to cash assistance recipients who need child care in order to work or enter education or training, or to families in their first year of leaving cash assistance due to employment or earnings.

• Access to *health care* was expanded for low-income children through the creation of the Children's Health Insurance Program (CHIP). Another policy change that has been gradually implemented since the late 1980s and has had significant implications for making work pay was the "delinking" of TANF and Medicaid. Under current law, eligibility for Medicaid is based on income. In contrast, historically, eligibility for Medicaid depended on receiving cash assistance. This policy discouraged welfare recipients from working because by becoming employed, welfare recipients would have to give up Medicaid coverage, and risk not being able to pay medical bills and not receiving needed medical treatment for their children (Yelowit 1995; Mofitt and Wolfe 1993).

The Earned Income Tax Credit

The strengthening of work support programs—and especially the expansion of the EITC in 1993—has been the most important recent innovation in American social policy that should be considered for adoption in Korea. The EITC has had a number of positive effects: lifting many children out of poverty, allowing low-income families to make an investment in upward mobility or asset-building purposes, and encouraging low-income families to work.

An analysis of Census data shows that in 1999, the EITC lifted 4.7 million people out of poverty, including 2.6 million children. These data show that the EITC now lifts more children out of poverty than all other means-tested benefit programs (including food stamps and housing subsidies) combined (Center on Budget and Policy Priorities 1999). In addition to lifting families from poverty, recent academic research that has examined how families expend their EITC payments finds that a substantial proportion of families use at least a portion of their EITC for upward mobility or asset-building purposes, such as for acquiring or repairing a car to commute to work or to search for and accept a better job, making capital repairs on a home (such as fixing a leaking roof), or paying for tuition for training or education (Smeeding et al. 1999).

The substantial expansion of the Earned Income Tax Credit in the 1990s played a significant role in inducing single mothers—the demographic group that makes up the vast majority of welfare recipients—to work. One of the two leading studies of this issue examined the large increase between 1984 and 1996 in the proportion of single mothers who work. It found that the EITC expansions implemented in this period were responsible for inducing more than half of this increase in employment. The study found that the EITC expansions had a stronger effect in increasing work than welfare policy changes did (Meyer and Rosenbaum 1999). The other leading study examined a shorter time-period, from 1992 to 1996. It found that both welfare policy changes and EITC expansions had large effects in increasing the employment of single mothers during this period, with welfare changes being the largest factor and EITC expansions the second largest (Ellwood 1999).

The EITC also has substantial political appeal. There is substantial support for "making work pay." Most people would agree that families with a full-time, full-year minimum wage worker should have enough income to avoid poverty, and the EITC is a critical component in allowing low-income working families to do just that. For many low-income working families, however, the EITC alone will not be enough to lift them out of poverty. Most families receive an EITC once per year when they file their tax returns. The EITC does not provide periodic support to meet ongoing expenses for low-income families. In addition to supplementing low wages with an EITC, the government should provide assistance with rent, food, and childcare for those who need it. These benefits could be supplied on a monthly basis either in the form of a cash earnings supplement, or in the form of a voucher for in-kind services.

V. Welfare Reform in the United States and Its Impacts

Prior to 1996, the primary public assistance program in the United States was an income transfer program called Aid to Families with Dependent Children (AFDC). Through the AFDC program, states provided payments for needy children who were deprived of parental support or care because their father or mother was absent from the home continuously, incapacitated, deceased, or unemployed. Payments also were permitted for the child's needy caretaker relative (usually the grandmother). Federal law set outer income and resource limits for AFDC eligibility, and the size of benefits was determined by each individual state. In 1997 the median benefit for a three-person household was $377 per month, an amount equivalent to 34 percent of the poverty line (US House of Representatives 2000). States were required to provide aid to all persons who were in classes eligible under Federal law and whose income and resources were within State-set limits. Recipients of cash welfare assistance through the AFDC program were also automatically eligible for food assistance through the food stamp program and health-care coverage through the Medicaid program.

When the federal government undertook welfare reform in the mid-1990s, some of the themes that were prominent in the welfare debates included:[6]

- the perception that AFDC did too little to encourage and require employment. Some critics argued that the program fostered family break-up and out-of-wedlock birth, and had created a "culture of dependency" responsible for an array of other social problems.
- the broad agreement that both parents should support their children. The vast majority of cash welfare recipients in the United States are single-parent (and primarily single-mother) households. For custodial parents, this typically meant an emphasis on work and cooperation with child support enforcement. For non-custodial parents (mostly fathers), this meant a set of initiatives to strengthen the effectiveness of the child support system.
- the perception that out-of-wedlock birth was presenting an increasingly serious social problem, and that the federal government should exert a strong leadership role in seeking to reduce the incidence of out-of-wedlock birth; and
- the perception much of the innovation and creativity in social policy was emerging from state experimentation rather than federal programs, and that federal law should be restructured to give more power and authority to states in the shaping and implementation of policy.
  The key ways that the welfare reform legislation, Temporary Assistance for Needy Families (TANF), differs from AFDC include (US House of Representatives 2000):
- *Funding*. TANF law provides a fixed family assistance grant for each State, plus some extra funds. AFDC law provided unlimited matching funds for AFDC benefits.
- *Time limit for benefits*. TANF sets a five-year limit on federally-funded aid, with a 20 percent hardship exemption. AFDC had no time limit.
- *Work requirements*. TANF requires that 50 percent of the caseload be engaged in "work activities" in most cases for 30 hours per week. States are penalized if that requirement is not met. AFDC did not have such a work requirement.

• *Sanctions*. States were required to impose sanctions on families who re-
fused to work or who did not cooperate with child support enforcement
officials.

Two basic program features of AFDC were retained by TANF. States decide
how needy families must be to receive aid, and States establish maximum
benefit levels.

   In addition to promoting work, the other goal of the 1996 welfare legislation was cutting spending. According to Congressional Budget Office estimates at the time of enactment, the bill would reduce outlays by $55 billion
between fiscal years 1997 and 2002. The primary savings in the bill were
reductions in food stamp spending (about $27.4 billion)[7] and welfare ben-
efits for legal immigrants. The reductions affecting legal immigrants who
were present in the country before welfare reform was enacted and were elderly or disabled at that time have, for the most part, been reversed through a
series of legislative acts. However, nearly all of the reductions that apply to
immigrants arriving in this country after enactment of the welfare bill continue to
apply. According to U.S. Department of Agriculture, the agency that administers
the food stamp program, hundreds of thousands of low-income immigrants no
longer receive food stamps as a result of these restrictions. President Bush
recently proposed a revision of some of these food stamp restrictions.

   While the immigrant restrictions target non-citizens, many U.S. citizen
children have been affected as well, because 80 percent of children with
immigrant parents are themselves citizens. Nearly one in ten U.S. families
includes at least one citizen child and at least one non-citizen parent. Even
though citizen children living in immigrant families and some immigrant
parents remain eligible for benefits, confusion about eligibility and concerns
about the immigration consequences of receiving benefits have caused a
substantial decline in participation among these groups.

   The food stamp cuts enacted during welfare reform also had a significant
impact on the working poor. The two provisions that saved the most money
disproportionately affected families that received smaller food stamp benefits.[8] Since working poor families tend to have higher incomes than families
receiving primarily welfare assistance, they received smaller food stamp benefits, and consequently were most affected. These reductions could be a factor contributing to the food stamp caseload declines — especially among the
working poor—because the transaction costs of securing food stamps may
nearly equal the benefit.

VI. Impacts of Welfare Reform

   In the United States, many have pointed to the dramatic decline in caseloads
of 60 percent since their peak in 1994 as the definitive indicator of its suc-

cess. Today, only a relatively small proportion of the U.S. population that is in poverty receives cash welfare assistance. In 1999, only 38 percent of poor children received TANF cash assistance, a drop of 34 percent since 1995. The ratio of the number of children receiving cash assistance to the number of poor children was substantially lower in 1999 than in any year since 1970. Similarly, the percentage of poor children receiving food stamps fell from 88 percent in 1995 to 72 percent in 1999. In any safety net program, the size of the caseload, or more specifically its reduction, is an inadequate measure of success.

A more definitive measure of the success of welfare reform has been the significant increase in work effort among single mothers. Single mothers are working more and earning more. In 1992, about one third of single mothers with young children were working. By 1999, the share had grown to more than half. Official child poverty rates have declined, and under a comprehensive measure of poverty that includes government benefits and taxes, the child poverty rate fell to 12.9 percent in 1999, the all-time low since this measure became available in 1979.

Not all these changes can be ascribed to the new welfare law. A strong economy and public policies that "make work pay" including the Earned Income Tax Credit and increased spending on child care also must be credited. Welfare reform coincided with the longest-running economic expansion in U.S. history—a time when hourly wage rates for the lowest-paid workers began to rise after falling for two consecutive decades, and unemployment rates fell as low as 3.9 percent. One would expect earnings to increase and child poverty to decline significantly under these conditions. Yet there is agreement that some families are floundering (Haskins 2001). The average disposable incomes of the poorest fifth of single mothers living only with their children and no other adults (about one million families) fell eight percent between 1995 and 1999, after adjusting for inflation, despite increased earnings (Center on Budget and Policy Priorities 1999). The impacts of the weakening of the United States economy on the well-being and employment opportunities of current and former welfare recipients are not yet clear, but are likely to be significant.

Tables 10-1 and 10-2 illustrate earnings and disposable income both before and after welfare reform for various types of families with children. Disposable income adds to wages all other forms of private income—child support and income from assets—plus government benefits less federal taxes less work expenses. However, child care expenses and subsidies are excluded because no information is obtained about those expenses by the Census Bureau. Families are divided into three mutually exclusive and exhaustive categories—single mother families living with their children and no other adults, single mother families living with other relatives or living with a male but not married to him, and all other families with children. In 1995, there were 17

Figure 10-3
Percent of Married, Single, and Never-Married Mothers Working, 1985-1999

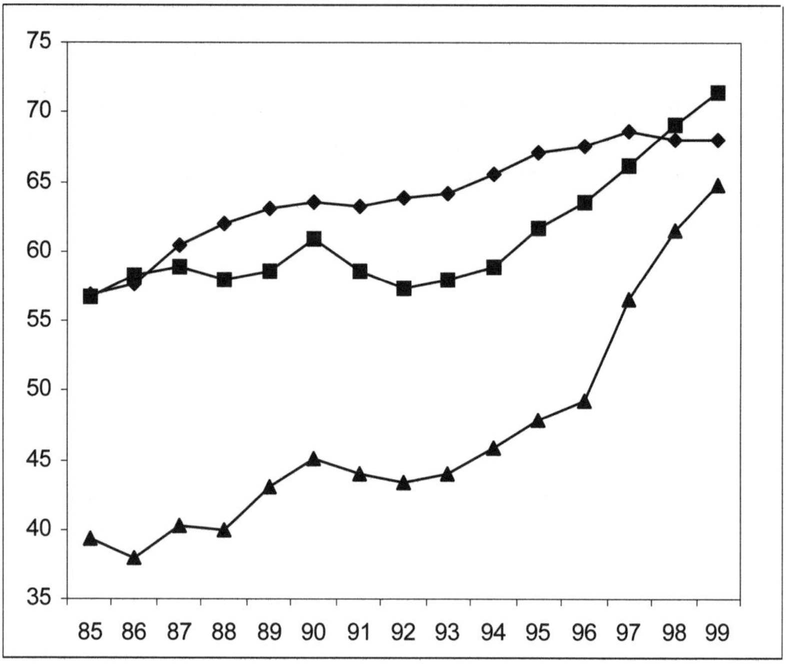

Source: Gary Burtless, The Brookings Institute

million individuals living in lone single mother families and 10.7 million individuals and 110.9 million individuals in the other two types of families respectively. By 1999, the number of individuals in lone single mother families had declined to 16.1 million, the number of individuals in other single mother families had declined to 10.5 million while the number of individuals in the third category of families had increased to 114 million individuals.

All of these families are arrayed by the ratio of disposable income to poverty and the results are shown in Table 10-1. For lone single mother families at the fifth percentile, disposable income declined from 42 percent of the poverty threshold in 1995 to 39 percent in 1999, a decline of six percent. Among other families with children at the fifth percentile, income increased from 85 percent of the poverty threshold in 1995 to 92 percent in 1999.

As can be seen from Table 10-1, there is a group of approximately 725,000 lone single mother families that are worse off today than they were before welfare reform. Given the very strong economy, and the increases in the EITC, why should there be any significant number of families that are worse off? The primary reason is that the earnings gains by the mothers have been offset by the decline in food stamps and cash assistance. Other types of families with children (with the exception of two percentiles in other single mother families) all had disposable income gains. The Census data provides snap-shots of the population at points in time; one cannot longitudinally follow the same families in this dataset. Some families may lose income while other families gain income, but as can be seen from Table 10-1, the net result of all of these income changes are only income gains among other families with children. Among lone single mother families, there were a substantial number of families who lost income between 1995 (pre-welfare reform) and 1999 (the last year for which data exists), despite a strong economy.

Table 10-2 summarizes these earnings and disposable income trends for the various types of families with children for 1993, 1995, and 1999. For the two years prior to the enactment of welfare reform in 1996, earnings and disposable income increased significantly. For lone single mother families, however, despite earnings gains disposable income fell by $697 between 1995 and 1999. These were the families primarily affected by welfare reform. For other families, there were both significant earnings and income gains.

While only a small part can be attributed to welfare reform, child living arrangements in the United States have also changed between 1995 and 2000. An analysis of the Census Bureau's Current Population Survey shows that between 1995 and 2000, the proportion of children younger than 18 living with a single mother declined from 19.9 percent to 18.4 percent—a statistically significant drop of 1.5 percentage points, or eight percent (Dupree and Primus 2001). In contrast, the proportion of children living with two married parents remained essentially unchanged during this period (ibid.). Both trends represent a significant change from the previous decade (1985-1990), when the proportion of children living with a single mother remained at essentially the same level and the share of children living with two married parents de-clined. The new data reverse steady trends over the last 25 years toward single mother families and away from two-parent families. Among lower income families, there was a significant increase in the percent of children living with two married adults, particularly among black and Hispanic families.

Income Gains are Critical to Enhance Child Well-Being

Welfare reform in the United States has worked for some families but not for others. As Tables 10-1 and 10-2 above demonstrated, welfare reform in combination with a strong economy and work supports like the EITC, has resulted in growing family incomes except for the poorest 14 percent of lone single mother families. Two recent reports which reexamined many previous welfare reform interventions in a number of different states which were all carefully evaluated using a randomized control and experimental groups found that income gains were critical to improving child well-being.

In the first study, the importance of increasing financial well-being for families that do work was emphasized by comparing the results of five separate studies covering 11 different welfare programs which fell into one of three categories: some programs mandated work without providingfinancial incentives, some which provided financial incentives for work but no man-

Table 10-1
Income to Poverty Threshold for Different Family Types by Percentile

Single Mother Families – No Other Adults				
Percentile	1995	1999	Difference	% Difference
5	0.42[9]	0.39	-0.03	-5.9%
8	0.54	0.49	-0.05	-9.5%
11	0.62	0.57	-0.05	-8.0%
14	0.68	0.66	-0.02	-2.7%
17	0.73	0.73	0.01	0.7%
20	0.77	0.81	0.03	4.5%

Number of families worse off in 1999 compared to 1995: 725,000.
Worse off is defined as a statistically significant difference of 1.7 percentage of poverty.

Other Single Mother Families				
Percentile	1995	1999	Difference	% Difference
5	0.45	0.48	0.03	7.3%
8	0.57	0.64	0.07	12.0%
11	0.64	0.74	0.10	15.3%
14	0.70	0.82	0.12	17.1%
17	0.77	0.90	0.13	15.8%
20	0.84	0.98	0.14	15.7%

Number of families worse off in 1999 compared to 1995: 72,000 (in percentiles 2 and 3; not shown).
Worse off is defined as a statistically significant difference of 1.9 percentage of poverty.

Other Families with Children				
Percentile	1995	1999	Difference	% Difference
5	0.85	0.92	0.07	8.8%
8	1.00	1.08	0.08	7.9%
11	1.13	1.21	0.08	6.9%
14	1.25	1.33	0.08	7.6%
17	1.33	1.44	0.11	8.0%
20	1.41	1.54	0.13	9.3%

Note: Families are mutually exclusive and exhaustive. Includes all families with children.

date, and some programs had both a mandate and financial incentives. This study found that mandating parental employment did not by itself improve the lives of the parents' children (Bloom and Michalopoulos 2001). Only in programs where the parents increased their employment and their income were positive effects in areas such as school achievement, behavior problems, and health and safety noted for elementary school-aged children.

Another study that synthesized the findings of 16 welfare-to-work programs, including the 11 cited in the previous study, found a more specific trend: every welfare-to-work program that lifted participants' average income by five percent or more had mostly good effects on children, while every program that reduced income by five percent of more had mostly bad effects on children (Sherman 2001). These effects on children varied by age. The positive results were concentrated on the middle years of childhood. None of

Table 10-2
Changes in Earnings and Average Disposable
Income: By Family Type (1999 Dollars)

Single Mother Families with No Other Adults					% Changes	
		1993	1995	1999	93-95	95-99
Poorest Fifth	Earnings	1,199	1,354	2,173	12.9%	60.%
	Disposable Income	7,714	8,532	7,835	10.6%	-8.2%
Second Fifth	Earnings	2,629	3,913	7,437	48.8%	90.1%
	Disposable Income	12,929	14,438	15,494	11.7%	7.3%
Single Mother Families with Other Adults					% Changes	
		1993	1995	1999	93-95	95-99
Poorest Fifth	Earnings	3,081	4,451	7,226	44.5%	62.3%
	Disposable Income	10,187	11,729	12,515	16.3%	6.7%
Second Fifth	Earnings	8,762	12,506	18,550	42.7%	48.3%
	Disposable Income	19,113	21,059	24,214	10.2%	15.0%
Single Mother Families with Children					% Changes	
		1993	1995	1999	93-95	95-99
Poorest Fifth	Earnings	9,338	10,632	13,198	13.9%	24.1%
	Disposable Income	13,325	14,941	16,607	12.1%	11.1%
Second Fifth	Earnings	20,771	22,794	25,289	9.7%	10.9%
	Disposable Income	22,318	23,687	25,857	6.1%	9.2%

Table 10-3
Changes in Child Living Arrangements by Income

	1985	1990	1995	2000	1985-1990	1995-2000
Overall						
Married Parents	74.3%	73.1%	69.5%	70.1%	**-1.2%**	0.6%
Single Mother	18.8%	18.9%	19.9%	18.4%	0.1%	**-1.5%**
Cohabiting Mother	1.5%	1.9%	2.6%	3.0%	**0.4%**	**0.4%**
Lower Income (Bottom 39 %)						
Married Parents	55.1%	52.9%	48.3%	50.5%	**-2.2%**	**2.2%**
Single Mother	35.0%	35.3%	36.6%	32.7%	0.3%	**-3.9%**
Cohabiting Mother	3.0%	3.7%	4.8%	6.0%	**0.7%**	**1.2%**
Higher Income (Top 61 %)						
Married Parents	87.1%	86.4%	83.8%	83.7%	-0.7%	-0.1%
Single Mother	8.6%	8.5%	9.5%	9.5%	-0.1%	0.0%
Cohabiting Mother	0.5%	0.7%	1.2%	1.1%	0.2%	-0.1%

the programs—even those that raised families' incomes—helped adolescents. Experts say that helping older children may require additional services (such as after-school activities), more flexible program rules, more income support, or a combination of these (ibid.). This study emphasizes that "the programs that raised family income were all *pro-work*. That is, the programs that lifted income did not do so simply by providing more government benefits for everyone. Instead, they created a more supportive environment for families that work. Supports included cash supplements for working families, job training, and considerable child care assistance. Program staff and written materials also emphasized the value and 'benefits of work.'"

Lessons for Korea from Welfare Reform in the United States

Politically, welfare reform in the United States is perceived as being enormously successful. Caseloads are down and the message conveyed through the press to the American public is how hard the clients are working and the barriers to employment that they are overcoming. As a result, opinion polls show that Americans are now willing to spend additional dollars to support the poor, particularly the working poor.

There are several important implications of welfare reform in the United States for South Korea:

- Through sanction policy and tough work requirements, dependency on public assistance programs can be limited.
- The public assistance caseload in the United States exhibited many and varying barriers to employment. A multi-faceted service strategy integrated closely with cash and other assistance programs is an essential ingredient to increasing employment.
- By focusing on poverty reduction not caseload reduction, and by making cash and in-kind assistance more accessible to the working poor, more income gains could be achieved among families and fewer families would experience income losses.

Dependency on Public Assistance Can Be Limited

Earnings supplements, childcare and other assistance (for rent or food) should be a matter of entitlement for low-wage workers. The combination of wages and these work supports achieve a minimal level of income. The receipt of benefits is conditional solely upon earnings. In contrast to the work support program, public assistance programs in the United States are conditional entitlements. Qualifying individuals are entitled to benefits so long as they comply with program requirements. The public assistance programs seek to improve the capacities as well as the living standards of clients. In addition to the work supports offered to low-wage workers, the public assistance programs include job training and work-readiness programs, counseling, and mental health and substance abuse treatment programs. Clients are required to meet program requirements such as participation in training, work, and job search programs in order to continue to receive benefits.

In some states, individualized employability plans or contracts are developed between the government and the client which outline what is expected from both parties. These plans are usually based upon assessments of what the client needs to secure and retain employment. The government agrees to provide the needed services, the client agrees to cooperate, show up for the required job search, training, substance abuse counseling or whatever other service may be needed. The client understands that public assistance grants will be reduced if the plan is not followed and appointments and progress are not made towards employment.

In addition, in most states, the client also understands that there is a definite time limit so that if she is not successful in finding a job, she will lose all cash assistance. While the evidence is clear that many more never married women (and many with substantial barriers) have joined the labor force, researchers have been unable to determine (and may never be able to definitively assess) to what extent the strong economy, the increased availability of child care and increases in the Earned Income Tax Credit versus various welfare policies (time limits, sanctions, changed expectations about work, and work supports) are each responsible for the increased attachment to the work force among former welfare recipients. In reality, each is partially responsible for the increase and the combination and interaction among these factors may have resulted in a situation where the whole is greater than the sum of the parts.

Over the last ten years, sanction policy has become an integral part of welfare policy. The GAO study implies that by the end of 1999, nearly 370,000 families had lost welfare benefits due to a full-family sanction and remained off aid. In addition, about four percent to five percent of the public assistance caseload experienced a partial sanction in each month. Relatively fewer families have hit their state or federal time limit. I would urge that you selectively adopt U.S. policy in Korea.

There have been a flurry of recent academic studies attempting to parse out what elements of the welfare reforms contributed to the employment gains. Given that many of these reforms were adopted simultaneously, the studies contradict each other (Kaushal and Kaestner 2001; Groger 2001; O'Neill and Hill 2001).

Sanctions[10]

As a part of the welfare reform laws passed in 1996, federal law requires all states to sanction families that refuse to comply with work activities or with child support requirements without good cause, either by reducing or terminating benefits. Some states also impose sanctions in their TANF programs for failure to comply with other requirements such as ensuring that children are immunized and attending school. States have considerable latitude regarding how sanctions are designed and applied. For example, benefits may be reduced or eliminated altogether; the benefit loss may apply to the parent's benefit or to the children's benefits as well; and the benefit reduction or elimination may be temporary or permanent. The following principles should guide the design and administration of sanctions:

The goal of sanctions must be to cause families to engage in productive activities that will help parents overcome their employment barriers if they have any and become employed. If sanctions are a part of public assistance policy—in the United States there is a political assumption that they are—they must be carefully designed. This is especially true because research indicates that sanctioned families, when compared to other families receiving welfare, have greater barriers to employment and are more likely to have multiple barriers. They tend to have lower education levels, more limited work experience, and a greater incidence of domestic violence, disabilities, and other physical and mental health problems. They also are more likely than other families receiving welfare to have several of these barriers at once. The following principles should offer a guide to design an administration of sanctions:

Program administrators must ensure that clients understand why they are being sanctioned and what they can do to avoid being sanctioned. The employment barriers described above may affect the ability of the parents to understand and comply with program requirements and thus may be the cause of the family's sanction. One way to implement this policy is through a pre-sanction review. A pre-sanction review can serve as an opportunity to evaluate the circumstances of a noncompliant family and provide more intensive services to help the family come into compliance. Addressing these issues before a sanction is imposed will make compliance more likely and could prevent the family from experiencing a deeper crisis resulting from the loss of income. Once a sanction has been imposed, it is important that a family knows how to cure it and have their benefits restored. This information should be provided orally by caseworkers and in clear written notices from the agency. Sanction notices often are difficult to understand, especially for families with limited English proficiency, low education or literacy levels, low intelligence, or learning disabilities.

Families should not face sanctions that eliminate their entire public assistance benefit the first time that they fail to comply with a program requirement. Instead, sanctions should be structured in a way that the initial sanction is mild and the sanctions escalate if the family continues to avoid coming into compliance and curing the sanction.

Even when a family has been sanctioned, the goal of program administrations should continue to be helping families to engage in productive activities that will help parents overcome their employment barriers if they have any and become employed. Unaddressed needs or barriers are likely to continue to prevent compliance both during the sanction period and even after a sanction has been lifted. For example, if a parent does not have transportation to the required work activity, compliance is unlikely until the transportation problem is addressed. Follow-up services also can prevent escalation of sanctions to more severe penalties.

The moment that a sanctioned family comes into compliance, that family's sanctions should be lifted and benefits should be restored immediately. When a family comes into compliance the sanction's purpose has been achieved, and the family's benefits should be restored immediately.

Do NOT Adopt Time Limits for Public Assistance

The time limits that were adopted as a part of welfare reform in 1996 are unnecessary (in my opinion), have limited efficacy, and are not fair to families that are working. They are an element of the safety net program in the United States that should *not* be adopted in other countries.

Time limits were adopted out of concern for dependency on public assistance. However, work requirements and sanctions are probably sufficient measures to address the issue of dependency. In addition, time limits are not fair to families that are working but still not earning enough to support themselves without a small public assistance grant. Work participation requirements and earnings disregards encourage welfare recipients to make the transition to work by combining earnings from work with a wage supplement in the form of small cash assistance payments. Because of time limits, however, recipients who make this transition and receive these modest wage supplements risk hitting the time limit and being ineligible for benefits at a time when they may need them in the future. The government should provide wage supplements to families that are working but not earning enough to support themselves and remain eligible for welfare benefits on an unlimited basis.

A Service Strategy Needs to Be Closely Coordinated with Assistance Programs

Generally, if appropriate services and accommodations are in place, individuals with disabilities should be able to succeed in the workplace. However, to accomplish this goal, welfare programs—both their policies and procedures—will have to address the reality that individuals who are disabled or have medical conditions may need additional help and may need assistance for longer periods of time.

Governments and others concerned about assisting low-income individuals with disabilities to be able to work and support their families should consider the following questions:

• Careful consideration should be given to the nature of the individualized assessment that the government agency uses. Is it designed to capture both strengths and barriers? Is it sufficiently refined to sort out whether a person has a learning disability or a low IQ? Is it administered by a person with the expertise to identify limitations and who is authorized to seek additional, outside assessments and diagnostic testing?

• Once an individual's needs are identified, are the government's programs designed to appropriately address those needs? What additional steps are needed to ensure that the state's procedures do not frustrate the well-intentioned parent whose disabilities make it more difficult to comply with complex rules and procedures?

• What steps is the government taking to identify and recruit employers whose jobs are well-suited to individuals with different disabilities, what steps have been taken to match the individuals with these jobs, and what steps are being taken to help employers understand the important role that accommodations can serve in ensuring that a person who is disabled will succeed in the workplace?

• Is the Korea thinking broadly about who best can provide the range of services and supports—often intensive in nature and of a longer duration than other parents require—for parents with disabilities?

There may be some individuals with disabilities for whom remunerative work at levels that allow one to support a family will not be possible or will not be possible in the near future. These families may face multiple barriers to employment and lack a connection to the labor force, but their disabilities are not severe enough for them to be considered permanently disabled. To address the needs of these families, the government should provide a higher cash assistance period after a given period of time (about two years) in addition to providing services to address their employment barriers.

Accessibility of Benefits

If these work support programs are to be successful, they need to be accessible to working poor families. In the United States, the low participation rate of working poor families in work support programs such as food stamps has become a key issue. By minimizing the administrative hassles of participation, government agencies can expect to improve working poor families' access to the benefits they need.

One way to reduce administrative hassles would be to create specific work support offices, where families would be able to get food stamps, child care, housing subsidies, and health insurance from one place. Application forms should be short and simple, and joint applications should be used wherever possible. Families should be able to complete a substantial portion of the application process by mail, telephone, and Internet. Once eligibility for a given benefit is established, the family should be certified to receive that benefit for a duration of six to twelve months.

The work support offices would provide income assistance only to families with employed individuals and some voluntary services to assist workers in obtaining a higher paying job. It could provide services, but not income assistance, to the unemployed. Income assistance could take the form of cash (EITC) or non-cash assistance (food and housing vouchers). In the United States, housing and food vouchers have more political popularity but they constrain to some extent consumption choices for low-income families. It is primarily a political judgement whether these benefits should be paid in cash or through food and housing vouchers.

In South Korea these work support centers could be an expansion of the 20 existing self-help assistance centers. The self-help centers currently act as a one-stop service center, providing job counseling, job training, job assistance, public works opportunities, and assistance to start up new businesses (Kwan 2000).

VII. Parental Responsibility and the Government's Role in Supporting Children

An overarching goal of the safety net in the United States is to hold parents responsible for supporting their children. This section describes the role of parents and the government in supporting the cost of raising children. Most people agree that the government should make some contribution to the costs of raising children, although the portion of the costs that the government should assume varies according to circumstances. Some government support services should be universal. When families are poor or children are disabled, this support would be more significant.

When children do not live with both of their parents, these questions become even more complicated. In the United States, a large proportion of children spend at least a portion of their lives living without both of their biological parents. As children get older, the proportion who do not live with both biological parents increases dramatically. At birth, about 17 percent of all children, or approximately half of the children born out-of-wedlock, do not live with both biological parents.[11] By the time children graduate from high school, approximately 50 percent to 60 percent of all children do not live with both biological parents because of divorce or termination of cohabiting relationships. In Korea, the proportion of children living in single parent households is substantially smaller: in 1995, some 89 percent of families with children were married-couple families, and only 11 percent of families with children were headed by single parents.[12]

In the United States and Korea, a disproportionate number of single parent families are poor. In the United States, children with a non-custodial parent are nearly four times as likely to be poor as children who live with both of their biological parents (Sorensen and Zibman 2000). In addition, only 21 percent of them live in families with incomes that exceed 300 percentage of the poverty threshold, while nearly half (49 percent) of children who live with both parents do (ibid.).

All parents have a responsibility to provide for their children regardless of whether they are custodial or non-custodial parents, and the government should enforce that responsibility. When parents are low-income, in addition to enforcing that responsibility the government should provide services to help parents meet those obligations. This section describes four policies: a universal child allowance, support for children whose parents can no longer care for them, child support enforcement, and providing earnings subsidies like the EITC to separated families.

Child Allowance

One concept is the creation of a child allowance—an annual credit that is available to support the care of all children, regardless of their family's income or living arrangements. The purpose of such an allowance would be to share in the costs of rearing children and to equalize the financial burdens borne by those who have children and those who do not.[13] The credit would equal $1,000 per child—the size of the recently enhanced child tax credit in the United States once it is fully phased in. Unlike the tax credit, however, the child allowance would be paid to families on a quarterly basis. In the United States, a child allowance is provided through the income tax system except for children in the very poorest and the very richest households. This child allowance would be child-centered: the credit would follow the child and provide income support to the adults raising him or her, regardless of whether it is a married couple, a single parent, or another relative of the child.

Support for Children Whose Parents Can No Longer Care for Them

Unfortunately, there are some children whose parents can no longer care for them. As mentioned earlier, some of these children are provided assistance through the Social Insurance system (children of deceased or severely disabled parents). Sometimes parents are unable to care for their children because the children themselves are extremely difficult to care for and are in need of specialized care. These children are typically institutionalized or placed in foster care. Sometimes parents can no longer care for the children because the parents become dysfunctional and no longer have the capacity to care for their children. In the United States, these children sometimes come to the attention of authorities because the children become victims of abuse or neglect; more often, though, relatives or others take over the care and maintenance of these children and the government is unaware. In many instances, however, these children are from lower-income families and are cared for by relatives who need assistance in raising these children. Special provisions need to be made to see that these children are properly taken care of. The foster care system in the United States provides for these children.

Child Support Enforcement

Parents who do not live with their children have an obligation to provide financial support to them. In the United States, federal legislation strengthening the child support system was passed in all but three years between 1981 and 1999. This legislation transformed each of the three key components of child support enforcement: paternity establishment, setting consistent child support orders, and obtaining child support payments. The legislation has made child support enforcement more effective: preliminary numbers indicate that between fiscal year 1995 and fiscal year 1999, paternity establishment increased by 60 percent to 1.5 million paternities established and child support collections increased by 46 percent from $10.8 billion to $15.8 billion (Department of Health and Human Services).

The current child support program has many tools at its disposal to enforce NCPs' responsibility to pay child support. In recent years, the program's enforcement activities have been strengthened at both the state and federal levels. The enforcement tools have become increasingly automated as well. Federal legislation passed in 1988 requires automatic withholding of child support obligations from the paychecks of non-custodial parents. To make wage withholding as effective as possible, legislation enacted in 1996 established the National Directory of New Hires which allows the child support office to closely track NCPs' employment. This directory contains information about all newly hired employees which the child support enforcement office then checks against a list of NCPs with outstanding child support orders. When a match is made, the child support office can issue a wage withholding order, so that the current support owed by the NCP is automatically deducted from his wages before he receives a paycheck.

Once non-custodial parents fail to pay child support and amass child support debts, states are authorized to take a number of additional steps. States can seize assets held in financial institutions and intercept periodic or lump sum payments from public sources such as unemployment compensation or lottery payments. They can place liens against real or personal property and suspend driver's, professional, occupational, and recreational licenses. Other enforcement techniques include withholding state and federal tax refunds payable to a parent who is delinquent in support payments and performing quarterly data matches with financial institutions to track down assets of delinquent NCPs.[14] States also can order NCPs to engage in work activities and use civil contempt procedures to incarcerate NCPs who do not comply with court orders to pay child support (Garfinkel 2001).

Child support is an important source of income for children who receive it. In 1996, children who had a non-custodial parent and whose families received child support received, on average, 16 percentage of their family income from child support. The average amount of child support received by these families was $3,795 (Sorensen and Zibman 2000). However, in 1997, two-thirds of children with a support order received financial assistance from their non-custodial parent. There are many reasons why low-income non-custodial parents fail to pay child support. One basic reason why many low-income NCPs do not pay child support regularly is that they are unemployed or under-employed, and have only a limited income from which to pay child support.

One way that government programs can help non-custodial parents take more responsibility for their children is to provide employment services for them, and use the penalties in the child support system as leverage to encourage NCPs to participate. These employment services are intended to increase the earnings and job stability of low-income NCPs, which should help these NCPs meet their child support obligations on a more regular basis. These employment services could include job search activities, job readiness ("soft skills") training, on-the-job training, publicly-funded jobs, and job retention services to help NCPs stay employed.

Earnings Subsidies for Separated Low-Income Parents

Currently receipt of the EITC in the United States is predicated on earnings and the presence of children. Childless workers receive a small EITC—in 2001 its maximum value was $353, an amount that is less than one-tenth of the maximum credit for a parent with two children, and the credit phases out when earnings reach $10,500. The size of this credit is appropriate for childless workers; however, non-custodial parents who are paying child support are contributing to the cost of raising their children, and thus I believe that low-income NCPs should be eligible for a separate earnings subsidy similar to the EITC that is contingent on the payment of child support. (Custodial parents and two-parent families would continue to be eligible for the existing EITC.)

A tax credit for low-income non-custodial parents who pay child support would provide an important benefit to these parents. Currently when they pay their child support orders in full, these low-income NCPs retain a relatively low proportion of their gross earnings as disposable income. This tax credit would encourage low-income NCPs to work and to pay child support without reducing the amount of child support that low-income custodial mothers receive.

The structure of this credit could vary. For illustrative purposes, the maximum size for the NCP tax credit at any given income level could be half of the size of the EITC for a family with the same number of children. To verify the payment of child support, the state child support agency would provide the NCP and the federal IRS or state department of revenue with an information form which would show two numbers: the total current child support due in the previous calendar year, and the total current child support collected during the previous calendar year. NCPs that paid the entire amount would receive the maximum credit for their income level. If an NCP paid less than the total amount of child support that he owed, the credit could be split between the custodial and noncustodial parents based on the portion that he did pay.

VIII. Administrative Issues

Let me conclude by sharing a few observations concerning the administration of a safety net.

Reporting Requirements

An important key to the success of a productive welfare plan will be how it is implemented and administered. Employers must be required to report the earnings of all employees on a regular basis, at least each quarter. Ideally, this should be accomplished on one form or electronically, not on several forms as in the United States. These reported wages form the basis of eligibility for the social insurance programs as well as the earnings supplements. Workers need to understand that they lose important protections if their wages are not properly reported. There should be significant penalties for non-compliance with these reporting requirements. Reporting of income from the self-employed can be a large compliance issue.

Benefit Structure

The structure of benefits for safety net programs will vary. There are several key issues that need to be weighed in determining the form and size of benefits that are made available. The concept of the "iron triangle" in poverty policy means that it is impossible for programs simultaneously to be generous (have a large guarantee level), be well targeted (limited only to those in need and therefore less costly from a government budget viewpoint), and have low effective tax rates. Achieving two of the goals always requires compromising on the third.

Requiring a household to report each month or very frequently will result in complete information on which to base benefits. This approach, however, places a substantial burden on households to remember each month's circumstances and retain and submit required pay stubs and other verification. When an individual, household, or family is determined eligible for benefits, how often do they need to reapply or re-certify their eligibility? Longer certification periods may be less responsive to a household's monthly fluctuations in income and other circumstances, but the reduced burdens on working households make the option well worth the trade-off. To some extent, these benefits could be reconciled through the tax system.

Benefits can be based on an individual's, family's, or household's circumstances at a given time. Typically, social insurance programs, which are temporary wage-replacement programs, are based on an individual's job history and current circumstances. In contrast, public assistance programs are based on family or household units. The choice depends upon government's concern with preserving neutrality with regard to living arrangements.

IX. Conclusion

A social safety net must seek to protect citizens from poverty and destitution due to economic conditions, discrimination, accidents, disability, death and individual characteristics that hinder obtaining employment; ensure a basic minimum standard of living; to provide a strong work incentive; to encourage parental responsibility and reflect the culture and values of a nation. To that end, Korea can better implement former President Dae-Jung's notion of productive welfare by drawing on the lessons learned in the United States to develop a system with three broad categories of support: a social insurance safety net which Korea already has, a work support system that reinforces work and provides a liveable income and a public assistance program that promotes self-sufficiency. Low wage workers should be entitled to work support such that they are able to maintain a decent standard of living for themselves and their children. Those individuals with serious barriers to employment should be conditionally entitled to benefits and other services provided they satisfy certain requirements. All clients of safety net programs should be treated with dignity and as valued members of society.

One of the primary lessons Korea can take away from the U.S. experience is that the provision of a basic minimum national benefit level need not result in significant increases in dependency and bloated welfare rolls. Through a strong emphasis on work—both work requirements enforced through well-designed and implemented sanction policies and rewarding work by low marginal tax rates—welfare rolls can be held in check. Individuals who are not in the labor force and who need public assistance have a multiple and varied pattern of employment barriers. These need to be addressed if the client is to succeed in the workplace. A well-run program which provides a relatively small number of transitional publicly funded jobs can assist in this process.

The provision of work supports through programs such as the Earned Income Tax Credit are politically popular, are critical to making work pay and to moving a family out of poverty. However, the United States needs to do a better job of getting these benefits—child-care, EITC, food stamps—to the working poor. This possibly could be done through work support offices which would seek to lower the administrative hassles these families face in receiving assistance. Parental responsibility is enhanced through the child support system which should be reformed to provide employment assistance and work supports as well.

Another lesson is that child well-being is only enhanced if the family's income is improved. In the United States, this implies that poverty reduction needs to be given a higher priority and caseload reduction a lower priority. While some researchers would argue otherwise, I would argue that Korea not follow the United States in adopting time limits. Dependency can be limited without resorting to this policy.

Finally, while I am not familiar with Korea's version of the Census Bureau, it is very important that a country measure its progress against poverty and evaluate its national programs on a regular basis, preferably annually. Gathering key demographic and income data by taking periodic snapshots of the population can assist policymakers in understanding whether the country is making progress in eradicating poverty. Household surveys linked to administrative data are key; the measurement of poverty requires developing a consistent measure of need and then examining the resources a family has in comparison to that need. If need exceeds resources, then the family is judged to be poor. Analyzing and publishing this data also will aid in the public's understanding of these policies.

Table 10-4
Prevalence of Employment Barriers

Barrier	% in Sample with Barrier	% Women Nationally with Barrier
Less than HS Education	31.4	12.7[1]
Low work experience (worked less than 20 percent of years since age 18)	15.4	
Fewer than four job skills (out of possible nine)	21.1	
Knows five or fewer work norms (out of a possible nine)	9.1	
Perceived discrimination (reports four or more of a possible 17 types of prior discrimination)	13.9	
Transportation problem (does not have access to a car and/or no driver's license)	47.1	7.6[2]
Major depressive disorder	25.4	12.9[3]
Post Traumatic Stress Disorder (PTSD)	14.6	
Generalized anxiety disorder	7.3	4.3
Alcohol dependence	2.7	3.7
Drug dependence	3.3	1.9
Mother's health problem (self-reported fair/poor health and age-specific physical limitation)	19.4	
Child health problem (has a health, learning, or emotional problem)	22.1	15.7[4]
Domestic violence (severe abuse from a partner within past year)	14.9	3.2-3.4[5]

[1] 1998 Current Population Survey: percent of all women ages 18-54 who do not have a high school diploma or equivalent.

[2] 1990 Census: percent of all women ages 18-54 who live in households with no vehicles available.

[3] 1994 National Co-morbidity Survey: percent of all women ages 15-54 who meet criteria for clinical case on each of these disorders.

[4] 1994 National Longitudinal Survey of Youth: percent of all mothers ages 29-37 with children who have one of six limitations.

[5] 1993 Commonwealth Fund Survey and 1985 National Family Violence Survey: the percentage of all women ages 18 and over who report current severe physical abuse.

Figure 10-4
Employment Probability by Number of Barriers

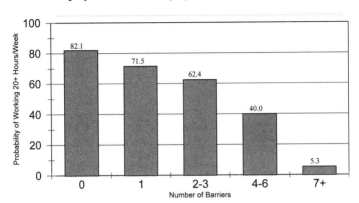

Note: Probability given that respondent is single, Black, lives in an urban census tract, is 25-34 years old, has one child age zero to two years old, has no children age three to five, and has received welfare for seven years. Predicted probabilities are based on regression coefficients

Notes

1. Tabulations of Census data by the Center on Budget and Policy Priorities.
2. Tabulations of Census data by the Center on Budget and Policy Priorities.
3. The effective marginal tax rate is defined as the percentage of each additional $1,000 in earnings that a hypothetical family or individual would lose in the form of taxes or benefits from all programs. For example, a family who loses $600 in benefits when income increases by $1,000 faces a 60 percent marginal tax rate. When marginal tax rates are high, families are penalized significantly for each extra dollar they earn.
4. *Wage and Income Trends: Up the Down Escalator*, Economic Policy Institute. Online at www.epinet.org.
5. *Ibid.*
6. These bullets draw heavily on Greenberg et al. (2000).
7. This includes about $3.7 billion of savings from denial of food stamp eligibility to legal resident aliens.
8. The two provisions that saved the most money were cutting the thrifty food plan by three percent and reductions in the standard deduction. The impact on the working poor from just the thrifty food plan cut can best be illustrated by the following. For a family that receives the maximum allotment, the benefit reduction equals three percent. For a family that receives a benefit equal to half of the maximum allotment, the benefit cut from this change equals six percent. For a family that receives a benefit equal to one quarter of the maximum allotment, the benefit cut equals 12 percent.
9. 0.42 means that in 1995 for single mother families with no other adults, income was 42 percent of the poverty threshold at the fifth percentile of families when families are arrayed by income to poverty threshold ratio.

10. This section draws heavily on Goldberg, Heidi, *A Compliance-Oriented Approach to Sanctions in State and County TANF Programs*, Center on Budget and Policy Priorities, February 2001
11. Approximately 32 to 33 percent of children are born out-of-wedlock. The number of these children whose biological parents are cohabiting parents is unknown. The Survey of Fragile Families, which covers low-income families, found that at the time of birth, approximately 50 percent of non-marital births live with cohabiting biological parents. Assuming that the cohabitation rate is the same at higher income levels, this implies that approximately 17 percent of all children born out-of-wedlock do not live with both biological parents at birth.
12. Tabulations from the 1995 Population and Housing Census, Korea National Statistical Office. These calculations exclude a small number of four-generation households because data breaking these families into single- and two-parent households was not available.
13. The Clearinghouse on International Developments in Child, Youth and Family Policies at Columbia University, http://www.childpolicyintl.org/familychildallowances.html.
14. For a complete list, see U.S. House of Representatives, Committee on Ways and Means, *1998 Green Book*, Washington: U.S. Government Printing Office, 1998, pages 552 to 553.

References

Bernstein, J., Brocht, C. and Spade-Aguilar, M. (2000) *How Much Is Enough? Basic Family Budgets for Working Families*, Washington, D.C.: Economic Policy Institute.

Blank, R. M. (1997) *It Takes A Nation: A New Agenda for Fighting Poverty*. New York and Princeton: Russell Sage Foundation and Princeton University Press.

Bloom, D. and Michalopoulos, C. (2001) *How Welfare and Work Policies Affect Employment and Income: A Synthesis of Research*. New York: Manpower Demonstration Research Corporation.

Center on Budget and Policy Priorities (1999) Tabulations of Census Data from March 1999 Current Population Survey.

Danziger, S., Corcoran, M., Danziger, S., Heflin, C., Kalil, A., Levine, J., Rosen, D., Seefeldt, K., Siefert, K. and Tolman, R. (2000) "Barriers to the Employment of Welfare Recipients." University of Michigan, mimeo.

Department of Health and Human Services (2000) Administration for Children and Families, Office of Child Support Enforcement, *Child Support Enforcement FY1999 Preliminary Data Report*.

Dupree, A. and Primus, W. (2001) *Declining Share of Children Lived with Single Mothers in the Late 1990s*. Washington, D.C.: Center on Budget and Policy Priorities.

Ellwood, D. T. (1999) "The Impact of the Earned Income Tax Credit and Social Policy Reforms on Work, Marriage, and Living Arrangements," paper presented at Joint Center for Poverty Research Conference, Northwestern University, Evanston, October 7-8.

Fields, G. S. (1999) "The Employment Problem in Korea," Ittacha: Cornell University, mimeo.

Garfinkel, I. (2001) "Assuring Child Support in the New World of Welfare," paper presented at The New World of Welfare Conference, Washington, D.C.

Goldberg, H. (2001) *A Compliance-Oriented Approach to Sanctions in State and County TANF Programs*. Washington, D.C.: Center on Budget and Policy Priorities.

Groger, J. (2001) *The Effects of Time Limits and Other Policy Changes on Welfare Use, Work, and Income Among Female-Headed Families*. Washington, D.C.: National Bureau of Economic Research.

Haskins, R (2001) "The Second Most Important Issue: Effects of Welfare Reform on Family Income and Poverty," paper prepared for The New World of Welfare Conference, Washington, D.C.

Kaushal, N. and Kaestner, R. (2001) "From Welfare to Work: Has Welfare Reform Worked?," *Journal of Policy Analysis and Management*, 20 (4).

Kwan, C. P. (2000) *Unemployment-Related Benefit Systems in South Korea*. Hong Kong: Research and Library Services Division, Legislative Council Secretariat.

Meyer, B. D. and Rosenbaum, D. T. (1999) *Welfare, the Earned Income Tax Credit, and the Labor Supply of Single Mothers*. Washington, D.C.: National Bureau of Economic Research, Working Paper 7363.

Moffitt, R. and Wolfe, B. (1993) "Medicaid, Welfare Dependency, and Work: Is There a Causal Link?," *Health Care Financing Review*, Vol. 15.

Kwan, C. P. (2000) *Unemployment-Related Benefit Systems in South Korea*. Hong Kong: Research and Library Services Division, Legislative Council Secretariat.

O'Neill, J.E. and Hill, M. A. (2001) *Gaining Ground? Measuring the Impact of Welfare Reform on Welfare and Work*. New York: Center for Civic Innovation.

Sard, B. and Daskal, J. (1998) *Housing and Welfare Reform: Some Background Information*. Washington, D.C.: Center on Budget and Policy Priorities.

Sherman, A. (2001) *How Children Fare in Welfare Experiments Appears to Hinge on Income*. Washington, D.C.: Children's Defense Fund.

Smeeding, T.M., Ross, K.E. O'Connor, M. and Simon, M. (1999) "The Economic Impact of the Earned Income Tax Credit (EITC): Consumption, Savings, and Debt," paper prepared for Northwestern University conference on EITC Research.

Social Security Administration (2000) *Annual Statistical Supplement*. Washington, D.C.

Sorensen, E. and Zibman, C. (2000) *Child Support Offers Some Protection Against Poverty*. Washington, D.C.: The Urban Institute.

Super, D. (2001) *Background on the Food Stamp Program*. Washington, D.C.; Center on Budget and Policy Priorities.

Sweeney, E. P. (2000) *Recent Studies Indicate That Many Parents Who Are Current or Former Welfare Recipients Have Disabilities or Other Medical Conditions*. Washington, D.C.: Center on Budget and Policy Priorities.

US House of Representatives, Committee on Ways and Means (2000) *2000 Green Book*. Washington, D.C.

Wage and Income Trends: Up the Down Escalator, Economic Policy Institute, Online at www.epinet.org.

Yelowitz, A. (1995) "The Medicaid Notch, Labor Supply, and Welfare Participation: Evidence from Eligibility Expansions," *The Quarterly Journal of Economics*, vol. 110.

Zedlewski, S. R. (1999) *Work Activity and Obstacles to Work Among TANF Recipients*, Washington, D.C.: The Urban Institute.

11

Financial Stability of the Health Insurance Scheme

J-Matthias Graf v.d. Schulenburg

I. Introduction

In all developed countries and societies of the world health care is considered as a special good, the allocation and distribution of which must meet specific regulations. Those regulations should guarantee that everybody has access to appropriate health care. The patients' willingness and ability to pay should not dictate how much and which services they receive in the case of illness. The following objectives are common for health care systems around the world:

- Equal access to health care for everyone;
- Cost-efficient production of health services;
- Effective medical care and patient management;
- Cost-control of public expenditures for medical services.

However, the way to achieve these goals varies. Korea and Germany have established social health insurance schemes. Other countries have relied on tax-financed national health care systems or free market allocation, but have social aid programs for special groups in society. All countries around the world have problems to achieve the general goals mentioned above. In particular, cost control seems to be a problem in all health care systems due to a rapidly aging population and advancement of new technology in medical care. In addition, the health care sector is characterized by a high degree of asymmetric information which makes an efficient planning, controlling and steering nearly impossible. This is certainly one reason why we observe a tendency for growing administration in the health care sector.

In this chapter, I will discuss strategies of achieving financial stability of social health insurance schemes. Because social health insurance is only one way of achieving equal access to medical care for everyone, the second section provides an overview of different ways of organizing health service financing. Each way has its own specific advantages and disadvantages with regard to financial stability. That is why most systems—including that of Korea and Germany—are mixed systems. The third section of this chapter shows some common organizational features and discusses them in the light of financial stability. As it is the aim of our discussion to learn by comparing the different approaches in the different countries, this section also compares the characteristic features of the Korean and German health insurance system. Although Korea and Germany are in two different parts of the world, these countries have a lot in common.

Both Korea and Germany suffered as a result of the Second World War and the division of their state. However, while Korea is still waiting for its unification, Germany was united on October 3, 1990. 40 years ago, on August 13, 1961 the Berlin Wall was built and it came down on 9th November 1989.

Table 11-1
Korea and Germany: An Overview

	Korea	Germany
Size	99,143 km²	357,022 km²
Population	South: 47m. (North: 24 m.)	West: 67m. East: 15m.
Density	472 persons/km²	230 persons/km²
Foundation of state	1948	1949
Per capita GNI (1999)	8,581 US $	12,905 US $
Economic growth rate (1999)	10.7 percent	1.6 percent
Number of doctors per 1000 population	1.46	3.55
Life expectancy (1997)	70.6 / 78.1	74.4 / 80.6
Health care expenditures as percent of GDP (1999)	5.4 percent	10.6 percent

Source: Institut der Deutschen Wirtschaft im Globalen Wettbewerb 2002.

Both countries have enjoyed a rapid economic growth, and have export-oriented economies, but have also been hit by an economic crisis, slowing down this growth. Both countries have achieved considerable success in social welfare and economic income levels through continued growth, but Germany seems to be about ten years ahead of the Korean economy and social development. This would also mean that Germany is a decade ahead in its problems, which have to be solved in society in general and in medical care financing in particular. Many problems, which are caused by the fast industrialization and urbanization such as environmental pollution and over-concentration of the population have been solved. However, the poor economic growth makes it more difficult to solve the growing demand for welfare services and medical care. While Korea tries to solve these problems by more central and organized planning and management, as with the foundation of the National Health Insurance Corporation (NHIC), Germany and the European Union see solutions in implementing more competition, and a decentralization of decision-making processes. For instance, in Germany competition between social health insurers was introduced in 1997 and private saving programs were introduced in 2001 to reduce the public pension system. To sum up, it seems to be worth observing each other and learning from this experience.

In the last section of this chapter, I will discuss several strategies to achieve financial stability in social health insurance.

II. Countries Have Chosen Different Ways to Finance Medical Care

Different nations have found various solutions for organizing the financing of medical care (Raffel 1997). Some nations employ a national health service financed by taxes, others base their health care system on social health insurance. The latter is financed by contributions from the insured and their employers. Most typical for a national health service is the British system, although social health insurance schemes, sometimes called Bismarckian type systems, are employed in many countries, including Korea and Germany. In those countries, most of the population is covered by one of the social health insurers. For instance, about 90 percent of the population in Germany and about 97 percent in Korea is covered by social health insurance.

The US system is often unfairly labeled as a "muddle through" or "(non) system." But even the US health care system can be called a "system" although it is based on a different concept, with a different set of values. In Europe and in many other countries around the world, we believe that everybody should have the same access to health services if they are needed. In the US, health care policy is characterized by the assumption that in principle everybody should care for himself or herself. The task of national policy is only to identify those groups in society which are believed to be under-compensated or under-served, those not being able to behave as normal consumers on health care and health insurance markets. For those groups, special isolated programs are then created and financed by tax money. In the US for instance, the Medicare program is concerned with health care for the elderly and the Medicaid program with health care for the poor, disabled and blind. Additional programs are enacted for unmarried mothers with dependent children and for children. The risk of such a policy is the overlap of those programs and the under-compensated health care for parts of the population.

Table 11-2
Types of Health Care Systems

	National Health Service (NHS)	Social Health Insurance (Bismarckian System)	Social Aid System
Countries (as on European car plates)	DK, E, GB, I, IRL, P, S, D (for civil servants) & most DCs	B, D, F, L, NL, CH & Japan, Israel, Korea	USA & South Africa
Financing	Taxes	Contributions	Out-of-pocket payments, taxes and other sources
Decision-maker	Government	Decentralized, but strong governmental impact	Markets, government and NGOs
Cost reimbursement	D (for civil servants)	B, F, L, NL, Korea	USA (most programs)
Benefits in kind	DK, E, GB, I, IRL, P, S & most DCs	CH, D, Japan, Korea	USA (managed care organizations)
Out-of-pocket payments	Low	Moderate, in some countries high (CH and Korea)	High
Cost control	Strong	Complicated	Difficult

One of the great challenges of the European Union is to create a harmonized social security scheme. The European Union is one economic market, one financial market and one labor market (12 of the 15 countries of the European Union have the same currency, the EURO). The financing of health care will be one of the key issues in this transition process. There is a uniform opinion among economists that a basic decision has to be made if health care should be financed by contributions from the insured and their employers or by general taxes.

As mentioned above, the problems of equity, efficacy and efficiency are discussed around the world. They are not singular for a certain type of system. Identical problems exist in many developing and developed countries. The financing system of health care has to take these goals into account. However, rationing medical care by budgets, price control, utilization control and market forces is necessary, too. Otherwise health care cost will explode. This is also not unique for a certain system.

The reasons for the cost driving forces are well known and can be summarized as follows:

1. Increase of demand for health services due to third-party coverage of expenses
2. Supplier induced demand
3. Increase of the number of elderly in society
4. Medical technological progress
5. Sisyphus syndrome in medical care

Some of these effects are actually intended by public health policy. The population should enjoy a comprehensive health service coverage, and should consume medical care if it is needed. In addition, it is intended that health care suppliers invest in their companies, i.e. physician offices and hospitals, so that they are able to offer more and high quality services to the patients. We do want to live longer, although we know that the elderly have a greater need and demand for health services than the young. Modern medical technologies and therapeutic concepts should be developed and used by our health care industry. The so-called Sisyphus syndrome describes the phenomenon that an increase in health services provided to the population leads to an increase in the sickness of the population, on average. This is because many diseases are chronic illnesses. Health services help the patient but do not cure him. In addition, health services prolong life and increase the chance that people will suffer from other diseases. That is why the more health services there are, the more the population requires them.

It is therefore no surprise that the introduction of a program which provides comprehensive coverage will induce an increase in national health care expenditures—as we have seen in Korea (Ministry of Health and Welfare 2001). Since the initialization of a universal health insurance coverage 13 years ago and the idea to introduce it step by step health care expenditures have increased sharply in Korea. And health care cost will also increase in future. In addition, out-of-pocket payments are still high in Korea (55 percent of total expenditure, 66 percent in outpatient and 44 percent in inpatient care). But these out-of-pocket payments will decrease. As a consequence, public health care expenditures will increase: a ten percent fall of out-of-pocket payment leads to a direct increase of third-party payment by ten percent. In addition it induces—as German research shows—additional demand between 10.7 and 34.6 percent depending on the level of co-payments and the type of services.

So, even if some of the effects described above are in line with the goal of health policy, there is a need for a cost-containment policy irrespective of the type of financing system (i.e. tax-financed or insurance-based). The success or non-success of these measures to increase efficiency and contain cost will be discussed in the last section.

III. Basic Models of Health Care Financing

As mentioned above, all third-party payment systems have a built in cost driving power (Schulenburg and Greiner 2000). The reason is that, as shown in Figure 11-1, patients consume services, while they do not pay the full cost of their consumption out-of-pocket. Under full third-party coverage they pay only with their consumption time. This is why waiting lists and long waiting times are very effective cost-containment measures in modern health care systems. Doctors and hospitals are either paid by the patient who is reimbursed by his or her health insurer (cash benefits) or they are paid directly by the third party (benefit in kind). In a cash benefit system there is a risk that health care providers and patients collaborate to the disadvantage of the third-party payer. This behavior has already been described by Adam Smith and is called "second degree moral hazard" in modern economic literature. In the case of benefit in kind there is the problem of the third-party payer having to verify if the services billed were really provided according to the standards. As Korea and Germany have benefit in kind as well as cash benefit, both risks apply for these systems.

Health insurance is only one way and one source to finance medical care. In most countries, a mixed system of private provision, health insurance and tax financing is adopted. Because there are interactions between the various types of financing modes, every change of one part of the system may have an impact on other parts of the system. For instance, if the coverage level of social health insurance is increased, private savings for health care expenditures may decrease and social aid programs may have lower expenditures. On the other hand, the number of health care suppliers might increase, which will lead to additional costs. Korea and Germany have mixed financing schemes, which makes every analysis on financial stability quite complicated. For instance, in the year 2000 the health insurance budget of the Ministry of Health and Welfare (MOHW) was 1,754 billion Won. In the same year the MOHW spent 1,032 billion Won on medical aid, and 236 billion on other health care issues. In Germany only 51 percent of all health care expenditures (about 270 billion Euros) are paid by the social sickness funds. The other half is financed by public sources (12 percent), social pension funds and social accident insurance (ten percent), private health insurance (five percent), employers (14 percent) and out-of-pocket (eight percent).

Figure 11-1
Third-Party Financing

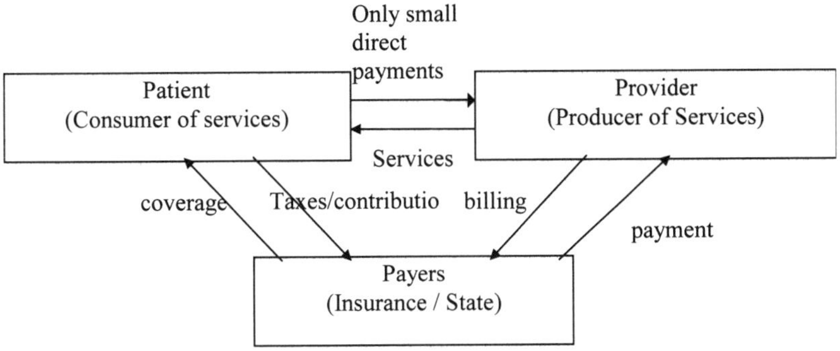

Only small
direct
payments

| Patient (Consumer of services) | Provider (Producer of Services) |

Services

coverage   Taxes/contributio   billing

payment

Payers
(Insurance / State)

Private Provision

Health services can be seen as goods which are traded on more or less free markets. In this case consumers pay the provider for the full cost of the service. No special market regulations are needed for health services. However, health services have various special characteristics:

Health services are consumed relatively seldom and therefore consumers are not very well-informed about the available alternatives or adequacy of a service for a particular problem. Their consumer sovereignty is therefore limited. They depend on the opinion of specialists such as physicians and other health care providers.

The cost of illness is often quite high, and it is uncertain as to when health services will need to be consumed. This means that it is in the interest of most people to take out an insurance to cover this uncertainty.

Health care services are not consumed at an equal rate over a lifetime or among different population groups. For this reason it might be desirable to redistribute resources across generations and social groups.

For these and other reasons (e.g. ethical reasons of equal access to essential goods such as health care) the market model, where consumers pay fees to the providers, which amount to the full cost of the services, is very rare and appears only on partial markets (e.g. for luxury services such as cosmetic surgery) or on informal markets (i.e. under corruptive circumstances).

Uncertainty and ignorance about the need for health care, combined with the high cost of particular health care services often result in so-called market failure. This expression is used by economists to describe circumstances in which there are constraints on the regular order of a market. Under these conditions, private provision does not work fully and some elements of government regulation are needed.

However, the introduction of out-of-pocket payments is helpful to improve the referral system by the creation of price signals, and to increase incentives for providers. This price mechanism also limits the tendency of health insurance systems to extend the number of health services provided. Some demand is also created by suppliers of care, drugs and other medical technology. Such expenditure does not necessarily ensure that the wishes of the population for better health services are met or that political goals such as longer life expectancy or better overall health status of the population are reached.

We can expect a decrease in the out-of-pocket payments in Korea and an increase in Germany. In Germany it is openly discussed that co-payments and deductibles will have to be increased in the future. This will make it even more difficult for the Korean government to stabilize expenditure of the national health insurance program.

Another type of private provision of health financing is the purchase of private health insurance with actuarial premiums. Usually this option is voluntary, but it is also possible for coverage with a private insurance company to be compulsory, the choice of insurer being left to the consumer (such as the regulation for automobile liability insurance in many countries). Private health insurers often have only limited opportunities to contain costs and are characterized by high administrative costs (due to promotion and control costs). On the other hand, these suppliers of health coverage can usually offer high-quality health care providers and a benefits package tailored to the individual needs of the citizen. These advantages are often bought with comparatively high premiums which exclude low income classes from joining the scheme. In Germany about eight percentage of the population have full private health insurance and another 15 percent of the population have supplementary private health insurance for those services which are not covered by the social health insurance. Figure 11-3 shows the basic structure of health care markets with private insurance. The insurer covers the health care costs of the insured according to the insurance contract. The insurer may have special arrangements with preferred providers (selective contracting), who provide services for better prices and according to pre-arranged standards. In Germany, a growing number of private health insurers have special contracts with clinics and rehabilitation centers.

Figure 11-2 provides an overview of the various basic models of health care financing. Table 11-3 provides a comparison of co-payments in Korea and Germany.

Figure 11-2
Basic Models of Health Financing Systems

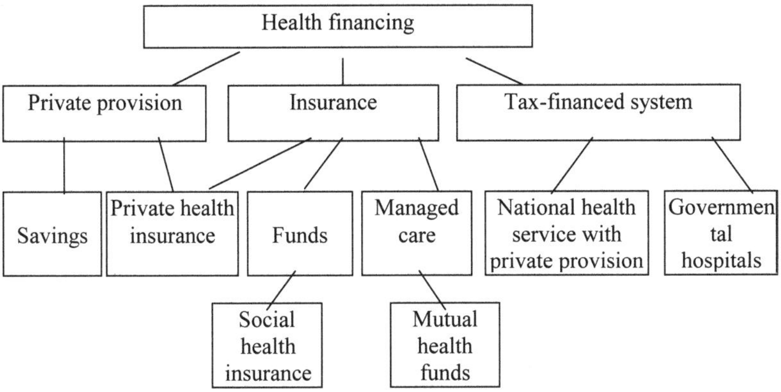

Table 11-3
Out-of-pocket Payments in Korea and Germany (simplified)

	Korea	Germany
Hospital	20 %	$ 8 per day for 14 days
Outpatient in a clinic	3,200 Won or 30 %	0
Outpatient in hospital	40 or 55 %	0
Pharmacy	1,000 Won or 30 %	$ 4 to $ 5 and the amount above the reference price
Treatment for simple fatigue	100 %	100 %
Average out-of-pocket payment	55 %[1]	7.8 %

Source: Verband der Angestellten Krankenkassen 2002.

Tax-Financed National Health Service

In purely tax-financed national health services, all revenue for financing the health system is provided by the state as part of the public budget (see Figure 11-4). Although it is not essential for this type of health financing system, all services are usually provided by public institutions such as state hospitals and health centers with employed physicians, nurses and technical staff. Private clinics or office-based physicians with their own practice are relatively rare in countries with a purely tax-financed national health service. However, the British and Swedish national health services have stimulated private provision of outpatient services and have adopted a more decentralized structure of financing and management.

Figure 11-3
Private Health Insurance Schemes

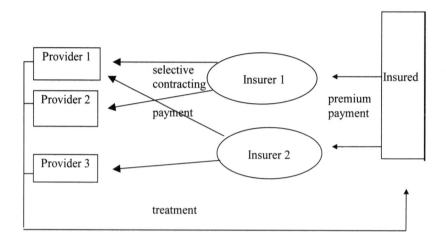

In a state-financed health system, the government or parliament can determine the balance between the amount of money allocated to the health care sector and that allocated to other essential public areas such as military defense, education and science. This leads to discussion about alternatives to health care services such as traffic safety or additional pollution control, which may also have a medical impact.

In practice it is often found that tax-financed systems are comparatively successful in controlling expenditure by powerful public control and cost-containment. On the other hand, competition in a state-financed system with public provision of services is obviously quite small. Therefore, the efficiency of the system in terms of quality of care is relatively low, and efforts to assess the needs of consumers are not rewarded. On the contrary, providers who attempt to make procedures more effective risk being punished by having their budgets for the next period cut by the amount saved.

Such systems always run the risk of under funding, as the health sector is subject to political debate on its budget each year. It is highly possible that other political goals might crowd out the allocation of an adequate share for health care. As the optimal proportion of the public budget to be allocated to the health sector is not known and cannot be calculated, it has to be set as a democratic decision following public debate. But this procedure may lead to under funding and unreasonably low resources for the health system. Thus waiting lists, e.g. for elective surgery, and frustrated staff (due to low income) are quite common in such systems.

It seems that Korea has intelligently combined the advantages of central planning and budgeting by the MOHW, the National Health Insurance Corporation (NHIC) and the Health Insurance Review Agency (HIRA), and the advantages of a comprehensive social health insurance financed by contributions. Although the German system is praised for its decentralized planning and the self-government of sickness funds and health care suppliers organizations (such as the powerful Insurance Doctors' Association), the German government is almost unable to guarantee financial stability of the system.

Figure 11-4
Tax-Financed Health Financing Schemes

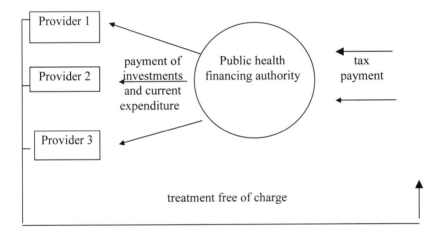

The health insurance fund pools the financial contributions of its members in order to protect the welfare of its members should they fall ill. Without access to insurance, many people are unable to obtain treatment, or must take up loans to pay for the required medical services. Health insurance also has the potential to increase the revenue available for health care and to redistribute the burden of illness among age groups, among healthy and ill people, and among groups of different income levels.

As shown in Figure 11-5, statutory social health insurance is typically financed by income-related contributions from employer and employee. Thus the contributions are not based on risk (as the premiums of private insurance companies are), but on the ability to pay. Social health insurance systems are generally tightly regulated, but are normally not a governmental institution, although they should at least have an independent position. Regulation includes a description of the beneficiaries, the benefit scheme, the internal organization of the fund (including responsibilities and decision-making authority), terms of financing by the contributors and payment to the

Figure 11-5
Social Health Insurance Fund

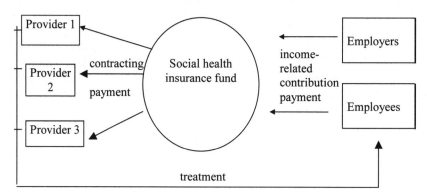

providers. The benefits are usually set on a national level and the contributions are calculated to finance the total cost of these benefits.

The payroll deductions are split between employer and employee in a certain percentage (for example 50 percent from both as in Korea and Germany). This is intended to encourage the employers to take some responsibility for cost-containment.

Statutory Social Health Insurance Fund

One problem with this type of payroll tax is that deductions may discourage employers from hiring more employees (which would increase unemployment) and that they may decrease the available income of the employee (which would reduce the demand for other goods in the economy). On the other hand, it is often more acceptable for people to pay for health services when they discern a direct relationship between their pre-payment and the of insurance benefits, rather than paying higher taxes for a national health service or a welfare program.

Most characteristic for the Korean and the German system is the financing medical services via social health insurance. Table 11-4 compares the two systems. As the survey shows, both health insurance schemes have much in common. The major differences are:

• Monopoly of NHIC in Korea, competition between sickness funds in Germany
• Low contribution rates in Korea, high contributions in Germany
• Central setting of fees for health care providers in Korea, negotiated fees in Germany
• High out-of-pocket payments in Korea, comprehensive first Euro-coverage in Germany

Table 11-4
Social Health Insurance in Korea and Germany

	Korea	Germany
Year of foundation	1977	1883
Compulsory insured	All employees	With income under 3,732 Euro
Population covered	97 %	90 %
Number of insured	45.9 million	71.3 million
Number of insurers	one NHIC	420 (1.316 in 1980) competition
Contribution system	percentage of income No ceiling 50 : 50 employer/employee	percentage of income Ceiling income 3,732 Euro 50 : 50 employer/employee
Contribution rate	3.4 % for employees 3.4 % for employers	5.5 % to 7.2 % for employees 5.5 % to 7.2 % for employers
Family dependents	Covered	Covered
Service provision	Mainly private Freedom of choice Inpatient care: statutory referral, but actually non-referral	Mainly private Freedom of choice Inpatient care: referral
Payment of doctors	RVS (Relative Value Scale) MOHW sets point value on recommendation of National Insurance Coordination Committee	RVS Negotiated flat payment per Insured to Insurance Doctors Association
Payment of hospitals	Fee for service, DRGs (Diagnosis Relate Group)	Per diems, DRGs, PMCs (Patient Management Category)
Major reform projects	Expansion of benefits Reform of RVS Expansion of DRGs Increase of contributions Cost-containment	Risk adjustment compensation between sickness funds New DRG-system for hospitals Cost-containment

Source: Schulenburg and Greiner 2000.

The division of contributions between employees and employers is a political question. It is possible for both groups to pay proportional, income-related contributions, or flat contributions which need to be adjusted periodically, or a mixed system of proportional and flat contributions as shown in Table 11-5:

Table 11-5
Proportional versus Flat Contributions

	Proportional contribution	Flat contribution
Employer	A	C
Employee	B	D

Proportional contributions are not necessarily superior to flat contributions and vice versa. Some pros and cons are listed in Table 11-6.

Table 11-6
Pros and Cons of Different Types of Contributions

	Proportional contribution	Flat contribution
Pros	Redistribution according to solidarity principle	Equal distribution of burden to finance health care costs
	More acceptable for lower income classes	Less excess burden on wages for higher income classes
Cons	Revenues of health care plan increases automatically with development of wages	Strong incentive for cost-containment as rates have to be adjusted to cover inflation
	Less acceptable for higher income classes	Increases cost of low wage labor at a higher rate than high wage labor
	The higher the dispersion of labor the less it will be acceptable	Causes problems for part-time workers

Another disadvantage of a nationwide social security fund is the lack of competition between various funds, which would lead to efficiency and more flexibility of administration of the social insurance. Therefore, higher financial stability may be achieved by introducing competition between different health plans or health insurers. This was done with some success in the Netherlands, Israel, Switzerland and Germany. If contributions are a proportion of income a risk adjustment compensation has to be introduced, otherwise health insurers try to select high income customers and avoid those with a low income.

It is also unlikely that a monopoly will be able to make selective provider contracts. Instead, all providers of health care have to be offered financing from the national fund, as there is no alternative scheme. Furthermore, it is likely that the fund will be subjected to political pressure.

Mutual Health Funds

In comparison to a social health insurance fund a mutual health fund is not a monopoly, but rather the citizens can choose between various public or privately administrated funds. These may be established by large industrial companies, branches of industries, trade unions or local government. As with the social health insurance fund, mutual health funds are financed by income-related contributions which redistribute monetary resources between the fund members according to their health service needs and ability to support the fund. If necessary or desired the government may subsidize the contribution payments of low-income citizens.

The mutual health fund is a non-profit organization which can be joined by every citizen who meets the admission conditions (e.g. a certain occupation or membership of a trade union). Thus, risk selection by the fund is prohibited (Ven 2001). To avoid adverse selection in one fund it might be necessary to establish a risk-sharing institution (working like re-insurer) which compensates funds with a relatively bad risk structure (e.g. in terms of age, disease structure or gender) and provides services for the funds such as health fund staff-training. This organization can teach mutual health funds managers basic skills such as accounting, statistics and marketing, and can also work as a supervising agency. In order to avoid risk selection the government can also set regulations which force employees to join the employers' health fund.

As shown in Figure 11-6, mutual sickness funds are self-governed with a board of employers' and employees' representatives who are regularly elected by the health fund members. The board is concerned with cost-containment and the provision of a high quality of services. It also decides on the scheme of benefits according to the needs of its insured, and on the contributions required by the fund to finance these benefits. The health funds make contracts with selected providers who treat the members free-of-charge (except for some co-payments to avoid an over-demand) and send the bill directly to the fund. For this, it is necessary to arrange fee-for-service schedules or other terms of payment between the health fund and the providers. These are regularly reviewed and negotiated, but have to be maintained for the term of the contract.

Figure 11-6
Mutual Health Fund

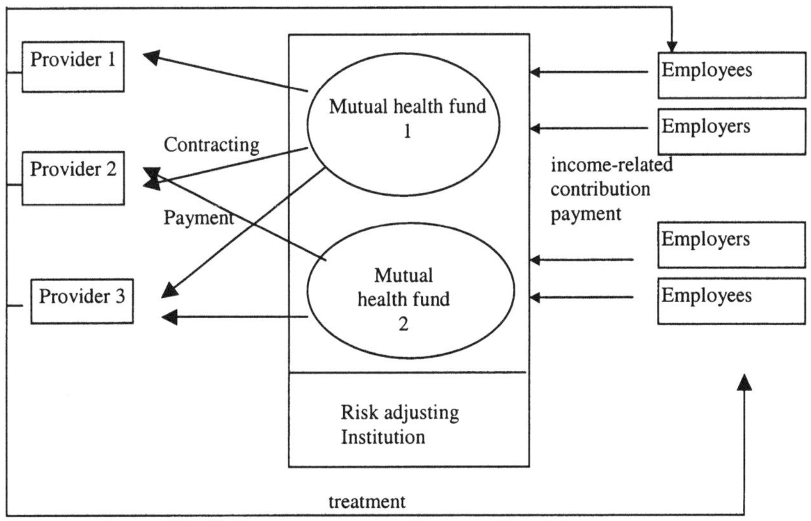

In some health care systems based on mutual health funds (such as Germany, Switzerland and the Netherlands) it is possible for the members to opt out of the funds and to apply for private health insurance coverage. This may be feasible for people above a certain income level or for all citizens who do not wish to be insured by a sickness fund (e.g. in Switzerland). On the other hand, the political goal of risk-sharing and solidarity within the society is violated when only those with a high income opt out of the system.

The mutual structure of health funds makes it easier to meet the needs of different groups within the population. They are less bureaucratic than social security health insurance as they are more clearly arranged and better controlled by the members and their employers. Therefore, their administrative costs are usually lower than the overhead costs of social security health insurance or private health insurers. Moreover, it is possible to create competition between the different funds, so the citizens can choose which fund best suits their individual needs and financial condition.

Nevertheless, health funds fail to insure people without formal employment. Although it is also possible to insure self-employed people and workers without formal employment, it is only feasible with a risk examination of the applicant and risk-related premiums, as otherwise the danger of adverse selection would be too large.

Managed Care Systems

Managed Care Systems are known from the US. In the US, Managed Care Systems are privately operated insurance programs run by business firms or by so-called Health Maintenance Organizations (HMOs). These schemes are pre-paid on the basis of annual capitation and provide comprehensive health care benefits for their members. In the US, nearly 50 million citizens are insured in almost 700 HMOs with a rising trend.

A basic element of managed care is selective contracting, which means that a greater number of patients are treated by specific providers who agree to provide services under contract with a purchaser of these services (health plan or employer). The providers agree under these contracts to undergo utilization controls (e.g. a specific length of stay in hospital is allowed by the insurer, and any extension needs a special approval) and to accept a discounted price or fee schedule. This system, of course, means limited choice for the enrolled persons, possibly adversely affecting patient satisfaction. Apart from the number of patients, which might encourage a provider to enter into contract with the HMO, other incentives are possible. For example, providers may receive a share of surpluses from the health insurance.

In managed care, purchasers of services (employers or insurers) directly manage the delivery of health services to a defined group of enrolled persons (e.g. diabetics, AIDS patients, hypertension patients). The system is characterized by competition on different levels: providers compete to offer services, and consumers choose health plans based on who can offer a given quality of care for the lowest price. In this way, managed care systems can allocate resources in desirable directions compared to unmanaged fee-for-service systems. Unnecessary hospitalization in particular can be decreased, and costly treatment alternatives such as inappropriate specialist care can be replaced by increased use of primary care.

In many countries, the basic idea of Managed Care Systems has been adopted. In Switzerland and Spain, Health Maintenance Organizations have been founded. In Germany we have about 250 so-called model projects or integrated service projects to find out how patients can be treated more effectively. Managed care, disease management, case management and evidence based medicine are currently the hot topics of the health care debate in Europe.

The different options for health care financing presented above have advantages and disadvantages. An optimal solution always depends on the particular circumstances of the country, its economic, social and historical background and the political goals and will. Apart from these structural considerations for the choice of a particular financing system (or a mixture of various types), it is also important to discuss the priorities which should be met by the health care systems. If, for example, cost-containment has top priority, a tax-financed scheme or a national health insurance which offers a wide range of instruments for government intervention appears to be the best. However, such a system will have more administrative problems and normally a poor quality of care. Moreover, an operational, relatively efficient civil service is required, as otherwise resource allocation will be far from optimal.

If freedom of choice for patients / insured and providers is a major goal of the system, mutual sickness funds and private health insurance should be considered, where the citizens can choose their health insurance and physicians on their own. Unfortunately, these systems are not very adept at avoiding cost escalation and tend to offer many incentives to increase utilization.

Statutory social health insurance does more to promote the idea of insurance than a tax-financed system which can lead to greater self-determination. On the other hand, as this financing type is a monopoly, the anticipated administration costs can be relatively high and the anticipated quality of the health providing system may be low. Another disadvantage of funds (public or private) as opposed to fiscal financing is the risk of under funding for preventative services, as the Ministry of Health has less direct influence on the health service budget allocation. This has been the experience of the Medicare program in the United States.

Competitive mutual health funds have a greater incentive than social security health insurance to contain costs (as they have no monopoly on the health financing market) and to provide appropriate care. Their performance depends to a large extent on the internal process of managing the system.

Managed Care Systems define themselves in a world of competition. If a market solution is not accepted as an appropriate allocation mechanism for the health care sector, this financing system should not be applied. On the other hand, market instruments are most common in systems where people do not expect the government to be liable for every public concern. If, for example, the patients are used to paying user fees for health services, they are more likely to accept a pre-payment to the provider (or a provider-based institution such as a staff-based HMO) than people who already enjoy free health care.

Another important question is the respective level of centralization or decentralization in a health care system. This issue examines how the power to make decisions and delegate responsibility is distributed among various levels, i.e. national level, regional level (districts) and local level (community). In many countries centralized planning systems have been replaced by competition between health care plans. To enable competition, risk adjustment and transfer mechanisms were introduced to subsidize those health insurers which insure mostly sick and low-income people. However, many countries have realized that competition works quite well in unregulated markets and in economic theory but does not work in health care and in practice. This topic is certainly on the health economic agenda in many countries.

There is no optimal system which meets the three goals equity, efficiency end effectiveness at the same time and in every segment of the health care system. Experience shows that particularly in less industrialized countries, the inefficiency of the government and other public bodies tends to increase, and public funds are often not administered appropriately. Tax-financed and government-managed health services will not be a good solution to cover the population in developing countries and even industrialized countries. Highly industrialized countries such as many EU-countries have had good experience with mandatory social health insurance and managed competition of health care plans. There is some doubt if these models would work in other countries. Every country has to make its own experience and has to make its own choice.

IV. Strategies to Increase Financial Stability of the Health Insurance Scheme

Germany has 120 years of experience with social health insurance. The experience of Korea is much shorter. But Korea has achieved a lot in the past two decades. General life expectancy has increased drastically and mortality rates including infant mortality have decreased. Smoking cessation programs and lifestyle changing programs have been introduced by the government and will have an effect on the wellbeing of the population. Health care resources have increased remarkably during the past five years and public health programs have been implemented successfully. All these initiatives have their price. There is no free lunch and never will be.

Cost-containment efforts are necessary to control cost and maintain the efficiency of the system. Two key questions as to what the right strategy will be to achieve these goals must be answered:

1.	What are the causes of inefficiency in our health care system?
2.	What can be done to solve the problem?

There are three general factors for inefficiency and instability in health care financing as a general answer to the first question:

1. Third-party financing leads to "moral hazard" behavior of patients. Therefore, cost-containment or other methods of limiting the consumption of health services are particularly necessary in health systems which are based on third-party financing. This is regardless of whether the third-party payer is a public institution or a private body. As a result, we have a triangle consisting of patient (consumer), provider (producer) and payer (either insurance or a state institution). To limit "moral hazard" out-of-pocket payments are introduced; this means the patient has to cover a small part of the cost of treatment (for example with co-payments).
2. The reimbursement system (the system by which payments from the payer to the provider are organized and calculated) determines the behavior of health care providers. Various remuneration schemes lead to a number of different incentives: budgets and flat payments lead to a decrease in quality and quantity of services provided to the patient. Per diems in hospital care lead to an increase in mean length of stay. Fee for service and DRG payments provide incentives for supplier induced demand.
3. The third cause of inefficiency is the lack of patient management concepts for chronically ill patients. Patient management requires the following tools: disease management, cost management, case management and demand management. It also requires a close collaboration of all health care providers.

The answer to the second question can be structured by looking at the following simple equations:

(1)	Expenditures	=	Income		
(2)	Demand	=	Supply		
(3)	Health Care Budgets	=	Prices	x	Utilization

The first equation simply explains that cost explosion in medical care is equal to income explosion of health care employees, and cost-containment means income containment for health care providers. Health care providers have never had an interest in cost-containment. To keep the financing of health insurance in balance, countervailing power has to be introduced. However, it is not wise for the government to become one of the parties. It is better if the government only sets the frame and takes the role of the moderator.

The second equation suggests that financial stability can be achieved by either stabilizing demand or stabilizing supply. Measures to stabilize demand are

Out-of-pocket payment,

- Co-payments,
- Waiting lists,
- Demand management.

Measures to stabilize supply are

- License for physicians,
- Requirement planning for hospitals,
- Positive and negative lists for services.

The third equation expresses the problems in monetary terms. It suggests that budgets are needed to control cost. Budgets are widely employed around the world (Schwartz et al. 1996). Alternatively, one can try to control cost with price regulation and utilization control. All those measures have a long tradition in health policy in Korea and Germany.

- Budgets for outpatient and inpatient care
- Reference prices
- Positive or negative lists
- Positive lists, negative lists
- Waiting time

One of the major tasks in Germany will be in the future, to define the basic package of health services covered by the social health insurance scheme, because the system will be unable to finance all health services available on the market and all innovations developed by the health care industry (Rutten and Busschbach 2001). Health technology assessment programs have to be established to provide the information to eliminate health services with low cost effectiveness ratio (Kielhorn and Schulenburg 2000).

V. Concluding Remarks

The ways to achieve the conflicting goals "equal access to health care for everyone" and "financial stability of the health care system" differ around the world. Korea and Germany have chosen a mixed system based on social health insurance. This gives a chance to learn from each other and to compare the different options to organize social health insurance. A detailed analysis shows, that the Korean and German health care systems have a lot of similarities but do also differ:

- Monopoly of NHIC in Korea, competition between sickness funds in Germany
- Low contribution rates in Korea, high contributions in Germany
- Central setting of fees for health care providers in Korea, negotiated fees in Germany
- High out-of-pocket payments in Korea, comprehensive first Euro-coverage in Germany

The challenges of both systems will be to contain cost by increasing the efficiency of providing medical care. Moral hazard, supplier induced demand, innovations with low cost effectiveness and a lack of patient management programs have increased cost and have led to a waste of scarce resources. Both systems need reforms with respect to their organization and the economic incentives to suppliers and consumers of health services. In addition a broad health technology assessment program has to provide the information to define the health service package covered by the health insurance scheme.

References

Institut der Deutschen Wirtschaft im Globalen Wettbewerb (2002) *Internationale Wirtschaftdaten*. Cologne: Deutscher Instituts Verlag.

Kielhorn, A. and Schulenburg, J.-M. v.d. (2000) *The Health Economic Handbook*. Tattenhal: adis international.

Ministry of Health and Welfare, Republic of Korea (2001) *Health and Welfare Services 2000*. Seoul.

Raffel, M. W. (ed.) (1997) *Health Care and Reform in Industrialized Countries*. Pennsylvania State University Press.

Rutten, F. and Busschbach, J. V. (2001) "How to define a basic package of health services for a tax funded or social insurance based health care system?" *The European Journal of Health Economics*, 2 (2).

Schulenburg, J.-M. v.d. and Greiner, W. (2000) *Gesundheitsökonomik*. Tübingen: Mohr-Siebeck Publishing House.

Schwartz, F. W., Glennerster, H. and Saltman, R.B. (eds) (1996) *Fixing Health Budgets: Experience from Europe and North America*. Chichester: John Wiley & Sons.

Ven, W. v.d (2001) "Risk Selection on the Sickness Fund Market," *The European Journal of Health Economics*, 23 (3).

Verband der Angestellten Krankenkasse (2002) *Ausgewählte Basisdaten der Gesundheitswesen*. Siegburg.

12

Evaluating the National Pension for Salary Earners and the Self-Employed

Alan Walker

I. Introduction

This chapter has four main aims. First of all, it explains the specific goals of the Productive Welfare approach with respect to the National Pension Scheme. Secondly, it outlines the recent changes made to the National Pension Scheme, some of which were designed to make it both more universal and equitable. Thirdly, the chapter considers the strengths and weakness of the current approach to pensions for private sector employees and the self-employed. Finally, some suggestions are made for possible future policy directions. The assessment contained in this chapter is based on the relatively limited information available and without the advantages of close first-hand examination of the operation of the National Pension Scheme or questioning anyone with responsibility for managing it and, therefore, must be regarded as a preliminary appraisal.[1]

Of course in discussing the National Pension Scheme we must be mindful of the fact that we are concerned with tomorrow's pensioners. Most older people in Korea today, especially those with the lowest incomes, depend on their own earnings or savings, family support and social assistance. Only a small proportion receives public pensions because, until recently, only government employees, teachers and the military were covered by public pensions. Prior to the introduction of the NPS in 1988 the only mandatory public pension scheme covering private sector employees was Retirement Allowances. This scheme was compulsory for firms with, first of all, ten employees and later for firms with five or more employees. It did not cover self-employed people.

II. Productive Welfare

The Korean Government should be congratulated on its Productive Welfare Strategy. This strategy is a sophisticated one derived from a careful analysis of competing welfare state models and based on clear principles. It has been very well summarized by Chung (Chapter 5):

> Productive Welfare can be defined as an active welfare policy aiming at social productivity improvement through economic value creation, based on the fundamental drive towards equality. That is, Productive Welfare begins on the firm premise that every single citizen in the society should be guaranteed and secured basic livelihood as one of their basic rights. With this premise, Productive Welfare acknowledges and stresses human development and self-actualization by means of education and work opportunity. Combing these ideologies, it aims at balanced development of equality and efficiency.

In contrast to some other countries in the region the Korean Government has openly acknowledged the limitations of development based only on economic growth. The Productive Welfare Strategy recognizes the limitations of the policy that prioritized growth. First of all in many countries, East and West, it has led to the widening of inequalities in income and wealth and, rather than the fruits of growth "trickling down" to the poorest, those at the bottom have been further impoverished. The Korean Productive Welfare approach turns its face against such theories (that have proved deficient in practice) and seeks a much more inclusive form of development: "If any group does not share in the fruits of economic growth, development is deficient." Secondly it is clear that a globalized world requires a more sophisticated blend of economic and social policies than those offered by neo-liberals in order to ensure both international competitiveness and social cohesion. Thus it is entirely appropriate that the Kim Dae-Jung administration has set its sights on "balanced social development" aimed at guaranteeing basic human rights and improving quality of life for all.

The goal of combining economic growth and social justice is one that many countries aspire to and some have achieved, most notably the Member States of the European Union (EU). The European model of development has long been described as one that combines growth and competitiveness with social justice—the two sides of the same coin. During the 1990s it was often represented in diagrammatic form:

Figure 12-1
The European Model of Development

Economic Growth and Competitiveness   +   Social Justice

The social policy strategy that places work at the heart of welfare is an increasingly familiar one as the developed countries strive to maintain their welfare states in the face of globalization and the ageing of their populations. We can see it in Australia's "Working Nation," the New Deal policies of the UK Labour Government ("making work pay" has been a dominant slogan) and, increasingly, in the approach being adopted by the European Union. All of them, of course, derive partly or wholly from the "third way" policies pursued by the Clinton Administration in the US and, certainly, the high rates of growth and employment achieved by the US in the 1990s have proved irresistible advertising slogans for this approach. However, the Korean Government has reached beyond the other main variants of work-based welfare or "welfare through work" in proposing to guarantee the right to work.

This is a difficult guarantee to deliver in a market economy—especially, as the report points out, in the face of globalization and technological change—but it is a bold step and rests on a principled belief in the dignity and other non-material benefits of labor. If the welfare through work strategy is to be successful it must be as inclusive as possible. Work must be made a realistic option for everyone and the many barriers to employment must be combated.

III. Pensions and Productive Welfare

Pensions are obviously a key element in any strategy to secure minimum living standards for all and to maintain human dignity, but they are not only an instrument of Productive Welfare, their sustainability depends on the success of the strategy. In particular, as noted above, an inclusive labor market is essential if pensions are to be both universal and sustainable. This is the stated intention of Productive Welfare in that its first component is a "fair labor market through which appropriate and fair working conditions can be achieved." In order to secure equal opportunities there must be active measures to combat discrimination and other barriers to employment (a point I return to at the end of this chapter). Pensions play a central role in the second component of productive welfare—redistribution—and, as the report points out, if distribution is left to the market, it will lead to exclusion and a breakdown in social cohesion. The third component of Productive Welfare—the encouragement of self-activation (the hand-up rather than the hand-out)—will help to ensure that labor force participation remains high and, therefore, that people are able to contribute to their own pensions. The fourth component—investment to enhance quality of life—will also help to deliver more secure pensions. Life-long education will enable citizens to continually adapt to the demands of a knowledge-based society and remain in employment while improved access to healthcare will help to ensure not only productivity but also the chance for healthy ageing.

This is the theory or ideology of Productive Welfare but what about its practice with regard to pensions? The Korean pension reforms are a key element in the expansion and strengthening of the social insurance system designed to reduce the impact of social risks, including old age. The National Pension Scheme (NPS) was established in 1986 and began in 1988. To start with it covered only workplaces with ten or more employees. On 1 April 1999, it was extended to all private employees and the self-employed, just 11 years after its introduction. The NPS covers those aged 18 to 60 who are resident in Korea. The scheme applies to private sector employees and the self-employed and excludes civil servants, military personnel and private school teachers, all of whom have their own Occupational Pensions Schemes (OPSs). The NPS also has two categories of insured persons: the compulsorily insured, such as employees and the self-employed, and those who pay contributions voluntarily, including housewives and students. Since 1988 the number of insured persons has grown continuously from 4.4 million to 16.1 million in 1999. Between 1998 and 1999, as a result of the extension of coverage, the numbers of insured nearly doubled.

The NPS for employees is funded by contributions from employers and employees (currently 4.5 percent each). Initially, however, contributions were set at a relatively low rate (1.5 percentage between 1988 and 1992). The contribution rates of the self-employed, including farmers and fishermen, and voluntary insured persons was three percent in June 2000 and is being raised by one percent per year from July 2000 until 2005 when it reaches nine percent. The self-employed pay their own contributions. The Government subsidizes the contributions of farmers and fishermen, a policy that will end in December 2004.

The NPS reflects the central goals of the Production Welfare Strategy in two main respects. First, following the 1999 reforms it aspires to universal coverage, so that the financial risk associated with old age may be spread throughout society, and to provide an income at least sufficient to maintain human dignity. Secondly, the NPS is a defined benefits scheme. Benefits (Old-age Pension, Disability Pension and Survivors' Pension) are calculated according to a combination of flat-rate (equalized) and earnings-related (individualized) elements with the former representing the average amount of the Standard Monthly Income of all insured persons and the latter the average of the Standard Monthly Income of an individual insured person. An additional five percent is added to both parts for each year in excess of 20 years. The standard level of pension benefits is estimated at 60 percentage of the income paid to the insured person who retires after 40 years of contributions and whose monthly income level is the median of the Standard Monthly Income of all insured persons. The amount of benefit received ranges from 60 percentage to 100 percentage of a person's income if the amount of monthly income is lower than the median of the Standard Monthly Income of all insured persons. If the person's income is higher than the median, the benefits will be less than 60 percentage of their income.

The Old-age Pension part of the NPS is paid at the age of 60 (55 for miners and fishermen) if the insured has contributed for at least ten years. The Basic Pension Amount is designed to ensure that a person with 40 years of contributions, whose income is the same as the median value of all insured persons, would receive 60 percentage of his or her average lifetime wage. The level of the pension is determined for each income group by the insured person's monthly income (the Standard Monthly Income). An Additional Pension is paid if the beneficiary is supporting a spouse, children under 18 or parents (including spouse's parents) who are aged 60 or over. Special arrangements are made for those who began contributing too late to build up the required contributions.

As noted in the introduction, in addition to the NPS Korea's Labor Law requires employers to pay every worker who has been employed for one year or more a minimum Retirement Allowance of 30 days (8.33 percentage) of the worker's average for every working year. The Retirement Allowance can be paid as a lump sum before retirement. Some employers promise to pay more than the legal minimum. Also, it is common for firms to seek tax relief on the reserves by establishing contracts with insurance companies on the proviso that the funds are lent back to the firm. Thus, even the funded element of Retirement Allowances is built on a rather shaky foundation.

IV. Reforming the NPS

Since it was established in 1988 the NPS has been extended gradually until it has achieved almost universal coverage. Initially it covered only workplaces with more than ten people and was extended, in 1992, to cover those employing five to nine workers. In 1995 coverage was extended to include farmers and fishermen, workers in small firms with less than five employees and the self-employed in rural areas.

As well as extending the coverage of the NPS a series of reforms, in the late 1990s have altered several aspects of the operation of the scheme. Following deliberations by the National Pension Reform Board (NPRB) major changes to the NPS were introduced in January 1999. The NPRB was convened in 1997 to recommend measures that would provide long-term financial sustainability, address the potential problems associated with extending coverage to the urban self-employed, provide methods of efficient management of reserves, coordinate links with the occupational schemes and design policies to deal with those older people not covered by the NPS. The NPRB held 13 conferences and nine meetings of the Special Committee in 1997 and involved representatives from the main trades unions, cooperatives, researchers and journalists in its numerous task forces. Unfortunately the NPRB did not produce a unanimous report, with the majority advocating a target replacement rate for average wage workers with full contribution histories from 20 to 40 percent and the minority recommending a higher replacement rate of 50 to 60 percent to be financed by increased contribution rates. The majority opinion was driven by a desire to prevent contribution rates from rising and would have maintained them at their 1998 levels until 2010 and, eventually, allowing them to rise to 12.65 percent by 2025 (World Bank 2000).

The recommendations of the NPRB were not accepted by the Government and, instead, after public hearings, the Ministry of Health and Welfare submitted a new reform package on May 8, 1998, one which according to the World Bank was closer to the minority than the majority of the NPRB. The main proposals were: an increase in the retirement age to 61 in 2013 and one year every five years thereafter until reaching 65 in 2033; a new benefit formula, which would use an accrual rate after 1998, which would generate a 55 percentage replacement rate for a worker with an average wage; no separation of the redistributive from the earnings-related scheme; and past years would be credited under the old formula (ibid.).

Table 12-1
Effects of 1999 Reform of National Pension Act on Replacement Rates
(percent)

	Pre 1999	From 1999	Percentage change
Average Wage	70	60	-14.3
150 percent Average Wage	57	60	-11.8
50 percent Average Wage	110	90	-18.2

Source: World Bank, 2000, p.23.

Most of these measures recommended by the Ministry of Health were included in the amendment to the National Pension Act on December 31, 1998. In approving the measures Congress made several important changes, including reducing the target replacement rate for an average worker to 60 (from 70 percent) instead of the recommended 55 percent and deciding not to increase the contribution rate in stages but to mandate five-year actuarial reviews. Table 12-1 shows the effects of the January 1999 reforms on target replacement rates and the consequent reduction in the redistributory impact of the NPS. Coverage of the NPS was further extended, in April, 1999, to cover those employed by small firms with less than five workers and the self-employed in urban areas (Yoon 2001).

As Table 12-2 shows, at the end of November 2000, a total of 16.5 million people were covered by the NPS, including 5.6 million employees and 10.8

million self-employed. The table also illustrates the high level of exemptions from contributions among the self-employed (45.2 percent) due to factors such as business closure, suspension or unemployment. At November 2000 the number of NPS beneficiaries was 0.6 million, some three-quarters of whom received Old-age Pension benefits. Since the implementation of the NPS a total of 7.2 million people have received a lump-sum benefit (ibid.).

Table 12-2
Numbers Covered by the National Pension Scheme (November 2000)

Private Sector	Self-employed			Voluntary	
Employees	Total Contributing	Exempt	Total	Insured	
5,680	5,963	4,926	10,889	114	16,683

Source: National Pension Corporation, quoted in Yoon, 2001, p.3.

V. Strengths and Weaknesses of the NPS

Having outlined the basic features of the Korean pension system for private employees and the self-employed and how it was altered by recent reforms, we can begin a preliminary assessment of its strengths and weaknesses. A key aim of any public pension system is to ensure financial security in old age and this is achieved principally by smoothing consumption between working life and retirement. At the same time public pension systems usually include an element of vertical redistribution to offset poverty in old age and to ensure that the living standards of all pensioners reach a minimum level. The pension systems of developed countries differ significantly with regard to their redistributory impact (OECD 1988; 2000). The Korean NPS combines both of these elements and, in line with the Productive Welfare Strategy, seeks to guarantee a higher quality of life for the poor, to reduce the effect of the social risk of old age and to ensure that all groups share in the fruits of economic growth. Within the context of both the national goals set by the Korean Government and global guidelines on provision for old age, such as the UN Plan of Action and Long-term Strategy on Ageing (in both its original 1982 and revised 2002 forms), this clear focus on achieving financial security in old age must be regarded as both a defining feature of the NPS and, from the perspective of future beneficiaries, its greatest strength.

The precise level of financial security is determined by the replacement rate and the target rate set by the Government for the NPS, 60 percent, compares favourably with those of other developed countries. However it is regarded in some quarters as being too generous (World Bank 2000). The NPS was designed to be redistributory both among different groups and inter-generationally. The benefit formula of the NPS is progressive and therefore provides a higher replacement rate (and a higher rate of return on contributions) to workers with lower lifetime earnings. The real value of retirement income is protected by indexing the pension to the consumer price index and the initial pension amount depends on the increase in real wages.

Secondly, as with other public defined benefit schemes, it is a great advantage to potential beneficiaries to be aware of the replacement rate they can reasonably expect from a lifetime's contributions. This contrasts with the defined contribution approach more common in private pension schemes in which a target contribution rate relies on the performance of stock markets and, therefore, contains an element of risk and uncertainty, as has been demonstrated amply by the negative impact of the recent downturn in equity performance, for example in the UK. Public defined benefit schemes may also be subject to "political risk" in the form of governments reneging on their own promises or, more often, those of previous governments as, again, is well illustrated by the recent history of pension reform in the UK (Walker 1989). We can say, without fear of contradiction, that there are strong differences of opinion about the best approach to pension funding. However, if the public defined benefit schemes are sustainable, they are likely to be preferred by beneficiaries.

A third strength of the NPS is its intention to attain universal coverage which, again, is in line with the Productive Welfare Strategy. Thus the January 1999 reforms reduced the minimum eligibility period required for pension rights from 15 years service to ten years. Also a split pension benefit system was introduced to safeguard pension rights for surviving spouses. The aim of achieving universal coverage will ensure that the financial risk associated with retirement is pooled throughout Korean society. This entails the considerable benefit of solidarity and is likely to be a source of social cohesion in Korea. As we have seen an important element of the redistributory aspect of the NPS is the intergenerational one and, if it can be maintained, is another source of social cohesion (ibid.).

In summary, the NPS is characterized by clear policy principles, such as universality, redistribution and solidarity and aspires to replacement rates that would, over time, minimize financial security in old age and place Korea in the top rank of public pension providers in the developed world.

Turning to the weaknesses of the pension system for private employees and the self-employed, there are six main ones, by far the biggest of which is the question of sustainability. In the unlikely event of the current contribution rate of nine percentage remaining unchanged, the NPS is projected to run into deficit from 2034 and to see its reserves depleted by 2048. Therefore future options for the NPS must address this central question of funding. In particular the lack of funding for Retirement Allowances makes them vulnerable. In the recession many firms were not able to pay the benefit guaranteed by law and, as a result, the Government introduced the Wage Guarantee Funds in July 1998. This fund is managed by the Minister of Labour and financed from a 0.2 percent tax on the wage bills of firms covered by the Retirement Allowance legislation. Where employers are unable to meet their obligations, the Government Fund pays the Retirement Allowance to the workers up to a maximum of three months.

Secondly, it is not entirely clear that the principal goals of the NPS, as derived from the Productive Welfare approach, are fully operational or, in other words, that the practice reflects the principles. For example, the combination of Retirement Allowance and NPS means that retirement incomes from these public schemes vary by age cohort and type of worker. According to World Bank calculations a Korean worker aged 50 in 2000 with 35 years of service would receive benefits of roughly equal magnitude from each of the two schemes. As the NPS matures workers will have spent more of their careers covered by the NPS and, by the time those entering the labor force in 1990 retire with full benefits the ratio of NPS to Retirement Allowance will be 2:1 (World Bank 2000). The combination of the two pension programs also produces higher replacement rates for some workers (as high as 85 percentage for a worker with 35 years of contributions). The operation of the twin public schemes—the Occupational Pension Schemes and the NPS—is also a source of inequity within the whole public pension system. Some aspects of these variations in accrued rights are transitory, related to the immaturity of the NPS, but some of them are structural features of public pension provision in Korea.

Thirdly, there is the issue of equity between employees and the self-employed due to the problem of assessing the incomes of the self-employed. At the end of 1999, the reported incomes of the self-employed were 69 percent of the reported incomes of employees (Yoon 2001). Low reported incomes by self-employed people result in disproportionately low contribution levels. This not only reduces the potential income of the NPS but also threatens the legitimacy of the scheme. Although some efforts have been made already to improve the accuracy of income reporting among the self-employed this must be an element in any reform package.

Fourthly, there are still groups of workers who remain outside of the NPS. In fact some 51 percentage of eligible urban workers are exempt from paying contributions. The majority of these exemptions are due to unemployment or premature retirement due to the recession. Some of those exempted from contributions are participating in some form of paid employment but have claimed exemption because they are not able to pay contributions. The high level of exemptions is obviously a factor in the financial sustainability of the NPS and it may also undermine the fairness of the scheme as perceived by its contributors. Many of those claiming exemption will be excluded from future old age pension coverage because they have not made sufficient contributions. In an attempt to mitigate this problem the national pension plan last year began to try to protect the underprivileged by placing them in small businesses with less than four employees.

Fifthly, there is the management system of the NPS. Since the scheme is in surplus the Government has been using its reserves as a source of direct borrowing. By the late 1990s two-thirds of the surpluses were automatically earmarked for this type of lending (World Bank 2000). The amendment to the Public Funds Management Act in 1998 phased out this automatic mechanism for channeling NPS surpluses to the Government. The NPS' surpluses are projected to grow over the next three decades and to peak in 2040. A question arises, therefore, concerning the investment of these funds, the answer to which will have an important bearing on the funds available to the NPS and the wider public sector. This also emphasizes the need for greater transparency in fund management.

Finally, the World Bank's analysis suggests that the fact that the Korean Government was forced to reduce the replacement rate promised only ten years earlier by 15 percent and increase retirement ages has undermined the credibility of the NPS (ibid.). It is impossible to assess the truth of this claim from a distance. However the changes are relatively minor and the NPS remains a substantial achievement and one that is likely to win the support of Korean citizens if it can experience a period of sustained stability.

VI. Future Policy Directions

The future of the NPS and, indeed, the entire Korean pension system is in question. In the wake of the financial crisis the World Bank advised the Korean Government to review not only the NPS but the entire pension system. The Government accepted this advice and, in December 1998, established the Pension Reform Task Force under the aegis of the Social Security Deliberation Committee and the Minister of Health and Welfare. The Task Force's terms of reference went way beyond the future of the NPS to encompass the balance between public and private pensions and the long term financing of the OPSs (ibid.). The Task Force set four objectives for the reform of the pension system: securing financial stability and sustainability; assuring adequate levels of pensions; assuring equity between generations, income groups and occupational groups; and assuring that the old age income protection system is comprehensive (Yoon 2001).

The Task Force also set out five policy directions aimed at pursuing these objectives. First of all it recommends the establishment of a multi-pillar pension system composed of a mandatory public basic pension as the first pillar, a mandatory private pension scheme as the second pillar and a voluntary private pension scheme as the third pillar. Secondly it proposes the introduction of a defined contribution scheme as the way to ensure long-term financial stability and to enhance individual responsibility. Thirdly, the Task Force argues that the Retirement Allowance system should be converted into a corporate pension scheme. Fourthly it recommends systematic reform to facilitate portability among different pension schemes, to improve fund management and to strengthen the supervision of pension schemes. Fifthly it suggests the absorption of the OPSs into the multi-pillar system and their linkage with the NPS (ibid.). These policy directions clearly reflect the advice given by the international economic agencies (OECD 1998; 2000; World Bank 2000), and, in particular, the first and second were urged strongly by the World Bank.

The model of multi-pillar pension systems with mandatory public and private first and second tiers and the replacement of defined benefits by defined contributions have achieved the status of global economic laws in the pensions field largely because of their sponsorship by the international economic agencies (World Bank 1994). Korea may well decide on a radical root-and-branch overhaul of its young pensions system but it is not clear from the evidence available that this radical option is essential. Moreover, before such a fundamental change is enacted it is important for the Task Force and others engaged in the pensions policy process to consider the advantages and disadvantages of the two main approaches to pension provision.

On the one hand, public defined benefit systems suffer from the danger of political interference and do not necessarily have a positive impact on the development of financial markets. They are vulnerable to demographic change and a decline in employment. But they do allow pensioners' incomes to rise along with general living standards if the political will exists to do this. They are superior with regard to the alleviation of poverty and the provision of insurance against inflation and investment risks. They tend to be socially inclusive: they can cover everyone, provide protection for gaps in earnings and also job changes.

On the other hand, privately defined contributions, or funded, schemes lack political and democratic accountability; entail higher levels of risk than public schemes; have high start-up costs; provide poor coverage for the vulnerable and those, such as female carers, with limited employment opportunities; have high public costs in terms of tax reliefs and other incentives; and generally entail higher administrative costs than public schemes. On the positive side, private defined contribution schemes are said to produce lower distortionary effects in the labor market than public ones and contribute to the development of financial markets. Some of the disadvantages of private funded schemes can be minimized by making them compulsory and by regulating them strictly, but there are no precedents internationally of compulsory private schemes covering more than two-thirds of the population. Also there is no guarantee that compulsory savings would yield sufficient income in retirement for large groups of workers (as the case of Singapore demonstrates).

A major change of direction for the Korean pension system would entail risks, particularly with regard to the retirement incomes of future pensioners. Moreover it may well compromise some of the intentions of the Productive Welfare Strategy such as universality, risk pooling and the maintenance of human dignity for all. But, if such a radical change is contemplated, as the Task Force's recommendations suggest, it is better to do it sooner than later because the transitional costs will be low and the disruption minimal. If the Korean Government decides on a more cautious approach (and caution is an excellent watchword with regard to pension system reform) there are several changes that would improve the operation of the NPS and help to overcome its weaknesses. They may also offset some of the fears about future sustainability.

First of all, it is essential to "join-up" the different elements of policy that have a bearing on pension provision. Much of the debate about pensions tends to be conducted purely in terms of the technical features of pension systems themselves, but employment and health are also major determinants of the demand and supply sides of the pension equation. In the European Union (EU) for example, public pension sustainability has been threatened by the trend towards early exit from the labor force (Walker 1997; OECD 2000) as well as by increased life expectancy. Korea is on a similar path to other developed countries with regard to life expectancy but not with regard to falling labor force participation among men.

Korean life expectancy has been below the OECD average but, by the end of 2030, it is likely to have caught up (OECD 2000). In 1960 life expectancy was 54 years for men and 57 years for women, and by 2030, it is expected to grow to 75 and 81 years respectively. As in other developed countries it is the combination of increasing life expectancy and falling fertility that is responsible for population ageing. Having started with a younger population than the OECD average the Korean population will age quite rapidly: from three percentage of the population aged 65 and over in 1960, to seven percent today, to 18 percent in 2030. However, unlike most other OECD countries, there has not been a large decline in labor force participation among Korean men. Moreover, according to OECD projections, there is not likely to be a significant decline in male labor force participation over the next 30 years. The pattern of labor force participation among women in Korea is similar to the OECD average: rising employment rates but not attaining the same level as men. When the demographic and labor market trends are combined it can be seen that Korea has a much higher projected share of its total population in employment than the OECD average and this is before the productive welfare strategy has reached its full effect. Thus the OECD projection of a 50 percent employment rate by 2030 (compared with an average 43 percent) may be significantly below the actual rate (OECD 2000).

It is essential that Korea maintains relatively high rates of labor force participation and at the same time seeks to minimize the negative impact of employment on health. In the EU and gradually elsewhere in the world the strategy that reflects these goals is labeled 'active ageing': the promotion of employment and other forms of activity and engagement in later life and the prevention of age-related barriers to employment or "age management" (Walker 1997; 1999; 2002; OECD 2000; WHO 2000). This entails a life-course perspective on the relationship between age and employment, rather than remedial measures, and emphasizes the need to connect all relevant policies. The Productive Welfare Strategy provides a perfect vehicle for joined-up policy thinking including in the pension field. Figure 12-2 shows the way in which the interconnectedness of the different policy fields is expressed in the EU (a model which replaced the simple one shown in Figure 12-2) while Figure 12-3 shows how it could be modified for Korean policy purposes.

Figure 12-2
The Policy Triangle

Social Policy

Economic Policy ———————— Employment Policy

Source: European Commission, 2000

Figure 12-3
The Korean Policy Triangle

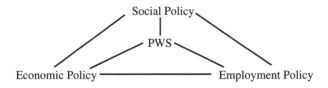

Social Policy

PWS

Economic Policy ———————— Employment Policy

Within this joined-up policy context the specific weaknesses of the NPS can be tackled more effectively. The Task Force has proposed four reform options and each of them contain advantages as well as disadvantages (Yoon 2001). All of them are projected to result in financial sustainability but at different contribution rates. Options 2 and 3 appear to be particularly attractive because they maintain the NPS as a common denominator for the whole pension scheme (Option 2) or create a universal basic pension (Option 3) and break down the barrier between the NPS and the OPSs. In addition to the four reform options the Task Force made a series of laudable general policy recommendations which include the need for urgent reform and a broad national consensus on levels of contributions and benefits: the conversion of Retirement Allowances into an occupational pension; a clear definition of the roles to be played by the public and the private sectors; a safeguard to provide old age protection for those denied benefits under the current system; and the need for reliable income data for the self-employed before pension reform is undertaken.

Regardless of the extent of the changes made to the NPS and OPSs it is essential that reforms are also introduced to the management and operation of the pension system. In particular it is important to ensure a much higher level of transparency in fund management. The governance structures of the NPS also need overhaul to allow greater independence in the management of investments, with clear lines of accountability and regulation, and to include representatives from both contributors and pensioners. Furthermore, the sustainability of a pension system depends on more than simple economic formulae suggest, it also requires the support of contributors and potential contributors. The Government must play a leading role in advertising the benefits of the NPS to the younger generations and in persuading them that it is a vital element of Korean citizenship.

VII. Conclusion

This review of the operation of the NPS has found that its establishment is a considerable achievement for the Korean Government. When it reaches maturity the NPS offers the prospect of financial security in old age and, therefore, reflects the fundamental human dignity aspiration of the Productive Welfare Strategy. However there is no doubt that the scheme suffers from several weaknesses and, as a result, further reform is needed. Reforms are required especially to ensure sustainability, to phase out Retirement Allowances as public provision, to end the distinction between the NPS and OPSs and to achieve greater transparency and democratic representation in the management and operation of the scheme. It is essential that these reforms are carried out in the context of a joined-up policy strategy in which economic, employment and social policies seek to achieve the same goal (Productive Welfare). Although Korea is being urged towards a radical overhaul of its pension system, it is clear from the available evidence and the work of the Pension Reform Task Force, that relatively minor adjustments to the operation of the NPS and other parts of the pension system would achieve the desired results including sustainability. The Korean pension system stands at the crossroads and which path is chosen remains a matter for the Government and the people of Korea.

Note

1. For what is contained here I am indebted principally to Dr. Chanyong Park, Dr. Byungsik Yoon and the World Bank, although none of them has the slightest responsibility for my interpretation of their work.

References

European Commission (2000) *Social Policy Agenda*. Brussels: European Commission.
OECD (1998) *Reforming Public Pensions*. Paris: OECD.
_____ (2000) *Reforms for an Ageing Society*. Paris: OECD.
Walker, A. (ed.) (1996) *The New Generational Contract*. London: UCL Press.
_____ (1997) *Combating Age Barriers in Employment*. Luxembourg: Office for the Official Publications of the European Communities.
_____ (1999) *Combating Age Barriers in Employment—A Guide to Good Practice*. Luxembourg: Office for the Official Publications of the European Communities.
_____ (1999a) "The Future of Pensions and Retirement in Europe: Towards Productive Ageing," *The Hallym International Journal of Ageing*, 1 (2).
_____ (2002) "A Strategy for Active Ageing," *International Social Security Review*, 55 (1).
WHO (2000) *Health and Ageing*. Geneva: WHO.
World Bank (1994) *Averting the Old Age Crisis*. New York City: OUP.
_____ (2000) "Generative Balanced Model of Welfare," Korea Institute for Health and Social Affairs. Seoul.
Yoon, B. (2001) "Introduction to Mandatory Old-age Income Security System in Korea," Korea Institute for Health and Social Affairs, mimeo.

13

Social Security Pensions in Korea and Japan

Noriyuki Takayama

I. Introduction

Korea is one of the countries that are faced with a very rapid aging of the population. While family-ties still play a major role in securing income after retirement, there is a growing demand for public pensions in place of family support. It has not been long since Korea introduced a universal pension scheme. The rapid aging of the Korean population along with further development and refinement of the pension system may impose financial difficulties in maintaining the current pension system around 2030 considering that there still remains the issue of the unbalance between contributions and benefits in the current pension program to be resolved.

The Korean pension scheme is similar to that of Japan. However, Japan has a longer history in handling the public pension scheme, has experienced population aging earlier, and already has experienced both shortfalls and success. Hence, Japanese public pension scheme and its experiences may be a good comparative study for Korea.

Section two of this chapter gives a brief outline of the National Pension Scheme of Korea. Section three compares the National Pension Scheme of Korea and the public pension scheme of Japan. Section four considers some implications the Japanese experience along with those of other OECD countries. The last section gives a concluding remark.

II. Pension Scheme in Korea

The earliest plan was established in 1960 for the civil servants. Three years later, a special program for the military servants was developed. Another

program started from 1975 targeted for private school teachers and their staffs.[1]
A more comprehensive scheme called the National Pension System came into
effect in 1988 for the private sector employees of ages 18 to 59, and its
coverage was extended to include the self-employed in rural areas in 1995.
The NPS was further extended to cover self-employed in urban areas in 1999.[2]
Programs are divided to cover different sectors of the population, and they are
run financially independent from each other. However, a small portion of the
population is still not covered by any public pension schemes. It consists of
non-active spouses of the person insured in any compulsory scheme, non-
active students or the draftees for military service of ages 18 to 26, and those
people protected under public assistance.

The contribution rate for the National Pension Scheme was initially set at
three percent in 1988, and has been gradually increased since then, reaching
nine percent in 1998. It is shared equally between employees and their employers. The contribution rate for the self-employed started at three percent in
1995 and has been increased by one percent per year from 2000 until reaching nine percent in 2005.[3] The contribution rate is determined based on the
Standard Monthly Income (hereinafter SMI), which has 45 grades from
220,000 won to 3,600,000 won as of 2001.[4] In certain cases, an insured person can be exempt from paying his/her contributions. These include people
suffering from business closure/suspension, unemployed, retired persons, students, those drafted in military service, patients in hospital and the poor.
Deferred contributions either in form of lump sum or installment basis may be
available for such people. The period of non-payment is not recognized as
the insured term. Government subsidy is provided to the National Pension
Scheme for covering its administrative cost. In the case of farmers and fishermen, the reduced contribution rate by one third of the lowest grade in the SMI
is being applied between 1995 and 2004, and the difference is being compen-
sated by the general revenue.

In Korea, there are old-age, disability and survivors' benefits, and a special
lump sum refund. The amount of each benefit is the sum of the basic pension
and any additional pension. The basic pension benefit is of the two-tier structure: the flat-rate benefit and the earnings-related benefit. The additional
pension benefit may be considered as family allowance, paid in a fixed amount,
solely based on the number of dependents. The methodology for the detailed
benefit calculation for basic Old-age Pension is given below.

The normal flat-rate basic benefit for old-age pension is 30 percent of the
average price-indexed SMI for all insured persons over three years prior to
pension contribution. This normal benefit will be paid to persons insured for
40 years. The flat-rate basic benefit is proportional to years insured. The
minimum contribution years required is 20. Consequently, those who have
contributed for 20 years will be applied with a flat-rate basic benefit being 15
percentage of the average SMI. The earnings-related benefit is proportional

to years insured (20 years or more) and to the average SMI of the insured person. The average SMI of the insured person is calculated over his/her entire period of coverage (and *not* for the last three years), adjusted by a wage index factor, and converted to the current earnings level. These conversions are carried out every year. The accrual rate for the earnings-related component of old-age benefits is 0.75 percent per year. Thus, a 40-year contribution will earn 30 percent of the career average monthly real earnings. For example, for a typical employee whose average SMI is the mean of the Standard Monthly Income of all insured persons, the replacement rate is estimated to be 60 percent after 40 years of contributions.[5] The benefit is indexed automatically each fiscal year (starting from 1 April) to reflect any changes in the consumer price index of the previous calendar year.

Old-age benefit is reduced for those insured for ten years or more but less than 20 years and this reduced benefit is nearly proportional to years insured.[6] Another reduced old-age benefit, called "Special Old-age Pension" was introduced to cover the special cohort group at the time of National Pension Scheme enactment. This specific cohort was unable to meet the minimum requirements of 10-year contributions because their age was already over 50 at the time. Subsequently, the special old-age pension is paid when a person of the above cohort reaches age 60 with contributions of five to nine years. The benefit ranges between 25 percent to 45 percent depending on the number of contribution years (five to nine), which is regarded as being proportional to the normal benefit of 20-year contributions.

Full pension can be currently claimed at age 60 by retired persons insured for 20 years or more. In 2013, the normal pensionable age is to be increased to 61 and then on, one year every five years, eventually reaching 65 in 2033.[7] On reaching age 60, an individual who has not fully retired can receive a reduced pension (called "Active Old-age Pension"). The reduction is not based on his/her current earnings, but based solely on age before 65. The reductions are by ten percent by one year; for example, ten percentage reduction for those of age 64 and 50 percentage for those of age 60, and so forth. Further, old-age pension can be claimed as early as 55 years of age if one is fully retired with contributions of ten years or more, though it is subject to actuarial reduction. The reductions are currently by five percent by one year before age 60. Consequently, the proportion of benefits to the normal amount is 75 percentage for those making an initial claim at age 55. One half of the old-age benefits accrued to a partner during the period of marriage may be granted to the divorced person of age 60, given the marriage lasted for at least five years. This will enhance the pension rights for women. If the divorced person remarries, the above claim will be suspended.

The Lump Sum Refund is payable to the following: (1) A person who had been covered by the National Pension Scheme but newly became a government official, (2) military personnel, (3) a private school teacher, (4) an employee of the specially designated post office, (5) one who emigrates to a foreign country, (6) one who is a survivor of the insured person but not qualified for the survivors' pension, and (7) one who reaches age 60 with contributions of less than ten years. The lump sum amount is based on the contributions and legally fixed interest.

When a person is eligible for two or more pension benefits (including the lump sum refund), only one benefit is allowed at his/her choice and the other benefits are not paid. Pension benefits are paid monthly to a beneficiary on the last working day of each month. In fiscal 2000, 91 percentage of beneficiaries were the recipients of the lump sum refund, whereas old-age pensioners were only 6.6 percent. In terms of the benefit amount, aggregate old-age pension benefits accounted only for 12.3 percentage of the total benefits due to the relatively short operational time for the Korean National Pension Scheme.

The National Pension Scheme is a defined-benefit plan, financed mainly on the pay-as-you-go basis with partial funding. As at the end of March 2001, it had fund reserves of 76.8 trillion won. The fund reserves have been invested mainly to construct social overhead capitals. They have been invested in the financial sector as well, including investments in private bonds, stocks, and shares. The medium- and long-term financial projections are to be conducted every five years from 2003, promoting the fortification of the financial sustainability of the National Pension Scheme in the future.

III. Comparison between the Japanese and Korean Pension Schemes

There are many aspects of similarity between the national pension scheme of Korea and the public pension scheme of Japan.[8] First, the coverage was widened step by step by setting up respective programs for different sectors of the population. The pension scheme was first set up for public servants, and then the coverage was extended to include private sector employees. The self-employed were the last portion of the population to be covered. Second, the pension benefit is more generous for public sector employees than for private sector employees, though since 1986, Japan has reformed the system to unify the benefit formula between public and private sector employees as far as the social security component is concerned. Third, the program is a defined benefit plan, financed mainly on a pay-as-you-go basis with partial pre-funding. Fourth, the program has a two-tier benefit structure; the flat-rate benefit and the earnings-related benefit. Fifth, the normal replacement rate is 60 percent and the benefit is CPI-indexed automatically. Sixth, the average age for the beneficiary for old-age benefit is to be increased step by step to 65. Seventh, the contribution rate has been increased gradually and will continue to do so in the future, though further hikes in the contribution rate of more than nine percent have not been announced yet in Korea. Eighth, while contributions are generally earnings-proportional, shared equally by employees and their employers, farmers and fishermen are exceptions where a flat-rate is applied for their contribution rate. Ninth, the fund reserves of the public pension programs have been invested mainly to construct social overhead capitals to boost economic growth. Tenth, reforms of public pension program are to be made at least every five years. Such frequent changes are necessary for fine tuning in order to take consideration of the rapidly changing socio-economic circumstances.

However, there exist several differences between the national pension scheme and the public pension scheme of Japan. The national pension scheme of Korea can be regarded as more advanced than the public pension scheme of Japan because of the following: a) private sector employees and the self-employed are covered within a unified program, both eligible for the earnings-related benefits i.e., the self-employed in Japan have no earnings-related benefit, b) the minimum contribution period for old-age benefit is ten years in Korea, whereas it is still 25 years in Japan, c) pension benefits are paid monthly in Korea, while they are paid every two months in Japan, d) upon divorce, pension payment is split equally in Korea. However, Japan has just started discussion on such a system, e) from the outset Korea has introduced the SMI which includes bonuses as the benefit/contribution base. In Japan the shift to incorporate the yearly income base will be from 2003, and f) Korea has no contracted-out plans for the earnings-related component. This issue caused much controversy, and after cautious consideration, Korean citizens came to a wise conclusion that the proposal of introducing contracted-out plans should be turned down. By contrast, Japan has made a misjudgement by introducing contracted-out plans. A majority of contracted-out plans in Japan are currently suffering from a serious deficit in pension liabilities.

Japan has much longer experience in handling public pensions and has managed to overcome some difficulties in terms of designing public pensions. It should be noted, among others, that: (1) since 1961, the portability of one's pension rights has been adjusted among the divided public pension programs in Japan. Since then, when an individual changes his/her job, that person will no longer lose the pension rights. Incidentally, the lump sum refund has been abolished in Japan except for the short-term foreign employees, who can recoup their contributions in lump sum subject to a maximum of three years' contributions. Abolition of the lump sum refund dedicates, in particular, to strengthen pension rights for women who are most likely to leave their career temporarily upon marriage or child-bearing, and return to labor market after child-raising. As mentioned above, the minimum contribution period for old-age benefits (25 years) is relatively long in Japan. With a lump sum refund, a majority of Japanese females would have been one of the most disadvantaged groups in old-age income security. (2) Japan has already set up a revenue-sharing scheme among different public pension programs. The public pension program for the military servants is fully integrated into the program of civil servants in central governments. Generally, military servants retire early, and start receiving their old-age pension benefits much earlier compared to civil servants. The advance benefits for veterans are fully financed from general revenue, and not from the social security contribution. Thus, any crisis in financing the pension program for military servants could be avoided. (3) There are other revenue-sharing schemes in Japan. Due to the fact that the self-employed have been decreasing in number, the pay-as-you-go pension program for them became even harder to maintain. Since 1986, the first-tier, flat-rate portion has been fully integrated into one program for all sectors of the population in Japan. It is financed on a pay-as-you-go basis with revenue-sharing by equal annual contributions per enrollee from all divided programs. Considerable amount of money is currently transferred every year from employees in the private sector to self-employed people. This transfer has been justified and accepted, since the majority of children of pension recipients in the self-employed group are currently employees in the private sector. (4) The same is true for fishermen, employees of Japan Railway company, Japan Tobacco company and National Telephone and Telecommunications company; they have been decreasing in number. They have all been included in the general program for employees in the private sector in order to avoid any bankruptcy of pension programs for financing the second tier, earnings-related benefits. From 2002, employees in cooperatives of agriculture, forestry and fishery will be included as well. (5) Public servants in Japan once enjoyed old-age pension benefits based on their final salary. Since 1986, the earnings-related pension for them has become lifetime average salary based, similar to one applied for employees in the private sector. Integration of pension benefit formula between public servants and the private sector employees has been accomplished. (6) Up until October 1994, pension benefits in Japan were adjusted in line with the hikes in gross wages, but since then, they have been linked with net wages. This implies a shift to define the replacement rate in terms of *net* earnings, inducing a more equitable balance of income between the working generation and the retired generation, in considering that of social security contributions and tax payments are increasing in real terms for the working generation.

IV. Implications of Experience of Japan and Other OECD Countries

Learning from the experience of Japan and other countries, Korea can implement reform measures to the public pension program before beneficiaries start to receive the full amount of old-age benefits from 2008. Also, it may be helpful for Korea to review the past painful experiences of OECD countries in order to avoid taking the same path. In this section, both short and long term issues will be discussed. Some suggestions for the future pension reform will also be made.

Overall, there seem to be eight short-term problems. First, the special program for the military servants is presently facing current account deficits. The government has been held responsible for making up deficits with general revenue due to an absence of a mechanism for the revenue-sharing scheme or integration. The Japanese case mentioned above may be useful in finding an adequate resolution to this problem and determining the optimal provision. Furthermore, contribution periods when an individual is involved in combat are currently counted as three times the actual period, and this generous way of calculation might pose a problem.

Second, there is a question of transparency in determining the income of the self-employed in Korea and the same applies for Japan. Low reported incomes by the self-employed raise the issue of equity between employees and the self-employed, subsequently causing dissatisfaction among employees. One suggestion might be to reduce the flat-rate pension benefit. However, this will lower old-age income security for the self-employed in turn. The problem of underreported income may be resolved through implementing a funding shift to a consumption-based tax, since consumption is based on the actual income and not on the income reported to the tax authorities.

Third, the drop-out problem especially for non-employed or self-employed people is serious.[9] This is quite contrary to the goal of achieving a state of "pension scheme for everyone," the nation's long-cherished dream. Japan also faces the same problem where some non-employed or self-employed people are forced to rely on public assistance in their old age, mainly due to their drop-out from the public pension program. Again, the solution to this problem may be a funding shift to a consumption-based tax for financing the flat-rate pension benefit.

Fourth, shifting to the net-wage indexation seems more advantageous. This shift has already been introduced in Germany and Japan in 1992 and 1994 respectively.

Fifth, implementing the improved benefit formula with adjusted pension requirements, well equipped with portability[10] among different program should be pursued with the assumption that the public pensions remain in defined benefit plans. Under this premise, the reform of the pension program for civil servants is urgently needed at this point. Their benefit is still wholly based on final salary and its accrual rate is considerably generous (i.e., the replacement rate is 80 percent for 35 years service). Furthermore, they can receive old-age benefits just after retirement regardless of age if they have continuous employment history of 20 years or more. Indeed, they are enjoying much greater benefits than the private sector employees in spite of deficits on current account of their pensions. The down-sizing of the public sector will be inevitable in the future. However, this will intensify financial difficulties in the pension program for civil servants even more. Thus, there should be some revenue-sharing scheme between programs for civil servants and private sector employees. The benefit formula and pension requirements should be in balance until then. Another thing to note is that it is possible for civil servants to have additional occupational pensions of their own, which are apart from social security.

Sixth, investment from fund reserves of public pensions should be done with careful consideration since it is most likely to be influenced by political situations, often causing non-transparent political scandals. The U.S. made a wise choice in that fund reserves are wholly invested in federal government bonds, which enables investment to be free from any political pressures.

Seventh, the old-age pension of Korea is rather unique: its reduction is solely dependent on age. The younger the active workers in their early sixties, the heavier their penalty become. The active old-age pension could virtually operate as a strong employment subsidy for employers. If its purpose is to promote delayed retirement, the penalty should be reformed: the younger the active workers in their early sixties, the less they are to be penalized. Alternatively the penalty (the reduction) should be wholly deleted in early sixties. If it is too extreme, then, a reduction of pension benefits by, for example, 50 percent with any additional earnings may be recommended.

Turning to the medium- and long-term issues, one cannot neglect adverse effects resulting from further increases in the contribution rate for public pensions. With the current level of pension benefits fixed, the future generations will be forced to pay increased contribution up to around 30 percent for public pensions.[11] Such contributions are more than three times the current contribution rate, posing great harm to the Korean economy. There could be some room for Korea to further increase the contribution rate for public pensions, but taking its adverse effects into account, any large increases in the contribution rate should be avoided in the future. There may be two alternatives; a funding shift or a change in the benefit structure. Some funding shift to a consumption-based tax is preferable, as stated above. It should be remembered, as well, that a consumption-based tax will be better in circumventing constraints on economic growth, compared with payroll tax or income tax (Takayama 1997). As regards possible changes in the benefit structure, let us look at international examples. One can observe a shift from the conventional two-tier benefit system to the earnings-related benefit with guaranteed income supplement in Sweden (see Figures 13-1 and 13-2). Canada has a two-tier system, with the income-tested flat-rate benefit for higher-income seniors. Australia has the earnings-related benefit with the means-tested flat-rate one. The United Kingdom is to introduce the second state pension or the pension credit for low-income groups. It can be regarded as a variant of guaranteed income supplement, the U.K. version. The essence of the new system is that the benefit is more closely related to contributions, which is more transparent and understandable to any generations. If introducing the no-tional defined contribution plan is combined with the above change in the benefit structure, further increases in the contribution rate above some percentage point will no longer be required.

The guaranteed income supplement is paid to those whose earnings-related benefits remain insufficient. It is financed separately from the earnings-related part. It can be financed from general revenue or an earmarked consumption-based tax. It is not a universal benefit, thus enabling considerable amounts of saving for public pensions. It is a benefit that meets with the social adequacy objective.[12]

In my opinion, a shift mentioned above reflects the current trend and should be considered by Korea, as well as Japan, in their effort to formulate benefit structures best suited to each country's socio-economic situation.

Along with the move mentioned above, private initiatives should be encouraged further with strong tax incentives. This is mainly because in the future, the middle- and high-income groups are likely to receive lower pension benefits from social security and therefore, considerable effort is still needed to compensate for this fall in income after retirement.

Korea has already mandated lump sum retirement allowances into its national policy. However, they are often of defined benefit type, possibly facing the risk of huge under-funded liabilities. The retirement allowances can be shifted to a hybrid plan (of the U.S. cash-balance-plan type) or to a defined contribution plan. Through this shift, investment-based pensions with higher rates of return can be provided although they may still face market risks. Some people advocate total conversion of lump sum retirement allowances into annuities. However, lump sum retirement allowances still seem quite important for Korean retirees. There should be freedom to choose between lump sum allowances and annuities.[13]

Figure 13-1
A Two-Tier Benefit System

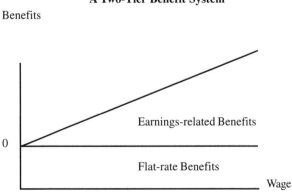

Figure 13-2
A New Benefit System

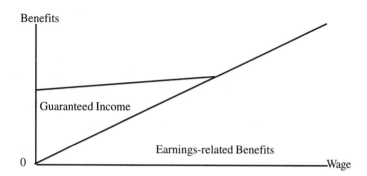

V. Concluding Remarks

This chapter has evaluated the Korean national pension scheme from a financial point of view. Special reference was given to Japanese experience, since the Korean scheme is very similar to that of Japan. Fortunately, the Korean national pensions are still at their start-up phase, and it is rather easy for Korean people to reform the pension scheme, making it more sustainable in the long run. Trivial flaws can be remedied with small pains. The future of Korean pensions is wholly in the hands of currently active generations in Korea.

Notes

1. Employees of the specially designated post offices are covered with the other special program, as well.
2. The persons working at the workplace with full-time employees of five or more are covered in the workplace, while those working at the workplace with full-time employees of less than five are covered in respective local areas along with the self-employed.
3. The person covered on the local basis pays the full amount of contributions.
4. 1 million won = US$ 801 = EURO 889 = UK£ 558 = 99,500 yen as at 3 December 2001. Note that the SMI is the monthly income of the *previous* year, determined by dividing the *total yearly income* of the workers concerned by 12.
5. The miners or fishermen currently can claim the full Old-age benefit from age 55.
6. See National Pension Corporation (2001) for more detail.
7. The replacement rate was first set to 70 percent, but was lowered recently to 60 percent for the average salary earners with 40-year contributions.
8. Takayama (1998; 2001) for details of the Japanese public pension program.
9. Yoon (2001) mentioned that recently 51 percentage of eligible urban participants did not pay pension contributions.

10. The portability is currently operated among three special programs, but *not* between the national pension and those three pensions. The unified public pension number is highly advisable to be implemented.
11. The long-term maturity ratio (number of beneficiaries/insured) is estimated to be over 50 percent (near 60 percent after 2040) under the current provisions of the national pension system (see Yoon 2001). With a purely pay-as-you- go financing, the required contribution rate would be more than 30 percent if the 60 percent replacement is to be maintained.
12. Korean people are currently discussing a reform plan to give "contribution period credits" to the unemployed, low income groups, students, military draftees and those in child birth or caring for the old. This might be on their way to attain the guaranteed income supplement within the pension system.
13. When South and North Korea are unified, the public pension programs will have to be integrated. Experiences of the German unification or the Okinawa case of Japan can be a lesson for that kind of integration.

References

National Pension Corporation, Korea (2001) "National Pension Scheme in Korea," available at the website (http://www.npc.or.kr/end/enpsk.html?code=./enpsk/).

Takayama, N. (1997) "Summary Comments by Rapporteur," a paper presented at ILO-OECD workshop on Development and Reform of Pension Schemes, Paris, available at the website: (http://www.ier.hit-u.ac.jp/~takayama/index.html).

Takayama, N. (1998) *The Morning After in Japan: Its Declining Population, Too generous Pensions and a Weakened Economy.* Tokyo: Maruzen Co. Ltd.

Takayama, N. (2001) "Pension Reform in Japan at the Turn of the Century," *The Geneva Papers on Risk and Insurance*, 26 (4).

Yoon, B. (2001) "Introduction to Mandatory Old-age Income Security System in Korea," Korea Institute for Health and Social Affairs, Korea, mimeo.

14

Environmental Justice and the Quality of Life

Bunyan Bryant

I. Introduction

Environmental justice refers to those cultural norms and values, rules and regulations, behaviors, policies, and decisions that support sustainable communities where
people can interact with confidence that their environment is safe, nurturing, and
productive. Environmental justice is served when people can realize their highest
potential.... Environmental justice is supported by decent paying and safe jobs;
quality schools and recreation; decent housing and adequate health care; democratic
decision-making and personal empowerment; and communities free of violence,
drugs, and poverty. These are communities where both cultural and biological diversity are respected and highly revered and where distributed justice prevails (Bryant,
1995:6).

The world is a much different place than it was 100 years ago when pollution took up a smaller space and the Earth needed less time to heal itself.
Today we pollute larger areas, and consequently the world takes a longer time
to heal. Increased consumption, pollution, and population growth mean that
human beings collectively and as individuals are wreaking havoc upon the
planet at an exponential rate. Our growing consumption of energy and materials and our discharge of waste for disposal are limited by a finite amount of
land and water. Communities of color and low-income communities bear a
disproportionate amount of toxic and hazardous waste compared with more
affluent communities.[1] Nonetheless, environmental justice advocates must
be most concerned with the reduction of pollutants in the aggregate as well as
the specific. In the aggregate, global warming differentially threatens people
of poverty and people of color. These people will be the most vulnerable to

disease, drought, coastal flooding, and other problems resulting from global warming. No one should be exposed to toxins or dangerous weather conditions resulting from global warming. We must pay particular attention to those groups who are most vulnerable in society. Additionally, pollution and environmental degradation are most serious in developing countries that do not have environmental protection laws or the infrastructure or expertise to handle toxins and hazardous waste. Also, developed countries often extract resources from these developing countries and use their land for waste disposal sites.

We must learn to "think outside of the box" to rid ourselves of these problems, many of which have global dimensions. This will unquestionably challenge our creativity and our resolve. We may have to look at our interactions with the world in a different way. Too long we have plundered the Earth for its treasures without serious consideration of long-term environmental effects. We must view the Earth and its inhabitants, human and non-human, as friends rather than as enemies; we must celebrate the diversity bestowed on us rather than destroying it. What we do to the complex web of life, we ultimately do to ourselves.

Although creative environmental and market strategies may be "good," they may not be enough to offset environmental problems and conditions of environmental injustice. This paper includes discussion on the shortcomings of knowledge and of the market along with creative environmental solutions. This paper also comments upon the Republic of Korea's Green Vision 21 and its Eco-2 Project. In addition, this paper comments on environmental solutions that are often designed to impact the aggregate while leaving specific situations of low-income communities unaffected. Furthermore, three phases are recommended to provide environmental protection in both the aggregate and specific. These three phases point us in the direction of an environmentally just society where all people are protected against environmental harm regardless of their income or where they live. Moving toward an environmentally just society requires developing an environmentally just income and the support of government and educational institutions. This paper is not designed to be inclusive regarding ideas for an environmentally just society, but rather it presents proactive ideas for stimulating our creative juices beginning with the role of knowledge.

II. The Role of Knowledge

Sustainable knowledge[2] has been used throughout generations to help societies adapt to harsh environmental conditions and to improve our quality of life. For the most part we have seldom questioned knowledge or its producers in any fundamental way because the assumption was that the creation of knowledge was for useful purposes or for the greatest good. Sometimes knowledge is created to defend us in war regardless of the short- and long-term consequences. If we are successful in defending ourselves, we often view this knowledge as "good" and "worthwhile" knowledge. But how do we effectively determine "good" versus "bad" knowledge? How do we determine whether or not knowledge is sustainable long term? "Good" or "worthwhile" knowledge is determined through the scientific process. "Good" knowledge is also determined through a rigorous peer review process where knowledge is or is not published. In the marketplace we buy things that reflect "good" knowledge and boycott other items that reflect "bad" knowledge. In other instances we determine "good" or "worthwhile" knowledge through trial and error. However, these methods for determining "good" or "bad" knowledge may not be adequate. What appears to be "good" knowledge today may not be good or adaptive knowledge 20 to 50 years from now. "Bad" knowledge embodied in commodities we create and in its by-products often end up in communities already overburdened with toxic waste facilities and polluting industries.

We are beginning to question whether certain kinds of knowledge are adaptive or sustainable.[3] To speak to the issue of sustainable development implies that there is also development that is not sustainable. In either case the basis of development is knowledge. We cannot develop sustainably or even non-sustainably without knowledge. Situations that are not sustainable may speak to the issues of environmentally unjust conditions. Are we producing sustainable knowledge?[4] Is the academy producing sustainable knowledge?[5] What are the long-term effects of knowledge? How does knowledge or its by-products create environmentally unjust conditions for some and not others? How do we define sustainable knowledge? More importantly, we must question how we know what we know and what we do choose to do with what we know. The use of knowledge for solutions to problems in one area may actually create problems in another area. As Barry Commoner stated:

> But each effort to solve one crisis seems to clash with the solution of the others - pollution control reduces energy supplies; energy conservation costs jobs. Inevitably, proponents of one solution become the opponents of the others. Policy stagnates and remedial action is paralyzed, adding to the confusion and gloom that beset the country (Commoner, 1976:1).

III. The Role of Markets

Although the markets, including science and technology, have brought us riches, they have also brought global warming, acid rain, nuclear and toxic waste, endocrine disrupters, and a host of toxic-induced and aggravated disease that threaten the quality of people's lives the world over. Pollution fails to respect geopolitical boundaries; the by-products from one country affect the ambient land, air, and water quality of surrounding countries. Though science and technology have been bountiful, the harvest from the cornucopia of resources has been poorly distributed. While one in every five people in developing countries is chronically undernourished (Miller 1999), the population of the North controls most of the world's wealth (Hawken 1993). This situation threatens to become worse because people are breeding and using highly cherished resources exponentially.

Markets are superb at setting prices, yet are incapable of recognizing the true cost of production which is seldom reflected in market prices. The cost of toxic-induced and aggravated disease is usually excluded from commodity prices. The market is designed to benefit humankind but not nature, as evidenced by the environmental destruction of our biophysical environment. Economic success is often tantamount to biological destruction. Companies often act to externalize all or part of their costs associated with production by passing on to society the brunt of the expenses and therefore creating a misallocation of resources (Daly and Townsend 1993). The more a company externalizes its costs, the greater the return on capital, and the more a company externalizes its pollution costs, the more vulnerable low-income people and people of color are to environmentally unjust conditions. If certain industries can internalize a considerable amount of their costs, then perhaps they can be subsidized to help make the market more environmentally responsive. We must find ways to protect people and the environment in which they live.

Markets often times with the support of the government have created conditions where low-income people often live on the margins and have little experience with living in safe, productive, and nurturing communities. They have little experience in holding decent-paying and safe jobs or living in communities with quality schools, recreation, housing, and health care. Markets are extremely good at what they do, and they harness potential motives such as greed and envy. Runaway and indiscriminate growth, including growth that degrades our biological capital and communities, results from successful markets (Hawken et al. 1999). A broader perspective and a complete rethinking and restructuring of the market are needed to be more responsive to the needs of society as a whole. Closing one polluting facility in a neighborhood that has several other polluting facilities or ignoring areas where poverty is rampant fails to address the issue of environmental injustice.

Creative Use of the Market and Taxes: A Short-Term Solution

Several solutions have been recommended to solve our environmental crisis. Emissions trading allow companies to use the market to buy pollution reduction credits from one another in order to reduce the amount of pollutants emitted in a given area.[6] While emissions trading is the mantra of many policymakers, the environmental justice community is highly suspicious of such programs. They feel it's the market that got us into this situation in the first place. Environmental justice activists point to the fact that while emissions trading has reduced pollution in the aggregate, it has not reduced pollution in specific areas. For example if Company A purchases pollution reduction credits from Company B so that Company A can maintain or increase its level of pollution, the communities in the immediate surrounding area of Company A will fail to get relief. The environmental justice community refers to these areas as "hot spots." In addition, considerable conflict has ensued between government regulators, industry, and environmental justice groups in the United States. The former two believe that command and control strategies stifle creativity and that environmental justice would be better served if the market were allowed to take its course. Environmental justice activists are skeptical of the accounting procedures companies use in calculating the number of pollution reduction credits. Environmental justice activists find more comfort in applying command and control strategies to environmental problems than to the market. Perhaps the Republic of Korea can use a combination of strategies. Emissions trading should not be the only strategy used alone. Emissions trading should be a part of a mixed strategy for environmental protection and Korea's productive welfare experience.

Shifting taxes from income to emissions, effluents, or solid waste disposals released into the environment; from inputs or materials known to be sources of environmental pressures; and from income to products linked to environmental degradation may be a viable strategy to offset conspicuous consumption and planned obsolescence and environmental destruction.[7] To increase the quality of life of Koreans through a productive welfare experience and to protect our biophysical environment against wanton destruction will require a tax structure that is radically different from the one found in Korea and in most industrialized countries. Taxing payroll and incomes fails to provide any positive incentives. In fact it is a perverse incentive to cheat in order to save money (Hawken 1993) and has a tendency to undermine the emotional support of government. Why should some people pay taxes and not others? Why should some people pay more than others when they are making the same amount of money or less? Collecting taxes from those who refuse to pay or to pay their fair share costs the system billions of dollars in lawyer and accountant fees, paperwork, administration and waste. This is lost money that could be used to support a productive welfare experience. In the U.S. it is estimated that for every dollar collected in taxes 65 cents is spent on compliance, forms, litigation, and data collection (Hawken 1993). Green taxes would be more efficient because they would circumvent the large government bureaucracy of compliance. Everyone who engages the market would have to pay a tax. No one would be exempt.

Because green taxes are incorporated in the price of the commodity, manu-facturers will have a powerful incentive to revise and improve methods of productions in order to avoid the green tax.[8] If social "bads" - such as the variety of pollutants, environmental degradation, and non-renewable energy consumption - were taxed, citizens and industry would have an incentive to avoid exposure to the taxes. Giving people and companies the right incen-tive is a purpose of the green tax. The incentive would be to save money and thus reward both the customer and the environment. For example if gasoline were taxed to a greater degree than it is now, then the car industry would perhaps be motivated to produce high mileage automobiles and increase citizens' use of car pooling, mass transits, and bicycles. But the green tax is regressive. Dealing with the issues of fairness, quality of life, and a produc-tive welfare experience requires a mixed strategy and an income tax levy on high-income people and companies. Simultaneously, it requires subsidizing the income of the poor so they can participate in society productively. A smaller bureaucracy could perhaps handle such a program freeing govern-ment to reduce the number of tax collectors by making direct payments to those most in need.

Raising taxes in any country could be political suicide for the governing party; people resist paying higher taxes even if it is in their long-term best interest. Having money to control their immediate needs is of more interest than paying taxes for some future need. It is difficult for society to exist without taxes to support the general welfare. Yet the Republic of Korea must design a tax system that will not only satisfy a productive welfare experience, but one that will support the general welfare of the biophysical environment. To exponentially exploit our biophysical environment will only undermine our social, political, and economic institutions, as well as Korea's new pro-ductive welfare program. No society can exist no matter how complex or civilized if it destroys the bedrock of the biophysical environment. Nature provides the air we breathe, the water we drink, and the land to grow food to provide nourishment for our bodies. We must fashion an environmental policy that internalizes the costs of pollution and of environmental degradation. No one, no matter how poor, should subsidize the external costs of production with toxic induced and aggravated disease or medical health care costs.

IV. A Flawed System - More So Than a Management Problem

We must also rethink our lifestyles and the ways in which we live. Indi-vidual consumption habits fuel a market economy based on greed. The mar-ket is adept at using the electronic media to program people's needs and buying habits. We are programmed to consume commodities we do not need or want. In some developed countries, namely the United States, the economy is based on planned obsolescence and conspicuous consumption (Packard

1960). Products are designed for a short lifecycle, and people are encouraged to buy new things even when what they have is satisfactory. Billions of dollars go into cultivating consumer taste while unnecessarily exploiting biophysical resources and increasing the waste stream. Tremendous amounts of energy are used each time something is manufactured, and huge volumes of waste are created as well. Business in its myriad forms plays a major role in plundering the Earth so we must call for a change in the way business views the world and for a paradigm shift that will make business more socially and environmentally responsive. Business should play a key role in increasing the quality of life for all Korean citizens regardless of their income or where they live.

Even if the Republic of Korea adopted the best environmental practices known to date, it still might continue to experience environmental degradation at a rapid rate. Better management of an imperfect system may not in the long run achieve environmental justice and a better quality of life for the people of the Republic of Korea. This imperfect system is based upon a flawed design of our production system more so than a flawed management system.[9] Business as practiced throughout Korea and other parts of the world designs and produces commodities and services that are antithetical to sustainable and environmentally just societies. For too long the focus has been on cleaning up toxic waste sites and using end-of-the-pipeline solutions such as pollution abatement and control technologies. Pollution abatement and control is a short-term answer to a flawed system that threatens the quality of life in Korea, particularly for those least served by the geopolitical system. We may find ourselves on the brink of ecological collapse due to profit-focused goals of business. The purpose of business should be to increase the quality of life for all humankind through service, creativity, and an ethical philosophy that respects Mother Earth. Making money simply for the sake of making money is destructive in the grand scheme of things particularly when those money-making activities contribute to environmentally unjust conditions and rob people of their ability to develop to their highest potential within the context of a sustainable and just society. Wherever one finds extreme wealth, one often finds extreme forms of poverty, crime, delinquency, and environmentally unjust conditions. Wherever one finds extreme wealth, one may also find alienation, despair, and free-floating anxiety. Extreme wealth in many instances has failed to bring meaning and satisfaction to people's lives.

The business community must transform itself to promote action-based knowledge that supports an environmentally just commerce. With vision and creativity, we have the capacity and ability to create a very different economy—one that restores ecosystems and protects the environment while bringing forth innovation, prosperity, meaningful work, and secure, safe, and environmentally just communities. We must disregard progress that fails to consider evolution, biological diversity, carrying capacity, health of the commons, environmental justice, and quality of life. With the evolutionary thrust of today's economy, the Republic of Korea may be subject to economic turmoil and upheaval if these concepts are not taken into consideration. Failing to transform the economy means conditions will continue to worsen in the long run for some people and eventually for all people including future generations. The conspicuous lack of ecological principles may mean what is "good" for business may be "bad" for nature, "bad" for people, and ultimately "bad" for business. We must not only become more concerned with the impact of business upon the environment, but we must go one step further and develop a restorative economy that is environmentally benign and supportive of just and sustainable social goals.

V. Thinking Creatively

The mantra of eco-efficiency has been duly noted as a key to energy efficiency and pollution reduction. This includes letting go of ownership so that a person never owns a large ticket item such as a refrigerator or a washing machine, but rather leases these items from a company that must collect them at the end of their life-cycle in order to recycle or dispose of them properly.

Although eco-efficiency and letting go of ownership are exciting concepts, we need to dig even deeper. These measures spring from "within-the-box thinking," but fail to bring about the basic changes needed to solve the long-term problems of social and environmental injustice. We must redesign the whole production system and the way in which we relate to environment and to each other. Our confusion will continue as long as we view environmental and social crises as specific and unrelated problems or questions. Specific solutions to specific problems may raise more questions than they answer. Other equally important questions are: Does global climate change really exist? Will global climate change differentially impact low-income communities and communities of color? Do automotive catalytic converters filter out toxic emissions or do they cause more damage than freon? Is economic growth harmful or does it provide resources for healing the planet? Will the costs of phasing out non-renewable energy sources outweigh the benefits? Do incinerator emissions cause cancer in humans? Do the benefits of chemicals outweigh their negative effects?

The questions posed above result from linear production processes. For the past 100 years humans have been disrupting the Earth's cyclical patterns at an accelerating rate, thus transforming our resources into useless garbage, some of which is obvious to the naked eye and some of which is microscopic. Rarely is garbage recycled back into society, nature, or industry. The volume of garbage is too large for nature to reuse, and some waste such as toxic metals and stable unnatural compounds cannot be recycled. Determining how one toxin reacts with another is difficult because the toxic levels for thousands of kinds of molecular garbage are unknown. Furthermore, their consequences may not appear for a long time. The full effect of today's pollution will not become evident until tomorrow. We must find creative ways to move far beyond our actions to protect the planet for future generations.

Critique of Korea's Green Vision 21 and the Eco-2 Project

In order to speak to productive welfare experience and quality of life, we must also speak to the productive welfare of the environment. Maintaining productivity and protecting the general welfare of people necessitates the care and nurturing of our biophysical environment. The market, democracy, or a productive welfare experience cannot be maintained in an environment that is degraded continuously by the production system. We must protect the general welfare of nature if we expect to survive on planet Earth. If we fail to protect the biophysical environment, we can expect to experience an increase in catastrophes of global warming, acid rain, endocrine disrupters, and toxin-induced and aggravated disease. If we fail to protect the biophysical environment, we will experience the undermining of our political, economic, and social systems. We must protect and use the bounty of nature wisely if we expect national stability and an enhancement in the quality of life for all Korean people.

In order to adequately address environmental justice issues, we must focus on both content and process. The latter may perhaps be more important than the former. The goal of many environmental justice activists is to be an integral part of the decision-making process to help define their destiny. Green Vision 21 makes a strong appeal that the government share environmental information with local residents and calls for greater participation by residents in environmental policy decision-making procedures. Green Vision 21 speaks to the community's right to know, particularly with respect to the discharge of toxic substances. It states that the government will encourage local community residents to organize citywide or countywide private supervision coalitions. The vision goes on to state that community organizations and schools will play a central role in supervising pollution in each water system. All of the concepts are on the right track, and Green Vision 21 must continue to be visionary in breaking new ground.

Although Green Vision 21 speaks to the issue of public participation, this important area should be revisited because oftentimes public participation is perfunctory. This means that decisions have already been made thus giving people only the appearance of being influential. To be effective, government and corporate entities must involve the community in a meaningful decision-making process. This is important because as professionals become more knowledgeable and specialized, they have a tendency to move the decision-making away from the village square. Because of their many years of training, they feel they are in the best position to make decisions - not the community. In the U.S., public participation in research endeavors is partially the result of traditional research which often fails to provide the answers needed for speedy identification and solution to problems. Researchers and policymakers cannot respond with confidence to questions of certainty and demands for immediate solution put forth by citizen groups. "Will my child get cancer from playing on a playground that was once a toxic dumpsite?" "Is my child's rash related to his playing on the school's playground?" "Is my coughing related to where I live?" Often questions like these cannot be answered to community people's satisfaction.

Professionals do have special knowledge, but to accomplish environmental justice goals policy decisions must be made in the village square, or they will most likely fail. When professionals make assumptions that people are irrational and lack the intelligence to understand complex issues, this often results in frustration and anger on both sides and thwarts any meaningful outcomes. When professionals make assumptions that people are smart and capable of understanding complex information, this can be an asset for solving local and national environmental justice problems. In the U.S. when communities were involved in the planning from the beginning and when they felt they had legitimate influence, the outcome of siting a facility or the cleanup process was much more civil, leaving people much better off. Additionally, when community groups understand the science and are motivated to participate, they can be very helpful. If they fail to understand the science and distrust the decision-makers, they can effectively thwart and frustrate officials attempting to site a facility in their community no matter what the advantages may be. To enhance their effectiveness in the decision-making process, lay people often consult with scientists, professionals, and the electronic media for different opinions. While Green Vision 21 and Eco-2 Project focus on many environmental content issues, environmental activists must be integrally involved in the discussion and the decision-making process. One of many roles of the productive welfare experience program is to advocate the training of new professionals in both content and process to work effectively with community groups. It is important that the community be involved throughout the process. They need to be involved in problem identification, questionnaire construction, data calculations, and analysis. This would be a bottom-up approach to policymaking rather than a top-down approach. Technical and top-down solutions to environmental justice problems are rarely effective, i.e. in the U.S. Community-based research provides opportunities for community and professional groups to work together effectively.

Both the Green Vision 21 and the Eco-2 Project are steps in the right direction, and the Republic of Korea should be commended. Green Vision 21 and Eco-2 Project represent a number of win-win strategies for building a just and sustainable Korea. While the implementation of many of these policies may yield cleaner results in the aggregate, they may have the opposite effect in specific areas. For example, the location and manufacture of new environmental technologies and their by-products could expose people disproportionately in surrounding areas. The development of clean fuels, advanced technology for water purification, new factories that produce low or zero-pollution vehicles, and new sewage treatment plants may also cause environmental problems for people in surrounding areas, even though most people in the larger aggregate will enjoy the benefits of these new and clean technologies. Where will new fueling stations for buses be located? Where will low sulfur fuel plants be located? How will the waste from the manufacture of these new technologies be handled? What impact will they have upon the people that live close to them? The government of the Republic of Korea should monitor and where possible ameliorate these potential "hot spots" so no one will be overburdened with environmental toxins. People should not be sacrificed on the basis of income or where they live.

To prevent disproportionate exposures to environmental hazards, an interdisciplinary team of people, including local residents or high-risk populations, should be involved in formulating environmental justice indicators by considering the following questions: What are the indicators that would suggest environmentally unjust conditions? What is the income level and proximity to environmental insults? What is the health status of people who are differentially exposed to environmental toxins in an area with polluting facilities? To what extent are people suffering from asthma, cancer, and other toxic-induced and aggravated diseases? What is the percentage of welfare recipients in the area? Without these environmental justice indicators, certain populations may be overlooked if the focus of environmental protection is only upon the aggregate or majority.

Green Vision 21 firmly supports environmental impact statements. To date, environmental impact statements often fail to speak adequately to environmental justice concerns. Such statements often calculate the potential environmental destructiveness or impact of a single industry. While these statements may be appropriate under certain conditions, they usually fail to take into consideration cumulative impacts. For example, before company A can move into an area, it must access the pollution levels of other companies within the area. If the aggregate pollution levels are too high, then Company A does not move in unless it can get the other companies to reduce their overall pollution levels, or company A must reduce its pollution potential to some predetermined level acceptable to government regulators. Companies and local governments in the States have resisted cumulative impact strategies because of their disincentive to investments and because environmental rules and regulations take time away from production. Research has shown, however, that environmental regulations have increased the number of jobs.

Although some jobs may be lost because of the expense to retrofit antiquated production systems, thus forcing them to close down, there is an overall net increase in jobs and investment in industries that produce new and cleaner technologies. Industry can be very creative and can rise to the occasion when necessary. In the U.S.A. we expect money spent on pollution control and abatement technology to equal the amount of money spent on defense. During an earlier downturn in the U.S., researchers found that jobs in the pollution abatement and control industries were more stable and survived economic slumps (Bezdek 1995).

Science and Technical Solutions

We live in a fact-fascinated, highly technological society. We expect technology to solve all our problems, but as mentioned before technical solutions to problems often become problems within themselves. In addition, while we think that "good" science will solve the problem, this is not always the case. "Bad" policy decisions are often made in the face of "good" science. To be successful in the application of science and to solve environmental justice problems consensus has been that politics must be aligned with science. In other instances policies based upon "good" science have not been enforced. Getting government to apply equal protection of the law in the United States means environmental justice groups have had to confront and protest governmental inaction. Is the government of the Republic of Korea willing to hold itself to the same standards as it does with business? More specifically, is it willing to evaluate itself and the contributions it makes to environmental degradation? Governmental credibility will be enhanced if it takes stock of its own contribution to environmental degradation and applies the policies it applies to others to itself. It is important that where necessary the Republic of Korea increases the number of laws and provides equal protection of the law in order to protect the environment and to enhance the quality of life of its citizens. If equal protection is not provided, this could result in contempt and public distrust of government.

New Environmental Technologies

With its technical know-how the Republic of Korea can become even more of a world leader in the production of pollution control and abatement technology than it is today. The Republic of Korea is already speaking to the possibility of creating an environmentally friendly production pattern for industry, one that includes cleaner production systems, advanced environmental technologies, and environmentally friendly substitutes for harmful raw materials. To cater to the country's environmental needs, the government should subsidize and nurture small and medium-sized environmental enterprises to produce environmental protection technology for the 21st Century. The manufacture of such technology in the short and intermediate term will help reduce Korea's balance of trade deficit. There is the need for such technology, particularly as developing countries move into the 21st century.

VI. Precautionary Principle

Below are three recommended phases that the government should implement to move the country toward a more environmentally just and sustainable society. During each of these phases or sub-phases, the precautionary principle should be considered. The precautionary approach is the principle of avoiding harm even where there is no absolute scientific certainty as to the cause of the particular harm. This approach is particularly important because it gives policymakers a tool to use other than the cause-and-effect model used in science. The causality model is based upon satisfying three conditions:

1. The cause precedes the effect in time,
2. The two variables are empirically correlated with one another, and
3. The correlation cannot be explained away as being due to the influence of a third variable that causes both of them (Babbie 1989).

Often this model of causality has failed to serve environmental justice advocates in good stead because in many instances causality is difficult to prove. Attempting to prove causality often leads to the paralysis of analysis and inaction. In addition, people concerned about their health are demanding "certainty" of whether a given chemical or toxin will cause them and their children health problems and/or they want an "immediate solution" to these problems or perceived problems. Continued debate regarding causality and the inability of scientists or policymakers to respond to the immediate demands of the community often creates even more resentment and community hostility toward decision-makers. Causality debates also cause resentment on the other side as companies defend themselves against blame by using scientific-sounding language such as "no proof of harm" or denying that their actions harm the environment. Another troubling point with causality is that the proof of cause and effect comes after the damage is already done, and thus high-risk populations must wait for scientific proof before a harmful practice or chemical is banned. This is morally wrong, particularly where humans are involved. Cigarette smoking is a case in point. After approximately 30 years of debate and numerous studies showing the association between smoking and lung cancer, the Surgeon General of the United States finally decided to state officially that smoking was harmful to one's health. In the meantime millions of people became ill or died from cigarette smoking. Let me be clear. I am not suggesting that science is not important. It is, but we should be aware of its limitations. When possible, we should use both science and the precautionary principle. When science fails to give us the answers within a certain prescribed time, then we must be prepared to use the precautionary principle and err on the side of caution rather than on the side of illnesses and death. Constructing an effective environmental justice program without the use of the precautionary principle would almost be impossible.

Three Conceptual Phases for Community-Based Research

The three conceptual phases of community-based research could be used to advance the goals of environmental justice. Although each phase should be from one to ten years, they may not always be distinct because of potential overlap. In some instances we may be moving forward while in other situations we may move backwards. In other instances, we may skip a phase that is not relevant. However, the overall thrust will be to move forward. These phases are useful for conceptual reasons and for taking stock of where we are and where we should be at any given time. They provide a framework for thinking about broad-based intentional changes, and each speaks to different needs and different resources for problem-solving purposes. Programmatic ideas that may work in one locale may not work in another. Individuals and groups will be required to fill in the specifics and use their creativity to help craft local and national environmental justice policies that are meaningful. In any event, we must always keep our eyes on the prize for a more environmentally just and sustainable society.

Phase I: The Teach-In

This should be an educational phase about environmental injustice and its threat to the planet. A series of National Environmental Justice Teach-Ins should be held involving citizens, corporate leaders, university professors, and students. People from health departments, universities, and nonprofit organizations would work in teams with community groups to educate themselves about environmental injustice. The teach-ins would take place in public universities, schools, and community centers across the country. Discussion should point out the varying effects of climate change on people based upon their access to resources and where they live. How does each individual contribute to global climate change? What is the implication of global climate change? Will everyone be impacted equally during these changes? More specifically, the teach-ins would focus considerably on local issues, problems, and possible solutions. Discussions should include energy inefficiencies, individual contributions to environmental injustice, and the impact of pollutants on various communities, particularly those of low-income. The teach-ins' objective would be partially to understand the lifecycle analysis of

products and materials so people become more aware of the energy inefficiencies and resulting disposal problems. The teach-ins' curriculum would
include focusing not only on the environmental harm that results from production practices, but also on the health, economic, and social effects, particularly of those disproportionately impacted by environmental insults. The
teach-ins would also educate people about clean and safe alternatives to the
present modes of production that improve the quality of life for everyone.
During this phase participants will take stock of the resources they have at
their disposal in order to become effective problem-solvers. Environmental
justice teach-ins can help people become more aware of their surroundings
and their contributions to waste and energy inefficiencies. Often we become
psychologically numb to environmental disasters, particularly those that
evolve slowly. We become oblivious to the toxic dumps; sewage treatment
plants; the incinerators poisoning ambient air, water, and land; and the waste
on the streets and in the alleys. We ignore life-threatening toxins that are
often invisible and odorless. People quickly adjust to such conditions as a
normal part of life. This initial phase should call upon the nation to clean its
landmass, rivers, and streams, and improve the quality of its air. Both the
government and the private sector should call upon volunteers to do environmental clean-up. Young people and senior citizens could work side-by-side
restoring their neighborhoods to be beautiful, clean, and safe. Technical clean-
up jobs involving certain toxins, however, should be reserved for those with
specialized training.

Phase II: Community-Based Research Teams

Phase II is characterized by three sub-phases: data collection, data analysis, and intermediate solutions. This phase is cyclical; community-based research teams in many instances will be involved in a revolving process of
data collection and analysis until the right solution is found. People in different communities will start and end these phases and sub-phases at different
times. Dealing with more complicated environmental injustice issues requires
a community-based research approach. In this phase a number of community-
based research teams should be formed and trained to collect and examine
information or to operate the necessary technology for retrieving relevant
information. Solving problems of environmental injustice requires not only
an interdisciplinary approach, but also interagency coordination because
government agencies are often specialized and work at cross purposes with
one another or the right hand doesn't know what the left hand is doing. The
lack of interagency coordination often confuses, frustrates and angers people
who receive contradictory information. Government bodies at varying levels
can save a considerable amount of time and frustration by effectively coordinating their efforts.

To help develop and carry out community-based research for building an environmentally just and sustainable society, the government of Korea should look to universities for help in training interdisciplinary research teams and finding ways to more effectively coordinate government agencies. These community-based research teams would consist of leaders from non-government organizations (NGOs); grassroots organizations, particularly from the community affected; professionals from the Ministry of Health and the Ministry of the Environment; faculty and students from colleges and universities; and teachers and students from high schools. Occasionally these teams would consist primarily of high school students[10] and teachers, and in other cases they would be primarily community people. Heterogeneous groups would be ideal.[11] The majority of team members should be community people with many from the affected area of concern. The Republic of Korea should mobilize citizens to formulate an assessment[12] of ambient air and water quality, the number and condition of brownfields as well as other environment insults that disproportionately impact low-income communities.

Sub-Phase A: Data Collection. Community-based research teams of diverse skills are to collect information on point- and non-point-source pollutants of lakes, rivers, and streams. This would also include examining point-source pollutants from pipes, ditches, channels, tunnels, wells, containers, concentrated animal feed organizations, landfill leachate collection systems, vessels, and other floating crafts from which pollutants may be discharged. Information should be retrieved from large industrial plants, sewage treatment plants, utility companies, incinerators, landfills, dry cleaners, and gasoline stations. Information should be collected on mobile sources such as off- and on-road gasoline and diesel fueled vehicles including aircraft, locomotive, construction equipment, and two-cycle motor engines. Pollutants from non-point sources should be collected as well.

Data from these sources should either be put into a Geographical Information System (GIS) for spatial analysis or be mapped out manually. GIS has the capability of mapping out ambient air plumes, polluted water sources, brownfields, polluted land mass or soil structures and their close proximity to low-income communities. Data collection of environmental degradation is only half the battle. The Republic of Korea must also collect data on the potential and actual health risks to its citizens. The identification of health risks must include not only risks to adults, children, infants, and pregnant women, but also to any population that is differentially impacted by environmental hazards based upon level of income. Identifying pockets of people disproportionately impacted by environmental hazards is important.

Sub-Phase B: Data Analysis. This sub-phase begins when all the relevant data have been collected. When the results are in from the laboratory, the teams will engage in data analysis to determine the meaning of the data and whether or not additional data are needed. The data analysis outcome should be written up as a discussion document or made as a PowerPoint presentation using charts and graphs as needed. Although not inclusive, the following questions should be considered to help out with the environmental justice analysis: (1) Are certain people bearing the cost of environmental burdens because they live in close proximity to polluting facilities? (2) To what extent are people who live in close proximity to hazardous waste facilities experiencing physical health problems? (3) More specifically, to what extent are people living close to hazardous waste or polluting facilities experiencing toxic-induced and aggravated disease? (4) To what extent are people living near hazardous waste or polluting facilities experiencing psychological stress? (5) What are the historic, scientific, cultural, legal, and political complexities that determine where people live and their exposures to environmental burdens? Following the data analysis, one- to three-day workshops or several conferences involving the larger community should be organized to discuss the results of the community-based research teams. These discussions could take place in a local school, community center, or a neutral place. If information is incomplete then more data must be collected.

Sub-Phase C: Intermediate Solutions and Choosing Alternatives. The next step in the process requires informed solutions once the data have been collected, analyzed, and disseminated. Another set of workshops should provide opportunities for community-based research teams to learn about possible short- and long-term solutions. This phase may be the most difficult as it requires people to choose among many alternatives. To make choosing among alternatives easier experts must be available for community researchers to consult. Several strategies should be considered. Energy conservation and energy efficiency strategies[13] can reduce the waste stream significantly. Significant amounts of material can be reused or recycled. Recycling, reducing, and reusing can save millions of gallons of oil and tons of coal per year since many of the products we consume are not really necessary. Product lifecycle analysis, where industry finds ways of cutting pollution from the beginning of a product to its end disposal, can save considerable energy. A green tax or command and control strategies may be recommended, through which the government would tax "social bads" and "social goods" and relieve workers from a payroll tax deduction. Industry in the United States has championed emissions trading in favor of command and control strategies.[14]

Phase III: The New Environmental Justice Revolution

This is perhaps the most important phase and a very difficult one as well. Quibbling over the many environmental issues would be unnecessary if the production of "goods" and "services" was changed to be consistent with the Earth's lifecycle. We often attempt to create knowledge to help us operate beyond the laws of nature by producing commodities inconsistent with nature's lifecycle.[15] We must look to nature to solve problems of environmental injustice because in nature there is little waste, if any. We need to understand how whole forests work and apply the myriad of relationships found in nature to the design of the industrial system (Anderson 1998), thus enabling us to build and operate factories on solar energy. The technology of the future will allow factories and communities to recycle raw materials that come from harvesting billions of square yards of waste from some other company. Not another drop of oil should be taken from the Earth, nor should another ton of coal be mined (ibid.). No waste should go to the landfills nor should pollution go into the air. We must design buildings and other structures in such a way that by their very existence, they demonstrate and teach environmental principals.[16] When we began to build systems that mimic nature, then we will be well on our way to producing sustainable and just communities. This requires using regenerative rather than depletive knowledge, conceiving designs that support interdependence with other living organisms and cradle-to-cradle lifecycles rather than a cradle-to-grave cycle (McDonough and Braungart 1998). This also requires using sustainable knowledge to enhance the quality of our lives and to prolong our survival on the planet. Knowledge based on a fossil fuel economy cannot be sustainable in the long run.[17] We must use knowledge to produce "goods" that are cyclical in nature and not linear in character, and we must use sun power to build and operate factories and whole communities.

The activities of the three phases described above are by no means conclusive. While these phases unfold, other activities above and beyond these phases should be considered. Environmental justice goes beyond hazardous waste protection by taking into consideration social and political issues as well. An overall coordinating committee may be helpful where several community-based research teams are operating within a city or town so that each team can share information and learn from one another's research. Additionally, teams should be formed within local industry to work on developing environmentally benign products. Representatives from these industries should be included at the citywide and/or higher coordinating level.

Addressing the Biophysical Environment is Not Enough

Addressing the biophysical environment is not enough. In order for environmental justice to be served we must address the issues of poverty[18] and income disparity. As previously noted, in countries where there is extreme wealth, there is also extreme poverty, crime, delinquency, and environmental injustice. In countries where wealth is distributed more equitably, there are usually significantly lower crime and delinquency rates, and more environmentally just situations. Barry Commoner raises the issue in one of his articles as to whether poverty breeds overpopulation or whether overpopulation breeds poverty. He found that when countries reach a certain level of economic well-being, population growth declines. People are better educated, more affluent, have better access to health care, are healthier, and live in better environmental conditions. Sharpe (2001) supports Commoner's findings when she states that population growth is the consequence of underdevelopment and could be curtailed by several factors including the eradication of inequities in income. Additionally, poverty may be a greater causal agent to one's health than any other virus or microbe. To achieve environmental justice as defined in the introduction of this article, we must make both the biophysical and human built environment livable, productive, and sustainable. To achieve these goals, poverty and racism, perhaps the worst forms of pollution, must also be addressed in order to ensure that no one group will be required to shoulder the social or economic burden for others.

Additional Short and Intermediate Programs

For all too long economic development has failed to take into consideration the effects of the environment upon our social, political, and economic institutions. Until recently environmental phenomena were seldom used to explain social phenomena or to account for the way we lived. Surviving here on planet Earth ultimately depends on whether social policy will take into consideration environmental concerns. To deplete and destroy our environment or to pass on what economists call "externalities" to society, particularly the poor, does not bode well for the future. Socializing environmental burdens without socializing the benefits is not in the long-term interest of the country. An unhealthy environment will result in an unhealthy people, numerous sick days lost, high mortality rates, and an ailing and inefficient economy. Therefore, a clean and healthy environment makes good business sense. The role of any social or environmental policy is to prevent the short-term destructive economic interests from superseding the long-term sustainable and productive interests of the country.

Redefining Work for an Environmentally Just Income[19]

One goal should be to extricate ourselves from work that is akin to slavery, and work that is boring, competitive, and destroys the Earth's treasures. Work can stifle creativity causing people to self-medicate as a way to combat boredom or to find relief through conspicuous consumption, much of which is often beyond their means. We should redefine work to be an environmental justice income by working a four-day rather than five-day week. On the fifth day people could have the option of working at a charity of their choice. This day would be set aside for creativity, teaching, learning, and healing the planet to ensure that environmental justice is served.[20] Helping people in need to increase the quality of their lives takes considerable effort. Those who choose to work a five day week could be eligible to receive a tax reduction for work completed above and beyond their full-time work by working in an accredited service organization that contributes to the greater good (Rifkin 1995). Another form of environmentally just income would be for the government to provide jobs for the unemployed to clean up the environment. In other instances the Korean government could offer tax credits to businesses that hire unemployed people for environmental clean-up.

Secondary Schools and Universities

Students in public and private schools should be required to enroll in environmental justice courses to become environmentally effective citizens. They need to learn how to walk softly upon the land and leave as few footprints as possible. Students should be required to examine historic, scientific, social, legal, cultural, and political conditions that give rise to environmental injustice and the actions that could ameliorate these harmful environmental conditions. Universities should require such courses and should also establish a Vice President for Sustainable and Just Knowledge to encourage research and the teaching of environmental justice. Secondary schools and universities could use their procurement power to purchase environmentally friendly products, thus sending a message to the community and the general public about the importance of environmental protection. For example, public institutions could purchase natural gas powered cars and recycled paper, and build and retrofit buildings to be environmentally benign. (For more on buildings see David Orr or the University of Michigan School of Natural Resources and Environment at www.snre.umich.edu.)

The National Government

The government of Korea must help to initiate and support an environmental justice movement to protect all of its citizens from the devastating effects of pollutants. Environmental degradation and injustice must be viewed as the moral equivalent of a natural disaster of the highest magnitude. Considerable resources must be available to universities and the private sector for researching, designing, and building an environmentally just society. Resources should be provided for moving families from contaminated sites that may pose potential dangers to their health.

Eco-2 Project and Green Vision 21 seem to be on the right track with their environmental cooperation projects with China, Japan, other Southeast Asian countries, and Europe. This includes Korea's transfer of environmentally clean technologies to other countries, joint science projects to study environmental effects such as global climate change, and participation in major international conventions that deal with environmental problems. It is critical that Korea follows through with these international environmental strategies as outlined in Eco-Project and Green Vision 21 because environmental pollutants fail to respect geopolitical boundaries. To effectively solve the pollution problems, Koreans must help their neighbors solve their environmental pollution problems as well.

Some developed countries are looking to foreign ports for waste disposal.[21] Although the Basel Convention managed to ban North-South transportation of hazardous waste, the Convention has yet to define hazardous waste. Furthermore, the Convention does not regulate South-South agreements or bilateral agreements. The Republic of Korea must have the goal of protecting its borders by refusing to allow commodities into the country unless the manufacturing and disposal of goods and services are consistent with the Earth's lifecycle. The Korean government can be even more of an international leader by championing the cause of global climate change and environmental justice. The world must know that all nations and all people are not impacted equally by global climate change. The Korean people can help the world move into the 21st Century with vision and with hope. It can be done.

VII. Summary

In this paper several development and policy issues regarding environmental justice have been raised. Critics of growth and development support sustainable development, yet a more fundamental question should be asked. Are we, along with the academy, producing sustainable knowledge? This question raises considerable controversy and should be seriously debated. Markets have played a role in producing wealth and improving the quality of life for some, but have failed to improve environmental protection and quality of life for the masses to any significant degree. Environmental justice activists place very little faith in the strategy of using tradable emissions either to right the "wrongs" of the market or to improve environmental protection because they create "hot spots." Also, there is the likelihood of dishonest reporting of emission trading by firms seeking emission reduction credits. We have designed a flawed system, one that is fundamentally difficult to correct even by excellent management. Eco-efficiency and letting go of ownership are reforms headed in the right direction, but this is not enough. We must "think outside the box" and design a system that mimics nature, and we must turn waste from one production system into raw materials for another. We must build cities and systems based upon solar energy.

Reaching our goals of an environmentally sustainable society means going through several phases and sub-phases. These phases and sub-phases are not carved in stone; some may overlap or even be skipped, but the overall intent is to move forward and change for the better. Community-based research is key in solving environmental justice problems, yet even that may not be enough. In addition, several other things must be done. We must redefine work so as to provide an environmentally just income. Public schools and universities must assume the responsibility to teach and create knowledge that is consistent with the Earth's lifecycle. The national government should actively support environmental justice efforts and keep products out of the country that cause social and environmental harm. We must deal with the population problem by encouraging sustainable growth and development to reach a certain threshold where population levels off.

Can all of these things be done? I hope so because hope gives meaning to our lives and fuels our ability to be creative. We must be creative and visionary. Failing to be visionary means we may be heading into a future where environmental injustice is magnified rather than reduced. It could be a future of environmental degradation, increased population growth, poverty, toxic-induced and aggravated disease, extinction of species, and the whole alphabet soup of problems. Failing to conduct the necessary research and to plan for the future could lead to an increase in crime, delinquency, and war as people compete for scarce resources. People could experience more free-floating anxieties, oppression, and uncertainty.

Actors upon the world stage have placed emphasis on developing the left side of their brain—the part that is more rational. Now these actors must spend time developing the right side of their brain—the part that is more creative. As the future unfolds, our work should focus on creativity, teaching, learning, and healing the Earth. We must develop a more spiritual connection to the Earth and to one another. If we plan for the future, we can open up some exciting possibilities. The 21st Century will bring forth some intriguing challenges for you. I am sure the Republic of Korea and the Korean people will rise to the occasion.

Notes

1. The proposition that environmental hazards impact everyone in America equally has been challenged empirically over the years. Many studies have examined the social distribution of pollution over the last three decades. The evidence has shown quite decisively that communities of low-income and particularly communities of color are more significantly impacted by such hazards than are their white and more affluent counterparts (Asch and Seneca 1978; Berry 1977; Bryant and Hockman 1995; Bryant and Mohai 1992; Commission for Racial Justice 1987; Council on Environmental Quality 1971; Freeman 1972; Gelobter 1988; Gianessi et al. 1979; Goldman 1994; Harrison 1975; Kruvant 1975; Mohai and Bryant 1992; U. S. General Accounting Office 1983; West 1992; Zupan 1973). The disproportionate impact of environmental insults on people of color and low-income groups is environmental injustice. When only people of color are disproportionately impacted (meaning that a much higher percentage of them are overexposed to toxins as compared to their white counterparts), it is often referred to as "environmental racism" (Bullard 1994; 1993; Bullard and Wright 1986).

2. In 1986 during a lecture on culture held in the School of Natural Resources and Environment, Roy Rappaport stated that culture is man's greatest invention because it allows knowledge to be transmitted over the generations and allows humans to accumulate knowledge to adjust to any place on the planet no matter how harsh the environmental surroundings. He reported that while culture has been adaptive for most of human existence, this may no longer be the case. He said culture has possibly become maladaptive because of the social and environmental threats posed to the Earth and to our existence. Culture cannot exist without knowledge. My question of whether we are producing sustainable knowledge is similar to Rappaport's hypothesis that culture may become maladaptive.

3. Knowledge is manifested or embodied in cultural symbols. Knowledge or its by-product in the form of pollution may disproportionately burden communities of color and/or low-income communities. We refer to this knowledge as "bad" knowledge or knowledge that is not sustainable for people of color and low-income communities because of its devastating effects.

4. Some would argue that it is not the knowledge but the use of certain knowledge that is the culprit. In this paper I do not make the distinction between knowledge and its use or between knowledge and its by-products. Knowledge that is non-sustainable can have catastrophic effects. Also, making the distinction between knowledge creation and its use absolves the creators of knowledge of any responsibility for the use of that knowledge. Perhaps those who produce or create knowledge should be held accountable whether that knowledge is sustainable or not.

5. Questioning whether academics are producing sustainable knowledge raises many issues that threaten academic freedom. If the academy is not producing sustainable knowledge, then how should we address the problem? What are the implications of academic freedom? Should we produce knowledge for the sake of knowledge regardless of its consequences? Should we produce knowledge knowing that it and its by-products may negatively affect people based on where they live or the color of their skin? The University of Michigan Senate Assembly is one example where knowledge constraints have been attempted. In the 1980s it adopted the End-Use-Clause stating that no faculty or researcher at the University should engage in research with the end use of killing or maiming people. This clause was created to stop war research on campus. The majority of the 70 faculty cast their votes in favor of this clause. However, the Board of Regents of the University rejected it

because they felt that this would place the University at an unfair disadvantage with other institutions. In other situations faculty members commonly go before the Human Subjects Review Committee to make sure that their research is ethically sound. Are there other ways to curtail the creation of non-sustainable knowledge? These are indeed hard questions to answer.

6. Stavins (2000); DeSimone and Popoff (1997). Many academics and policymakers state that the market (emissions trading) can be used for environmental protection even though the market may have helped cause ambient air, water, and land quality to decline. Environmental justice activists fear that people living in close proximity to the company that obtains the credit may be differentially exposed.

7. The introduction of green taxes into the market helps ensure sustainable development. We must obviate acts of environmental destruction by making these acts expensive, and we must reward restorative acts. Green taxes attempt to provide those in the marketplace with the true cost of production. The purpose of green taxes is not to increase tax revenue, but to shift from taxing income to taxing the purchase of commodities, pollution, environmental degradation, and non-renewable energy consumption. The purpose of a green tax is to give people and companies powerful incentives to avoid environmental destruction (Hawken 1993:171; DeSimone and Popoff 1997; Ayres and Weaver 1998). Positive incentives such as a green tax can encourage energy consumers to use more efficient combustion methods and alternative forms of energy where possible. A green tax could also be used to raise the price of energy sources proportionately to the emission of hydrocarbons.

8. Green taxes could motivate industry to increase its profits since taxes can be avoided by making more energy efficient products. Inefficiency and pollution are often a sign of lost profits.

9. I compare this imperfect system to a sinking ship. No matter how skilled the management, the ship will eventually sink. Skill managers may delay the inevitable for a while, but the ship will be lost. However, if the ship is not sinking, skilled managers would be important to get us where we want to go efficiently without worrying about a sinking ship. Hawken (1993) also believes that the system is flawed more so than management.

10. Community-based research is a unique opportunity to use the community as a laboratory. Students learn about chemistry, biology, geography, sociology, and civics by testing ambient air and water quality. They learn how to problem-solve and how to hold government agencies responsible for environmental protection and health. The results of this research may strengthen their community for greater environmental justice protection.

11. Where possible, any heterogeneous group that includes community people should be in the majority so community people won't be politically impotent or disquieted. Community people should not feel intimidated by professionals and should feel comfortable participating in group discussions.

12. Many countries do not have the technology to conduct the assessment required. However, some simpler technologies can be useful. Water quality and soil testing kits are available at reasonable prices. For more information on monitoring rivers and streams contact Earth Force, 1908 Mount Vernon Avenue, Second Floor, Alexandria, VA 22301,USA. www.earthforce.org. This organization does water monitoring work with students and teachers in over 135 countries. The Bucket Brigade Manual gives instructions for combining a bucket with a vacuum cleaner part to sample air quality. The cost to build one for sampling ambient air quality is about $100. The bucket can provide samples for a number of organic and inorganic

gases to be analyzed in health departments. The manual can be purchased from Communities for a Better Environment, 500 Howard Street, Suite 506, San Francisco, CA 94105, USA. www.igc.org/cbesf/ or www.bucketbrigade.org.

13. High efficiency appliances ranging from light bulbs to heat pumps use only a fraction of energy required by conventional versions. Saving energy also reduces pollution because the cleanest fuel is that which is never burned. Fuel cells are compact, quiet, super-efficient, and super-clean devices for converting fuel into electricity chemically rather than through burning.

14. From the very beginning of the environmental movement in the United States, industry has fought against environmental regulations. Industry fought against the 1970 Clean Air and Water Acts and subsequent acts claiming that environmental rules and regulations place it at a disadvantage with overseas competitors. Manufacturers contended that environmental regulations were too time consuming and cut too deeply into profit margins. They blackmailed workers by threatening plant closures if the workers failed to side with industry against environmental regulations and environmentalists. Yet countries like Japan and Germany have some of the most stringent environmental regulations in the world, and they have experienced booming economies. In the United States, the State of California has the highest number of and most stringent environmental regulations, and yet seems to prosper (for more information on this see Moore and Miller 1994). Even now, the U.S. economy with all of its up and downs over the last 30 years is at an all-time high. Command and control strategies or environmental regulations help create jobs; they force industry to be more creative. Nevertheless, industry is in favor of letting the market take care of ambient air quality through emissions trading, arguing that this approach allows for more flexibility and creativity in solving the problem. Environmental justice advocates question the effectiveness of such trading because it creates "hotspots" in areas where people live and where companies are allowed to maintain their present levels or even increase their levels of pollution. Environmental justice advocates feel the market got the country into this situation, and they don't trust the market to get us out.

15. Karl Henrik Robert, one of Sweden's foremost cancer researchers, observed that often the scientific community was divided on the safety of chemicals. Some scientists claimed that certain chemicals were safe while others disputed this. Robert posited that if the safety of these chemicals was confusing to the scientific community, then certainly the layperson would be confused as well. How could the layperson be certain about the safety of these chemicals if the scientific community was confused? To address this dilemma, Robert called together a number of people in the scientific community for a conference to formulate questions that would guide research and production practices. Providing guidelines for research and production would enhance the confidence of the scientific and lay communities that chemicals or materials for human consumption or use are safe. From this conference four questions were articulated: 1) Is the material or chemical naturally found in nature? If not, then should it be manufactured? 2) Is the chemical or material persistent? If the material is going to be around for a long time, should it still be manufactured? For example, nuclear waste plutonium 239, one of the most toxic substances known to humans, has a half-life of 24,000 years. 3) Is it biodegradable? As with the above example, plutonium 239 is linear and inconsistent with the Earth's lifecycle and is therefore not biodegradable. 4) Can its tolerance level be predicted? If the substance is too poisonous, should it be produced?

16. Commercial buildings, homes, and communities can be designed to be more efficient. Designing and planning communities can also be used as an opportunity for

community organizing involving the people in designing eco-efficient homes and communities. A cost accounting of each building or home should be made. For example, where did the materials come from? How much energy was involved in the making and transporting of the materials? What was the energy saved in recycling materials? How much energy did using recycled rainwater and using trees as natural cooling systems save? Each building or home should be a curriculum for education within itself. Buildings and homes should teach the older and younger generations about energy, the environment, health, and environmental justice. For more information on this subject see Orr 1994. The outcome will mean much more to people who are integrally involved in the planning of their communities.

17. Many experiments and projects at varying levels of development are in progress. Clean technology includes fuel cells that will make the combustion engine obsolete. Cars are being designed to run on compressed air or recycled vegetable oil. Cow dung is being used to fuel a commercial power station in England, and houses are being built from straw. Energy is obtained from the sun and from tidal waves. Although it's too early to tell, the projects mentioned here may fall under the category of sustainable knowledge. For more information on the above see The Millennium Debate. www.millennium-debate.org/alternative.

18. In some instances urban land trusts and a variety of cooperatives with an environmental justice focus should be used to offset poverty.

19. An environmental justice income would be consistent with a Productive Welfare Experience because healing the Earth requires ridding society of conditions that foster toxin-induced and aggravated disease. People have fewer opportunities to move toward self-actualization if they must support externalized costs of production practices that threaten their health and livelihood.

20. For more information on the subject of work and income see Robert Theobald's guaranteed annual income or Milton Friedman's negative income tax. While these income programs do not ask people to work in exchange for income, the environmentally just income would. Work is the rearrangement of space and the transforming of energy into both useful products and waste. Much of today's work creates considerable amounts of environmental harm. People need work that is creative and restorative.

21. Because of increased environmental regulations, fewer disposal sites, and increased prices for hazardous waste disposal, developed countries have targeted developing countries in dire need of foreign exchange for waste disposal sites. This has caused a considerable amount of controversy as developing countries, which lack experts for monitoring the handling of waste disposal or suitable places for disposal, have begun to trade off the health of their communities for foreign exchange. While governments in some developing countries allow their countries to be waste depositories, African politicians and journalists speak of "toxic terrorism," "garbage imperialism," and "neo-colonialism." As a result, these developing countries under pressure from citizens and international environmental organizations have taken action. In some cases people have been jailed for participating in international waste trade. Shipping countries or countries of origin have been ordered to remove their waste. Sometimes ships carrying hazardous waste cannot find ports and consequently have wandered the seas for months before finding a disposal place. For more information on this see Bartz 1989; Duflour and Denis 1988; Hackmann 1994; Hiltz and Ehrenfeld 1991; Rublack 1989; Vilcheck 1992. The Basel Convention states that countries, primarily developed, must discontinue sending shipments of waste to developing countries. For other shortcomings of the Convention see Clapp 1994; Puckett 1995.

References

Anderson, R. (1998) *Mid-Course Correction.* Atlanta, GA: The Peregrinzilla Press.

Asch, P. and Seneca, J. (1978) "Some Evidence on the Distribution of Air Quality," *Land Economics,* 54 (3).

Ayres, R. U. and Weaver, P. M. (eds) (1998) *Eco-Restructuring.* Tokyo: UNU Press.

Babbie, E. (1989) *The Practise of Social Research.* 5th ed. Belmont, CA: Wadsworth Publishing Company.

Bartz, D. (1989) "Toxic Waste Dumping on Latin America," *NACLA Report on the Americas,* 7-9.

Bell, B., Gaventa, J. and Peters, J. (1990) *We Make the Road by Walking: Conversations on Education and Social Change.* Philadelphia, PA: Temple University Press.

Berry, B. (1977) *Social Burdens of Environmental Pollution: A Comparative Metropolitan Data Source.* Cambridge, MA: Ballinger Publishing Co.

Bezdek, R. (1995) "The Net Impact of Environmental Protection on Jobs and the Economy" in B. Bryant (ed.) *Environmental Justice: Issues Policies, and Solutions.* Washington, DC: Island Press.

Bryant, B. (ed.) (1995) "Introduction" in *Environmental Justice: Issues, Policies, and Solutions.* Washington DC: Island Press.

Bryant, B. and Hockman, E. (1995) "Hazardous Waste and Spatial Relations According to Race and Income in the State of Michigan," University of Michigan, School of Natural Resources and Environment, mimeo.

Bryant, B and Mohai, P. (1992) *Race and the Incidence of Environmental Hazards.* Boulder, CO: Westview Press.

Bullard, R. (1994) *Unequal Protection: Environmental Justice and Communities of Color.* San Francisco, CA: Sierra Club Books.

Bullard, R. and Wright, B. (1986) "The Politics for Pollution: Implications for the Black Community," *Phylon,* 47.

Clapp, J. (1994) "The Toxic Waste Trade with Less-industrial Countries: Economic Linkages and Political Alliances," *Third World Quarterly,* 15 (3).

Commission for Racial Justice of the United Church of Christ (1987) "Toxic Wastes and Race in the United States: A National Report on Racial and Socio-Economic Characteristics of Communities with hazardous Waste Sites," New York: United Church of Christ Commission for Racial Justice.

Commoner, B. (1976) *The Poverty of Power: Energy and the Economic Crisis.* New York: Alfred A. Knopf.

Council on Environmental Quality (1971) *The Inner City Environment.* The Second Annual Report of the Council on Environmental Quality, U. S. Government Printing Office, Washington DC.

Daly, H. and Townsend, K. (1993) *Valuing the Earth.* Cambridge, MA: MIT Press.

DeSimone, L. D. and Popoff, F. (1997) *Eco-efficiency: The Business Link to Sustainable Development.* Cambridge, MA: The MIT Press.

Duflour, J. and Denis, C. (1988) "The North's Garbage Goes South," *World Press Review,* 35.

Freeman, M. (1972) "The Distribution of Environmental Quality," in A. V. Kneese and B. T. Bower (eds) *Environmental Quality Analysis.* Baltimore, MD: Johns Hopkins University Press for Resources for the Future.

Friedman, M. (1967) "The Case for the Negative Income Tax," *National Review,* March 7.

Gelobter, M. (1988) "The Distribution of Air Pollution by Income and Race," paper presented at the Second Symposium on Social Science in Resource Management, Urbana, Illinois.

Gianessi, L., Peskin, H., and Wolff, E. (1979) "The Distributional Effects of Uniform Air Pollution Policy I," *The U.S. Quarterly Journal of Economics.*

Goldman, B. (1994) *Toxic Waste and Race Revisited: An Update of the 1987 Report on the Racial and Socioeconomic Characteristics of Communities with Hazardous Waste Sites,* Washington DC: Center for Policy Alternatives.

Hackmann, J. (1994) "International Trade in Waste Materials," *InterEconomics,* 29.

Harrison, D. Jr. (1975) *Who Pays for Clean Air: The Cost and Benefit Distribution of Automobile Emissions Standards.* Cambridge, MA: Ballinger.

Hawken, P. (1993) *The Ecology of Commerce: A Declaration of Sustainability.* New York: Harper Business.

Hawken, P., Lovins, A. and Lovins, L. (1999) *Natural Capitalism.* New York: Little, Brown and Company.

Hilz, C. and Ehrenfeld, J. (1991) "Transboundary Movements of Hazardous Waste: A Comparative Analysis of Policy Options to Control the International Waste Trade," *International Environmental Affairs,* 7.

Kruvant, W. (1975) "People, Energy, and Pollution," in D. K. Newman and D. Day (eds) *The American Energy Consumer.* Cambridge, MA: Ballinger.

McDonough, W. and Braungart, M. (1998) "The Next Industrial Revolution," *The Atlantic Monthly,* 82-92.

Miller, G. T. (1999) *Environmental Science,* Seventh Edition. New York: Wadsworth Publishing Company.

Mohai, P. and Bryant, B. (1992) "Environmental Injustice: Weighing Race and Class as Factors in the Distribution of Environmental Hazards," *University of Colorado Law Review,* 63 (4).

Moore, C. and Miller, C. (1994) *Green Gold: Japan, Germany, the United States, and the Race for Environmental Technology.* Boston, MA: Beacon Press.

Orr, D. (1994) *Earth in Mind: On Education, Environment, and the Human Prospect.* Washington, D.C: Island Press.

Packard, V. (1960) *The Waste Makers.* New York: D. McKay Co.

President's Council on Sustainable Development. (1996) *Sustainable America: A New Consensus of Prosperity, Opportunity, and Healthy Environment for the Future,* Executive Summary, Washington DC: Government Printing Office, Mailstop SFOP, Stock number 061000008578.

Puckett, J. (1995) "The Basel Ban - The Pride of the Basel Convention: An Update on Implementation and Amendment," a GreenPeace document prepared for the Third Conference of Parties of the Basel Convention.

Rappaport, R. (1986) "Culture," lecture given at the University of Michigan, School of Natural Resources, Ann Arbor, Michigan.

Rifkin, J. (1995) *The End of Work: The Decline of the Global Labor Force and the Dawn of the Post Market Era.* New York: G.P. Putman's Sons.

Robert, K.H. (1991) "Education a Nation: The Natural Step," *InContext,* Spring: 10-15.

Rublack, S. (1989) "Controlling Transboundary Movements of Hazardous Waste," *The Fletcher Form.* 13.

Sharpe, V. A. (2001) "Environmental Justice: Ethics and Allocation of Benefits and Burdens," paper presented at the University of Connecticut. Garrison, New York, sharpeva@thehastingscenter.org

Stavias, R. (ed.) (2000) *Economics of the Environment: Selected Readings.* New York: W.W, Norton & Company.

Theobald, R. (1967) *The Guaranteed Income.* New York: Anchor Books.

U.S. General Accounting Office (1983) *Siting of Hazardous Waste Landfills and Their Correlation with Racial and Economic Status of Surroundings Communities.* Washington DC: U.S General Accounting Office.

Vilcheck, M.(1991) "The Controls on the Transfrontier Movement of Hazardous Waste from Developed to Developing Nations: The Goals of a Level Playing Field," *Northwestern Journal of International Law & Business*, 11.

West, P. (1992) "Invitation to Poison? Detroit Minorities and Toxic Fish Consumption from the Detroit River," in B. Bryant and P. Mohai (eds.) *Race and the Incidence of Environmental Hazards.* Boulder, CO: Westview Press, Inc.

Zupan, J. (1973) *The Distribution of Air Quality in the New York Region.* Baltimore, MD: Johns Hopkins University Press for Resources for the Future, Inc.

15

Culture and the Quality of Life in Korea: Strategies for Promoting Cultural Policy

Adriaan van der Staay

I. A Second Look at Culture and Development

The discussion on culture and development seems to have entered a new, more cultural phase. It is nearly half a century ago that Margaret Mead published her *Cultural Patterns and Technical Change* (Mead 1955). In it she drew attention to the anthropological context into which modernity was injecting itself. But nobody yet seemed able to imagine that modernity could reach so far and so deep, and that the new culture of modernity could replace and wipe out cultural forms that had existed for centuries, if not millennia.

From the 1950's onwards culture would be seen as a factor of resistance, a formidable opponent to change. The traditional way of life was an obstacle to be overcome by any possible means, if one wished successfully to reap the fruits of modernity: wealth, health and respect in an ever widening circle of developed nations. Economic development could be achieved as a matter of course by ignoring culture. Villages could be uprooted and displaced, religious sensibilities counted for nothing measured against the promised gains of development. Monuments as ancient and sacred as the temples of Abu Simbel in the Nile valley could not stop new nationalist leaders from adopting Russian models of development: flooding whole areas irrevocably and building dams for the production of electricity. Europe, and still mainly European UNESCO, tried to mitigate the cultural consequences of ruthless development. In saving the temples of Abu Simbel culture was recognized as being important but also museumized. Culture would be saved as a legacy from the past, but the future clearly belonged to development.

One cannot say that there was a fundamental change in this attitude, but the practice became more sophisticated. The brutal eradication of existing culture, if it stood in the way of development, seemed lacking in intelligence and efficiency. The costs were relatively high. Disaffection of population, even local resistance and revolt, told the developers that the going was not that easy. Taking culture into account to a certain degree might be advisable and smooth the path of progress. Could local customs and institutions not be used, and harnessed to the yoke of development? Out of the studies of culture as an adversary grew a new appreciation of culture as a factor in development. People and their values might prove beneficial to the development process after all. This clearly was not a sufficient change of heart. It left intact the paramount doctrine of development that it was unquestionable benefit in itself.

Yet out of this approach of taking account of people and their culture grew an awareness that people mattered after all. In this, the insight of the Dutch development advisor, Prince Claus of the Netherlands, struck a clear note. People, he told international development organizations, cannot be developed; they can only develop themselves. This brought a fundamental change of perspective to those who share his views. Not only were people made interesting, and no longer seen as obstacles, or merely collaborators in development, they were the originators of development. People and their cultures were not only recognized, but they were seen as the prime movers of the development process. This of course tied in with the widespread movement of empowerment, starting in the 1970's, which saw the giving of power to minorities as one of the tools of development. The poor, women, ethnic minorities, sexual minorities had to be empowered to achieve their own liberation. This was at least the belief in progressive circles. It was a minority belief not widely shared, and certainly not in the centers of powers related to development, by governments, the International Monetary Fund or the World Bank.

However, the recognition of the importance of people and their values was a decisive step forward in thinking about development as such. If people were to be empowered to develop themselves, they should be given the right to impose their own values. Values became important as an expression of self, of identity. If development was after all something not imposed on people, but wanted by them as opposed to former dogmatic top down development, would not development have to take into account their diversity of cultures? Indeed a number of more or less declamatory roads to development were proclaimed: non- aligned development, Burmese development, Islamic banking, Asian values supporting Asian Tigers, and so on.

This people-power reasoning led not only to a diversification of the meaning of development, but also to the proverbial tower of Babel, i.e. to mutual incomprehension and the danger of relativism. Relativism here is meant as the giving up of any hope of finding common values in the achievement of development. This relativist, even cynical approach to the multifarious ways to development, in which development could be the means to any cultural result, struck a deep hole in the center of development. It meant that development was no longer in possession of some guiding culture, western or otherwise. Development had briefly entered its nihilistic phase, and had become in a sense valueless, without value. An aim only unto itself.

This crisis at the center of development philosophy was bravely tackled at a monster conference (Mondiacult, The World Conference on Cultural Policies organized by UNESCO in Mexico City) held in 1982. The Mexican hosts of this conference may not have foreseen the wide-ranging implications of the reversal of values that was embedded in its so-called Declaration of Mexico. Basically, the message was very simple. If economic development had lost its way, some central core of belief should be reinstated. Culture could be the aim of development, not its means. On the global level, values should be found to guide development. After all, if peoples' lives were the aim of development, the collective will of the people should guide the development process. Culture beats economics.

As a participant at this conference, I must admit having overlooked the far-reaching impact of our Declaration and the watershed-like divide that this reversal of roles between culture and development indicated. On the one hand it was easily observable that power in the world was still, as it is today, in the hands of the economic elite that gathers at the World Economic Forum of Davos. The crowing of cultural luminaries like France's Jacques Lang (then minister of culture and prominent at Mondiacult) could be constructed as a symptom of weakness. Moreover the failure of communist countries to establish political hegemony over economic development did not bode well for a new attempt to ride the economic tiger. All this made for scepticism. I returned from Mexico with the depressing feeling that we had achieved not much more than the pitting of the word culture against the manifest realities of economic development.

Somehow I was wrong. In the twenty or so years after Mexico the discussion of the relationship between culture and development seemed to change, just as the triumph of economic development seemed to become almost complete. Perhaps it was the very success of economic development in certain countries that made obvious a hollowness in the development process. Though the means might deliver the wished-for effects, and nobody seemed to wish to change course completely, world capitalism started to look at itself in the mirror and did not quite like what it saw. It saw a world in many ways out of control, with dwindling natural reserves, a devastated ecology, growing pollution and global warming. It saw persistent inequities in the distribution of power, economic or otherwise. It saw huge population shifts away from traditional agriculture into the broken-back economy of mega-cities. It also increasingly had to cope with public opinion and critical movements which rattled its cozy self-confidence. Most importantly, people all over the world were worried. They did not reject the brave new world of economic development, and indeed were voting by their feet and flocking to the biblical fleshpots of Egypt, wherever these appeared. But they felt worried nevertheless, not about the past, but about their future and that of their children.

I think this is much the situation today. The twin regulatory processes of the market and democracy have acquired great prestige, the first for its efficiency, the second for its avoidance of insoluble strife and as a platform. If one wants efficiency and harmony in the development process, one should clearly lean towards the market and democracy, and forget about command economies or dictatorships. But both regulatory frameworks tell us little about the future. At any moment the market or democracy may go haywire. Therefore there is a great cultural challenge at the core of present-day thinking, to define the future of mankind as a whole. How far can population, indeed the economy, grow; can geo-sphere and biosphere deteriorate; can cultural traditions disappear; can values be left out of the development equation without courting catastrophe? These are important questions which have to be debated.

There exists no world parliament to effectively debate all this, since the structure of the United Nations family of organizations is, as the word implies, an assembly of states, sending their diplomats and occasionally experts to peacefully settle differences. The United Nations is not a world parliament. Whatever may be globalized in this world, it is not the will of the people. There is not a single forum for the vox populi. The world may not be ready for this type of gathering; one would still be at a loss to assemble the founding fathers for it. But the clear need exists to take into account the wishes of the people and their values, if one wants to solve the battle between culture and development.

In this wide framework of future construction, a small book (or rather a small part of a medium-sized book) took up the challenge of answering the questions which values should guide development. The book was the result of a contorted process of decision-making that started with the strangely heroic Mondiacult conference of 1982. It goes under the innocuous title of "Our creative diversity" and was the result of work by a committee of international experts. It tried to act as an embryonic world parliament by listening to countless shouts and murmurs in many corners of the world. It tried to define the outlines of global ethics, a set of common values that should guide development. For this we must thank the economist Paul Streeten, who conceived of this non-economic approach to development. In recent years the ethical approach to the process of development has gained in prestige, while the status of the purely economic approach to the world's future has been questioned. The Nobel Prize awarded to the Indian economist Amartya Sen has confirmed this alternative approach.

If one takes seriously what was described above, and considers culture as the prime mover of the development process, at least for the time being, one should have the courage to state a few obvious facts. People all over the world are struggling to find answers to new problems. It is quite probable that certain answers will be more successful in coping with these problems than others. The answers will not only be different from those of the past, but also not immediately widely known or respected. It behooves good governance to make these good practices known as quickly as possible, and to discuss their implications and values. This can only be done by intelligent scouting. There is no bureaucratic formula for this scouting process. It depends on scouts in many parts of the world, a network that carries the information, platforms of communication for testing the value of these solutions, but of all things it depends mainly on eyes, ears, noses of intelligent people to discover them. So the scouting of exemplary solutions to the problems of culture and development becomes a strategic priority and even a must. Especially if this implies the positioning of development in a wider cultural context. This would immensely enhance and amplify the so far abstract discourse of finding a global ethics to guide development.

II. Eight Strategic Suggestions for a Cultural Policy

Cultural Policy and Centers of Power

If we define cultural policy as the changing of a cultural situation by more or less powerful means, we should first consider where the power of cultural policy lies. This is a strategic question for those who have the ambition, as Korea seems to, of including the whole population and the whole of leisure in cultural policy initiatives.

There appear to be three major powerbrokers in the cultural field: the cultural marketplace, dominated by an economic elite; the public sphere, dominated by the political elite and its administration; and the voluntary associations or movements, dominated by social elites, that are emerging in many parts of the world.

A well thought out cultural policy would try to balance these three factors, so that they would work together. A different balance may be achieved in different places. In Europe, for instance, which has a strong and long history of public intervention, the lifestyle of the population is still dominated by the cultural influences of the market. In the Netherlands, which also has a long tradition of cultural policy at the local level, the influence of the market in the cultural lifestyle of the population is balanced by voluntary associations. Of the hundreds of local museums the great majority have been created by private initiative and are run by voluntary associations. These associations organize major festivals, bringing together hundreds of thousands of people participating in cultural or sports activities. In any year amateur participation dwarfs participation in official, professional art many times over. The power of official cultural policy is limited.

I think, without knowing the Korean situation, that it is reasonable to assume that public arts and public programs will always be a relatively weak player in the leisure time activities of the population as a whole, though of course one of great importance. This importance is conveyed by such means as giving official recognition to certain activities; in education and information; by institution building, sometimes supported by the law; and by providing support and setting up commissions. These are the classical mainstays of cultural policy. By these means cultural policy can strengthen continuity, quality, diversity, innovation, in the overall cultural situation, in a way the market or voluntary movements will not always be able to do well.

In our area of rapid globalization we should perhaps accept that the market is the cultural force that is making the most rapid advance, that the public sphere has yet to become strong and that voluntary organizations are an emerging influence in cultural growth.

Scientific Analysis and Cultural Policy

Scientific information can be very helpful in developing cultural policy. Statistical databases and surveys, together with policy oriented analysis, can give the public player in the field of leisure and culture a much better view of what the field actually looks like. This scientific analysis cannot be taken for granted. It does not exist everywhere. Many professional people in the arts or in the administration of culture do not look outside their direct field of interest. I can understand that. But for policymakers it is strategic to have this overview of the field.

It is possible to gain a quantitative picture of developments in leisure time from scientific surveys. Analysis of *time budget data* has helped modernize culture in my country, Netherlands, for instance by indicating at what time of the day people have free time available for shopping or other leisure time activities and when they do not. Another instrument with which to obtain information about culture is the *value survey*, by which I mean a specialized form of survey normally associated with public opinion research for politics or the market. From existing value surveys we can, for instance, learn that the lifestyles and values of young people in China or Japan are changing and diverging from those of the adult population. As young people tend to carry this lifestyle over into their grown-up lives, we may assume that the future cultural situation is already present in its embryonic form. Youth lifestyle movements, and especially the values they adhere too, seem to me extremely significant for cultural policy development.

Value analysis is, for instance, to be found in the two recent World Culture Reports by UNESCO (1998; 2000). For these reports it was not feasible to arrange new value surveys, so secondary analysis of existing databases was substituted. Even if they were less than perfect, they do provide an insight into what people are thinking in many countries. The main impression one gets is that the populations surveyed are more varied in their opinions that we would usually suppose. It also emerges clearly that youth is very open to new ideas.

For UNESCO it was not feasible to commission a worldwide value survey. At the national level the Netherlands does have this unique opportunity, as far as its own population is concerned, through its Social and Cultural Planning Bureau, an advisory body which commissions time budget surveys and public opinion surveys on a regular basis (Staay 2000b). The surveys touch on religious and ethical questions, moral dilemmas, women's liberation, attitudes towards migrants and so on. They make it possible for governments to take the long view, and not to give in to sudden hypes in the media or politics, or sectarianism.

My two examples, time studies on leisure and public opinion polls on values, are not what normally comes to mind when we think of cultural statistics. These statistics are interesting in themselves and should be available. But if you want to step outside the usual boundaries of cultural policy, as seems to be the Korean ambition, and reach out to the population as a whole, you should also have new scientific tools for knowing what is out there. These data should be used and analyzed by a special policy-oriented scientific unit or network.

There is another aspect to the dispassionate study of the values, opinions and behavior of the population. It also strengthens the *democratic process*. Though public opinion may well be reflected through political channels, these channels will select what they think important; that is their task. But it helps to look at public opinion with a dispassionate eye and get the picture directly.

Recently world leaders have been surprised by demonstrations of young people outside the venues of their gatherings. They need not have been surprised if they had taken account of public opinion surveys. Analysis has shown for years that there seem to be two extremes to the classical political spectrum in Europe, one to the left and one to the right of a moderate center. Those at the far right are frequently not very well educated, materialistic and have no interest in politics, those to the far left are mainly well educated, idealistic and are interested in politics (Staay 2000b). The very simple conclusion of this summary description (which in its brevity approaches a caricature) is that the majority of the protesters at, for instance, the Genoa Summit

are potential participants in the democratic process, by virtue of their education, idealism and interest in politics. On the other hand, those on the far right
seem to be less so inclined, and are more difficult to assimilate in the democratic process. Knowing public opinions strengthens the democratic process.

Culture for the Millions

If we are to take the Korean ambition of providing culture for the millions
seriously, we should perhaps start by recognizing that the market, and especially the commercial electronic media, are already doing this. They are already occupying the high ground. A few weeks ago, while I was visiting a
small scale publisher of quality books in Morocco, I looked down from the
13th floor and was astonished to see the whole sprawling city of Casablanca
covered with and even disappearing under satellite dishes. These millions of
eyes and ears are not connected to quality books. They are connected to
mostly commercial culture.

What culture? A year ago I visited the producers of a number of the soap
operas watched by viewers in the Middle East. These soap operas are created
in Mexico City, and their export to the Middle East has become a major
industry in Mexico.

This international world of disk-vision creates an interesting situation in
which there is a gap between disk-vision and daily life, between recognized
culture and unrecognized culture, between the culture of the cultured and the
culture of everybody else. But it is inconceivable that the presence of disk-
vision culture, which consumes much of the leisure time of the population,
will not in the long run influence their values and behaviors. If we were to
take up the challenge of asking what positive influence public cultural policy
could exert here, we would improve a central aspect of leisure.

However there are two other areas which are of great interest to all of the
population and which, at least in Europe, are not always seen as part of
cultural policy: architecture and nature.

Architecture and Public Opinion

The urban dwelling and the town itself are the context of life for ever more
people. The majority of the world population already lives in an urban setting. What we call public space, which is the space everybody can make use
of, envelops an important part of our everyday life, for example in commercial shopping malls and traffic highways. Specifically, public transportation
and official buildings come to mind when one thinks of how cultural policy
could enhance the everyday quality of life for the population.

I am aware of the fact that I am speaking in a part of the world which has, or
perhaps had, the oldest and most refined tradition of building cities and

houses of all—the Chinese, Korean, and Japanese traditions. At the same time these traditions have nowhere been more rashly uprooted for some form of globalized building than in East Asia. A cultural continuity has been broken. Priority should be given to preserving those quality parts of the urban landscape that are still there, and retaining the skills to preserve them. This has been understood by some courageous individuals, voluntary and professional associations. Cultural policy should support them.

Thirty years ago, when I was working as the director of the Rotterdam Arts Foundation, I worked in a city with hardly anything left of its architectural heritage, because of the war. Everything had to be rebuilt. I made improvement of the cityscape a main priority, because this links quality with the greatest number of people. Creating a political awareness that quality counts, that good town planning, good transportation, good building immensely enhances the human and aesthetic quality of life is not easy.

In the case of Rotterdam, which calls itself the largest port in the world, it was only natural to internationalize the issue of quality. International critics, architects, discussions and conferences, innovative pilot projects, insoluble problems tackled by geniuses, major international events were all marshaled to elevate the critical awareness of local political and public opinion. This awareness had hardly existed before, though, of course, people would judge privately, and not without merit or reason. I think this architectural initiative of the 70's, which has now grown beyond recognition, has made Rotterdam a much more interesting city to live in. Yearly events of architecture, exhibitions, books and films, institutions and buildings have clearly created a participation in the quality of architecture that did not exist before. Architecture and city planning is a cultural responsibility too.

The quality of life of a city depends largely on the role nature is allowed to play. It is both a traditional given and a future challenge. Gardens, parks, landscape all contribute greatly to the quality of life. Because of its implications, and because it is discussed too little in cultural policy, I will discuss this matter in a little more depth.

Nature and the Urban Setting

It is hard to see how one could have a culture of quality without a culture of nature. Did not the Chinese humanist Lin Yu Tang simply ask the question: how can a man live without a garden? *Landscapes, parks and gardens* have delighted civilized people for thousands of years. Yet landscapes, parks and gardens seldom attract much attention in cultural policy today. And what is even more telling: cities and dwellings are created, in which gardens or parks are marginalized. These horticultural delights still exist for the rich and famous. But as a private luxury. This leaves us with great modern cities where it is frequently impossible to communicate with nature, to look at the sun, the moon, the stars, to see mountains or water, or look at the unfolding of flowers and participate in the antics of animals and birds. We have entered a cultural period in which the man-made world dominates. When we talk about public spaces, we seldom include gardens.

This has many causes, one of which is purely cultural. Economic growth and demographic pressures coincided with a building and planning movement, *international modernism*, that seemed to give cultural legitimacy to the eviction of nature from the city. The last century was the century of a utopian modernism that relished a world that would be man-made, and neglected the natural world. Its great spokesman Le Corbusier kept nature at a distance, as a green backdrop, and did not create gardens.

So much of the defense of the garden had to come from private citizens, rich or poor. But it seems to me that something, at least in the Western world, is changing. People in Europe are getting richer and, having left the city for a house in a natural setting, having filled their houses with man-made things, they are again creating gardens. Moreover, parks have become the backdrop for many activities, sports, and festivities. Golf courses with their designed parks are proliferating. Yet this does not reach the level of spirituality you are looking for. In all this, man dominates and nature is seen as another form of consumption. It does not quite re-establish contact with nature.

There are signs, albeit a minority movement, that the garden is being rediscovered as a point of contact between nature and culture. There is of course the ecological movement, which holds nature to be sacred, and which considers nature parks as a kind of shrine. There is also this curious American movement of the therapeutic garden, which seems to recognize that the garden has much to offer in re-establishing mental and physical health in people. There is an upsurge of interest in books about garden history.

If one was to make the landscape, the park and the garden a pivotal feature of cultural policy in Korea, this would no doubt contribute greatly to the quality of life there, and perhaps to the mental health of its people. Moreover, I am aware that the cultural tradition of the garden in East Asia naturally lends itself to the fusion of the man-made environment and nature. The two great garden traditions of the world may perhaps be called the *paradise garden* tradition of the West and the *landscape garden* tradition of the East. This latter tradition has, by its fundamental acceptance of man as part of the landscape and by the discovery of miniaturization, made it quite easy to insert natural elements into the man-made world. In 1990, at the international symposium about the Authentic garden, I had the pleasure of listening to your compatriot Byong-E Yang. He first introduced me to the specific language of the Korean garden. I was struck by the openness of ancient Korean gardens to natural phenomena, like river beds and rocky embankments.

It would be interesting to know what decentralized cultural policy could do with this idea of giving landscape and garden a central importance. On the one hand traditional agriculture may provide a link to the protection of the quality of the landscape, on the other hand voluntary associations might be interested in enhancing the quality of miniaturization of landscape. And both together might influence local awareness of the importance of nature.

Slow Food

I wonder if cooking is not a neglected field of culture and development. In recent years the art of preparing good food and eating it has become something of a cultural and political battlefield. This is evident in the reaction of many to globalization and the provision of high-tech simplistic food by McDonalds. Increasingly the importance of keeping authentic traditions of national and regional cuisine is emphasized. Yet, like all culture in a globalizing world, cooking is changing fast. For two centuries already Indian cooking has become much hotter by the introduction of the South American pepper. In the last century the pizza has travelled from Naples to the US and back to Italy transformed. Today there is a cosmopolitization and creolization of food. There are nationalist battles going on around the origins of shoarma and kebab.

In a rather more serious vein I could point out the increased importance of the study of the history of the art of cooking. Recently the cultural historian Claudia Roden was awarded the Prince Claus Award for her work on the Mediterranean and Middle Eastern kitchen.

Being Jewish and from Egypt, she now has a definite impact on the all too globalizing hotel kitchen world of Egypt, in teaching them to rediscover the original recipes of the countryside. In the same way she helps with the emancipation of the Sephardic tradition of eating and cooking in Israel. Cooking is a matter for cultural policy.

Indeed cooking not only concerns all families, but it also strongly concerns the self-definition of a culture. So if the Korean new cultural policy were looking for a subject that would interest local communities and (culinary) elites at the same time, it might well be regional cooking. Actually, underneath the rediscovery of traditional and regional cooking lies a broader concern than the question of local traditions in a globalizing world. It is one that concerns the whole lifestyle of our emerging cultures.

The association of fast food with globalization is not accidental. It points to a world in which fast living reaches into every corner of our lives. The fast work time is linked to a fast leisure time. This fast culture never stops, seven days a week and 24 hours a day. This fast-track orientation of our emerging culture is well symbolized by fast food. So it is worth noting that a countermovement, called Slow Food, has arisen in Italy, which is now expanding to a wider area around the slow art of traditional cooking. The production of quality ingredients, the knowledge of where to get them, the careful preparation of food, the rituals concerning the eating of good food, have branched out into a concern with the quality of our daily lives. This has found its way into a journal called Slow Food, but also into yearly festivals at which slow food is celebrated. This may well indicate that fast track society is reaching certain cultural limits, and may be in search of moments of immobility and repose, recuperation and even meditation. So the question of the art of cooking is not that far removed from the question of immaterial quality after all.

Cultural Identity and Learning from Others

Indeed for cultural policy, cultural identity is a motivating force. Most people have several loyalties. They define their identities first by their family allegiance, then by the local identity, then by their nation, and finally by some international standard. Research has shown that these cultural identities need not be exclusive. Yet the local cultural identity may have a great motivating force, as we can witness in sports. So some form of regional or international competition may drive the local population to develop cultural skills. This happens in traditional societies, like on the island of Bali, Indonesia, where local musical groups compete with each other. But it is also a driving force in modern societies, as the Olympic games show.

Yet there is a paradox within the concept of cultural identity. Local ambition may be a motivating force, but does not by itself lead to cultural competence. There is no magical path to achieving quality. There is no magical way of being recognized by others for one's ambition. One can only lift oneself to a higher level of competence or value or recognition by being *taught by others*. And though people cannot be culturally developed, but can only develop themselves, as a wise man said, they can still only develop themselves by accepting being taught by others. In my example, the Balinese village that wants to acquire proficiency in music or dancing will send out its young people to other villages that are renowned for their skills. Or they will invite traveling teachers.

So the paradox of cultural identity is that it is both an energizing force and a fundamental impediment to cultural development. Cultural identity will be an obstacle to cultural growth if it does not reject its limits, and accept openness to others, and the necessity of change.

Cultural Scouting

Looking around us from a global point of view, we can see cultural identities, for instance Korean culture, yet we see every identity in flux. If we look backward at those same cultural identities, taking the long view, over thousands of years, we see something else. We mainly see people acquiring *new elements of culture*. Technical skills, but also new values. We see cultures change. Existing cultural identities may be fiercely defended, but they have largely been taken over from others in bits and pieces. For instance, England today will defend its cultural identity vis a vis continental Europe, despite the fact that it took much of its culture from there. Though we should not ignore the importance of identity questions in the short term, the most important fact in the long-term development of culture may be cultural change, meant as the acquisition of new skills and values. This is not widely understood. We perhaps need a 21st century Charles Darwin to explain *cultural evolution by cultural selection.*

People all over the world are struggling to come up with new answers to new problems. It is quite probable that certain solutions will be more successful in coping with these problems than others. These successful answers will be different from those of the past. They will not be immediately widely known or respected. It behooves good governance to make these good practices known as quickly a possible and to discuss their implications. This can only be done by intelligent *cultural scouting* (Staay 2000a). Since 1997 the Prince Claus Fund for Culture and Development is active in this field, and has decided to put international cultural scouting at the center of its concerns. There is no bureaucratic formula for this scouting process. It depends on scouts in many parts of the world, a network that carries the information and perhaps platforms that will test the value of these solutions. But above all it depends on the eyes, ears and noses of intelligent people to discover them. It is this scouting avant-garde, in a world of as yet virtual culture and development, that Korea could and should be part of.

References

Mead, M. (ed.) (1955) *Cultural Patterns and Technical Change*. Paris: UNESCO.

Staay, A.v.d. (2000a) "A Second Look at Culture and Development," The Hague, *Prince Claus Fund Journal*, 4.

Staay, A.v.d. (2000b) "Public Opinion and European Unity: A Learning Experience," in A.v.d. Staay (ed.) *Experiencing Europe*. Maastricht: European Centre for Work and Society.

UNESCO (1998) *World Culture Report 1998*. Paris.

UNESCO (2000) *World Culture Report 2000*. Paris.

Part III

Conclusions

16

Productive Welfare:
Its Significance and Implications

Ramesh Mishra

This concluding chapter seeks to present an overall assessment of the nature of the Productive Welfare (PW) paradigm and highlights some of the key issues arising out of the development of social policy under its auspices. The assessment offered here is based mainly, though not exclusively, on the chapters presented in this volume—chapters which cover a wide range of topics and express differing viewpoints concerning many of the issues.

The chapter is divided into two parts. The first part is concerned with the evaluation of the nature and significance of PW as a paradigm of social policy/welfare. The second part looks at the development and implementation of policies associated with the paradigm in the area of social security (i.e. social insurance and assistance) which may be said to represent the core of social protection in the welfare state.

I

The Nature and Significance of Productive Welfare

It may be useful to consider briefly the economic and political context of the development of PW. Let us begin with the economic aspects. The acute financial crisis of 1997 provided the main impetus for the development of PW and related policies. What "caused" the crisis remains a matter of contention and debate (Singh 1999; Kwon 2001). There is little doubt, however, that openness of the Korean economy in terms of capital flows, financial non-transparency, and imprudent foreign borrowing by the private sector were among its proximate causes (Grabel 1999; Gough 2001). In any case what the crisis showed very clearly was the vulnerability of the country's system of "social protection by other means" (SPOM) (Mishra, Chapter 3). In short, steady and high rates of economic growth, private sector full employment with job security, and company-provided welfare, which had served as partial substitutes for a comprehensive system of social welfare thus far, were seriously undermined. This is not to underestimate the role of state programs of social protection which had also been in the process of gradual development. Nonetheless SPOM as well as traditional forms of kinship obligations and support remained important elements in the overall security and well-being of the people (White and Goodman 1998). With the sudden collapse of SPOM it became painfully clear that Korea's system of social protection was in many ways grossly inadequate to cope with the economic insecurity and deprivation resulting from the crisis. Moreover if the country was to embrace globalization fully it could no longer rely on SPOM to serve as a substitute for state welfare in the future. As a member of the OECD group of nations and as a recipient of a substantial bailout loan from the IMF—which demanded more economic openness and labor market flexibility—Korea could scarcely afford to turn its back on globalization (Grabel 1999; Kim 2000). More openness meant greater economic volatility with its ineluctable consequences for employment, labor market and economic growth. Clearly SPOM could no longer be relied upon as a major constituent element of economic and social security.

Turning next to the political context of PW, the election of a member of the opposition party to the Presidency in 1998 was an unprecedented event in the country's history. Kim Dae-Jung, the new president, was committed to change, i.e. to ending the domination of the economy, and beyond that of society by the large conglomerates (*chaebols*), to make the economy more open and competitive, and to strengthen democracy. Moreover the president had aligned himself with the aspirations of labor for social justice. This meant, inter alia, correcting the overemphasis in the past on economic growth and the neglect of social development and equitable distribution of the fruits of growth (Kim 2000; Kwon 2001).

Thus economic and political developments came together to give birth to the ideology and policy of PW. The PW paradigm seeks to combine equity with efficiency, growth with redistribution and economic development with social development. But is this really the case? For as some of the contributions to this volume show, the nature and significance of PW as a social policy paradigm remains somewhat contentious. To some extent it is the eclectic nature of the paradigm itself that lends itself to varying interpretation.

Thus according to one viewpoint, the vision articulated by PW is in line with the global shift from the "welfare state" towards the "enabling state."

The latter is concerned with harnessing welfare to the objectives of international competitiveness and higher productivity, and to strengthening individual responsibility and work incentives (Gilbert, Chapter 2). In short PW looks like an approach that would turn welfare into a handmaiden of the global competitive economy. Gilbert's interpretation is based primarily on a reading of the official statements and other authoritative pronouncements on PW which appear to emphasize production, work incentives and the like rather than welfare per se. Moreover, he argues, PW's idea of harnessing non-state actors to the task of social welfare seems to imply that responsibility for social protection is to be downloaded from the state on to individuals and the civil society at large.

A second—and an almost opposite—view of PW is that it has a good deal of affinity, if not a family resemblance, with the Scandinavian social democratic approach to welfare (Kuhnle, Chapter 4). In its professed objectives of establishing social protection as a "right," extending social insurance coverage to all citizens, ensuring a minimum subsistence income to everyone in need and making the system of social welfare redistributive, PW suggests a social democratic approach to welfare. Moreover, PW's emphasis on labor market participation and work, when taken in conjunction with other principles and objectives, is not all that different from that of the Scandinavian model of welfare. The latter, especially in its most celebrated Swedish version, has always emphasized the importance of labor market participation—not least from the viewpoint of economic and financial viability of the welfare state. Thus training and the upgrading of the skills of the unemployed, in order to integrate work and welfare successfully, has been a part the model. Although translating the broad objectives of PW into concrete policies is a process that is still unfolding, the basic principles and practice taken together point to the development of a comprehensive system of social protection. Under the auspices of PW, state commitment to welfare in general and the scope of state welfare programs in particular is already very substantial especially when placed in the context of East Asia.

A third view—and this may represent more of a Korean perspective/perception—is that essentially the PW paradigm seeks to avoid the "excesses" of both the "social democratic" and the "neo-liberal" orientations to welfare. In its emphasis on a "balanced" and "productive" approach it represents a new model more closely attuned to the conditions of 21st century (Chung, Chapter 5). In short, PW is a Korean rendition of the Third Way. The latter, espoused by political figures such as Bill Clinton and Tony Blair and legitimized intellectually by sociologists such as Anthony Giddens (1998), seeks a new balance between individual and collective responsibility and emphasizes an "affordable" or "sustainable" form of welfare state. It shows a good deal of concern with the effect of welfare on work incentives, productivity and the like in the context of international competitiveness. Undoubtedly, as acknowledged by the official statement on the nature and rationale of PW (Office of the President 2000) the PW paradigm derives at least some of its inspiration from the Third Way. Thus like the Third Way it too aspires to a sort of middle way between the right and the left. And in this sense it also has a clear affinity with the older socio-liberal approaches or models of welfare pluralism and the mixed economy of welfare. They too seek a balance between freedom and security, between individual and collective responsibility and between the civil society and the state in the provision of welfare (Pinker, Chapter 6). Arguably, the balance between the state and civil society sought by this approach is not so different from that envisioned by pioneers of the mixed economy of welfare such as Beveridge and Keynes (George & Wilding 1976).

Be that as it may, between them these three views of PW bring into focus the different facets of the paradigm. Undoubtedly in the Korean and East Asian context, the emphasis on universality, social rights and equity suggest a new departure, if not towards the social democratic welfare system of Scandinavia then at least away from the "conservative-corporatist" approach to welfare—associated with Japan and other East Asian countries—reliant on forms of SPOM. However as Gilbert (Chapter 2) reminds us "the devil is in the detail." The fine print is important, as is the international context in which the PW has emerged, viz. a shift towards the enabling state. Indeed as some of the Korean contributors point out (Lee et al., Chapter 8 and Park, Chapter 9), there is a sizable gap at present between the principles and practice of PW. Thus nominally the coverage of unemployment and work injuries insurance is nearly universal but in fact a far lower percentage of workers actually qualify for benefits. There is a similar disparity between, on the one hand, the concept of minimum income for all and, on the other hand, extensive kinship obligations for mutual support and extremely stringent conditions of eligibility for assistance. However to some extent this disparity is connected with the question of implementation and the effective administration of programs, a subject to which we shall return.

Notwithstanding these reservations it appears that, on balance, PW and the policies associated with it do represent a substantial development of social protection in Korea under state auspices (Yeon-Myung 2001). The significance of this development could well extend beyond the national borders. For the successful implementation of PW will signal a new departure in respect of social protection in the region and indicate the feasibility of a universal and comprehensive welfare state, anchored in the idea of social solidarity and social rights of citizenship, in East Asian countries. Moreover the circumstances in which the expansion of state welfare has taken place in Korea are no less remarkable, viz. a serious financial crisis followed by a bail out loan under the auspices of the IMF. This is a state of affairs generally associated with fiscal austerity and social retrenchment rather than social development which makes the Korean case doubly significant (Yeon-Myung 2001). First, unlike the advanced welfare states in Western countries which, in broad terms, have seen the erosion of social protection in the context of globalization, Korean welfare state is undergoing a significant expansion. This underlines an important point, viz. that globalization, in short financial and trade openness and closer integration with the global economy, tends to undermine SPOM (Mishra 1999 and Chapter 3). National strategies of welfare, based on mercantilism and a relatively closed economy, become difficult to sustain in a globalized economy. Hence choices have to be made about what should replace them, e.g. a minimal safety net based on a residual approach to welfare or a more comprehensive welfare state. Secondly, it underlines the point that the consequences of globalization for social welfare are mediated by the political economy of the nation state (Gough 2001). Thus Korea, unlike for example Mexico in 1995, with its strong pre-crisis fundamentals and the track record of fiscal prudence has been able to negotiate a strategy of expanding the social sector (Kwon 2001). Here political factors have played a role no less important than the economic. A progressive president took office shortly after the crisis of 1997 and chose to move towards a rights-based approach to welfare and state responsibility for comprehensive social protection, in part as a basis for building national solidarity. Thus expanding the unemployment insurance program and liberalizing the public assistance system was not simply a stop gap policy measure to cope with the situation arising out of the crisis. These measures formed an integral part of the PW paradigm—a component in the social strategy of adjustment to a more open, globalized economy (Gills and Gills 2000; Kwon 2001). Inter alia the latter presupposes a more volatile and flexible labor market with greater risks of unemployment, job insecurity and wage inequity. PW commits the state to socialize these risks and to help the labor force to adapt to change.

A contrast with Japan is instructive here. The Japanese system of social protection combines a "conservative-corporatist" approach to welfare with forms of SPOM, viz. full employment and job security, seniority wages and company-provided welfare (Gough 2001; Esping-Andersen 1997). Indeed Japan is seen as the prototype of the East Asian version of SPOM with pre-crisis Korea as a variant. Unlike Korea, however, the Japanese economy still remains relatively closed with uniquely national forms of business practices and relationships (Katz 1998). Despite a protracted economic crisis the country has largely clung on to its form of SPOM and change has been slow and limited thus far (Junji 1997; OECD 2000a). The scope of state welfare has been extended somewhat lately, notably in respect of long-term care of the aged and the disabled, but overall the future pattern of social protection in Japan, including the role of SPOM, remains uncertain (Peng 2000). Korea, on the other hand, has decided to move away from its mercantilist and autarchic past—in respect of the economy as much as in respect of social protection. Whereas Korea seems to have turned the crisis of 1997 into an opportunity to "modernize" its economy and welfare and prepare the country for globalization the same cannot be said of Japan's economic and financial crisis which has now lasted for over twelve years. In any case Japan's situation underscores the point that in a globalized economy corporate restructuring and unemployment are practically unavoidable. "Lifetime employment" and its corollary company welfare are unlikely to be sustainable options. For example, as Takayama (Chapter 13) points out, many corporate pension funds in Japan are in serious trouble and cannot meet their liabilities without government help. Yet thus far Japan has been unable or unwilling to restructure its economy in order to meet the challenges of the 21st century (OECD 2000a). Put simply Korea appears to be ready to "modernize" its economy and welfare in a way that Japan is not, at least not yet. In the past Korea has been influenced by the Japanese model of economy and welfare. Could it now be the turn of Japan to follow Korea's lead?[1]

II

Part I of this chapter was concerned with the general assessment of PW as a paradigm of welfare and its significance for Korean social policy. In Part II we shift our attention to the development of policies and the changes in the system of social protection brought about under the auspices of PW. In short, if the first part of the paper was concerned with the principles and objectives of PW—its promise so to speak—here we are concerned with its performance. How far has the government succeeded in implementing policies in line with the objectives of the paradigm and what are some of the key problems arising out of the process? Furthermore what light does a review of policies and their progress throw on the nature of the paradigm itself?

Clearly limitations of space do not permit a review of all public policy areas discussed in the earlier chapters of this book. We shall instead concentrate on one broad area of policy, viz. social security, arguably the core area of social protection. Social insurance and social assistance constitute its two main components. Both have seen far reaching reforms in recent years. We look at each in turn.

Social Insurance

All four insurance schemes in Korea—pensions, health, unemployment, and industrial injuries—have undergone substantial changes. Generally speaking, coverage has been extended, benefits improved and conditions of eligibility liberalized. Coverage is virtually universal in health insurance and nearly universal in pensions insurance. With the extension of coverage in

1999 to all private sector employees and the self-employed the numbers insured for pensions nearly doubled (Walker, Chapter 12). However some public sector pension schemes remain separate. The minimum eligibility period for pension rights was reduced from 15 to 10 years of service. On the other hand the replacement rates were reduced slightly and the element of redistribution scaled down. However as Walker (Chapter 12) sums up, the pensions scheme "is characterized by clear policy principles such as universality, redistribution and solidarity"; moreover it "aspires to replacement rates that would, over time, minimize financial insecurity in old age and place Korea in the top rank of public pension providers in the developed world." In the case of health insurance conditions of eligibility have been liberalized making its effective, as distinct from nominal, coverage universal. More significantly perhaps the four hundred or so health insurance societies—with differing rates of contribution and forms of management—have been replaced by a single health insurance scheme run by the public sector with unified standards of contribution across the nation. Employment insurance has of course undergone a rapid expansion of coverage. First introduced in 1995, the scheme now covers nearly all wage earners. With the surge in unemployment following the crisis of 1997, coverage was extended—nearly doubling the number of insured—conditions of eligibility were relaxed and the benefit period lengthened (OECD 2000b). The scope of industrial injuries insurance, which began in 1965, has been expanded gradually and benefits improved. Since the crisis of 1997 its coverage has been extended further. Some of the measures, notably those associated with Employment Insurance and labor market policies, were in the nature of a temporary response to the crisis of 1997. With the resumption of growth and the fall in unemployment they have been wound up or scaled back (OECD 2000b). However, the bulk of the reforms in the area of pensions, health, employment, and industrial injuries insurance are in the nature of long-term institutional changes in social protection related to the principles of PW.

No doubt before the crisis of 1997 and the advent of the Kim Dae-Jung administration, all four branches of social insurance were in place with health insurance representing the most 'advanced' scheme of social protection in the context of a developing country. Nonetheless, by any standards, the change over the last five years has been remarkable. The principles of universality, social inclusion and unified administration have made major strides, thus strengthening the basis for national solidarity and social integration. By pooling risks and contributions universal coverage should also strengthen the financial basis of the insurance schemes. Measures to encourage labor market participation with the aim of maintaining near-full employment should also help sustain the financial base of social insurance.

Social Assistance

The National Basic Livelihood Act passed in October 2000 guarantees a minimum living standard to all whose income falls below a certain level. According to a Korean scholar it is "the most representative and practical reform" of the social safety net under the philosophy of Productive Welfare (Yeon-Myung 2001). The new scheme departs radically from its predecessor under which the working age population and the able-bodied were not eligible for public assistance. True, there exists a stringent means test, kinship obligations to support needy relatives are quite extensive and the stigma of social assistance remains a considerable deterrent. Thus one-third of those below the poverty line do not receive assistance (OECD 2000b). On the other hand the scope of social assistance is undoubtedly much wider as shown by the tripling of the number of beneficiaries in 2001 (Park, Chapter 9). Moreover social assistance is no longer a form of state charity meant for a small residue of population. Rather it is a measure which entitles the poor to a minimum income and lays a corresponding obligation on the state to provide the same. True, those able to work are required to satisfy certain 'workfare' type conditions, e.g. participation in job training or in self-support programs. But these do not appear to be intended as a deterrent. Apparently workfare type programs affect only about 3 percent of the 1.5 million public assistance beneficiaries (Yeon-Myung 2001). In sum, parallel with the changes in social insurance the reforms in public assistance have also moved Korean welfare towards a more comprehensive, rights-based system.

Some Emerging Issues and Problems

As Park (Chapter 9) observes so aptly, Korea is trying to implement within a relatively short time frame a comprehensive system of welfare which has taken "advanced nations several decades" to develop. The rapid expansion of the scope of social protection, greater unification of insurance schemes and other changes have, not unexpectedly, given rise to or underlined a number of problems. There is a sizeable gap between policy and practice; the administrative infrastructure and database is inadequate; effective long-term financing and sustainability of the services is by no means assured; lastly there is a problem of securing compliance with and building consensus around policies based on PW. These issues are examined below.

As noted earlier, the effective coverage of insurance schemes lags behind the much greater nominal coverage. For example, the participation of the self-employed in the pensions scheme remains low. Moreover about one-half of the eligible urban workers were exempted from paying contributions either because of unemployment or early retirement. Thus both in regard to contributions and benefits there seems to be a "drop out" problem which weakens considerably the principle of national pensions for all (Takayama, Chapter 13). The effective exclusion of a sizeable population has implications not only for equity and financial soundness but also for the legitimacy of the national pensions scheme (Walker, Chapter 12).

Employment Insurance and industrial injuries schemes also suffer from the same problem. Thus although coverage has been extended to over two-thirds of the wage earners and eligibility rules liberalized the percentage of workers effectively insured against unemployment is a good deal lower (Lee et al., Chapter 8). Moreover the proportion of the unemployed actually receiving benefits—only 11 percent in 1999—is extremely low. (Lee et al., Chapter 8). Not only do many temporary and daily workers remain outside the system but also strict eligibility rules and administrative deficiencies exclude many beneficiaries. In the case of industrial injuries schemes effective coverage also remains low—estimated at less than half of the work force—for a variety of reasons (Lee et al., Chapter 8).

Not unexpectedly, the administrative capacity of social insurance and assistance services has failed to keep pace with the demands made by the rapid expansion in the scope of these services. The main weakness seems to be understaffing but the lack of adequate training of personnel is also evident in a number of areas (e.g. job counseling) (Lee et al., Chapter 8). The information base remains seriously deficient regarding the income of the self-employed which affects the functioning of insurance as well as assistance services. There are other gaps in the database concerning, for example, the employment record of temporary and daily workers. The reliability of many employers' reports regarding the wage and employment status of other employees also remains doubtful (Park, Chapter 9).

On the question of financing and long-term sustainability of services the national pensions scheme has been the principal focus of attention. A relatively recent scheme it has a substantial surplus at the moment. However, in light of the expanded coverage, liberalization of eligibility conditions and the decision to retain the defined-benefit formula there are concerns regarding its medium and long-term funding (Takayama, Chapter 13). Contributions, at nine percent of earnings already, will have to rise a good deal in the future and the question is what level of contribution might be sustainable. The government has wisely decided to review the situation every five years (Walker, Chapter 12). Health insurance also faces the problem of adequate funding. For the moment the government has chosen to increase the subsidy rather than raise contributions but this may be no more than an interim measure (Park, Chapter 9). Clearly cost-containment and other measures for stabilizing health care expenditure remain important and will need further attention in coming years.

In sum, the problem of adequate funding, financial stability and long-term sustainability of the expanded system of social protection will need careful attention and monitoring, not least because the "balanced" approach of the PW paradigm demands that revenue and expenditure are in line. However, the overall tax burden in Korea, although similar to other developing countries, is low by OECD standards (OECD 2000b). During the last three years strong economic growth has reduced the budget deficit—caused by the sudden spike in public spending to cope with the crisis—and the government is committed to eliminating the deficit in 2003. Before 1997 Korea never experienced a budget deficit, thanks to high rates of economic growth and a relatively low level of social spending. Despite increases in social outlay resulting from the PW approach there is no reason to believe that the overall level of social expenditure is not sustainable—at least in the short run. With the economic recovery and the fall in unemployment temporary labor market measures— put in place to meet the emergency—are being phased out. Moreover the general improvement in the economy and employment should help to ease the financial burden of social insurance and assistance. Nonetheless, the government along with the social partners and the civil society, need to ensure that there is a high level of voluntary compliance with the payment of higher taxes and contributions. Thus far Korea, in company with other East Asian developing countries, has been a relatively low tax country. It is important therefore to garner public support for the socialization of a higher proportion of income in order to pay for a more comprehensive system of social protection. It is important to emphasize that the latter is meant to benefit all sections of society and thus the nation itself. In short the earlier, crisis-induced, period of innovation and expansion in welfare needs now to be followed by a phase of consolidation and the institutionalization of the reform.

Note

1. The Japanese situation differs in important respects from that of Korea. Japan's economy is still the second largest in the world with balance of payments in surplus and a strong currency. There is nothing comparable to the external "shock" (the IMF loan and its conditionality), which was instrumental in precipitating Korea's reforms. The peculiarities of Japanese politics as well as the systemic nature of Japanese welfare capitalism militate against radical reform.

References

Esping-Andersen, G. (1997) "Hybrid or Unique? The Distinctiveness of the Japanese Welfare State," *Journal of European Social Policy*, 7 (3).
George, V. and Wilding, P. (1976) *Ideology and Social Welfare*. London: Routledge.
Giddens, A. (1998) *The Third Way*. Cambridge: Polity Press.
Gills, B.K and Gills, D. S. (2000) "Globalization and Strategic Choice in South Korea's Economic Reform and Labour" in S. S. Kim (ed.) *Korea's Globalization*. Cambridge: Cambridge University Press.

Gough, I. (2001) "Globalization and Regional Welfare Regimes: The East Asian Case," *Global Social Policy* 1 (2).

Grabel, I. (1999) "Rejecting Exceptionalism: Reinterpreting the Asian Fnancial Crisis" in J. Michie and J. Grieve Smith (eds) *Global Instability*. London and New York: Routledge.

Junji, B. (ed.) (1998) *The Political Economy of Japanese Society*, Vol. 2. Oxford: Oxford University Press

Katz, R. (1998) *Japan: The System That Soured*. Armonk, N.Y. and London: M.E. Sharpe.

Kim, S. S. (2000) *Korea's Globalization*. Cambridge: Cambridge University Press.

Kwon, H. (2001) "Globalization, Unemployment and Policy Responses in Korea," *Global Social Policy* 1 (2).

Mishra, R. (1999) *Globalization and the Welfare State*. Cheltenham: Edward Elgar.

OECD (2000a) *Economic Surveys 1999-2000: Japan*. Paris.

OECD (2000b) *Economic Surveys 1999-2000: Korea*. Paris.

Office of the President (2000) *DJWelfarism: A New Paradigm for Productive Welfare in Korea.* Seoul.

Peng, I. (2000) "A Fresh Look at the Japanese Welfare State," *Social Policy and Administration* 34 (1).

Singh, A. (1999) "'Asian Capitalism' and the Financial Crisis" in J. Michie and J. Grieve Smith (eds) *Global Instability*. London and New York: Routledge.

White, G. and Goodman, R. (1998) "Welfare Orientalism and the Search for East Asian Welfare Model" in R. Goodman, G. White and H. Kwon (eds) *The East Asian Welfare Model*. London and New York: Routledge.

Yeon-Myung, K. (2001) "Welfare State or Social Safety Nets?: Development of the Social Welfare Policy of Kim Dae-Jung Administration," *Korea Journal* 41 (2).

Contributors

Bunyan Bryant is taking his major faculty appointment in the School of Natural Resources and Environment at the University of Michigan. He also has an adjunct position with the Center of Afro-American and African Studies at the University of Michigan. Professor Bryant has written the book, *Environmental Advocacy: Concepts, Issues and Dilemmas* (1990), and a manual entitled *Social and Environmental Change: A Manual for Community Organizing and Action.*

Kyungbae Chung is former president of the Korean Institute for Health and Social Affairs (KIHASA) and his research interests include social insurances, particularly pension size and operation, social welfare and welfare economics. He received his Ph.D. in economics from University of Pittsburgh. He has published *Productive Welfare, Philosophy and Policies* (1999*), Social Safety Net for Korea* (1999), and *Productive Welfare: A New Welfare Paradigm* (2001).

Neil Gilbert is professor of social welfare at the School of Social Welfare, University of California at Berkeley, faculty leader of the Center for Comparative Family Welfare and Poverty Research, and was the founding director of the Family Welfare Research Group. His numerous publications include twenty-two books and 100 articles. His book, *Capitalism and the Welfare State* (Yale University Press) was well received with reviews in the *New York Times* and the *New York Review of Books.*

Jai-Joon Hur is a research fellow at the Korea Labor Institute. He graduated with a Master's degree from Seoul National University, Korea, and with a Ph.D. from the University of Paris X, France.

Nanak Kakwani is professor at the University of New South Wales, Australia, and a leader in the field of econometrics theory and welfare economics, having extensively researched inequality and poverty, public finance and development economics. He was elected fellow of the Academy of Social Sciences in Australia and awarded the prestigious Mahalanobis Memorial Gold Medal for outstanding research in quantitative economics.

Hokyung Kim is a research fellow at the Korea Labor Institute. He graduated with a Master's degree and a Ph.D. from the University of Texas at Austin.

Stein Kuhnle is professor in comparative politics and head of Department of Comparative Politics at the University of Bergen, Norway. He is also associated with the Stein Rokkan Center for Social Studies at the University of Bergen. Recent publications include *Survival of the European Welfare State* (2000) and (with Sven Hort) "The Coming of East and South-East Asian welfare states," *Journal of European Social Policy* (2000).

Won-Duck Lee is president of Korea Labor Institute. He has served as senior expert member of the Labor-Management Relations Reform Committee, consultant to the president, and advisor to the minister of labor. His recent publications include *Labor in Korea in 21ˢᵗ Century* (1998) and *Participatory Co-operational Labor-Management Relations and New Labor Policy* (1996).

Ramesh Mishra is Emeritus Professor of Social Policy at the School of Social Work, York University, Toronto. He has published extensively on theories of the welfare state and on comparative social policy. His books include *The Welfare State in Crisis* (1984) and *Globalization and the Welfare State* (1999). Currently, he is working on the implications of globalization for social protection in emerging market economies.

Chanyong Park is director at the Korea Institute of Health and Social Affairs (KIHASA). He received his Ph.D. in economics, majoring in Welfare Economics, from IEP de Paris, and his research areas include poverty, income distribution and social assistance. His numerous publications include *Schemes for Reforming Income Maintenance System to Strengthen the Social Safety Net* (2000) and *Current Poverty Issues and Counter Policies in Korea* (1998).

Robert Pinker is a professor and a graduate of the London School of Economics and Political Science (LSE). Appointed to a chair of social studies at Chelsea College in 1974, he subsequently returned to LSE as professor of social work studies and on his retirement in 1996 he was appointed Professor Emeritus. Academic publications include: *Social Theory and Social Policy* (1971), *The Idea of Welfare* (1979,) and *Social Work in an Enterprise Society* (1990).

Wendell E. Primus joined the Center on Budget and Policy Priorities in June 1997 as director of income security. Dr. Primus served as deputy assistant secretary for human services policy in the Office of the Assistant Secretary for Planning and Evaluation. Previous to this position, Dr. Primus was chief economist for the Committee on Ways and Means and staff director of the Subcommittee on Human Resources of the U.S. House of Representatives.

J-Matthias Graf v.d. Schulenburg is professor of business administration and director of the Institute for Insurance Economics at the University of Hanover. He has published many books and articles in scholarly journals in the fields of risk and insurance, health economics and empirical microeconomics. He has worked in particular on health insurance issues and methodological questions of economic evaluations of health services. He has done more than 30 pharmaco-economic studies.

Hyun Hwa Son is an economist at the World Bank, She graduated with a Master's degree and a Ph.D. from the University of New South Wales, Australia.

Adriaan van der Staay is Emeritus Professor of History and Arts at the Erasmus University Rotterdam, Netherlands. He has served on numerous cultural and arts boards in Europe, including acting as president of the European Center for Work and Society. He is also serving on the Board of the European Cultural Foundation. He served as director of the National Social and Cultural Planning Office of the Netherlands from 1979 to 1998. Recently, he was a member of the Scientific Committee of the World Culture Report for UNESCO.

Noriyuki Takayama is professor of economics at Hitotsubashi University. He is currently engaged in Microdata Analyses of the Aging/Declining Population and his research interests are economics of social security/private pensions. His recent publications include *Pension Reform in Japan at the Turn of the Century* (2001) and *The Economic Status of the Elderly in Japan: Microdata Findings* (1997).

Alan Walker is an acknowledged expert on aging in Europe and has been professor of social policy at the University of Sheffield since 1985. He is president of the International Sociological Association's Research Committee on Ageing and an expert adviser to the UN's Programme on Ageing. Recent Publications include *Managing an Ageing Workforce* (1999) and *Ageing And Welfare Changes In Europe* (1997).

Index